THE NEW NATUR

A SURVEY OF BRITIS

C000200174

A HISTORY OF ORN.

THE NEW NATURALIST LIBRARY

A HISTORY OF ORNITHOLOGY

PETER BIRCHAM

Collins

This edition published in 2007 by Collins,
an imprint of HarperCollins Publishers

HarperCollins Publishers
77–85 Fulham Palace Road
London w6 8jb
www.collins.co.uk

First published 2007

A cip catalogue record for this book is available
from the British Library.

Set in ff Nexus by
Rowland Phototypesetting Ltd
Bury St Edmunds, Suffolk

Printed in China by Imago
Reprographics by Saxon Photolitho, Norwich

Hardback
isbn-13 978-0-00-719969-3
isbn-10 0-00-719969-4

Paperback
isbn-13 978-0-00-719970-9
isbn-10 0-00-719970-8

Contents

Editors' Preface

THE VOLUMES OF the New Naturalist library have generally examined particular places, habitats, or groups of species. The naturalists themselves have of course had walk-on parts, but very few of the 103 previous titles have taken as their main theme the people who have studied the wildlife, or the story of how our knowledge of the subject has developed. This addition to the series is different. It sets out to survey the history of ornithology in Britain spanning a millennium, to assess the worth of its components and their place in the grand scheme of things, and then to present the outcome with appropriate balance and in a palatable manner. This is indeed a mammoth task, but it is one that Peter Bircham has accomplished most successfully, producing a cover-to-cover read of continuing interest and fascination from what might be deemed to be the driest of base materials. He has also accomplished the task with style, his enthusiasm for both the underlying researches and the compilation of the text shining through each chapter.

With a background in continuing education, and based in Cambridge, Peter Bircham is well placed to handle the necessarily extensive sifting of both the archival and present-day researches and researchers, and to present the product to great effect. Inevitably, detail from the Middle Ages is scanty, but from the sixteenth century onwards the quantity of material to be sifted grows rapidly. Not only was there more interest in the natural environment and its inhabitants, but much more information was placed on record in one way or another. Then, as now, there were disputes over vernacular names and over taxonomy, with cyclic prevalences of splitters and lumpers, although at a rather more basic level than today. Many readers will be astonished at how little the concerns of the ornithologists have changed, and at how recently some of today's everyday birds were separated one from another.

Through time, the gradual attitudinal shift from hunting and collecting towards conservation is revealed, although sadly this transition has not yet been fully accomplished. Revealed too is the gradual, but now rapidly accelerating, shift from 'what's hit is history, what's missed is mystery' of the stuffed specimen to the technology of field identification of the live bird in the wild, brought about by a combination of observer skills and optical developments which allow feather-by-feather analysis. This, as the reader will discover, is not without intrigue, even dishonesty, along the way.

The pen-pictures of the ornithologists themselves show a gradual progression, from a handful of enthusiasts and scholars in the earliest days, to the mainly wealthy amateurs with ample time for field observation of the eighteenth, nineteenth and early twentieth centuries, then on to not much more than a handful of university academics before the post-1950 burgeoning of both the pursuit of birdwatching and the science of ornithology. The status of the amateur birdwatcher has been raised, first from crank to harmless eccentric, then to an interesting component of the social community, and finally to a respected contributor to a rapidly accumulating amateur/professional science base. The more extreme exertions of today's twitchers, seeking rarities often in far-flung places, may be viewed by some as a return to the eccentricity of old, but none can deny the field skills of those seeking and identifying these vagrants to our shores. And the science of ornithology has grown alongside the skills of the observers, so that by the start of the twenty-first century the study of birds has developed to the point where it can play a key role in fundamental biological investigation.

Peter Bircham skilfully unfolds a kaleidoscopic and highly readable account of ornithological personalities over the centuries, and of the contributions they have made to ornithology in Britain. No reader will be left complacent, nor will they put this book down without having extended their background knowledge, including numerous gems of revelation and surprise. This is a most welcome addition to the New Naturalist library.

Author's Foreword and Acknowledgements

A s a tutor for what is now called the Cambridge University Institute of Continuing Education, I once asked an evening-class group if there was any topic that they would particularly like me to cover in the course – probably just called Bird Study in those days. One lady mentioned Gilbert White and said that she would like to know more about the history of ornithology in this country. I was surprised, and with not much enthusiasm I wandered across to the Zoology Department Library, with which I was vaguely familiar.

When I entered the small inner office the librarian, Ron Hughes, a small slim man with a round face and black-rimmed glasses, looked up from a large Victorian desk that was covered with papers, and when I told him I would like to use the library he produced a card for me to fill out. This was followed by a quick induction in his Welsh lilt, and finally he asked if I had any particular interest. When I told him that I was interested in old books about ornithology he directed me to the inner room, where the Newton Library is housed, containing the great collection of Alfred Newton, the first Professor of Zoology in Cambridge. I can't recall Ron's exact words, but they were something to the effect that 'you'll find all you need in there, boy.' He was not wrong! I had about four weeks to prepare my lecture on the subject, but by the time the evening came I had already realised that there was a whole book's worth of material in Newton's papers alone. That was seventeen years ago.

All research leads to more research. This book has led me to more and more sources about the historical aspects of our ornithology. I am perfectly aware that this is a topic where new information will come to light from time to time, so that at whatever point I complete my writing there will be omissions.

Furthermore, others may know of published or unpublished sources not mentioned here. In the end there is also the difficult task of choosing which material to include and which material to exclude, and keeping it all to a reasonable number of words. I decided to restrict the book to those things that I consider to be of fundamental importance. For the earlier period this was not difficult, but from the nineteenth century onward I have been forced to jettison some material that others might consider to be just as significant as that which I have included. It boils down to a personal decision. Recently both Stephen Moss and Ian Wallace have produced books that cover much of the ground of the twentieth century (Wallace's contains many interesting personal insights from the post-war period), and I have attempted not to reproduce what they have written, although inevitably there are overlaps.

A book of this kind would be dull if it adhered to the serious side of bird study alone. Some amusing incidents are revealed when one reads the many documents and recollections that I have been privileged to see, and I have deliberately put some in the book to show that supposedly stuffy characters from the past also possessed a sense of humour. Towards the end of the book we find a couple of examples of the human condition – dishonesty – that most intrigues people.

The point of entry to the subject is self-limiting, as little information is available for the early part of the story, but the point of departure has been rather less easy to determine. However, as the book is intended to be historical I have used the rather arbitrary notion that I shall, in general, not include analysis of the work of any living ornithologist (although living ornithologists do get a mention from time to time). Time is required to gain a real evaluation of people's work: discoveries that seem ground-breaking in their day can be revealed to be less than significant with the passage of time, and studies dismissed at birth can subsequently be seen to be important. In effect the cutoff point is around the 1970s to 1980s. The concluding chapter embraces modern ornithology, but only in so far as it relates to the material covered elsewhere in the book.

Throughout the text I have retained the English names that preceded the recent changes – except in the list in the Appendix, where I have used the new nomenclature as modern lists all do. To retain the 'old' names was a deliberate decision, since in my view many, if not most, readers will be far more familiar with the 'old' names, and the 'new' names are as unattractive as they are misconceived. But I must try not to sound like many of the crusty souls who appear in this book!

ACKNOWLEDGEMENTS

This book has been a joy to write and research. Many people have given me snippets of information over the years, or directed me to new sources – particularly Chris Thorne, Nick Davies and the late Roger Clarke. These three also read the whole manuscript at various times in its existence, Richard Billington read the almost-final draft, and all made many very valuable and helpful comments: my thanks to all four. Thanks are also due to the staff of the Balfour Library in the Department of Zoology in Cambridge, particularly the late Ron Hughes and more recently Jane Acred and Claire Castle; also to Dr John Flowerdew, who kindly allowed me to use the material for illustrations, and to Neal Maskell, who photographed some of the paintings. I must also thank Ray Symonds in the Cambridge University Zoology Museum, who allowed me access to some of the museum's holdings and manuscripts; also to the staff of Cambridge University Library, although I suspect they haven't much clue about me since I was just another reader asking for obscure material, and the staff of the Library at the Natural History Museum, where James Fisher's original papers are stored.

I am most grateful to the photographers who very generously provided some stunning new images to grace these pages – Richard Billington, Jim Lawrence, Chris Martin, and especially Rebecca Nason. The following individuals and organisations kindly gave permission for the reproduction of the other illustrations: the Balfour Library, Zoology Department, University of Cambridge; the British Library; the British Museum; the British Ornithologists' Union; the British Trust for Ornithology; the Clarendon Press; Emmanuel College, Cambridge; HarperCollins; the Harry Ransom Humanities Research Centre, the University of Texas at Austin; David Hosking; the Linnean Society; Methuen; the Natural History Museum; the National Portrait Gallery; Norwich Museum; Oxford University Press; Phaidon Press; T. & A. D. Poyser; the late Derek Ratcliffe; the Royal Society for the Protection of Birds; Lady Philippa Scott; the Wildfowl & Wetlands Trust; Witherbys Publishing.

Two people gave me help with specialist topics: Mark Cocker kindly commented on my assessment of Richard Meinertzhagen (not always agreeing with me!), and the late Colin Harrison shared with me the results of his studies into the palaeontology of British birds – a sadly neglected area of interest. The late Derek Ratcliffe, in his capacity as the specialist editor for the New Naturalist Library, made many helpful suggestions and additions and provided great encouragement, a role taken on in the later stages by Jim Flegg, and both suggested re-shapings that have improved the end product immensely. Peter Beaven at the British Trust for Ornithology kindly spent a day unearthing the boxes of lantern slides from which I have drawn some of the illustrations, and the BTO kindly agreed to my using them. Jeremy Greenwood helped with the history of the BTO. At HarperCollins, Helen Brocklehurst, Emily Pitcher and Julia Koppitz have patiently dealt with my enquiries, and Hugh Brazier has used an expert eye to greatly improve and correct the text to make the book more readable. My thanks to them all for the help that they have given.

Above all, I have to say a special thanks to Michael Walters. Following a conversation at a meeting of the BOU on the History of Ornithology we began a correspondence that served both as an exchange of information and as a debating forum. Michael was writing a book on the global history of ornithology, while mine was always restricted to Britain. Coming to the subject from separate ends of the spectrum, we have enjoyed some robust exchanges over many of the issues both in this book and in his *Concise History of Ornithology*. Perhaps, one day, our correspondence about the history of ornithology will be part of the History of Ornithology in Britain!

This book is dedicated to the memory of Susan Taylor, a schoolteacher, who found a spark and left a flame.

CHAPTER 1

Up to the Sixteenth Century

'The White Rabbit put on his spectacles. 'Where shall I begin, please your Majesty?'
he asked.
'Begin at the beginning,' the King said gravely, 'and go on till you come to the end;
then stop.'

Lewis Carroll, *Alice's Adventures in Wonderland*

THIS BOOK IS concerned with the scientific study of birds in Britain. It is not a book about birdwatching *per se*, a topic covered by a number of recent publications (Moss, 2004; Wallace, 2004). It is difficult to define the point at which a birdwatcher, or birder, becomes an ornithologist, since the dividing line between the two is very thin. Nevertheless, someone who goes in search of birds only for the pleasure of seeing them is not an ornithologist in the true sense. It has been said that an ornithologist, while not always aware of what species he or she is watching, knows what it is doing and why, while a birdwatcher, largely ignorant of the underlying purpose of the bird's activities, can identify the species, age, sex and race of the bird – an exaggeration, of course, but one with a grain of truth. What is not an exaggeration is to say that almost every ornithologist began as a birdwatcher attempting to tell one species from another.

The early part of the story of bird study in Britain follows much the same pathway, for at the beginning the preoccupation of the first ornithologists was to find, identify and give names to the birds of these islands. To follow their discoveries we have to rely on archaeological evidence, and on the writings of the earliest chroniclers, since the period from the Ice Age through to the Middle Ages is largely unrecorded. Only in the sixteenth century do we find the first published accounts devoted specifically to British birds, but from that point onwards, as we progress through the centuries, we find an increasing wealth of information to draw upon, until by the close of the eighteenth century there is some real ornithology to report – and by the twentieth it is impossible to include more than a snapshot.

Almost all British scholarship began around the Norman invasion, and British ornithology was no exception. Some information has been gleaned from the few remaining writings of the pre-Norman occupants of this island, but this retrospective knowledge is not always fireproof and relies often on supposition and interpretation, to say nothing of translation. To take the advice of the King of Hearts and begin at the beginning is therefore not quite as straightforward as it sounds. Nevertheless, with a little background information, 1066 is as good a firm starting place as any. But before we consider the earliest British birdwatchers there is good reason to examine, briefly, the classical background.

THE CLASSICAL BACKGROUND

The significance to this book of the two great civilisations of Greece and Rome is that they provided the basis of our knowledge of many subjects, particularly scientific study, and that includes ornithology. Among the many classical philosophers were two whose work had, and in nomenclature still has, an enormous influence on developing science. One (Aristotle) was Greek, and the other (Pliny the Elder) was Roman.

Aristotle (384–322 BC) and Pliny (AD 23–79) were among the first scholars to write about birds. Between them, particularly Aristotle, they laid a foundation of knowledge which formed the basis of most British ornithological publications until the later part of the eighteenth century, and many of the names they used for the birds they described remained in common usage, so that eventually they were incorporated into the scientific names used for classification.

Aristotle combined his own observations with those of other learned men, which he used, together with accounts given to him by farmers and fishermen, to compile short life histories of the species known to him. He was unusual for his time in that most other philosophers of the period formed their theories and then gathered information to confirm their preconceived ideas. Aristotle used the information that he gathered as the basis for his theories, and although he was not infallible his work has, in many respects, withstood the test of time.

Pliny produced 37 books on natural history, containing almost everything known on the subject up to that time – but much of his writing has proved to be incorrect. The following short extracts give a flavour of Aristotle and Pliny. Here is Aristotle writing about the kite (Fig. 1):

> *Milvi [red kite] lay for the most part two eggs each but sometimes three and hatch as many young. But that kind which is named Aetolial [black kite] at times lays even four.*

And here is Pliny on the same subject:

> *Milvi are of the race Accipitres though differing in size. They seem moreover to have taught mankind the art of steering by the turning of the tail, nature thus showing in the sky what might be useful in the sea. Milvi lie hidden in the winter months yet not until hirundines depart. They are reported also to be affected with gout around the solstice.*

FIG 1. Red kite, from Greene's *Birds of the British Empire* (1898).

This mixture of accurate observation and fanciful tales is typical of these writers, especially Pliny. It seems likely that some of the Romans who conquered or lived in Britain would have been sufficiently well educated to know of the work of Aristotle or Pliny, but there is no documentary evidence that any of the Romans in Britain carried out any study of birds in this country. We learn virtually nothing about our birds from the contemporary accounts of the Romans, but archaeological analysis, using the bones of birds found around Roman towns or encampments, offers some insight into the birds of the time: for example, evidence relating to the presence of pheasants.

It was long suggested that the Romans brought the pheasant to Britain. This is disputed by Rackham (1986), who placed the responsibility for the introduction of the pheasant with the Normans. Bones of pheasant have been found in Roman settlements, but Rackham has argued that these birds were kept enclosed, and that it was the Normans who released them into the countryside and provided the means to maintain their populations.

The period between the departure of the Romans in AD 410 and the arrival of the Normans is often known as the Dark Ages. The pursuit of knowledge had advanced under the Romans largely as a result of the structure of Roman society, in which labour was specialised much as it is today, and this allowed men of scholarship to pursue their chosen field of study. The social organisation of Britain in the Dark Ages did not allow this. It was a period of considerable turbulence, with many of the tribes of Europe invading parts of Britain and creating small settlements. Most prominent among these were the Angles and the Saxons, who began to arrive around AD 570 and gradually integrated to form a new race – the Anglo-Saxons.

THE ANGLO-SAXON PERIOD (570–1066)

The Anglo-Saxons were a very spiritual and cultured people, and many elaborate artistic works remain from their time, such as decorated goblets and items of jewellery; but it is within their literature that our knowledge of birdlife at the time is contained. Much of Anglo-Saxon writing was the work of holy men, and the influence of Christianity was strong. From the writings of monks we learn that around AD 530 St Serf had a tame robin that was killed by the boisterous play of his pupils.

We know that St Columba was reported to be familiar with the migration of cranes, and he is said to have nursed an injured crane back to health. Then there was St Cuthbert, who must qualify as the first bird protectionist in Britain, who in 676 established a nature reserve and holy place on Inner Farne (one of the Farne Islands) in Northumberland. Cuthbert knew the white-tailed eagle (called the erne), the carrion crow and eider ducks – which are omnipresent on the islands and which have become known colloquially as St Cuthbert's ducks. Another scholar, Aldhelm of Malmesbury, c.685, knew woodpigeon, nightingale, swallow and chaffinch. Of the nightingale he wrote, 'mean is my colour, but none hath scorned my song.' In around 699 St Guthlac made his way to the Fens of East Anglia to live a life of contemplation, and his biographer records a mutual attraction between Guthlac and wildlife, mentioning cuckoo, raven and swallows – which apparently perched on the saint's shoulder.

The earliest evidence of falconry in Britain comes from around AD 700, provided by a reference to St Boniface supplying King Aethelbald of Mercia and King Aethelbert of Kent with 'accipitres and falcones' (see below).

Among the Anglo-Saxon written works the most famous is probably the poem *Beowulf*, and this contains an early reference to the 'ganotes' (gannet), a species that is frequently mentioned in early literature (Fig. 2).

However, the most ornithologically revealing of all the Anglo-Saxon writings is the 124-line poem *The Seafarer*, thought to have been composed around AD 650 but only written down, in the form in which it has survived, in about AD 1000.

FIG 2. The gannet, also called the Solan(d) goose, from the Willughby/Ray *Ornithology* (1676).

I heard nothing there but the sea booming
the ice-cold wave, at times the song of the swan.
The cry of the gannet was all my gladness,
the call of the curlew, not the laughter of men
the mewing gull, not the sweetness of mead.
There, storms beat the rocky cliffs; the icy-feathered
tern answered them; and often the eagle,
dewy-winged, screeched overhead. No protector
could console the cheerless heart.

From this translation (Crossley-Holland, 1984) we learn the names of the species of birds known to the Anglo-Saxon writer at the time. However, James Fisher (1966) offered an alternative, inspired ornithological interpretation, based on locating 'the seafarer' as a visitor to the Bass Rock sometime between 20 and 27 April. Fisher argued that, with some ornithological knowledge of that site, a more accurate translation would run as follows:

There I heard naught but seething sea,
ice-cold wave, awhile the song of swan.
There came to charm me gannets pother
And whimbrels trill for the laughter of men,
kittiwake singing instead of mead.
Storms there the stacks thrashed, there answered them the tern
With icy feathers; full oft the erne wailed round
Spray feathered . . .

Fisher's version changed curlew to whimbrel and defined gull as kittiwake; he also changed eagle to erne – the old name for the white-tailed eagle (Fig. 3) – and went on to explain that the swan in the second line is likely to be the whooper swan, which, in April, is to be seen in parties migrating north to the breeding grounds in Iceland; during which they are often to be heard calling out in contact. Later in the narrative the cuckoo is mentioned, making a total of six species of bird in the poem. Whichever of these two versions you prefer, the work clearly shows a knowledge and affinity with the birds of the Seafarer's home.

Further evidence concerning the birds of pre-Norman Britain comes from a list of Saxon names for the animal kingdom which appeared in Archbishop Aelfric's *Vocabulary*, accompanied by their Roman equivalents. Examples of the birds, with probable identities, are shown in Table 1.

FIG 3. White-tailed eagle by Archibald Thorburn, from Swaysland's *Familiar Wild Birds* (1883–8).

TABLE 1. Saxon and Roman names for birds, from Archbishop Aelfric's *Vocabulary* (late tenth century).

SAXON NAME	ROMAN NAME	PROBABLE IDENTIFICATION
swan	*Olor*	swan (?mute)
ylfete	*Cignus*	swan (?whooper)
gos	*Auco*	goose
ganra	*Anser*	gander
ened	*Anas*	duck (?mallard)
fugeldoppe	*Mergulus*	merganser
scealfr	*Mergus*	cormorant
hranga	*Ardea*	grey heron
storc	*Ciconia*	stork
goshafuc	*Aucarius*	goshawk
earn	*Aquila*	eagle
stearn	*Beacifa*	tern
pawe	*Pauo*	owl?
ule	*Strix*	owl (?tawny)
lauerce	*Alauda*	lark
nightegale	*Lucinia*	nightingale
swertling	*Ficedula*	blackcap
crawe	*Cornix*	crow
goldfinc	*Auricinctus*	goldfinch

Many of these names (Saxon and/or Roman) are still in use today. The Roman names have mostly been incorporated into the modern scientific nomenclature, and the Anglo-Saxon names have been adapted and changed over time.

In another Anglo-Saxon document, the *Colloquy of Aelfric* (written in Latin in the tenth century, and translated into Old English sometime before 1050), in answer to the question 'how do you catch birds?' the man replies: 'sometimes with nets, sometimes with snares, sometimes with bird-lime, sometimes with a call, sometimes with a hawk, sometimes with a decoy.' Diverse methods of bird-catching are by no means modern.

A bill of fare from Waltham Abbey dated 1059 mentioned crane, thrush, partridge, pheasant, magpie and goose. James Fisher used this and other sources to estimate that by the time of the Norman conquest in 1066 up to 75 different bird species had been identified, named and documented as occurring in Britain.

THE NORMAN PERIOD

The Norman Conquest saw the beginning of the slow and sometimes painful process of creating a country with a civilised structure, united under a single monarch. This process took not only time (centuries) but also much of the energies of the people. It is therefore hardly surprising that the study of birds was not of prime importance.

Ultimately the organisation of small village communities under a feudal lord, with a priest for every settlement, provided some opportunities for study, and it is almost always those who studied doctrine or medicine (or both) who were the scholars, and thus the birdwatchers, of the period.

From the beginning almost all the ornithological writers were engaged in the business of reporting (and re-reporting) information largely supplied by others. There is very little evidence of original observation at this time. Sometimes they reworked the old classical writers – Aristotle was particularly popular – and they often repeated age-old fables and stories heard in their travels.

In this period the first writer of note was Alexander Neckam (1157–1215), in whose publication *De naturis rerum* there are references to osprey, goshawk, crane and nightingale. However, Neckam is an example of those whose work was more fantasy than fact. More reliable is the testimony of a monk, Reginald of Durham, who wrote in 1167 of the tameness of the birds on the Farne Islands, birds which 'the English call "Lomes", which nest in the houses and even under the beds and come clamourously to those who call them.' The name 'lomes' was said by both Gurney (1921) and Raven (1947) to mean guillemots, but the birds referred to by the monk were probably eider duck, as it seems unlikely that guillemots would be found nesting under beds.

Thomas of Ely in the *Liber Eliensis* (in the part that gave his account of Hereward the Wake), written at some unknown date in the eleventh century, described the creatures harvested by the fenmen – including coots, grebes, cormorants, herons and ducks. Sadly this lacks the specific detail we would like, although we know from other sources that cranes were present in the Fens, and in the thirteenth century there are several records of hawking for them – indeed Gurney reported, as mentioned above, that about the middle of the eighth century the King of Mercia requested Archbishop (St) Boniface of Mons (Belgium), who was an Englishman, to send him two falcons trained to kill cranes. Since the kingdom of Mercia was mainly in the Midlands/Lincolnshire this implies a wider distribution of the crane (Fig. 4) than just East Anglia, at least in Saxon times. However, it is important to note that it is not impossible that

FIG 4. Common crane, from Edward Topsell's *Fowles of Heaven* of the early seventeenth century, first published in 1972.

the name crane may have been applied to herons in some cases. Holloway in his *Historical Atlas* (1996) suggests that the use of the names crane and heron was sufficiently imprecise to cast doubt on the crane ever being resident in Britain, but this suggestion is contradicted by a large amount of evidence, particularly from fossils and bones, which was subsequently summarised by Boisseau and Yalden (1998). These writers have also pointed out that several place names and village names reflect the presence of cranes, such as Cranford in Berkshire and Cranshaw in Lancashire, and many places named Cranmoor(e).

One of the most valuable contributions of this time came from Giraldus Cambrensis (c.1146–c.1220), a Welshman born in Pembrokeshire, educated in Paris and ordained in 1172. Most of his writings were the product of his travels and as a consequence were more accurate than those of many of his contemporaries since, in part at least, they were based on some personal observation.

His work on birds contained some astute and noteworthy observations: for example, he was able to describe the separate physical characteristics of whooper and mute swans, and he noted the most obvious example of sexual dimorphism, that in birds of prey the female is invariably larger than the male. In his book *The Itinerary of Archbishop Baldwin Through Wales* (undertaken in the late twelfth century but published in 1585) he described finding the green woodpecker and the golden oriole (Fig. 5) in the Principality, the latter being a surprising bird to find so far west compared with its distribution today – yet with its 'yellow colour and sweet whistle' there can be little doubt of his identification.

FIG 5. Golden oriole, from F. O. Morris's *History of British Birds* (4th edition, 1896).

He noted also the absence of the nightingale in Wales, and in his book about his travels in Ireland (Fig. 6) he observed that despite the care taken by falcons and sparrowhawks over nesting places their nests did not become more numerous and their numbers did not increase – undoubtedly the earliest report of natural population regulation. Although these observations were in contrast to the more fantastic writings of his contemporaries, Giraldus understandably incorporated some of the more common erroneous beliefs of the time in his work, such as the idea that barnacle geese hatched from the barnacles on the rocks, and that storks spent the winter in the mud at the bottom of the water in lakes. This latter idea was a general belief concerning the disappearance of some birds in winter – the concept of migration not being widely credited.

Raven (1947) described Giraldus as 'pompous, monstrously conceited, quarrelsome, vituperative, credulous and inaccurate'. It is therefore hardly surprising that his ecclesiastical career was troubled. He died at St David's in or around 1220. In his travels to Ireland (1183–6), Giraldus noted the following additional species: merlin, hobby, shrike (presumably red-backed), grouse (presumably red), capercaillie, kingfisher, raven, carrion crow, quail, woodcock, snipe, corncrake and wild swan (whooper).

A further, excellent description dating from 1251 has been gleaned from a manuscript by Mathew Paris, a monk of St Albans:

> At the turn of the same year, at the season of fruits, certain wonderful birds never before seen in England appeared, particularly in orchards. They were a little bigger than larks and ate the pips of apples and nothing else … they had the parts of the beak crossed and with them split the apples as with pincers or a pocket-knife.

FIG 6. Drawings said to be of cranes (the bird on the left clearly is, but the bird on the right appears to be a heron). Originally from Giraldus Cambrensis' twelfth-century *Topography of Ireland*. From Gurney's *Early Annals of Ornithology* (1921).

This is almost certainly the first description of an irruption of crossbills. Some species, of which crossbills are a prime example, nutcrackers another, are subject to periodic exceptional breeding success in years in which there is a bumper seed crop. This leads to a so-called irruption, when surplus birds disperse beyond their normal range. The crossbills in this instance were most likely from the Continent. The monk records this event not because he was in any sense an ornithologist: his interest was due to the crossbills' attacking the apples, which were at the time economically important to the monastery since they were used in the making of cider – which may well have been made commercially and not just for monastic consumption. This is the first recorded instance of what became known, early in the twentieth century, as 'economic ornithology' – the unfavourable interaction of birds with humans, especially in agriculture.

Among other writers, Bartholomaeus Anglicus, a Franciscan, wrote about the natural world in his book *De proprietatibus rerum* (c.1260). His references to birds were rather few in number and he drew much of his information from Neckam – and thus repeated much of the fantasy that Neckam had propounded. *De proprietatibus* was well known at the time and was much quoted by other writers – inevitably continuing all the old wives' tales.

In 1274, Jurors sent to assess the island of Lundy for the Crown (the owner of the island) sent a report that included:

> *The rock of Gannets is worth 5s there are other birds but they are sold. There is also one eyrie of Lanner Falcons [Peregrines?] which have sometimes three young ones, sometimes four, sometimes more, and sometimes less. The eyrie the jury knew not how to estimate and they build their nests in a place in which they cannot be taken.*

In this quotation we find an early instance of a problem that will be encountered again and again, namely the confusingly inconsistent use of names. Here we have the name lanner falcon. Since the bird now known as the lanner falcon (*Falco biarmicus*) has not been recorded in the wild in Britain, the bird in question was almost certainly the peregrine falcon (Fig. 7). The name lanner, and its variants, appears frequently in older publications.

Information about the birds of Britain throughout this period comes more often than not from sources concerning birds being eaten, as in a poulterer's price list of 1275 which suggests cranes at three shillings (15 p in today's money), bittern at sixpence (2.5 p), heron and teal also sixpence, and curlew threepence.

The monastic and manorial accounts of this time are particularly rich as sources of information on colonial-nesting birds. For example, we discover that there was a heronry at Chilham in Kent in the 1280s, as there is today. Heronries

Falco peregrinus.
The Peregrine or
haggard Falcon.

FIG 7. Peregrine falcon,
from the Willughby/
Ray *Ornithology* (1676).

were also documented at Whinburgh, Cantley and Wormegay in Norfolk,
where each parish also noted breeding sparrowhawk, bittern and spoonbill –
presumably on undrained wetland, of which there must have been a great deal.
From the account of the visit to Lundy mentioned above we discover that the
gannetry there was in existence in 1274. Again it must be emphasised that these
facts were noted not from an ornithological perspective but for the possibilities
of plundering the nests and taking the young for food, or as a kind of inventory
of the breeding birds, to indicate how many of the full-grown birds might be
expected for catching and eating, or to be taken for falconry.

THE LATER MEDIEVAL PERIOD

Among the most significant writers of the fourteenth century were the poets
Geoffrey Chaucer and William Langland, both of whom included many
references to birds in their works, the former being more acquainted with
wild birds and the latter with domesticated birds, hawks and pest species.

Chaucer's *Parlement of Foules*, written between 1382 and 1383, was essentially
a poem about love, and seems to have been prepared for a St Valentine's Day
celebration. The long narrative, while not having birds as its primary subject,
not only makes mention of 36 species but also, in a poetic way, tries to give
a system of classification which is almost certainly the first in the English
language. In a translation by Brian Stone, we read that

> ... the Birds of Prey were set
> In highest place, and next came those more small,
> Like birds who followed Nature's laws and ate
> Such things as worms whose names I do not call;
> And lowest in the glade sat water-fowl
> But on the green sat birds that live on seed
> So many, it was strange to see indeed.

This represented, perhaps, the first attempt to separate birds into sections,
and to decide on an order of 'importance' in which to present them – in short,
a classification of a kind, based on the food that they ate. Further on, the poem

FIG 8. An engraving of men harrowing, from the *Luttrell Psalter* of 1340, with the birds
overhead likely to be rooks, carrion crows or possibly gulls. From Gurney's *Early Annals
of Ornithology* (1921).

describes the birds in a partly anthropomorphic way that nevertheless gives an indication of characteristics that we can recognise, and furthermore gives early instances of some simple ecology:

> *There was the tyrant with the feathers dun*
> *And grey, I mean the Goshawk, fell in deed*
> *To birds with his outrageous ire and greed.*
> *… the sturdy Sparrowhawk too*
> *Foe of the Quail; the Merlin who explores*
> *Ways all the time the small lark to pursue;*
> *The Starling who betrays all secret matter;*
> *The Swallow, murderer of the creatures small*
> *Whose honey comes from flowers fresh of hue;*
> *The watchful goose; the Cuckoo ever unkind.*

Chaucer also provided evidence for a modern study into the evolutionary battle between the cuckoo and its hosts (Brooke and Davies, 1987). One of the most curious elements of cuckoo parasitism is the way in which those cuckoos that parasitise dunnocks fail to lay a mimetic egg. A possible reason for this might be that the dunnock is a relatively recent host and that the cuckoo has not had time, in an evolutionary sense, to develop an egg to match that of the dunnock. Chaucer, however, shows that as long ago as the fourteenth century cuckoos were parasitising dunnocks when he addresses these words to the cuckoo:

> *Thou mordrer of the heysugge [dunnock] on the braunche that broghte thee forth.*

The *Monk's Drawing Book* and the *Sherborne Missal*

In the Middle Ages books were often illustrated, with drawings alongside text, or even pages of drawings. The *Monk's Drawing Book*, in the Pepys Library at Magdalene College, Cambridge, is a fourteenth-century 'model book' comprising pages of illustration of all manner of things. Approximately eight pages consist of pictures of birds, of which some, such as the herring gull, are identifiable, while others are open to conjecture.

Likewise the *Sherborne Missal*, produced for the Benedictine Abbey of Sherborne, Dorset, some time just after 1400, had 48 illustrations of birds among the many decorations placed in the margins of the text, all done by (or overseen by) a Dominican Friar named John Siferwas (Fig. 9). The quality of the illustrations is variable; each has the name of the bird in Middle English alongside, and some,

(a)

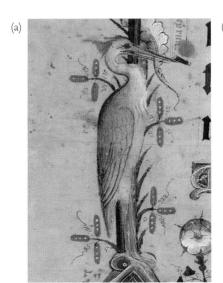

(b)

(c)

(d)

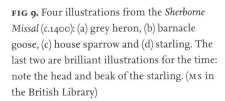

FIG 9. Four illustrations from the *Sherborne Missal* (c.1400): (a) grey heron, (b) barnacle goose, (c) house sparrow and (d) starling. The last two are brilliant illustrations for the time: note the head and beak of the starling. (MS in the British Library)

particularly those reproduced in this book, have a quality that exceeds that of many illustrations in the publications of the next four hundred years. At this time (and for much of the subsequent three centuries) illustrations in general were rather poor, except for those showing species with distinctive shapes and features such as crane, some raptors, and some species of ducks and geese.

Local historical information

There was an extremely practical source of ornithological information in the early medieval period. This was the household accounts, known as court rolls, kept of the administration of the various halls, castles, monasteries and manors in the land – and they prove informative.

The Account Rolls at Durham Monastery from the fourteenth and fifteenth centuries described populations of crows and rooks being thinned out and the birds subsequently eaten. There was a single record of the skylark, suggesting perhaps that this species was less common then, although an Italian visitor to London in the sixteenth century noted that skylarks were caught and eaten in large numbers. The Durham Rolls named magpie, mallard, teal, fieldfare, merlin, goshawk, heron, whooper swan, mute swan kept by the monks, wild goose (species unknown), shelduck, eider, plover (species unstated but probably lapwing), curlew, woodcock, snipe, crane, capercaillie, black grouse, red grouse, pheasant and grey partridge (Ticehurst, 1923). All these species were, in general, obtained for culinary purposes, with the exception of the merlin and goshawk (used in falconry).

In his book on the history of Sawston, a village in Cambridgeshire, T. F. Teversham, a local historian interested in birds, quoted an extract from court rolls of around 1450 referring to 'Profits of the Common Severall to the Lord':

> Ptrych [partridges] enough yf they be kept from Traudlyng
> Bytonys [bitterns] bredyng yn Midelmore and Tryplowemore
> Larkys, nought all winter.
> Malardys [mallards], Herons and Storkys – good hawking …
> gete plenty crows and dawes [jackdaws].

An important issue raised by this extract is the status of the white stork (Fig. 10). 'Storkys' were almost certainly common cranes. Turner (Chapter 2) stated that the white stork was not known in this country, but the common crane was found in the fens of Cambridgeshire and Norfolk. Sir Thomas Browne (Chapter 4), writing of the birdlife of Norfolk, mentioned both crane and stork but gave the

FIG 10. White stork, from the Willughby/Ray *Ornithology* (1676).

impression that while the crane was a regular visitor the stork was rare. So rare that the reported nesting of a pair of white storks on St Giles Cathedral, Edinburgh, in 1416 was noted – although to this day this record is regarded with suspicion. While it may be hasty to be emphatic about it, all the available evidence suggests that the white stork was not found in this country and that the names crane, stork and heron were used without precision.

Yapp (1982) provided information on birds kept in captivity, particularly from prohibitions mentioned in the statutes of some Oxford colleges. The 'keeping of larkes' was forbidden at Queen's (1340), keeping 'thrushes or other singing birds' was forbidden at Magdalen (1450), and at Corpus Christi it was forbidden to keep 'singing birds such as those thrushes called Song Thrushes, Nightingale, Starling and Blackbird within college or without'.

In the *Liber Albus*, compiled in 1419, which contained the price levels set for poulterers to charge, we find the following (in old money):

a cygnet 4d	plover 3d	12 finches 1d
teal 2d	curlew 6d	river mallard 3d
bittern 18d	snipe 1d	heron 16d
woodcock 3d	whimbrel 18d	partridge 4d
4 larks 1d	pheasant 12d	12 thrushes 6d

Other instances of the culinary interest in birds can be gleaned from the accounts of a variety of celebratory feasts, such as the wedding breakfast of Henry IV in 1403 and the coronation dinners of Henry V in 1413 and Henry VI in 1422. To celebrate the enthronement of George Neville as Archbishop of York in 1465 a total of 17,512 birds of sixteen species were consumed. This was the order:

Swans	400	Cranes	204	Geese	2,000	Bittours	204
Plovers	400	Heronshawes	400	Quayles	1,200	Fessauntes	200
Peacocks	104	Partridges	500	Mallard	4,000	Woodcocks	400
Teal	4,000	Curlews	100	Egrittes	1,000		

The foules they call Rees [reeves] 2,400

It must have been quite a feast.

Another identification problem is that of 'egrittes'. It is possible that they were indeed what we know today as egrets, and that these 'egrittes' had been imported from the Continent especially for the occasion, or maybe that they were present in Britain, possibly found in the Fens. Bourne (2003), reviewing the work of Fred Stubbs, a nineteenth-century ornithologist, has recently suggested that evidence from poulterers' records and other sources makes it almost certain that little egrets were present in this country, although there is no scientific evidence to date to suggest that they were. The name egret or egritte may have been used for any birds of the heron family, but in this case both herons and bitterns are named as well, so it can hardly be either of those species. Bourne (1981) described a similar gastronomic session that took place just over the Channel at Calais in October 1532, when 40,000 birds were reportedly consumed when Henry VIII met Francis I of France. These included birds described as 'brewes', which Bourne has pointed out were also listed by London poulterers, and which he has identified as night herons (Fig. 11), even going so far as to suggest that these birds might have been obtained in Britain and

FIG 11. Night heron by Archibald Thorburn, from his book *British Birds* (1915–18). Was this the 'brewe' of medieval times, as suggested by Bourne?

therefore could have been much more commonly found than today. As with the little egret, however, there is no scientific evidence of this.

The *Book of St Albans*, printed in 1486, contained some technical niceties in its treatises on hunting and hawking, including a reference to sparrowhawk and goshawk as the true hawking birds, and a list that suggested an eagle for an emperor, a gyrfalcon for a king, a peregrine for a prince, a merlin for a lady and a hobby for a young man.

Thomas Elyot, a politician born around 1490, Sheriff of Oxford and Member of Parliament for Cambridgeshire, produced several books, one of which gives a good description of the 'Caprimulgus' (nightjar), in addition explaining the origin of the species' vernacular name of 'goatsucker':

> *birds like to gulls which appear not by day, but in the night they come into goat pens and do suck the goats whereby the udders of them be mortified.*

Finally in this era I must mention John Leland, whose 'itinerary' in or around 1538 included notes on several birds. On the Farne Islands in Northumberland

he found 'certain big foules called St Cuthbert's birds' (eiders) (Fig. 12), and
commented on the 'puffins, birds less than ducks', which were 'found breeding
there in the cliffy rocks'.

Names remained inconsistent. *Coturnix*, for example, in an interpretation
by John Trevisa in a 1397 edition of the Bartholomew book *De proprietatibus*, is
described as 'having fixed times of coming ... dreading the Goshawk', and so
on – yet it is given the English name curlewe, when clearly the narrative refers
to the bird we know as the quail (present scientific name *Coturnix coturnix*). Then
there is the name *Upupa*: Trevisa's description is of the hoopoe (scientific name
Upupa epops), but he calls the bird the lapwinge (an accurate description of the
hoopoe's flight pattern). These problems are further exacerbated when one
author quotes another, thus carrying the confusion into a further generation.
Nevertheless, the large number of names in the written records by this time
indicates that they were used commonly – which in itself implies that these
species must have been recognised by a significant proportion of the population
for a long period preceding.

So the observations began to emerge, almost despite the writings of some
of the scholars of the time, and by the sixteenth century the number of birds

FIG 12. A curiously stylised drawing of an eider (or St Cuthbert's duck), from the
Willughby/Ray *Ornithology* (1676).

known to be British would have been over a hundred. Yet in the mid sixteenth century there was not a single comprehensive book on birds. This situation was remedied by the man now regarded as the father of British ornithology, William Turner.

CHAPTER 2

The First Bird Book

No annals of ornithology would be complete without proper reference to the labours of William Turner, who has been called the Father of British Ornithology, for with the aid of this enquiring and industrious man we may make some tolerable attempt to sketch the status of British birds in the sixteenth century.

J. H. Gurney, *Early Annals of Ornithology* (1921)

I N THE PERIOD OF the late Middle Ages two fundamental social developments took place that created the environment for the serious study of birds in Britain to begin. The first was the expansion of the universities at Oxford and Cambridge, which allowed men to pursue academic studies of their choosing. Although the universities were mostly concerned with subjects such as philosophy and theology, the study of natural sciences and medicine gradually became acceptable. The second important development was a technical one, the development of printing. This had begun in Britain around 1470, and was to bring into the public domain books that had hitherto been restricted to only the most learned of men. However, those in power regarded general education with such suspicion that publishing was restricted to London, Oxford and Cambridge. Yet this was the renaissance. Columbus was discovering America, and in England the Tudors, triumphant in the Wars of the Roses, were to bring stability of government and a new prosperity to the country.

In the study of birds there was a gradual, if somewhat disjointed, advance. This began with the book published by William Turner who, like many other learned men of his time, studied a variety of subjects, most particularly theology and natural science. Despite the trials and tribulations of his personal life,

Turner was able to lay the foundations in Britain of both botany and ornithology in his comparatively short lifetime.

WILLIAM TURNER: *A SHORT AND SUCCINCT HISTORY OF THE PRINCIPAL BIRDS NOTICED BY PLINY AND ARISTOTLE* (1544)

William Turner, the son of a tanner, was born in Morpeth, Northumberland in or about 1508. It is clear from his subsequent writings that even as a child he was interested in the flora and fauna of the countryside. He described the nest of a robin based on a sighting as a boy. He noted the nesting of kestrels on the church tower at Morpeth (Fig. 13) and described the typical local birds of his home area such as the dipper, which Turner called the water craw, corncrakes calling among the flax and cormorants nesting at the mouth of the River Tyne.

Turner went to school in Morpeth and was noticed by Thomas, 1st Lord Wentworth, who arranged for Turner to go to Pembroke Hall (as it was then) at Cambridge University in 1526. Here he studied for his BA, and he was elected a Fellow in 1530. While at Cambridge he studied botany, and in 1538 published his *Herbal*. Also while at Cambridge he came under the influence of the two religious reformers, Ridley and Latimer, who taught him much of the Protestant doctrine of which he became a passionate adherent throughout his life – the cause of considerable difficulties for him. He was ordained a Deacon at Lincoln Cathedral in 1536, and around the year 1537 he married Jane Ander, the daughter of an Alderman of Cambridge. Sometime in 1540 he left Cambridge on a preaching tour and spent time in Oxfordshire where, after a short while, he was imprisoned for preaching without a licence.

On his release, presumably as a result of his experiences, he left England and travelled to Italy, where he attended botanical lectures at Bologna; and he took an MD degree, either at Bologna or at Ferrera, all within a year at most. From there he travelled to Switzerland, where he made the acquaintance of Conrad Gesner, a man who had an enormous influence on the progress of natural history across Europe. Gesner was the first and the greatest of the compilers, and Turner became one of his principal correspondents. The knowledge compiled by Gesner was to lead to the most comprehensive publication on the fauna of the known world at that time; the *Historia animalium*, which ran to 15 books of which the third was dedicated to birds and published in 1555. By early 1544 Turner was in Cologne, where he published the work that established his reputation as an ornithologist (preceding Gesner's volume on birds).

FIG 13. Kestrel, noted breeding on the church tower at Morpeth by William Turner. From Swaysland's *Familiar Wild Birds* (1883–8).

Turner's *Short and Succinct History* was written in Latin, with the grandiose title *Avium praecipuarum quarum apud Plinium et Aristotelem mentio est brevis & succincta historia*, and while it was based on information from the two classic philosophers, its great historical importance is that it contained large amounts of original information drawn from Turner's own observations. The book included many species that had not previously been described as British birds, and it can reasonably be considered to be the first British bird book, as well as almost certainly the world's first printed book devoted entirely to birds. It was reissued in 1823 by George Thackeray, Provost of King's College, Cambridge, but the reprint became as rare as the original so A. H. Evans, another Cambridge academic, produced a new version in 1903 with the Latin on the left-hand page and an English translation on the right. The translations given here are taken from the edition by Evans.

In alphabetical order, Turner's book described some 110–120 birds, most occurring in England. It is not possible to be precise about the number since one or two species were not given English names and the Latin names were not always those of today. Under the Latin name heading were names in Greek, German and English. Some of the English names, especially their spellings, make interesting reading: tele (teal); water craw (dipper); turtel duve; cukkow (cuckoo); sparhauc (sparrowhawk); bramlynge; see gell (*Larus* sp.); white semaw with a blak cop (black-headed gull); petridge (partridge); phesan (pheasant); wodspecht (woodpecker); cout (coot); nut-jobber (nuthatch); sterlynge (starling); solend guse (gannet); nyghtyngall (nightingale); redetale (redstart); blakbyrd (blackbird); quale (quail; Fig. 14).

Turner's observations were remarkable. First and foremost they were obviously drawn from his fieldwork, and in this respect they differed markedly from almost all his contemporaries, whose observations were not so much observations as quotations. Secondly, and of considerable importance, Turner made it clear where he had seen each of the species mentioned, and explained that some did not occur in England. For example, 'the stork, though one of the best known of birds among the Germans is to nearly all my countrymen of Britain as unknown as the most unknown bird', and

> *I know of two sorts of kites, the greater and the less; the greater is in colour nearly rufous and in England is abundant and remarkably rapacious. This kind is wont to snatch food out of children's hands in our cities and towns. The other kind is smaller, blacker, and more rarely haunts cities. This I do not remember to have seen in England, though in Germany most frequently.*

Coturnix.
The Quail

FIG 14. Quail, from the Willughby/Ray *Ornithology* (1676).

So neither the black kite nor the white stork occurred in Britain as far as Turner knew (Fig. 15). This is evidence that encourages the view, expressed in the previous chapter, that mention of storks was simply confusion (with cranes, or possibly herons).

Turner also expanded on the features of species identification given by the classical writers. For example, Aristotle and Pliny mentioned only a single crow (*Cornix*) but Turner adds:

> There is also a sea-crow, which some call the winter crow, with black head, tail and wings and the remainder grey [hooded crow] ... there remains another crow, a grain-eater with white beak but black otherwise [rook].

Further examples of his observations on the status of some species in Britain include comments on the woodcock, which Turner records did not breed, and cranes (Fig. 16), which he records did:

Woodcocks are never seen with us save in the winter wherefore I have naught to say about their young or mode of nesting. They are chiefly caught in England in the woods at daybreak or at dusk, by means of nets hung in some place devoid of trees, and dropped when the bird comes.

Cranes moreover breed in England in marshy places I myself very often see their pipers [young] though some people born away from England urge that this is false.

Turner also noted similarities of plumage in young birds, writing of the redstart that:

The female and its brood are so much like the young of Rubecula [robin] that they can scarcely be distinguished by the sharpest eye. But by the motion of the tail they may be recognised.

Furthermore, Turner went on to dispel the theory of transmogrification, proposed by both Aristotle and Pliny, whereby the bird that is the robin in winter mysteriously turns into the redstart in summer.

FIG 15. Red kite, recognised by Turner as being the only kite in England. A drawing by Archibald Thorburn, from Swaysland's *Familiar Wild Birds* (1883–8).

FIG 16. Common crane, from the *Sherborne Missal* (c.1400).

His observations on the great grey shrike (Fig. 17) amount to a detailed account of both ecology and behaviour that deserves quoting at length:

In size it equals the least of the thrushes and to one observing from afar seems wholly grey. And yet inspecting it more nearly the chin the breast and the belly appear white and from the eye there reaches to the neck, although somewhat oblique, a long black patch. It has short wings and flies as if by bound upwards and downwards. It lives on beetles, butterflies and biggish insects, and not only these, but also birds after the manner of a hawk. For it kills Reguli [goldcrests and firecrests] and finches and as I once saw thrushes ... It does not fly down the birds that it kills and strike them with its claws like hawks, but ambushes them and attacks them and as I have often noted aims at the throat ... Moreover unlike other birds when it has an abundance of prey it stores some up against a shortage. It impales and hangs big flies and insects that it has caught on the thorns and spines of bushes ... It is of course only a winter visitor with us but nests freely in the Rhineland.

Turner also noted the presence of albino herons:

The Pella [heron] builds its nest in England on the lofty trees that grow not far from the banks of streams. The upper part of the body is blue, the lower is, however, somewhat

FIG 17. Great grey shrike, from Thomas Bewick's *History of British Birds* (1797).

white. It routs eagles or hawks, if they attack it suddenly, by the very liquid mutings of the belly, and thereby defends itself. Of this kind I have seen some white, though they are rare, which differed from the aforesaid neither in size nor shape of body, but in colour only. Furthermore the white has been observed in England to nest with the blue, and to bear offspring. Wherefore it is clear that they are one species.

These are not misidentified egrets, as you might expect, as Turner makes clear. Furthermore he shows understanding of one of the important features that define a species in that two morphs (colour types), however different in plumage, breed with fertility. Today white morphs are virtually unknown in the grey heron (*Ardea cinerea*), although they are found in the closely related *Ardea herodias*, the North American great blue heron. Turner also noted two white ravens he found in Cumberland (Cumbria) in 1548.

These short extracts give a flavour of the work as a whole and show Turner's unprecedented skill as a field ornithologist. The book represents a masterly work by the earliest British ornithologist (according to our knowledge), and if it had no other interest it is remarkable, as Fisher pointed out, in naming 105 species of British bird – including 14 previously undocumented species (see Appendix).

Turner continued his botanical studies on the Continent until the death of Henry VIII and the accession of Edward VI in 1547, when he returned to England and became chaplain and physician to the Lord Protector, the Duke of Somerset. He lived at Kew, where he established a botanic garden (not the famous one). With Protestants ascendant, Turner prospered. He was incorporated MD of Oxford and appointed a Prebendary of York. However, it is clear that his only wish was to be given some post, either ecclesiastical or academic, whereby he would be free to pursue his studies and to publish his work. Around the year 1550 attempts to get him a college mastership at Oxford came to nought. Out of frustration, and because of his ailing health, he expressed the wish to return to Germany but instead was appointed Dean of Wells. In 1551 he published the first part of his *New Herbal*, and a year later was ordained priest by his old friend Ridley – now Bishop of London. Yet this was just the calm before the storm. Following the death of Edward VI in 1553, Mary took the country back to Catholicism and Turner virtually fled to the continent again until Elizabeth became queen in 1558, when he returned once more to the Deanery at Wells. At Wells he pursued his studies and published the second part of his *New Herbal* in 1562, only to be suspended for non-conformity in 1564. Finally he retreated to London, retaining his stipend – just – until his death four years later.

William Turner's botanical knowledge and interest probably outweighed his ornithological work. Yet while other men were active in the botanical area, as an ornithologist he was alone. In his writings he recognised no fewer than 238 species of plants and over 120 species of birds (not all British), and at his death he was engaged in further work on publications about both fish and birds, as well as in more botanical studies.

JOHN KAY (CAIUS): *OF SOME RARE PLANTS AND ANIMALS* (1570)

While of lesser interest in the development of ornithology than Turner, Caius is nonetheless a figure of some significance. Like Turner, Caius was a dedicated correspondent of Conrad Gesner. Indeed, much of Caius' investigative work seems to have been prompted by requests from Gesner both for written factual material and for illustrations, which it seems Caius drew himself. Although a lot of this information was included in Gesner's *Historia animalium*, Caius himself felt compelled to publish it also in his own name.

Born in Norwich in 1510 and educated there, John Caius progressed to Gonville Hall at Cambridge in 1529. His aim was to study subjects that would lead to ordination, yet an interest in Greek persuaded him to remain at Cambridge, and he was awarded a Fellowship in 1533, at some point adopting a Latinised spelling of his name. In 1539 he went to Padua, where he studied medicine for four years and was greatly influenced by Vesalius, the renowned anatomist. He received his MD in 1541 and lectured on the subject of Aristotle for a couple of years. He returned to London in 1545 and lectured on anatomy to surgeons, becoming a leading physician. In 1557 he refounded Gonville Hall, which became Gonville and Caius College, and two years later he was elected Master of the College and President of the Royal College of Physicians (Fig. 18).

Of Some Rare Plants and Animals (*De rairorum animalium atque stirpium historia*) was published in 1570, and was, unlike Turner's book, based very little on observations in the wild. Many of the creatures included were viewed by Caius at menageries in or around London and at various other places. Caius' book was, however, more factual than the many fanciful pre-Turner publications. For example, he refuted the story that the osprey had one foot taloned and the other webbed (a fable from Neckam and others), stating that both feet have talons. Yet he believed certain legend-like attributes. He repeated the fable that when the osprey is hunting, the fish turn upside-down in the water to show their white undersides, so that the osprey may have a free choice of target! From Caius we learn that ospreys were common around the coast, and he claimed to have kept one for a week until it died of starvation.

FIG 18. John Caius (Kay), co-founder of Gonville and Caius College, Cambridge, and author of *Of Some Rare Plants and Animals* (1570).

FIG 19. Puffin, a species kept by Caius. (Photograph by Rebecca Nason)

He also kept a puffin (Fig. 19), and gave a good description of the bird, saying that it refused to fly unless within sight of the sea. He suggested that the puffin hibernated 'like the cuckoo and the swallow'. This suggestion was doubtless prompted by the fact that puffins spend their non-breeding lives out at sea and would not have been seen at all in the winter in normal circumstances.

Caius was particularly interested in the names of birds, and was quite pedantic about their usage. This is not surprising since, as can be seen from Turner's work, colloquial names abounded and a single species might have six or seven different names in use in different parts of the country. Caius, for example, chided people in the use of the name cormorant, stating that 'corvorant' was correct, derived from *Corvus marinus* or water crow (not to be confused with the water craw of Turner!).

Yet despite his pedantry Caius got himself into a considerable muddle concerning geese. First he stated that 'brend' (as in brent goose) is a descriptive term for a mottled colour. Next he explained that the barnacle goose was so named because it was believed to hatch from a barnacle (a repeat of the fable). However, these two facts – a pseudo-fact in the case of the latter – became garbled in a letter to Gesner, in which he stated that the brend is the juvenile phase of the barnacle.

He gave good descriptions of the sea-pie (oystercatcher) and the dotterel, explaining how the latter could be caught by candlelight when it curiously imitated the actions of its pursuer, making itself easy prey. It was caught in quite large numbers on passage and considered a 'dainty dish'. Overall, Caius' work was a mixture of accurate and inaccurate information.

Both Turner and Caius were academics, both were involved with medicine, and both had associations with Cambridge University and Conrad Gesner – but there is no evidence to suggest that they were more than vaguely aware of each other's existence. Whether this was due to their differing views on religion, or simply to the fact that their paths never crossed, is not recorded – yet it remains a strange unexplained mystery that with so much in common they seem to have been virtually unacquainted.

OTHER WRITERS OF THE PERIOD

With the development of printing, learned men were able to produce books for a wider readership – but sadly few of these writers produced any significant information that was in any way novel; most writings were mere reworkings of the material already published. Thus, once written, misinformation was continually disseminated. The following are a few of the more reputable productions.

Edward Wotton's *De differentiis animalium* of 1552 was a compilation job, described as 'the first scientific work on animals by an Englishman', but according to Gesner it 'teaches us nothing new'.

Thomas Cooper's *Thesaurus linguae Romanae et Britannicae* of 1563 was in the form of a dictionary, re-issued many times. Cooper attempted to sort out some of the nomenclature problems, most notably with *Upupa*, which as we have seen Trevisa had confusingly named in English 'the lapwynge' but which was in fact the hoopoe (Fig. 20). Cooper states that it is

> *a birde no bigger than a thrush and hath a creste from his bill to the uttermost part of his heade which he stroutheth up or holdeth downe accordynge to his affection. Wherefore it can not be our Lapwynge as it hath been taken for.*

Thomas Muffet's *Health's Improvement* of 1595 listed over a hundred species of bird, with information drawn (sometimes almost verbatim) from Gesner's books, and thus indirectly from Turner and Caius. Muffet (his name is also variously

FIG 20. Hoopoe. (Photograph by Chris Martin)

spelt Muffett, Moufet or Moffet) was born in Shoreditch and attended Merchant Taylor's School before going to Trinity College, Cambridge, in 1567 (aged 14). At Cambridge he studied medicine under Caius, from whom he almost certainly gained his interest in natural history. After a period of travel he settled as a physician in London and moved in the highest circles. In around 1592 he moved to Wiltshire and became MP for Wilton. He was considered to be the British entomological pioneer. His *Health's Improvement* was not published until the following century, edited by a fellow physician, Christopher Bennet. Muffet's comments on birds are mainly concerned with their edibility, giving details of their diet and of how they taste, as can be seen by his entry on puffins: 'birds and no birds, that is to say birds in shew and fish in substance ... permitted by Popes to be eaten in Lent'. About cranes Muffet wrote:

> Cranes breed (as old Dr. Turner writ unto Gesner) not only in the Northern Countries
> amongst the Nation of Dwarfs but also in our English Fens ... Certain it is that they
> are of themselves hard, tough unfit for sound men's tables ... yet being young, killed
> with a Goshawk and hanged two or three daies by the heels, eaten with hot galantine,
> and drowned in sack, it is permitted unto indifferent stomachs.

Quite where the 'nation of dwarfs' is to be found is not entirely clear. Muffet mentioned migratory flights of woodcock and snipe, mainly because of their effect on flavour, commenting that the birds, 'especially at their first coming in, or rather when they have rested themselves after their long flight from beyond the seas, are fat.' On other subjects he made some original observations:

> Godwits are sold at four nobles the dozen ... Lincolnshire affordeth plenty of them ...
> Curlues feed wholsomly upon cockles, crevisses, muscles and periwinkles.

Muffet also described the 'houpes' (hoopoe) as being 'found once', suggesting that the species was as unusual in Britain then as it is today. A further observation concerned the rock dove, which he described in some detail, clearly from personal experience – the significance being that the subsequent Willughby/Ray *Ornithology* (see Chapter 4) described it only from an account given them by a correspondent.

From the same period is a picture book called *Portraits d'oyseaux et animaux etc.*, from the library of Thomas and Edmund Knyvet, father/son members of a Norfolk family with an interest in natural history. The illustrations are largely derived from the work of a Frenchman, Pierre Belon, whose *Histoire de la nature des oyseaux* was published in 1555, and the book belonged to the Knyvet family early in the seventeenth century. Interestingly, at an unknown date someone added English names to the Latin, as below (with my comments in square brackets):

Collurio: the Warriangle [great grey? shrike]
Caprimulgus: the Night Raune, a Night Clapper, a Shrike owle [nightjar]
Boscas: the Widgenne [*boscas* was later used – wrongly – as the specific name for the Mallard before *platyrhynchos*]
Vanellus: the Lapwinge, a Bastard Plover, a horne Pie [lapwing]
Himantopus: the Oxe-eye [oystercatcher]
Oedicnemus: the Stone Curlewe or Field Courlewe [stone curlew]
Cornix: the Devonshier Crow [carrion crow]
Monedula: the Chofe, a Caddow, a Dawe [jackdaw]
Upupa: the Houpper or houping bird [hoopoe]
Sitta: the Nutthacker [nuthatch]
Ficedula: the Bullfinche [*Ficedula* is today a generic name of flycatchers, e.g. pied flycatcher, so why the bullfinch?]
Ruticilla: the Redstert, a Prest's Crowne [redstart]
Pyrrhula: the Aupe [bullfinch again. The name 'aupe' or 'aup' was commonly used for the bullfinch, and *Pyrrhula* is the present scientific name]
Parus maior: the Collmouse, Tydie [coal tit? but today *Parus major* is the great tit]
Parus sylvaticus: the Capon Wagtayle [confusing, but could be long-tailed tit]
Fringilla: the Chafefinch, a Jack Baker, a Sheld Appell, a spink
Apus: the Martlett [swift]

Throughout the sixteenth century, information about birds continued to be recorded in the accounts of manor houses, for example from the home of the Le Straunge family at Hunstanton in Norfolk from 1519 to 1578, documented by Gurney (1921). The location of this manor house, so close to the Wash, explains the presence of many of the species in the accounts. Those mentioned were golden plover, lapwing, 'wylde goose' (probably pink-footed goose), 'brantes' (brent goose), 'redshanke', mallard, 'a swanne' (whooper or Bewick's, since mute were kept tame), 'cockle dokes' (literally cockle ducks, said by Gurney to be common scoter, but could equally have been eiders), 'sepys' (sea-pies – oystercatchers), woodcock, 'spowe' (whimbrel according to Gurney), 'wydgyn' (wigeon), 'tele' (teal), 'curlewe', dotterel (might have been dotterel on passage, or possibly ringed plover), 'sea dotterel' (turnstone), 'styntes' (stints were probably any small sandpiper, including, or perhaps mainly, dunlin), 'knotte', 'snypes', grey plover (probably the first mention of this species in Britain, dated 1523), 'fleddowe' (godwit – bar-tailed most likely), great bustard, crane (for which there were quite a few entries, one stating 'three cranes from the fouler of Tichewell'), 'popeler' (spoonbill), hernes (grey heron), 'buttour' (bittern – only one record), partridge (grey partridge – many records), pheasants (many records), 'quaylle' (only a few records), 'stockdowes', woodpigeon, blackbirds, larks (killed by a hobby), coots (also killed by a hobby), 'seemew' (probably black-headed gull, but the proximity to the coast leaves open the possibility of other species). For hunting other birds they used goshawks, 'spar-hawkes' and peregrine. One tenant in the midst of a cash-flow problem paid his rent with twelve 'sparouse' (house sparrows). Also mentioned in some entries were unspecified species under the catch-alls of either 'grete byrdes' or 'litell byrdes'. Some entries even specified the means of death such as 'kylled wt ye crossbowe' or 'kylled wt ye gunne', and there is also evidence of the use of nets to catch waders in the maintenance accounts, which show payment to various people for 'twyne for ye stynte nett'. Other species were also netted, as is indicated by the purchase of 'ffesaunt nettes, ptrich nettes, hoby nettes' – these latter were most likely nets set for skylarks (Fig. 21) as the hobby drove them in.

FIG 21. Skylark. (Photograph by Rebecca Nason)

UNPROTECTION OF BIRDS ACT

The prevailing attitudes to wild birds in the sixteenth century are shown by a 1534 Act of Henry VIII (set out in a publication of 1594 and quoted by Mullens, 1922) which described the rewards given for 'the destruction of noisome foule and Vermine':

> any heades of old crowes, chouhges [jackdaws], pies [magpies], or rookes ... for the heades of every three of them a penny; and for every five egges of any of them unbroken, a pennie; and likewise for every twelve stares [starlings] heades a pennie ... for everie head of merton [merlin?], hawkes, fursekite [?], moldkite [?], buzzard, scag [?shag], cormerant, or ringtail [harrier sp.] two pence ... for every iron [erne = white-tailed eagle] or osspraces [osprey] head four pence; for the head of every woodwall [woodpecker], pie, jay, raven or kite a pennie, the kings fisher a pennie, for every bullfinch or other bird that devoureth the blouth [blossom] of fruit, a pennie.

Despite rather strong encouragement for the destruction of birds, the Act went on to point out that while engaged in the business of destroying those on the vermin list some other species were *not* to be disturbed. Protected species included 'hawkes [rather illogical, since they were also on the vermin list], herons, egrittes, paupers [? pipers, i.e. young cranes], swannes or shovelers [spoonbill; Fig. 22] and doves'. There was also a prohibition on the taking of some of the species on the destruction list in 'anie Parke', and against the killing of kites or ravens in 'anie citie or towne corporate or within two miles of the same'.

Kites and ravens were scavengers, and as such acted as sanitary agents – hence the need to protect them. It is also notable that the name 'egrittes' appears in this list – again the implication that egrets were to be found in Britain.

By the end of this period the study of birds had begun to diversify, progressing from identification and status to a more enquiring state, with evidence of a growing interest in certain facets of bird behaviour. By the end of the sixteenth century, ornithology was crying out for the arrival of a systematic approach to bring more order to the subject. This would be provided by the book produced by Francis Willughby and John Ray.

FIG 22. Spoonbill by Archibald Thorburn, from Lilford's *Coloured Figures of the Birds of the British Islands* (1885–97).

CHAPTER 3

The First British List

As some day it may happen that a victim must be found,
I've got a little list – I've got a little list.

W. S. Gilbert, *The Mikado*

SOME KNOWLEDGE OF the species of birds found in Britain emerges
from the sources discussed in the preceding chapters, and by studying
the poems, scientific books, estate accounts and other material it is
possible to compile a list of the birds that were known in each period. Indeed
some works such as Aelfric's list may have been an attempt at such a compilation.
Extrapolating from all these sources, Fisher estimated that by the close of the
sixteenth century 150 species had been named; my list (see Appendix) gives 152.
In this chapter I examine two significant lists of the late sixteenth and
seventeenth centuries. The first is unpublished, taken from a copy of a book by
Gesner that was owned by a man named Nicholas Carter, but the second is the
genuine article – the first published British List.

THE CARTER LIST

In 1921 the ornithological historian Hugh Gladstone purchased a copy of
Conrad Gesner's *Icones animalium*, published in 1560. Gladstone discovered
that his copy had belonged to one Nicholas, and subsequently Bernard, Carter,
and that, around the year 1600, either Nicholas or Bernard Carter had annotated
some of the species in the book, adding English names and comments on
nomenclature – in effect producing a list of the birds he knew to occur in

Britain. The Carter annotations provide a valuable source of information on the state of ornithological knowledge at the start of the seventeenth century. Gladstone's attempts to discover more about the Carters sadly yielded nothing further. The complete Carter list is as follows. The Latin names are as published by Gesner, followed by Carter's English names and comments, with Gladstone's (1924) and/or my own comments in square brackets. Like Merrett (below) the Carter list included domestic birds and even 'the bird of paradise', but these are not included here.

Aquila – an Eagle [presumably golden eagle]

Aquila Anataria – A Bald-bushard [marsh harrier]

Astur – A Gos-hauke; Male, a Tercell of Gos-hauke

Accipiter minor – A Spar-hauke or Sparrow-hauke

Tinnunculus – A Kestrill, or Wind-hover, a Stanegall or Steingall

Milvus – a Kite; a Gleid; a Puttocke

Buteo – a Bushard [buzzard]

Falco – A Falcon; Male, a Tercell Gentle [peregrine]

Aesalon – A Merlin; Male, a Jack-merlin

Dendrofalcus – A Hobbie

Lanius – Hauk-Robbin unless I am mistaken a solitary bird [shrike]

Vespertilio – A Batt; a Reermouse or a Flindermouse [yes! Bats were birds in the sixteenth century and, as we shall see, even in the nineteenth century to some misguided souls]

Grus – a Crane

Corvus – A Raven which lives on Prey

Cornix – A Dung-hill Crow; or a Carion-crow

Monedula – A Daw; or a Jack-Daw; a Cadesso; a Chough; a Money-stealer

Caryocatactes – A Rouke; perhaps from its hoarse cry [in fact the illustration showed a nutcracker, and the Latin name is that of a nutcracker, but the quality of some of the pictures was so poor that Carter could be forgiven for misidentification, and he may not have been familiar with the nutcracker if it was then, as it is today, a sporadic visitor] (Fig. 23)

Graculus coracias – A Cornish Chough

Pica glandaria – A Jay

Pica – A Py; a Magg-py; a Haggester; a Py-annet; a Nan-py; a Piot

Turdus minor – A Whindle; a Redd-wing, a Bow-thrush

Turdus viscivorus – A Misle-bird; a Jarre, from its hoarse cry

Upupa – I once saw a little bird in every respect like this figure however dead; it was called by men the Whooping-bird and is considered portentious [hoopoe]

Merula – An Owsle; a Black-bird

Merula Torquata – A Fieldfarr [in this case the picture was of a ring ouzel and the Latin name is now that of the ring ouzel]

Cuculus – A Cuckoo; or a Goake

Sturnus – A Starling; a Stadle or a Sheep-starlin

Picus viridis – A Wood-pecker; A Hewhole, or a Yough-all; a Hickway [green woodpecker]

Picus varius – A Nutthacke [the illustration showed a spotted woodpecker, species undetermined]

Oriolus – A Woodpecker; or a Speiught [here the illustration was, as you might expect from the Latin name, a golden oriole]

Picus Varius – A Nuttrobber [this time the illustration *was* a nuthatch, generally called a nuthack – various spellings]

Certhius – Climbtree; a Climber [treecreeper]

Iynx – More properly a Nutt-hack and by some a Glenn-bird or a Wry-neck, a bird of magic, etc

Picus Muralis – A Climber the less [? woodpecker sp.]

Loxias – the Wimble bird [crossbill]

Passer – A Sparrow

Emberiza – A Bunting [corn bunting]

Carduelis – A Goldfinch

Linaria – A Linet

Fringilla – A Caff-finch

Acanthis – A Thistlewarpe [redpoll]

Citrinella – A Yellow-ambar [yellowhammer]

Chloris – A Greenfinch

Parus major – An Aup ['aup' was an alternative for bullfinch but in this case applied to the great tit]

Parus caeruleus – A Titt-mouse [blue tit]

Parus monticola – An Ox-eye [coal tit]

Luscinia – A Nightingale

FIG 23. Nutcracker, from the Willughby/Ray *Ornithology* (1676). Obviously drawn from a specimen, and of much better quality than most of the illustrations in the book.

Erithacus – A Redd-breast; a Robin-ruck or a Robin-redd-breast; a Ruddock

Pyrrhulas – A Bull-finch

Troglodytes – A Wren or a Jiny-wrenn

Hirundo – A Swallow

Cypsilus – A Swift

Hirundo rustica – A Martin

Urogallus – A Cocke of the Wood [capercaillie]

Meleagris – A Ginny-henn [guinea fowl – presumably kept domestically]

Perdix major – French Partridge [red-legged partridge]

Perdix Minor – A Partridge

Lagopus – The White Partridge [ptarmigan]

Palumbus minor – A Stockdove

Palumbus major – A Ringdove; a Wood-pigeon; often a Cowshott

Turtur – A Turtle-dove

Otis – A Bustard [great bustard]

Alauda – A lerke [skylark]

Alauda cristata – A Tit-larke badly drawn [in fact it was a crested lark and not the 'titlark' or meadow pipit] (Fig. 24)

Coturnix – a Quail

Anser ferus – A Wilde Goose amongst which it seems there is an even smaller species of Goose in England; Brante-geese

FIG 24. Meadow Pipit. (Photograph by Rebecca Nason)

Anser – A Goose; male, a Gander and in the north a Stegg

Anas – Male, a drake; female, a ducke

Anas fera – A Drake

Querquedula – A Teale

Cygnus – A Swan

Corvus aquaticus – A Cormorant

Merganser – A Bergander ['bergander' was a shelduck]

Anser arborum – A Goose

Mergus – A Cormorant [again!]

Colymbus major – The great Didopper or after the Dutch Arse-foote; a Loune
    [? diver sp.]

Colymbus minor – A Dapchick; a Puffin; a Didopper

Fulica – A Coote

Pelecanus – A Shoveler [spoonbill]

Recurvirostra – A Rheeme [avocet]

Larus – A Sea-gull; a Cobb; a Gray-gull

Sterna – A Skirre [tern]

Hirundo sylvestris – A Martin

Capra – A Lapp-winge and by some a Teuwhit or a Greene Plover, but the crest is
    extremely badly drawn nor is the beak well

FIG 25. A 'white' wagtail, which is the nominate form of pied wagtail found on the Continent and a visitor to Britain. From the Willughby/Ray *Ornithology* (1676). This drawing may be from a specimen collected by Willughby during the journeys he made with Ray to the continent (see Chapter 4).

Ispida – A Kingsfisher

Gallinula – A Cock-snite or a Judd-cock [not entirely clear, as snipe appears below. Is this a jack snipe?]

Erythropus – A Redd-shanke or a Touk

Rusticula – A Woodcock; by fowlers a Small-cock

Gallinago – A Snite or a Snipe

Limosa – A Rebeck [could be a godwit – the Latin name is right]

Ardea – A Herne or Heron or Heronshaw

Ardea stellaris – A Bittern or rather Boutern; a bird resounding

Ciconia – A Stork

Motacilla – A Wagg-taile, a Dish-washer, a Seed-bird, a Wagg-stert [pied wagtail] (Fig. 25)

Motacilla flava – A Yellow Dish-washer [yellow wagtail]

Bernacla – and also in some parts Rode-goose or Coal-goose. The legs, thighs and feet longer than they should be [barnacle goose]

Carter's list includes at least 86 species. Within the list avocet, yellow wagtail and redwing are mentioned for the first time as British birds. Were it not for uncertainty with woodpeckers and golden oriole the total could have been 90 or more. It is possible that Carter knew other British birds that did not appear in Gesner's book, since his entries were determined by the birds that Gesner included.

The text that Carter annotated was entirely in Latin, although Gesner had previously given English names for several species in his *Historia animalium* of 1555. Many of the names added by Carter were different from those used by Gesner in his earlier book, suggesting that Carter's additions included several more colloquial names that were not known to Gesner.

CHRISTOPHER MERRETT AND HIS *PINAX RERUM NATURALIUM BRITANNICARUM*

The first comprehensive list of British Birds was published in 1666, ten years before the emergence of the Willughby/Ray *Ornithology* (see Chapter 4). The author, Christopher Merrett, was born in Gloucestershire in 1614. In 1631 he became a member of Gloucester Hall, Oxford, before moving to Oriel College two years later. He took his BA degree in 1635 and went on to study medicine. Merrett then moved to London, where he became a member of the Royal College of Physicians in 1651, and he lived and had a practice at Amen Corner.

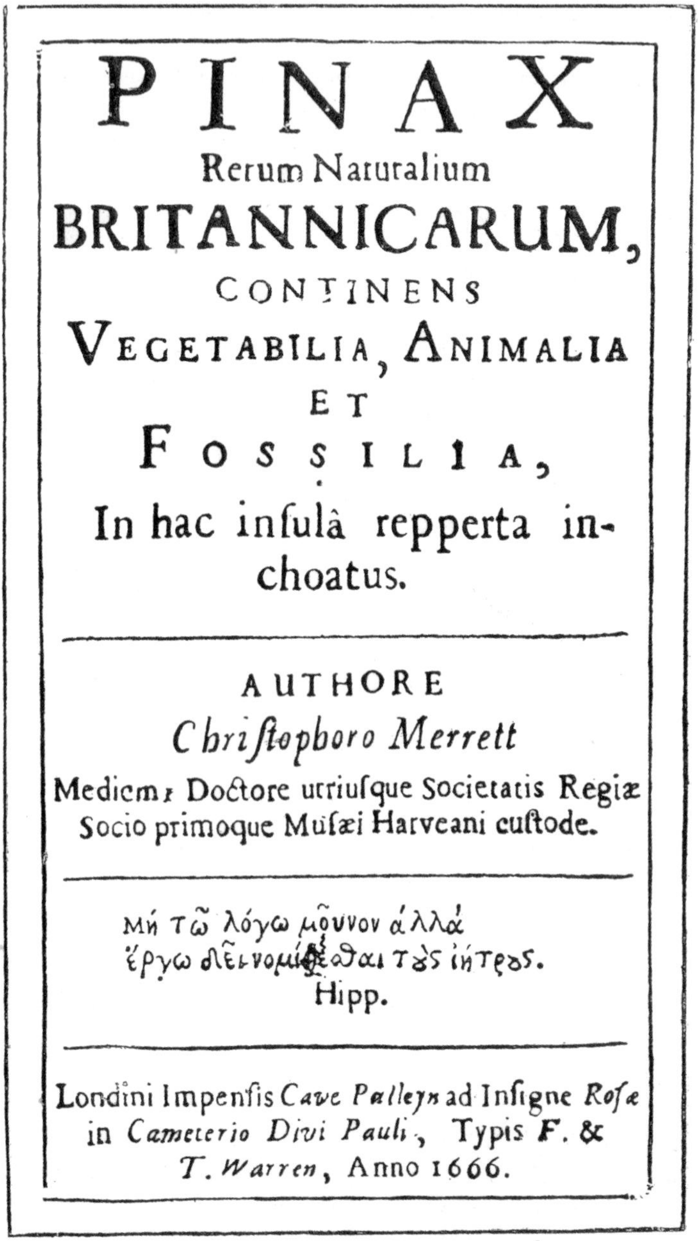

PINAX

Rerum Naturalium

BRITANNICARUM,

CONTINENS

VEGETABILIA, ANIMALIA

ET

FOSSILIA,

In hac infulâ repperta in-
choatus.

AUTHORE

Chriſtophoro Merrett

Medicmɾ Doctore utriuſque Societatis Regiæ
Socio primoque Muſæi Harveani cuſtode.

Μή Τῶ λόγω μοῦννον ἀλλά
ἔργω δἐιτνομιⱥⱥⱥⱥⱥⱥⱥⱥⱥⱥ Τⱥⱥ ίήΤⱥⱥⱥ.
Hipp.

Londini Impenſis *Cave Pulleyn* ad Infigne *Roſæ*
in *Cæmeterio Divi Pauli*, Typis *F.* &
T. Warren, Anno 1666.

FIG 26. Title page of Merrett's *Pinax* (1666). From Mullens, *British Birds*, 1908b.

He was also listed among the first members of the Royal Society. He died in August 1695.

During his life Merrett was the author of many works on both natural history and medicine, and his *Pinax rerum naturalium Britannicarum* (Fig. 26), which was an attempt to catalogue all living things found in Britain, included the first published list of British birds.

The list itself was more or less restricted to the names of the species he knew to be found in Britain, in both Latin and (in some cases, but by no means all) English. For some species the briefest comment was added, and where there were comments it is clear that the information was drawn from other sources, chiefly the works of Giraldus Cambrensis, Ulisse Aldrovandi, whose *Ornithology* had been published sixty years earlier, and John Jonston (Jonstonus), the first edition of whose *History of Birds* had been published in 1650. Both Aldrovandi and Jonstonus were compilers, the former with greater originality than the latter; but their works were considered less and less worthy over time. Merrett also, it seems, was no original ornithologist.

It seems worthwhile to give Merrett's list in full, since it is not readily available elsewhere and provides interesting reading – mainly because of the various anomalies. This version is taken from that published by W. H. Mullens in 1908. Some explanation of the names, based on comments by Mullens, is provided in round brackets, with any additional comments of my own in square brackets. The spelling and use of capitals etc. are those of Merrett.

In addition to the named birds, Merrett included a few brief descriptions (in Latin) but with no specific names in either Latin or English. Regrettably some of these entries remain obscure. In addition, there appears to be duplication of one or two species, and where the male and female have different plumages they were often regarded as separate species and thus given separate names. Merrett's list demonstrates some similarity to the scientific nomenclature of today, while being also littered with anomalies.

Aquila, the Eagle [golden eagle, or was it the white-tailed eagle? – probably the latter was more widespread]

Accipiter, the Hawk [which hawk? – all the obvious ones appear elsewhere in the list]

Haliaetus, the Sea Eagle (osprey) [Merrett mentioned Cornwall]

Lanarius, the Lanar, found in Sherwood Forest and the Forest of Dean [possibly peregrine, although perhaps just an error by Merrett]

Accip. Palumbarius, the Goshawk

Accip. Fringillarius & Nisus, the Sparrow-hawk, the Muschel

Tinnunculus, a Stannel, or Stonegall, a Kestrel or Kastrel

Falco, the Faulcon found in Pembrokeshire (peregrine)

Coccyx Cuculus, the Cuckoe or Guckoe

Lanius, the Butcher Bird or murdering-Bird (red-backed shrike?) [or great grey shrike?]

Milvus, the forked tail'd Kite, a Glede, a Puttock [red kite]

Subuteo, the ring-tail'd Kite (hen harrier?)

Buteo Triorchis, the Buzzard

Peronos, the Bald Buzzard, or Kite (marsh harrier?)

Noctua, the night, or little grey owl bubo a like fowl [little owl]

Ulula, the white hooping Owl, or Owlet, or Howlet (barn owl)

Strix, the Screech, or Screeching Owl (tawny owl)

Corvus, the Raven

Corvus, Cornix nigra, Cornix simpliciter our common or Carrion Crow

Cornix frugilega, spermalogus, a Rook

Cornix aquaticus (dipper?)

Cornix Cinerea, the Royston Crow [hooded crow]

Graculus vel Mondula, a Jackdaw, a Chough [jackdaw]

Coracius Arist, the Cornish Chough [chough]

Pica Glandaria, a Jay

Pica, the Magpie, Pyot, Py-anet

Pica Marina, the Sea Pye (oystercatcher)

Vespertilio, a Bat, Flittermouse, Rearmouse [as in Carter's list]

Loxias, the Shell-Apple (crossbill) [Merrett mentioned Warwick]

Caprimulgus, the Goat-sucker [nightjar – Merrett mentioned Hampshire and that it was rare]

Pavo, the Peacock

Gallo pavo, the Turkey-cock

Phasianus, the Pheasant

Urogallus, major Cock of the Wood (capercaillie) (Fig. 27)

Gallina Coryllorum, the Hasel Hen, Grous [red grouse]

Gall. Africana, the Guiney Hen [guinea fowl]

Otis, Tarda, Bistarda, the Bustard [great bustard – Merrett mentioned Newmarket Heath]

Attagen, a Godwit [species undetermined – Merrett mentioned Lincoln]

Perdix Ruffa, the Partridge [grey partridge]

Coturnix, the Quail

Rusticola minor, the Snipe or Snite

Gallinago Rusticola minor, the Jack Snipe

FIG 27. Capercaillie, possibly the finest of all the illustrations painted by Archibald Thorburn for his four-volume *British Birds* (1915–18).

Rusticola major, Scolopax. Gallinago. The Wood-cock

Ralla-Anglor, the Rail, or King of the Quails (corncrake)

Upupa, the Hoopee [hoopoe – Merrett mentioned the New Forest in Hampshire and Essex and stated that it was rare]

Gallus, a cock [domestic cockerel]

Gall. Palustris, a Moor-hen (black grouse)

Gallina rustica [not possible to identify]

Fulica, a Coot

Ispida, the Kings-fisher

Gallina Aq. (the figure in Jonstonus is a moorhen)

Gallina serica (the figure in Jonstonus is a godwit)

[there follows a list of domestic dove/pigeon types with such exotic names as
Culver, Cropper, Jacobins, Carriers, Shakers, Runts, Helmets, Smiters and *Tumblers*]

Turtur, the Turtle Dove

Palumbus major torquatus, a Ring-Dove, or Quist, a Cowshot [woodpigeon]

Oenas seu vinago, a Stock-Dove, or Wood-Pidgeon [stock dove]

Passer domesticus, the House-Sparrow

Passer pusillus in Junglandibus degens [tree sparrow?]

Junco, the Reed Sparrow (reed bunting)

Carduelis, a Gold-finch

Calandra, a Bunting (corn bunting)

Coccothraustes (hawfinch) (Fig. 28)

Fringilla, the Common, or Chaffinch, a Sheld apl or Spink

Monti-fringilla, the Bramble, or Brambling

Chloris, the Green-finch

Citrinella, the Yellow-hammer

Linaria, the Linet

Luteola, a Siskin [Merritt reported that Turner found it in Cambridgeshire]

Alauda, the Lark [skylark]

Alauda pratensis, the tit-Lark [meadow pipit]

Alauda cristata, the wood-Lark

Rubicilla, a Bull finch, a Hoop, and Bul Spink, a Nope

Turdus vulg., the Song Thrush, a Thrussel

FIG 28. Hawfinch.
(Photograph by
Richard Billington)

Turdus Viscovorus, the Mistletoe Thrush or Saith

Turdus Illas, the Wind Thrush (redwing)

Trichas, the Feldefare [Merrett stated *Turdus pilaris* of Aldrovandus]

Merula, the Black Bird or black Ousle

Sturnus vulg., the Stare or Starling

Sturnus Cinereus [probably an immature Starling, says Mullens, and Merrett would not be the first person to fail to recognise this species in its dull juvenile plumage]

Caeruleo, a Clot Bird, a Smatch, or Airling, a Stone-check (wheatear)

Picus viridis, the Green Wood pecker, or Hickwall

Picus varius major (great spotted woodpecker)

Picus varius minor (lesser spotted woodpecker)

Picus murarius, the Creeper, or Wall Creeper [is this really the wall-creeper? If so, was it a British bird? Chances are not, although Willughby/Ray stated that it had been reported in England]

Picus cinereus (nuthatch)

Jynx, seu Torquilla, the Wryneck

Certhia, the Ox-eye Creeper (treecreeper)

Passer troglodytes, a Wren

Curruca, the Hedge Sparrow [is this a dunnock (hedge sparrow) or a whitethroat sp.?]

Hirundo, the House Swallow

Hirundo Riparia, the Sand Martin, or Shore-bird, a Bank Martnet

Hirundo agrestis sive Rustica, a Martin [house martin]

Hirundo Apus, a Black Martin, or Martlet, a Rock or Church Martnet (swift)

Parus major, the Common Titmouse, the great Titmouse, the great Ox-eye [great tit – but the Carter list suggests Ox-eye as the name for the coal tit. Ox-eye is also used by Merrett for a treecreeper, and the name appeared in the Knyvet list as an oystercatcher!]

Parus caeruleus minor, the less Titmouse (blue tit)

Parus ater, the Coalmouse [coal tit]

Parus ater, the least, or long taild Titmouse

Motacilla, a Water Wagtail [pied or grey wagtail? The latter is not definitely mentioned for the first time until Willughby/Ray, so pied is more likely]

Motacilla flava (yellow wagtail?)

Rubetra, the Stone Chatter, or Blackberry-eater [stonechat]

Rubecula, the Ruddock, Red-breast and Robin Red-breast

Ruticilla, Phaenicurus, the Red-Start

Oenanthe, the Wheat ear or White tail [again]

Luscinia, Lusciniola, the Nightingale

Morinellus, the Dotterel [Merrett mentioned Lincoln]

Cygnus, the Swan [whooper or mute?] (Fig. 29)

Anser domesticus, the Goose

Chenalopex, vulpanser, a Bergander (shelduck – burrow-gander)

Anser ferus [goose sp. – no idea which]

Capricalca, Capricalze Scotis, (capercaillie) [second mention – this time Merrett
    included it among the geese]

Bernicla Brenta, the Brent Goose

Gustarda Avis Scotica (great bustard) [again]

Anser Bassanus, a Soland Goose (gannet)

Anas Domesticus, the Duck

Harle, the black Diver, A Shell drake (goosander or red-breasted merganser)
    [Merrett mentioned Norfolk]

Cygnus.
The Swan.

FIG 29. This appears to be a
mute swan, from the
Willughby/Ray *Ornithology*
(1676), but it is given the name
Cygnus, normally associated
with the whooper swan – the
head of which was also
illustrated in the *Ornithology*
and called the 'elk' (see Fig. 121).

Anas fera, the Wild Duck (mallard)

Anas fera fusca (Mullens stated that the figure in Jonstonus looked like a scoter but that Merrett may have meant the Pochard, as in Willughby/Ray)

Anas Platyrhincus (shoveler based on the illustration in Aldrovandi – not mallard)

Querquedula, the Teal

A *Gaddel* (gadwall) [the name is followed by a description in Latin suggesting this species is similar to the teal, but no Latin name is given]

Penelope major, the Widgeon

Colymbus major, the great Ducker (great northern diver).

Colymbus etc., Norwegis Lumme, Razor bill, Worm [the name Lumme may be Loon and therefore this may be another species of diver; alternatively it may indeed be the razorbill]

Colymbus Cristatus (great crested grebe?)

Colymbus medius, the Dive-dapper or Arsfoot [diver or grebe sp. – arsfoot is used for both] (Fig. 30)

Colymbus minimus, the Dab Chick [little grebe]

Mergorum serrati-Rostratorum (Mullens suggests goosander or merganser) [Merrett mentioned Warwick]

Mergus Turn. (Mullens explained that Turner's mergus is the cormorant) [Merrett mentioned Norfolk]

Corvus aquat. The Cormorant *Carbo aquat.* Shags [Merrett put both species in the same entry and repeated that this species is Turner's *mergus*]

Onocrotalus, the Pelicane (Mullens pointed out that they were kept in St James's Park from around 1660 and Sir Thomas Browne recorded one 'shott in a fenn' and that 'because it was so rare some conjectured it might bee one of those which belonged unto the King and flewe away') [so not quite as strange to be included as might first appear]

Pelicanus, Plataea, a Shovelard, a Spoon bill [spoonbill – Merrett mentioned Lincoln]

Larus major and *minor albus*, the Sea Mew, Gul, Sea Gul, or Sea Cob (common gull) [Another Latin description follows, with the prefix *Larus* and a suggested name of 'ganet' – Mullens was certain a skua was meant and probably the great skua]

Puphinus Anglicus, the Puphin [puffin – Merret mentioned Cornwall and Anglesey]

Ciconia, the Stork

Ardea cinerea, the Ash coloured Heron, or Hern, or Hernshaw [grey heron]

Ardea Alba, a Mire Drumble [Mullens suggested a spoonbill, but is this the 'egritte' or egret, or is it a white morph of the grey heron as described by Turner? Confusion is caused by the fact that 'mire dromble' was an ancient name for the bittern]

FIG 30. Black-necked grebe, from Donovan's *Natural History of British Birds* (1794–1819) (see Chapter 5). Might this be the *colymbus medius* of Merrett's list?

Ardea stellaris, the Bittourn [bittern]

Ardea minor (little bittern?)

Avis pugnax, a Rough, a Reev [ruff – Merrett mentioned Lincoln]

Haemantopus, Red shanks [redshank]

Arquata, Numenius, the Curliew

Arquata congener a Stone Curliew [Merrett mentioned Hampshire]

Vannellus, the Lapwing, bastard Plover or Pewit [Merrett mentioned Essex]

Vanello congener ... [Merrett described this bird as smaller than a thrush with a long crest – it is hard to tell the identity, and mention of Cornwall is no help]

Pluvialis cinerea, the Grey Plover

Pluvialis flavescens hujus meminit [not identifiable]

Pluvialis vulg. the Whistling Plover, or green Plover (golden plover) [possibly a
    lapwing again, but most likely the golden plover, as Mullens suggested]

Rallus Itallorum (rail sp.)

Trynga etc. (sandpiper) [Merrett mentioned Warwick but that scarcely helps to
    identify the species]

Trynga paulo minor [no real information]

Merulam aquat (dipper) [again mention of Cumberland matches the identity]

Charadrios ab incolis, Sea Lark (probably ringed plover or dunlin)

Grus, the Crane

Crex, a Daker Hen (corn crake) [again – Merrett mentioned 'Anglia' and
    Northumbria where it has been seen and heard]

[Three long descriptions follow from a report of three birds seen in Lincoln
described to Merrett by a man called Hutchinson, a London bird dealer. Mullens
suggests that the first is a smew, the second possibly a garganey and the third a
goosander/merganser]

Altogether this amounts to around 122 identifiable species, with another
twenty or so that, given better descriptions, could possibly also have been
British birds. Although Merrett's list seems at first sight to be comprehensive,
and might be interpreted as a resumé of the birds known in Britain in the mid
seventeenth century, the most interesting feature is the birds that are not there.
It does not include some species known to Carter, such as merlin, hobby, and
possibly redpoll and avocet. Where, for example, are the warblers? We know
that the blackcap (*swertling* in Anglo-Saxon) was known at this time. Where is
the goldcrest? Where is the erne or white-tailed eagle that has appeared with
such regularity in previous publications? Or is recent interpretation wrong,
and is the *Aquila* the white-tailed eagle – in which case the list has excluded
the golden eagle?

There is no indication as to how the order in which Merrett's birds are
presented was arrived at, although there is *an* order about it, with birds such as
ducks and waders being grouped together, and Merrett uses catch-all headings
such as *Insectivorae* – although this heading includes tits and the dotterel. Since
it preceded the Willughby/Ray *Ornithology* there was no standard reference for
Merrett to use, except perhaps Turner, Gesner or Aldrovandi. Merrett's list
and Carter's show similar starting points (Carter's sequence was of course predetermined by that in Gesner's book), with birds of prey followed by corvids

(crows), but after that they diverge. Chaucer, in his *Parlement of Foules*, also began with birds of prey, but there the similarity of order ends. There was, it seems, a general acceptance that birds of prey were the premier genera, but a lack of consensus as to what followed.

It is a risky business guessing the identity of some species listed by Merrett, and to rely on today's distribution and status in doing so may be to base those guesses on a false premise. It would be much more interesting ornithologically, and by no means impossible, if the species were indeed as suggested in the original text. The final word of caution is that it is possible that the species were those suggested in the original – but that they did not actually occur in Britain. Merrett may well have been misinformed, as is hinted at by his critics.

Contemporary opinion of Merrett's work was not always complimentary, suggesting that Merrett relied on information from correspondents, much of which was inaccurate or possibly even invented. John Ray referred to 'Merrett's bungling *Pinax*', which is a good hint that the anomalies highlighted here were recognised at the time. It is probably reasonable to suggest that the *Pinax* was bungled due to the fact that Merrett knew enough to prepare the list but not enough to do it properly. To paraphrase Doctor Johnson, however, the important thing about the *Pinax* is not that it was done badly, but that it was done at all.

CHAPTER 4

The Willughby/Ray Ornithology and Other Seventeenth-Century Works

Although Christopher Merrett published the first attempt at a British List of birds, this was so unreliable that its main achievement was to goad Willughby and Ray on in their efforts to produce something accurate and scientifically arranged.

Max Nicholson in *The Ibis*, 1959

B Y THE END OF THE sixteenth century, British ornithology was in desperate need of both a sense of order and some scientific discipline, and this is exactly what was provided by the comprehensive, accurate and well-ordered treatise produced by Francis Willughby and John Ray.

John Ray (Fig. 31) was essentially a botanist. He was born in 1627 at Black Notley in Essex, the son of the village blacksmith. He was educated first at the local school and then at Braintree Grammar School, where he seems to have prospered. Like Turner before him, he came to the attention of a man with influence, in Ray's case the local vicar, who is thought to have had a hand in Ray's entry to Cambridge. In 1644, at the age of sixteen, he went to St Catharine's College, where his academic studies began during a period of great change, as the Civil War was at its height. Ray soon found himself uncomfortable at St Catharine's, and in 1646 he transferred to Trinity College, where he was more at ease in the less rigid atmosphere.

Ray studied languages, becoming extremely proficient in Latin (all his main works were written in that language), and later he studied both Anglo-Saxon and Celtic, in which respect he was something of a pioneer. His interest in biology

FIG 31. John Ray, from an original in the British Museum.

was already evident, and he undertook dissections in the rooms of a friend (some were of birds, including bittern, curlew and yarwhelp [godwit]), becoming proficient in anatomy. He is said to have searched in vain for a tutor in botany. He graduated around 1647–8 and was elected a minor Fellow of Trinity in 1649, where he was given several responsibilities and was variously lecturer in Greek, mathematics and humanities.

It was about five years later that Ray's serious botanical studies began, when he started to visit the fens and woods around Cambridge; visits which led eventually to his first publication about the plants of Cambridgeshire (1660). However, it was the arrival at his college of an undergraduate from Middleton in Warwickshire that brought Ray the most fruitful friendship of his life.

Francis Willughby (Fig. 32) was born in 1635, the son of Sir Francis Willughby and Lady Cassandra, daughter of the Earl of Londonderry. He came from an entirely different background to Ray, being wealthy, privileged and well connected, a member of the land-owning aristocracy. Virtually nothing is known of his early life, the first noted event being when Willughby became a Fellow Commoner of Trinity in 1652 at the age of seventeen. It has been suggested that he was Ray's pupil, but circumstantial evidence indicates that both he and Ray were sequentially pupils of a Dr Duport, and that may well be how they became acquainted. In any event, Willughby was undoubtedly attracted to Ray's personality and force of mind.

Willughby took his BA in 1655 and his MA in 1659. He was obviously working with Ray by this time, as he received an acknowledgement in Ray's *Catalogus plantarum circa Cantabrigiam*.

While a Fellow at Trinity, Ray began to travel around Britain, usually accompanied by Willughby and often by his pupil Philip Skippon. Ray journeyed to Derbyshire and north Wales in 1658, to the north of England and the Isle of Man in 1660, to York, Scotland and Carlisle in 1661, to Sussex, Wales and down to Land's End in 1662. These journeys were the start of Ray's serious botanising, and he made such accurate notes of the plants he discovered that, as recently as the 1950s, botanists were able to return to the localities and re-find the plant species.

Although ordained in London in 1660 (Fellows were generally compelled to be ordained), Ray was beset by the political and religious controversies of the time, and whilst he was very happy with the academic part of university life it is clear that the background religious turbulence continually distressed him.

FIG 32. Francis Willughby, from J. F. Denham's *Memoir of Francis Willughby*, which appeared in Jardine's *Naturalist's Library*.

In 1662, Ray found himself in what turned out to be a decisive difficulty concerning the Act of Uniformity. All clerics were expected to sign a document accepting the Act, but Ray refused on moral grounds and felt compelled to resign his Fellowship, bringing to an end his association with Cambridge.

Whilst it is impossible to imagine what Ray might have achieved had he remained at Cambridge, he used his release from academia wisely and wasted little time before, together with Willughby, he left for the Continent. In April 1663, accompanied by Skippon and Nathaniel Bacon – a cousin of Willughby – they journeyed through the Low Countries, up the Rhine to Vienna, then to Italy, where they spent the winter. The following year the party divided, with Willughby and Bacon crossing to Spain, after which, at the end of 1664, Willughby returned home. Ray and Skippon, meanwhile, travelled to Sicily, Malta and then Rome, where they stayed from September 1664 until January 1665. They then journeyed to Switzerland in June 1665 before spending the autumn at Montpellier and arriving home in the spring of 1666 via Paris and Calais.

At this time it was common to find captured birds, both dead and alive, for sale at markets in the larger cities. Both Ray and Willughby bought specimens, which they meticulously dissected, including species such as a black stork at Frankfurt, great bustard at Modena and common cranes in Rome. The plumage and structure of these birds were all noted in minute detail, even to the extent of noting the parasites that were discovered living internally and externally on each specimen.

In 1667, having returned to England, Ray and Willughby travelled from Worcester to Hampshire through the West Country. In 1668, as well as travelling around Essex and Cambridgeshire, Ray went to Westmorland and Yorkshire on his own. In 1669 Ray visited Surrey, Oxford, Kent and Shropshire at various times, and in 1671 he made a visit to the Yorkshire Dales and to Berwick in Northumberland.

For Ray his resignation from Cambridge had serious financial consequences, since he was without much independent means of support. This meant that he was compelled to live and work, when not travelling, among his friends. In effect he spent most of his time at Middleton, the home of Willughby's family, where he was employed as tutor to Willughby's children.

Willughby did not have a strong constitution and suffered several illnesses, the last of which ended his life on 3 July 1672. Their mutual friend, Bishop John Wilkins, described Willughby very fully:

His rare natural abilities joined with his indefatigable industry, brought him to very great skill in all parts of learning, and particularly in those sciences which are most abstruse and uncommon to vulgar capacities; the most subtle parts of mathematics and natural philosophy; and more particularly the history of animals, birds, beasts, fishes, and insects, in which he distinguished himself almost beyond example, and became the glory of his age.

Willughby bequeathed Ray a legacy of £60 per annum, a useful sum in those days, and Ray continued as a tutor to Willughby's children until the death of Francis' mother, who did all she could to see that her son's work was continued. After Lady Willughby's death the rest of the family seem not to have been so committed, and Ray's association with the family ceased and he returned to his native Essex.

It appears to have been Willughby's death that provided the catalyst that inspired Ray to write up the results of their labours, leading to the publication of the famous *Ornithology*.

THE ORNITHOLOGY

First published in Latin in 1676 as *Ornithologia libri tres* and in English, with emendations, in 1678, the text of this book amounted to 441 pages. It comprised three volumes and contained some of the most comprehensive descriptions of birds published up to that time. As W. B. Alexander stated in his review of Charles Raven's 1942 biography of Ray, 'the ornithologist unfamiliar with these works will doubtless be surprised to discover how much information on birds and their habits was known to the authors.'

The *Ornithology* had two great strengths. The first was that for the first time a real attempt was made to provide a systematic approach to the subject. The Willughby/Ray classification system used as a foundation the simple Aldrovandi division of land birds and water birds, but it developed a greater sophistication by introducing subdivisions, using physical characteristics, to separate the birds into various classes (Table 2). This formula provided a stouter framework than anything before it and, given the paucity of information on which it was constructed, the scientific prowess behind it is clear. The Willughby/Ray classification endured, and today the principle of using physical characteristics remains an integral part of the modern classification system.

The second of the book's great strengths was that the information it contained was reliable, and it eliminated the legends included in most of the

TABLE 2. Classification of birds, from the Willughby/Ray *Ornithology* (1676).

LAND BIRDS

---

1. Those with crooked beaks and claws
   a. diurnal birds of prey (eagles, hawks, falcons, vultures, shrikes and birds of paradise)
   b. nocturnal birds of prey (owls and goatsucker)
   c. frugivores (parrots, macaws, parakeets)
2. Those with straight beaks
   a. large and flightless (ostrich, cassowary, dodo)
   b. middle size, large bills, flesh feeders (crows, kingfishers, woodpeckers)
   c. smaller bills, white flesh (poultry), dark flesh (pigeons, thrushes)
   d. small birds, soft-beaked insect-eaters or hard-billed seed-eaters.

WATER BIRDS

---

1. Those that frequent watery places
   a. piscivorous (heron, crane, stork)
   b. long-billed, crooked (curlew) or straight (woodcock, snipe)
   c. middle-sized bill (sea-pie, redshank, stints)
   d. short-billed (plovers)
2. Those that swim
   a. cloven-footed (moorhen and coot)
   b. long-legged (flamingo and avocet)
   c. three-toed (auks)
   d. four toes webbed together (soland goose, cormorant)
   e. back-toed loose, blunt-billed (mergansers, shearwaters), sharp-billed short-winged (grebes, divers), sharp-billed long-winged (gulls, terns), broad-billed, large (swans, geese), broad-billed, small (sea-ducks, river-ducks)

---

previous publications. It listed and described around 230 species, most of them British, and most of them illustrated (Fig. 33). Willughby had collected together a number of pictures and had also commissioned others, from which Ray selected those that he considered most suitable.

The English nomenclature used in the *Ornithology* remained rather confusing, with several names used for some species. For example, birds seen on the Bass Rock were named soland geese (the name always used for gannets), but strangely the authors did not make a connection between these birds and those seen in Cornwall, which they called gannets. There was also considerable confusion over the names of auks, with much, and various, use of the term 'puffin', which seemed to cover both the bird which we now know as the puffin and the Manx

Merula aquatica
The Water Ouzell.

Upupa
The Hoopoe.

FIG 33. Illustration from the Willughby/Ray *Ornithology* of hoopoe and dipper ('water ouzell'). The former is an excellent drawing, leaving no doubt as to the identification; the latter, while recognisable in part, is drawn in a shape and posture that is common to many of the illustrations but not typical of the species portrayed.

shearwater; the authors recognised that these were separate species but gave the name 'puffin' to the Manx shearwater, while the bird we know as the puffin was called the Prestwich puffin – yet the illustration of the shearwater was labelled 'the Sheare-Water' (Fig. 34). Most probably seabirds were relatively unknown to both Willughby and Ray.

Divers (Fig. 35) were given three names: 'arsfoot', which was also used for grebes, 'loon', now the North American preferred name, and 'diver'. The name woodpigeon was given to the bird we know as the stock dove, the woodpigeon of today being called the ring dove. The woodpeckers were given many names: woodspite, pickatrees, rain-fowl, highhoe or heghoe, hew-hole, witwall and hickwall. The redwing was called the windthrush, because it came to this country at the time of the equinoctial gales, and so on.

The Sheare-Water.

FIG 34. Illustration of a (Manx?) shearwater from the Willughby/Ray *Ornithology*. This drawing is extremely good and is one of a dozen or so that show real likeness to the bird in question, said to be the work of Sir Thomas Browne.

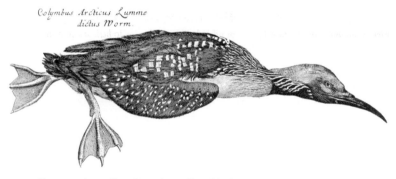

FIG 35. Great northern diver from the Willoughby/Ray *Ornithology*, possibly a drawing that came from Sir Thomas Browne. Compare this good drawing, albeit of an obviously dead specimen, with the very poor one of the same species from Sibbald's *Prodromus* (Fig. 40).

When considering the large number of English names included, it is important to remember that the Britain of those times was a much more parochial and regional place than it is today, and doubtless dialectal and colloquial variations abounded. The parson in Northumberland and the squire in Sussex would most probably have different names for many species. Willughby and Ray would have picked up the variants on their travels, or possibly from correspondents. For a book to sell it needed to relate to its potential buyers, and thus the range of names was probably included for commercial reasons as much as for completeness.

The species descriptions comprise the main body of the book, and contain many interesting passages. For example, of the cuckoo (Fig. 36):

> what becomes of the Cuckoo in the winter time, whether hiding herself in hollow trees or other holes and caverns she lies torpid, and at the return of the spring revives again; or rather at the approach of winter, being impatient of the cold, shifts place and departs into hot countries, is not as yet to me certainly known … but seeing it is most certain that many sorts of bird do at certain seasons of the year shift places and depart into other countries, as for example Quails Woodcocks Feldfares Storkes etc. why may not Cuckoos also do the same. For my part I never yet met with any credible person that dared affirm that he himself had found or seen a Cuckoo in winter time taken out of a hollow tree or any other lurking place.

And the bittern:

> they say that it gives an odd number of bombs [booms] at a time viz., three or five; which in my own observation I have found to be false. It begins to bellow about the

FIG 36. Cuckoo. (Photograph by Rebecca Nason)

FIG 37. Illustration from the Willughby/Ray *Ornithology* showing a variety of methods for catching birds, mainly game birds but also sparrows and, rather surprisingly, nightingales – although the method for this latter species looks rather primitive and one wonders what the success rate would have been.

beginning of February, and ceases when breeding time is over ... in the autumn after
sunset these birds are wont to soar aloft in the air with a spiral ascent, so high till they
get quite out of sight, in the meantime making a singular kind of noise, nothing like to
lowing.

The work had other features, such as 24 questions asked by Willughby – a
fascinating example of which is 'Do all birds of the same species have the same
colour iris?' It included an account of the remarkable nesting places of British
birds, as well as suggested methods for catching birds, including a duck decoy,
and it presented the rudiments of falconry in one of the appendices. Indeed,
some of the illustrations showed bird-catching methods (Fig. 37).

WHO WROTE THE *ORNITHOLOGY*?

There has been considerable academic discussion over the subsequent centuries
concerning the authorship of the *Ornithology*, centred on whose was the more
significant contribution. Like many of these questions, the answers have varied
over time, depending on the fashion of the day and who was answering.

What hard evidence remains comes mostly from Ray himself and one or
two other contemporary sources. Ray's introduction to the book seems to explain
his and Willughby's respective roles, and he stated that Willughby provided
the bulk of the information. He even went so far as to say that Willughby, at the
time of his death, was not in favour of publication because he considered his
work incomplete. Willughby's writings were probably in note form, and these
notes were almost certainly prepared for publication by Ray. There can be no
doubt that the words that appear in the book were physically written down by
Ray. William Derham, who published a biographical memoir of Ray based on
conversations with the naturalist just before his death, confirmed those views,
and it all seems straightforward enough.

Yet Raven, in his biography of Ray (1942), was strangely ambivalent in his
assessment of the authorship. In certain sections of his book Raven gave much
credit to Willughby. Yet, in concluding his chapter on the *Ornithology*, Raven
stated that much of Willughby's reputation is due to the impression of him
given to the world by Ray who, said Raven, was a man generous to a fault. Quite
how he knew this, nearly three centuries later, is not recorded. Raven quoted a
controversy going back to the mid nineteenth century when, after the formation
of the Ray Society and the consequent hero-worship of Ray, many scientists felt
that Willughby's role had been unjustly diminished. Raven suggested that these

scientists may well have exaggerated Willughby's contribution in compensation. Raven was probably referring to this piece from the pen of William Swainson:

> Willughby was the most accomplished zoologist of this or any other country, for all the honour that has been given to Ray, so far as concerns systematic zoology, belongs exclusively to him. In botany, and in no other science, was Ray the author of a system, for he confessedly adopted Willughby's both in ornithology and ichthyology.

Raven himself gave a very different assessment of their relative merits, and stated:

> the evidence makes it certain that Ray was a scientist of genius and probable that Willughby was a brilliantly talented amateur. There is no evidence at present that they were in the same class as naturalists.

This assessment appears to be based more on Raven's assessment of Ray than on any tangible evidence or knowledge of Willughby. Contrary to Raven's statement, there is considerable evidence that Willughby was as good a zoologist as Ray was a botanist, and my own inclination is to agree with Swainson's assessment.

Whilst almost every facet of the *Ornithology* shows the highest order of scholarship, the most important feature in retrospect was the system of classification, and it has been suggested by many that this was down to Ray. There are many references in the literature to ornithological works that follow 'Ray's classification'. Yet, here again, Ray's own words suggest otherwise – 'both birds, beasts, fishes and insects [were] digested into a method of his [Willughby's] own contriving.' There is no ambiguity or ambivalence. Ray says that Willughby was responsible for the classification. Derham, who knew Ray and had no reason to mislead the world, confirmed this, pointing out that 'the noble design which by agreement between Mr Willughby and Mr Ray fell to Mr Willughby's share, was dispatching the history of animals.'

Ray also made it clear that he alone was responsible for the inclusion of the appendices. The first was a list of the birds suspected to be from fables and not to exist, and this was followed by two sections on falconry drawn largely from Simon Latham's earlier book. Indisputably these were the weakest part of the work, and in some ways incompatible with the strong scientific base of the rest. With the benefit of hindsight, they were probably an error of judgement, though they may have been included in an attempt to attract greater custom.

There can be no doubt that Ray included additional material sent to him by various named people, including Sir Thomas Browne (see below), Philip

Skippon (his old travelling companion) and a certain Mr Jessop, all of whom he acknowledges in the book.

Perhaps the last word should come from Ray himself. Concerning Willughby's attention to detail in describing the plumage of birds, which Ray found far too scrupulous, his comment was, 'yet I dared not to omit or alter anything'. My view is that Willughby should be considered the author of the work and Ray the editor, who wrote the manuscript and updated and supplemented the original information. Thus it is called the Willughby/Ray *Ornithology* throughout this book.

Ray's later years

Following Willughby's death, Ray felt obliged to publish not only the *Ornithology* but also a book on fishes, *Historia piscium*. Ray's work at Middleton also produced the English Botanical List and a collection of English proverbs; these, together with other works and second editions of his Botanical List, were all produced within five years of his friend's passing. At this time Ray also married a member of the Middleton household, Margaret Oakely, in 1673.

In 1675, his tutorial task completed, Ray and his wife returned to Essex, living at first at Falborne Hall near Black Notley, where it seems likely that he was tutor to the son of the owner, Edward Bullock. Two years later, on the death of his mother, they moved into her house at Black Notley. Ray continued to be interested in birds and in 1694 completed a *Synopsis methodica avium*, which contained much from the *Ornithology*. This was not published until 1713, after his death, due to a problem with the bookseller to whom it was entrusted. Ray remained at Black Notley until his death in 1705. We are left to wonder what he and Willughby might have been able to achieve, either separately or collectively, had Ray remained among the academics of Cambridge and had Willughby lived longer than his mere 37 years.

OTHER WORK OF THE SEVENTEENTH CENTURY

Edward Topsell was a London parson whose interest in natural history resulted in the publication of two books, *The Historie of Four-footed Beastes* (1607) and *The Historie of Serpents* (1608), both of which were translations of the work of Conrad Gesner. Topsell was born in 1572 at Sevenoaks, Kent. A graduate of Christ's College, Cambridge, he went into the church and in 1604 was appointed perpetual curate (presumably limited to his lifetime!) of St Botolph's, Aldersgate. He died in 1625.

FIG 38. Coot, from Edward Topsell's *Fowles of Heaven.*

The manuscript of Topsell's *The Fowles of Heaven or Historie of Birdes* was never completed, and what little there was of it saw light of day only when it was published in 1972 by the University of Texas, edited by Thomas Harrison and David Hoeniger. This modern version of Topsell's book comprises 240 pages, dealing with birds of the alphabet letters A, B and C only (Fig. 38), beginning with 'alcatraz' (pelican) and ending with 'cuckoe'. For the text Topsell drew largely from the Italian naturalist Ulisse Aldrovandi (1522–1605) (who himself derived much material from Gesner), Pliny and Aristotle.

Topsell's bird book probably dates from 1608–25, after the publication of the *Serpents* book. The drawings within the manuscript vary from unrecognisable to fairly accurate, and they were hand-coloured. The text consists of a list of birds in alphabetical order with a written passage accompanying. There is the customary mixture of physical description and nomenclature, with a section on the culinary merits of each species and some religious references. Much of it is fantasy, and the ecology is sometimes a bit haywire – we are informed that barnacle geese feed on fish, that bullfinches feed on 'wormes', but also (accurately) on 'blossomes of apple and peare trees'. The description of the mating of cranes is splendid:

*[Cranes] flie into Aegipt and whotter places, there they are inflamed with lust and
mingle in generation. So the Cockes leape their hennes and the hennes receave and beare
the Cockes not like Dunghill-hennes, or pea-hennes shrinkinge to the earth but
standinge upright.*

Harrison and Hoeniger's judgement was that 'had the *Fowles of Heaven* been
published, it would have popularised the subject through the pious eyes of the
translator but affected the serious study of birds very little.' They discovered a list
of birds that Topsell proposed to cover – similar to that of Merrett (see Chapter 3)
but not specifically restricted to British birds.

Walter Charleton's *Onomasticon zoicon* of 1668, written in Latin, was almost
certainly overshadowed by the far superior work of Willughby and Ray. It has
around 56 pages devoted to birds, and amongst interesting species that had
hitherto not been mentioned Charleton named the 'Spanish partridge with bills
and legs red' (red-legged partridge) and stated that it was common on the island
of Guernsey. He described '*Mereops* the bee eater' and stated that it was a rare
visitor. And the book contained what is probably the earliest detailed reference
to the avocet:

*Avosetta, Italiorum Spinzago d'aqua, Recurvirostra, the scooper ... on the approach of
winter they congregate in flocks on the western coasts of England and after a month or
two disperse to shores perchance less cold.*

The *Onomasticon* is notable because it contained bird illustrations, presumably
by Charleton himself. These illustrations were competent, especially when
compared with the more primitive drawings in the Topsell manuscript, and
far better than many published at a later date, including some of those in the
Ornithology. Illustration at this time remained constrained by artists using only
specimens as raw material, resulting in some birds being presented in strange
and unnatural poses.

This era also witnessed the first attempt to document the fauna of Scotland.
Robert Sibbald's *Prodromus historiae naturalis* of 1684 was largely derived from
other sources, and was criticised by a contemporary as drawn from 'the
communications of ignorant and credulous correspondents'. Some of its
contents, however, were original. The indication that the great auk occurred
in Britain pre-dated that of Martin Martin (see below). Sibbald (Fig. 39) gave a
full description of the black-winged stilt, possibly the first, and he described
the existence of migration: 'certain of them [birds] migrate others do not depart
or hide themselves far away from the place they usually frequent.'

FIG 39. Robert Sibbald, author of *Prodromus historiae naturalis* (1684). From Mullens, *British Birds* (1912b).

Among the surprising species noted by Sibbald are black kite, eagle owl, chough, green woodpecker, lesser spotted woodpecker, nuthatch, great bustard, nightingale, crane, bittern, spoonbill and garganey. While some may have occurred in Scotland (Fig. 40), many almost certainly did not, showing the danger of relying upon the testimony of correspondents.

Martin Martin's *A Late Voyage to St. Kilda* (1698) contains several notes about the seabirds of the island. Pre-eminent among them is his description of a bird presumed to be the great auk:

> *above the size of a Solan Goose of a black colour, red about the Eyes, a large white spot under each, a long broad Bill; it stands stately, it's whole Body erectd, it's wings short, flies not at all; lays its egg upon the bare Rock, which if taken away, she lays no more for that Year; she is whole-footed, and has the hatching Spot upon her Breast, i.e. a bare spot from which the Feathers have fallen off with the Heat in hatching; it's Egg is twice as big as that of a Solan Goose, and is variously spotted Black, Green, and Dark; it*

comes without regard to any Wind, appears the first of May, and goes away the middle of June.

This description is slightly inaccurate in physical detail – the white spot is not under the eye, and Martin makes no mention of the white underside of the bird – but it provides ample evidence of the bird's habits and slow reproductive rate, features that help to explain its extinction when placed under pressure by humans. However, it is worth noting that there is a view today that the bird described by Martin Martin may not have been the great auk but another species of *Pinguinus*; we know from bones from Holland that at least one other species existed at one time.

Among the other entries in the *Late Voyage* are details of both gannet (solan goose) and fulmar:

FIG 40. Great northern diver, from Sibbald's *Prodromus* (1684). From Mullens, *British Birds* (1912b). Compare the quality of the illustration with Fig. 35.

And when the young Fulmar is ready to take Wing, he being approached, ejects a
quantity of pure Oyl out at his Bill, and will make sure to hit any that attacks him, in
the Face ... [the Inhabitants] surprise him also from behind by taking hold of his Bill,
which they tie with a thread, and upon their return home they untie it with a Dish
under to receive the oyl.

Further on he makes reference to the use of the birds by the islanders as a
source of food:

the number of Solan Geese consumed by each Family the Year before we came there
amounted to Twenty two thousand five hundred in the whole Island, which they said
was less than they ordinarily did, a great many being lost by the badness of the season.

This seems a very large number of gannets, especially if 22,500 were consumed
in a bad year.

Martin Martin's book about St Kilda was followed by a more extensive work,
A Description of the Western Islands of Scotland, which was published in 1703.

In 1661, Joshua Childrey, who described himself as an antiquary,
schoolmaster and divine, published his book *Britannia Baconica, or the Natural*
Rarities of England Scotland and Wales. Childrey offered a rare insight into
migratory behaviour: discussing the reason why birds leave and then return,
he hypothesised that it was due to a lack of food. He also described a plague
of mice in Essex and of the strange owls that accompanied them (presumably
short-eared). A further piece of considerable interest, considering the state
of knowledge at the time, is an observation that 'if the winter prove very mild
then the winter birds (fieldfares, etc) come not quite home to us; if it prove
extreme sharp then they flye beyond us southward.'

THE FIRST COUNTY AVIFAUNAS

The seventeenth century also saw the beginning of a more parochial approach to
ornithology. One example is the work of Richard Carew, whose *Survey of Cornwall*
(1602) covered many aspects of the county, including an avifaunal list (Fig. 41).

Carew noted the absence of nightingales in the county – 'whether through
some natural antipathie betweene them and the soyle or rather for that the
Country is generally bare of covert and woods' – and like Mathew Paris before
him he recorded an invasion of crossbills:

THE
SVRVEY OF
CORNWALL.

Written by Richard Carew
of Antonie, Esquire.

LONDON
Printed by S. S. for Iohn Iaggard, and are to bee fold
neere Temple-barre, at the figne of the Hand
and Starre. 1 6 0 2.

FIG 41. Title page of Carew's *Survey of Cornwall* (1602). From Mullens, *British Birds* (1908a).

not long sithence, there came a flock of birds into Cornwall, about the harvest season, in bignesse not much exceeding a Sparrow, which made a foule spoyle of the Apples. Their bils were thwarted crossewise at the end, and with these they would cut an Apple in two, at one snap, eating onely the kernels.

He also noted many species of seabirds and waders:

Coots, Sanderlings, Sea-larkes [said to be ringed plover], Oxen [dunlin] and Kine [?knot], Seapies [oystercatcher], Puffins, Pewits, Meawes [black-headed gull], Murres [guillemot], Creysers [?], Curlewes, Teale, Wigeon, Burranets [shelduck] Shags, Ducke and Mallard, Gull, Wild-goose, Heron, Crane and Barnacle.

He wrote of the chough:

> *I meane not the common Daw but one peculiar to Cornwall, and there-through termed*
> *the Cornish Chough: his bill is sharpe, long and red, his legs of the same colour, his*
> *feathers blacke, his conditions, when he is kept tame, ungracious, in filching, and hiding*
> *of money, and such short ends, and somewhat dangerous in carrying sticks of fire.*

Carew's described birds of prey consisted of 'Marlions [merlin], Sparhawkes,
Hobbies and Lannards'. Are 'lannards' a variation on lanner? 'Lanner' was
used for birds on Lundy (see Chapter 1) and it might possibly have been a West
Country colloquial name. Turner did not use it, but Merrett did. The name is
not mentioned in the Willughby/Ray *Ornithology*, yet in a book on falconry
Simon Latham (1618) also stated that lanners bred in England. Again it seems
highly unlikely that the birds named here are what we now call lanner falcons,
whose range is restricted to the extreme south of Europe, North Africa and the
Middle East.

Carew's entry for the woodcock (Fig. 42) is interesting in its acknowledgement
of the seasonal movement:

> *They arrive first on the North-coast ... From whence as the moyst places which supplie*
> *them food beginne to freeze up, they draw towards those in the South Coast, which*
> *are kept more open by the Summers neerer neighbourhood: and when summers heate*
> *drieth up those plashes, nature and necessitie guide their returne to the Northern*
> *wetter soyle again.*

The birds of Norfolk were documented by Sir Thomas Browne (1605–82), the
medical doctor and well-known literary figure and polymath. Browne had a
collection of skins and eggs, most of which were obtained in Norfolk, and he
also provided some of the illustrations in the *Ornithology*. His observations on
the natural history of Norfolk were published in 1902, over 200 years after his
death, in a book by Thomas Southwell entitled *Notes and Letters on the Natural
History of Norfolk*. The first part of this book is devoted to birds and includes
many interesting passages. Browne noted, among other things, the breeding of
spoonbill in Suffolk and recorded that they formerly bred at Reedham and were
taken 'not for theire meat but theire feathers'. Cormorants evidently still bred
also at Reedham, some being taken for use by Charles II as catchers of fish – so
inland breeding, presently considered to be a novel development, is in fact
nothing new. He talked of great bustard and dotterel as being good dishes but
redshank not, and he noted the absence of French or red-legged partridges.

FIG 42. Woodcock by Archibald Thorburn, from Lilford's *Coloured Figures of the Birds of the British Islands* (1885–97).

He gave the first record of the roller, a specimen of which he received, and mentioned common cranes being seen in winter. Strangely, he also mentioned stork 'in the fennes and marshes', by which he presumably meant cranes. Perhaps the 'storks' were reported to him as such. He kept ruff for almost a year in his garden and recorded that they would fight to the death in the confined space, that the males lose their ruff at the end of the summer, and that the female was the reeve.

Browne described the habits of ospreys and kites in a way that indicates they were commonly encountered at the time:

> There is also a lesser sort of Agle called an Ospray wch houers about the fennes and broads and will dippe his claws and take up fish oftimes for wch his foote is made of an extraordinarie roughness for the better fastening and holding of it and the like they will do unto Coots.

The most important piece of observation concerns migration:

> Beside the ordinarie birds which keep constantly in the country many are discoverable both in winter and summer which are of a migrant nature, and exchange their seat according to the season, those which come in spring coming for the most part from the southward, those which come in autumn and winter from the northward ... nor to

*come only in flocks of one kind but teals woodcocks felfars thrushes and small birds
too, come and light together, for the most part some hawkes and birds of prey attending
them.*

This constitutes a very accurate description of migration, which, living in
Norfolk, Browne was well placed to observe and record. The existence of
migration was not much accepted at the time, and indeed was still argued against
a hundred years later.

In 1677, a year after the appearance of the Willughby/Ray *Ornithology*, Robert
Plot published *The Natural History of Oxfordshire*, which included a list of birds to
be found within the county. There was nothing particularly scientifically new
in the list, its interest being derived from the geographical limit of the county.
He followed the success of this first book with *The Natural History of Staffordshire*
(1686); once again, the bird list was unexceptional, although the detailed entry on
the breeding of the black-headed gull (Fig. 43) was subsequently used by William
Yarrell in his nineteenth-century masterwork (see Chapter 8).

Charles Leigh, another doctor 'of physick' (i.e. a medical doctor), produced a
work similar in every way to those of Plot for Lancashire, Cheshire and the Peak
District in 1700. Mullens described the ornithological observation contained in
this volume as 'useless and trivial'.

These books marked the beginning of county natural histories, and county
avifaunas, many more examples of which appeared in the following hundred
years. The publication of these county lists showed that interest in ornithology
was growing. Nevertheless, the ornithology itself was still riddled with

FIG 43. Illustration of a gullery, from Plot's *Natural History of Staffordshire* (1686). Note that
the young black-headed gulls are being rounded up, presumably to be taken as a 'crop'.
From Mullens, *British Birds* (1909a).

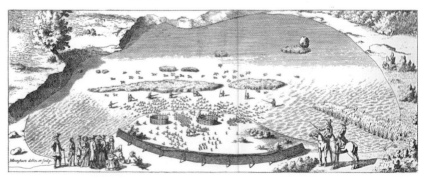

inaccuracies and in some cases superstitious nonsense. By the end of the seventeenth century the confusing use of English names was drawing to an end. With a baseline established by the Willughby/Ray *Ornithology*, the interest in birds needed to be developed with a more scientific approach, and the dawn of the age of exploration led both to a number of high-quality studies of birds and to the beginning of two hundred years of obsession with a 'natural classification'.

CHAPTER 5

The Systema naturae: Dawn of a New Age

The employment of the true and natural method for the identification of creatures according to genus and species is the prime and sole aim of natural history.
Peter Artedi, *Philosophia icthyologia*

AT THE TURN OF the eighteenth century, only the *Ornithology* and perhaps Merrett's list in the *Pinax* had added substance to the foundation put down by Turner. Some basic facts about the way certain species lived had been recorded, but precious little else. As the century progressed, a steadily growing interest in birds was reflected in both the quantity and the quality of the publications, and we find real bird study under several different headings. That this was linked to a rise in the standard of living is beyond dispute. The beginnings of mechanisation, although primitive by the standards of the later Victorians, drove the industrial and agricultural development that was largely responsible for improvements in people's work opportunities and food availability. Not least, as far as ornithology is concerned, there was an increase in education and leisure time for the landed gentry and professional men – and thus scientists, country squires, doctors and parsons began contributing to our knowledge. Doubtless the 'mass' production of printed material also played a big part in this process, as did the development of scientific societies, but the single most important factor in ornithology across the Western world was that this was the age of exploration.

By the early eighteenth century the world was developing apace. Travellers were leaving the shores of Europe on expeditions to unexplored regions where, for ornithologists, there were new birds to be seen, drawn, killed, stuffed and taken home to be studied at leisure. As a result of the expeditions, but also based on locally obtained specimens, the landed gentry began to amass collections, not to attract visitors, but for the enjoyment and status that they gave to the owner. Dead birds in boxes, live birds in cages, bird specimens mounted and displayed – all these had to be catalogued and placed in order. Yet what order? Alphabetical? Water birds followed by land birds or vice versa? What about the names? Should it be nightjar, caprimulgus, or goatsucker (Fig. 44)? You could name your specimen goatsucker, only to find that your neighbour had called his specimen of the same species a fern-owl – when it wasn't an owl at all.

For the naturalists of the time it became imperative for all living things to be alloted a place in a standardised system (thus the study was called systematics) and to have universally recognised names.

The *Ornithology* had broken new ground, showing that it was possible to divide birds into categories based on anatomical features. This allowed greater

FIG 44. A fern-owl, caprimulgus or goatsucker, known to us as the nightjar. From a drawing in *Birds and Bird Keeping* (anon., late nineteenth century).

differentiation than just land birds and water birds and, after much discussion (and not a little opposition), this device was gradually accepted. However, the *Ornithology* did little to solve the problems of nomenclature, which continued to cause great confusion within Britain, let alone across Europe. It was a young Swedish botanist who provided a solution.

LINNAEUS AND THE *SYSTEMA NATURAE*

Carl von Linné (Linnaeus) was born in 1707, the son of a church minister in southern Sweden. His father was interested in natural history and taught his son a little botany. Linnaeus went to university at Lund but for various reasons this proved unsatisfactory. He moved to Uppsala, where he made the acquaintance of Peter Artedi (Arctaedius), and he made a number of excursions across Sweden (and into Lapland) noting the flora and fauna. In 1734 he became interested in the daughter of the physician of the town of Falun and they became engaged on the proviso that he qualify as a doctor.

At this point Linnaeus left Sweden and travelled in Europe, going first to Holland. He took with him his first attempt at a system of classification and nomenclature, the *Systema naturae*. Linnaeus, with help from Artedi, had developed a system of classification based on a very simple concept. Each living thing was assigned a name, derived mainly from Latin, and placed in position in a system divided into four hierarchical sections which, in descending order of importance, were called class, order, genus and species. The choice of Latin as the base language for this process was almost predetermined by its use at that time as an international language – indeed, many British ornithological works were still written in Latin.

At Leiden, Linnaeus's work so impressed a botanist named Jan Frederik Gronovius that he paid for its publication, and thus in 1735 the first edition of the *Systema naturae* was published. Not the least feature of the work was its economy with words; one of Linnaeus's obsessions was that scientific works were far more verbose than their content required.

The most important systematic difference introduced by Linnaeus was the use of defined levels of division within a hierarchical structure that slotted all living things into a fixed position relative to each other. At the lower level (above species) he used the term 'genus' to mean a group of related species such as thrushes (previous writers, Willughby and Ray included, had used 'genus', without much definition, to cover large unrelated groups). Linnaeus then added two higher categories of 'class' and 'order', which enabled the system to group the related genera in orders all under the general umbrella of the class.

The characteristics used to separate the natural world were chiefly morphological. Thus Linnaeus divided the class *Aves* (birds) into orders, such as *Passeres* (perching birds), which in turn were divided into genera such as *Columba* (pigeons and doves), *Turdus* (thrushes; Fig 45, 46), *Parus* (titmice), etc. So the separation of birds according to whether they were found on land or water all but disappeared.

Much as Darwin was to encounter considerable opposition to his *Origin of Species* in the nineteenth century, Linnaeus's system was subject to great criticism from the older generation of naturalists. However, because it solved so many problems, the younger naturalists were happy to adopt it, and it was not long before it became the standard form of arrangement. Like many systems, it was, has been, and still is constantly under review, and many naturalists have added to it or modified it – but in essence it lives on.

However, the system could not be applied to birds without a reasonable grounding in ornithology, which Linnaeus did not have. This led to obvious shortcomings in the way in which he constructed the classification of birds, and possibly goes some way towards explaining why ornithologists continually drew up variations, particularly in the number and differentiation of the genera.

In all aspects of human endeavour the genius is demonstrated not in the moment of conception but in the longevity of the concept. The great discoveries live long lives, and despite the modern technological approach to the detail of classification, the fundamental structure of class, order, genus, species remains intact. But Linnaeus had an equally clever – and simple – addition to come.

Twenty-three years after the publication of the first edition of the *Systema naturae*, Linnaeus produced a new simple formula that has become known as binomial nomenclature. Each living thing was given a double name, rather as human beings were at the time. For example, in the case of thrushes the generic name was (and still is) *Turdus*, and this was followed by a unique specific name, as in the blackbird, *merula*. Thus the binomial *Turdus merula* defined the blackbird. This addition, which improved his system immeasurably and helped to stem the tide of criticism, was finally published in 1758, in the tenth edition of the *Systema naturae*, which was for several decades used as the standard.

FIG 45. Song thrush: obviously related to the redwing (Fig. 46), in the genus *Turdus* (thrushes). (Photograph by Rebecca Nason)

FIG 46. Redwing. (Photograph by Rebecca Nason)

THE ENGLISH CONTRIBUTION: THOMAS PENNANT AND JOHN LATHAM

Almost a hundred years passed after the Willughby/Ray *Ornithology* before anything comparable saw the light of day in Britain, in the form of Thomas Pennant's *British Zoology* and John Latham's *General Synopsis of Birds*. Neither of these works embraced Linnaean binomial nomenclature, and neither author seemed inclined much towards Linnaean classification, although it must be said that the binomial nomenclature was scarcely five years in publication when Pennant began to publish his work.

Thomas Pennant

The list of birds in Merrett's *Pinax* of 1666 was probably the first devoted solely to British birds, but it was finally superseded by Pennant's *British Zoology*, which was published over a long period beginning in the 1760s and in several editions, the last of which was supervised by his son-in-law Hanmer with the help of Latham in 1812.

Pennant's work was of a higher quality than that of most of his contemporaries, largely because it was based on his observations, and on the observations of reliable correspondent observers, not least among them Gilbert White (see Chapter 6). The book was enhanced by the inclusion of coloured illustrations; these were not the work of the author, but this was one of the first books to be illustrated in this way.

Thomas Pennant (Fig. 47) was born at Downing on the Welsh borders in June 1726, and educated at Oxford, though he never finally took a degree. He said that his interest in natural history was kindled by the gift of a copy of the Willughby/Ray *Ornithology* when he was about twelve years old. In 1755 he began a correspondence with Linnaeus, and two years later he was elected a member of the Royal Society of Uppsala on the personal recommendation of Linnaeus, after the publication of a geographical paper. He described this as 'the first and greatest of my literary honours. I value myself the more on its being conferred on me at the instance of Linnaeus himself [who] spoke of my works in terms too favourable for me to repeat.'

In 1761 he began the publication of his *British Zoology*, a task that lasted most of his life with various different editions. Pennant travelled quite widely, in 1765 visiting the French naturalist Buffon and the German naturalist-explorer Peter Simon Pallas, with obviously stimulating results on both sides. In 1766 he met Sir Joseph Banks, the famous natural historian, and they became friends,

FIG 47. Thomas Pennant: an engraving from a portrait by Gainsborough in 1776. From the Graham Watson Collection in Emmanuel College, Cambridge.

as indicated by Banks's gift to Pennant of a copy of William Turner's *Avium praecipuarum* – a book that even by that time was considered to be scarce. Banks also gave Pennant help with the later publication *Arctic Zoology*. In 1767 Pennant was elected a Fellow of the Royal Society and in 1769 he travelled to Scotland, his journeys being written up and published by Ben White (Gilbert's brother) in several editions over the years, as was his journey to north Wales nearly ten years later. In 1770 he published a further hundred or more plates of the *British Zoology*. He was awarded an honorary doctorate of Oxford University and in 1773 published his *Genera of Birds*, which was followed by a fourth volume of the *British Zoology*. During this period he worked also on the three-volume *Arctic Zoology*.

In the years that followed he mostly reworked some of his earlier publications and continued to publish works on a variety of topics until in 1793 came the eccentrically titled book *The Literary Life of the Late Thomas Pennant, Esq. by Himself*. The title is particularly curious since at the date of publication he was by no means 'late', surviving another five years until his death in 1798.

There has been some discussion in the past about the lack of recognition that Gilbert White, as a correspondent who supplied much of the information in the

British Zoology, received from Pennant. Although the role of Pennant and White in mutually stimulating each other's enquiries is well known, the contributions of one to the other are not really demarcated. Pennant makes reference to White on occasion but White, for his part, did not include the letters he received from Pennant in his *Natural History of Selborne*, although undoubtedly they would have enhanced the production. It may be that White, aware of Pennant's greater fame, made a conscious decision not to include them for fear of being upstaged; or perhaps he simply did not keep them, although that seems unlikely. Pennant was less than generous in his acknowledgement of White, though the kind of acknowledgement that might be seen to be appropriate today was not a common custom at that time. Furthermore, Pennant was a national authority on natural history while White was unknown at the time. Perhaps the Victorians, who idolised White, failed to put the Pennant/White relationship into the context of the time. However, Pennant did have something of a reputation for sharp practice. He fell out, temporarily, with Sir Joseph Banks when he used illustrations that belonged to Banks in one of his publications; his correspondence with Pallas came to a sharp conclusion when Pennant used information from Pallas without acknowledgement; and last but by no means least there is a story that shows Pennant at his worst. Noblett (1982), quoting the ornithological historian A. M. Lysaght, reports that Pennant was introduced to the Reverend George Lowe, who lived in Orkney, and persuaded the clergyman to write a natural history of those islands; when Lowe sent him the manuscript Pennant lifted the best parts and put them in his *Arctic Zoology*, compounding the felony by returning the original manuscript to Lowe and advising him that no publisher was interested in it!

Yet Pennant was able to record observations in a manner that echoed Turner and Willughby, as in this interesting piece about Revesby in Lincolnshire, the home of Sir Joseph Banks:

> *The birds which inhabit the different fens are very numerous. Besides the common wild duck, wild geese, Garganies, Pochards, Shovelers and Teals breed here. I have seen in the East Fen a flock of Tufted Ducks ... the pewit Gulls [black-headed gull] and black Terns abound ... I saw several of the great crested Grebes on the East Fen these called Gaunts and met with one of their floating nests with eggs in it ... the black and dusky Grebe [?black-necked?] and the little Grebe are also inhabitants of the fens together with coots, water-hens [moorhen], spotted water-hens [spotted crake] water-rails Ruffs Redshanks Lapwings or wipes red breasted Godwits and Whimbrels ... Opposite to Fossdyke Wash during summer are vast numbers of Avosettas called there Yelpers.*

FIG 48. Great crested grebe. (Photograph by Rebecca Nason)

This account of the avifauna of part of the Lincolnshire fenland, almost unique in the detailed identification of the species observed, demonstrates the contrast between the fenland of two hundred years ago and today. The implication that black-necked grebes bred is interesting. Great crested grebes (Fig. 48) were probably not as common then as they are today, but with today's rarities spotted crake, black-tailed godwit, ruff and black tern all recorded, and more extraordinarily whimbrel and 'vast numbers' of avocets, Pennant's description conjures up a picture of a watery paradise unrecognisable today beyond the limits of the East Anglian coastal bird reserves.

Pennant's status within British ornithology has diminished with the passage of time and his fame today is based on little more than his being one of the correspondents of Gilbert White. But to his contemporaries he was pre-eminent and for a period afterwards he was considered one of the titans of British ornithology.

John Latham

The other 'giant' of the time was John Latham (Fig. 49), whose *General Synopsis of Birds* started publication in 1781, twenty years after Pennant's *British Zoology*.

Latham was born at Eltham, Kent, on 27 June 1740. His father was a surgeon and he was educated at Merchant Taylors' School. Of his early life very little seems to have been documented, but we know that after leaving school he studied anatomy under John Hunter (the most influential and celebrated physician of the time) and subsequently worked as a doctor in Dartford, Kent, where he seems to have been very successful; so successful in fact that he was able to retire (to Romsey, Hampshire) at the age of 56. His interest in natural history must have been established earlier, since by the time he was 31 he was a correspondent of Thomas Pennant and, according to the records, was made a Fellow of the Royal Society in 1775. He was also a founder member of the Linnean Society in 1788 and was greatly impressed by the work of the Swede. His ornithological claim to fame rests on two publications which, together with Pennant's work, were to form the framework for the ornithologists in this country into the nineteenth century, until they were replaced by the far superior works of Montagu, MacGillivray and Yarrell.

Latham's interest began as a collector, and among those with whom he exchanged specimens was Sir Ashton Lever, one of the principal early collectors of zoologia in this country along with William Bullock and Sir Joseph Banks. Lever and Banks gathered specimens from many sources, but particularly from the expeditions of the celebrated Captain James Cook in the 1780s. Cook

FIG 49. John Latham, from a portrait in the British Library.

was always accompanied by a naturalist of some sort, once indeed by Banks. Lever's collection was exhibited in a museum in Blackfriars, London, where its haphazard arrangement was noted by many visitors. Some compared it unfavourably with the rival enterprise of William Bullock, who presented labelled specimens, usually in a manner as close to their natural surroundings as he could. Latham used these and other collections to derive material, and added the source of the specimens to his descriptions.

Latham specialised in describing and cataloguing the new discoveries, along with species already known, and this culminated in the publication of *A General Synopsis of Birds* in three volumes between 1781 and 1785. In it Latham used a hybrid system of classification, espousing Linnaeus's groupings (and adding more), but ignoring some of the basic tenets of Linnaeus by retaining both the Willughby/Ray division of land and water birds and the use of English nomenclature, rather than Latin binomials. Views of Latham's work have declined with time. William Swainson, whose work on the biographies of zoologists (1840) contained some pithy comments on many authors, perhaps summed up a contemporary view:

> *The works of Latham will be long quoted, because, although exhibiting more of unwearied zeal and extensive research than of critical acumen or comprehensive judgement, they have become interwoven with the science he cultivated, and are cited by almost every writer ... we are obliged to say that the vastness of his plan, which aimed at no less than the description of all known birds, was too great for his talents. His memory was not good; hence he frequently described the same species by different names; and he placed too much faith in drawings which led to the same error.*

The German ornithologist Erwin Stresemann (1975) was blunt, describing Latham's book as 'a mass-production job with every consequent failing; the descriptions are superficial and often so disfigured by errors as to be completely unrecognisable and the locality data are unreliable.'

As far as Linnaean nomenclature was concerned Latham later either relented or saw the way the pendulum was swinging, and he Latinised the names in his *Index ornithologicus* of 1790, and went on to add two supplements in 1787 and 1802. Between 1821 and 1828 he published an eleven-volume work, *A General History of Birds*, which was mainly an enlarged re-writing of the *Synopsis*.

Latham, like many before him and a few after, was not much of an *observer* of birds, if at all – more a collector of facts who wrote them up. He corresponded with, and directly copied from the work of, the Frenchman Brisson. The failings in his work are almost certainly a direct result of his lack of field experience. Unsurprisingly, therefore, despite the fact that his work was for a period among the standard reference texts, Latham's work did not stand the test of time. Recently Farber (1997), an American historian, gave Latham much credit as a contributor to knowledge. The view on John Latham in his own country, however, is of a compiler who performed a service through his cataloguing of newly discovered species, but whose work was limited in usefulness by inaccuracy. Latham's disinclination to adopt Linnaean nomenclature cost him a posterity that was snatched by a more enterprising man, J. F. Gmelin.

Latham's loss was Gmelin's gain. Gmelin, a German, has significance in a history of British ornithology because in 1788 he began what he called the thirteenth edition of the *Systema naturae*. He took information from published sources, particularly Latham, and used the Latin-based binomial nomenclature to create an authoritative book. What is more, because he was the first to give scientific names to those birds first described by Latham, Gmelin has always received credit for them!

BRITISH AVIFAUNAS OF THE EIGHTEENTH CENTURY

The books of the later part of the eighteenth century were very much precursors of those grander volumes published in the first half of the nineteenth. Most of the writers were still compilers, lifting information, sometimes wholesale, from the work of others, which inevitably reduced the long-term value of their work. This is a selection of the minor offerings of the eighteenth century.

In 1769 a book titled *Outlines of the Natural History of Great Britain and Ireland* was published by John Berkenhout – later reprinted under the same title with the prefix *Synopsis*. In 1771 Marmaduke Tunstall produced his *Ornithologia Britannica*, which was merely a list of names. Beginning in the same year, William Hayes published a *Natural History of British Birds*, a folio of forty plates with text which according to Alfred Newton showed much ignorance on the part of the author (Fig. 50).

In 1776 Peter Brown, a professional artist, produced his *New Illustrations of Zoology*, which received approval from William Swainson in his review of the works of British ornithology fifty years later. Swainson thought the plates were superior, on the whole, to those of Edwards (see below); but the descriptions, he said, were so short as to be nearly useless.

In 1789 John Walcott produced a *Synopsis of British Birds*, illustrated in

FIG 50. Lapwing, from Hayes's *Natural History of British Birds* (1771). Typical of its time, the illustration has many faults, not least the unnatural pose, which is most likely the result of the subject being a (poorly) mounted specimen. That said, the bird is instantly recognisable.

colour, and William Lewin commenced his *Birds of Great Britain* in seven volumes, the last of which appeared in 1794. Lewin was described by Swainson as the best zoological painter and one of the most practical naturalists of his day (Fig. 51). It was also in 1794 that Edward Donovan began his *Natural History of British Birds*, which was completed in 1819, but it was rather scathingly treated by Swainson, who considered the work expensive, the figures 'destitute of grace or correctness', and the text 'verbose and not above mediocrity'. *Harmonia ruralis*, published by James Bolton around 1795, was an account of British song birds that ran into several editions for up to fifty years.

Critics in the nineteenth century all agreed that none of these works was sufficiently original to remain of interest, and to the average student of British ornithology they will be unknown. A book by Thomas Lord, published in 1791, was described by Swainson as so bad that it was difficult 'to conceive figures worse executed than those contained in this book now seldom seen'.

A number of books published in Britain with a more international interest are rather better known. Mark Catesby's *Natural History of Carolina* was published in two folios with coloured plates between 1731 and 1743. Eleazar Albin's *Natural History of Birds* appeared in three volumes between 1731 and 1738; it lacked good ornithological knowledge but, the author being a professional artist, it had some good illustrations (Fig. 52).

Finally there was George Edwards, who deserves a special mention since his work is probably the best known of the various less important offerings. Born in Stratford, Essex, in 1693, Edwards is often considered to be the first of the bird illustrators able to bring a new accuracy to the pictures. He was also a competent ornithologist who travelled widely on the Continent, where he spent some time recording and observing all forms of natural life. While in England he seems to have drifted into drawing and painting birds, mainly because he was

FIG 51. Great grey shrike, from William Lewin's *Birds of Great Britain* (1789–94). One of the best of some fairly ordinary illustrations.

not satisfied with the efforts of others. In December 1733, at the instigation of Sir Hans Sloane (see below), he was appointed Librarian of the Royal College of Physicians, which gave him the opportunity for further study since the library was stocked with many rare books on natural history. He began publishing his *Natural History of Birds* in 1743, and after the first volume sold well he produced three further volumes in 1747, 1750 and 1751 (Fig. 53). His intention was to stop there, but in 1758 he published a fifth volume under the new title *Gleanings of Natural History.* The sixth came out in 1760 and the seventh and final volume in 1764. A generic index was added and Linnaean nomenclature was provided by Linnaeus himself, who was a friend of Edwards.

In 1750 Edwards was presented with the Gold Medal of the Royal Society for his *Natural History of Birds,* and later he was elected a Fellow and gave papers at various meetings. After a gradual decline in health, in which he began to lose his sight, he died in July 1773. Yet he remains one of the first British bird artists.

FIG 52. Hoopoe, from Albin's *Natural History of Birds* (1738–41). A good portrait, but the quality of the colouring varied from book to book. This copy is a good one; others could be watery or inaccurate.

FIG 53. Grey wagtail, from George Edwards's *Natural History of Birds* (1750).

COLLECTIONS AND COLLECTORS:
SLOANE, BANKS AND LEVER

In the late seventeenth and early eighteenth century, wealthy men began to collect what have subsequently been termed ornithologia. These collections comprised birds, both dead and alive, their eggs, and illustrated catalogues and books about birds. In Britain the largest collection, and the most impressive according to Linnaeus, was that of Sir Hans Sloane (1660–1752). Sloane was born in Northern Ireland of Scottish descent and travelled to London to complete his medical training. Yet it was as a naturalist that he made his mark. He was an admirer and friend of John Ray and had sent botanical specimens to him from a trip to France. As a young doctor, Sloane had accompanied the Duke of Albermarle to Jamaica, where he (Sloane) gathered many of the natural history specimens that formed the basis of his collection. Predominantly a botanist, he also sponsored the expedition made by Mark Catesby to the southern colonies of America (Carolina, Georgia and Florida) and the Bahamas from 1722 to 1726. Sloane became Secretary of the Royal Society and editor of its *Philosophical Transactions* and, following the death of Sir Isaac Newton, its President. He left both his library and his collection to the nation, including some 1,172 ornithological items – beaks, bones, eggs, nests etc. The Sloane collection subsequently formed the basis of what became the British Museum (Natural History), but unfortunately its state of preservation was poor and due to lack of attention it degraded and was eventually discarded.

Sir Joseph Banks (1743–1820) travelled to the northeast coast of America in 1765 and then accompanied Cook on a trip around the world to South America and the Antipodes, where Banks made a great collection of flora and fauna. After a short break he set out for Iceland and took in many Scottish Islands on the way, with more collecting as he went. He was elected President of the Royal Society and led the organisation deeper into natural history, a movement that was not always appreciated by some of the physical scientists. Banks left his collection and library to his librarian, Robert Brown, and after Brown's death to the British Museum.

Sir Ashton Lever (1729–88) differed from Sloane and Banks in that his collection, which contained items from Cook's voyages, was housed in his museum with the aim of making money from paying visitors. This was not a success, and when Lever sold it (by lottery) the 'lucky' purchaser found it no more successful, so in 1806 the collection was sold, the sale taking two months and comprising nearly nine thousand lots.

While systematics developed apace, for the first time other branches of ornithology were also receiving attention. In a Hampshire village a country parson was meticulously observing and recording the events in the countryside, with a very strong emphasis on matters ornithological. These studies were what we would today call ecology – the relation of the birds to the environment in which they live – and bird ecology developed in parallel to the advances in systematics.

CHAPTER 6

The First Ornithological Ecologists: White, Jenner and Blackwall

I would anxiously guard against an exclusive attention to the collecting and arranging of specimens to the neglect of what is much more instructive and valuable: I allude to the study of their habits, manner, economy, instincts, and notes.

John Blackwall, 1822

THE EIGHTEENTH CENTURY saw the start of a gradual separation in British ornithology. On the one hand were the systematists, working on specimens and collections of dead birds in boxes or live birds in captive collections, identifying and storing, cataloguing and arranging; while the other group were the field ornithologists who watched birds in their natural habitats and noted and analysed their behaviour.

In England, in the Hampshire village of Selborne, one man, whose name is now known throughout the world, was busy watching and noting the habits of the birds – Gilbert White, the father of British ornithological ecology.

GILBERT WHITE

The fundamental strength of White's work was that it was original, informative and based firmly on his own observations. That is not to say that he did not incorporate the reports of his neighbours and parishioners, but when he used reported information he notated it as such.

Gilbert White (Fig. 54) was born in the vicarage at Selborne on 18 July 1720. His mother was the daughter of the incumbent and his father was a barrister; Gilbert was the first of their eleven children. He went to school at Basingstoke

FIG 54. Gilbert White, aged 27, by his friend T. Chapman. (British Museum)

before going to university at Oxford, where he eventually became a Fellow of Oriel College in 1747.

White then undertook certain modest journeys but was often afflicted with travel sickness, which discouraged him from further travel, and this seems to have been the prime reason for his birdwatching being confined to his home ground.

Like Turner and Ray before him, but in much less controversial times, White's life was linked with the church; he was ordained in 1749, and a significant proportion of his income was derived from curacies at Farringdon (near Selborne), which he undertook in 1755, and at Moreton Pinkney in Northamptonshire in 1757. Both these parishes were in the gift of his Oxford college. Much of his early life was divided between Oxford and Selborne, but an attempt to be elected Provost of Oriel in 1757 met with failure, much to White's disappointment. Probably as a direct result, the time he subsequently spent in Oxford dwindled.

In 1751 he began to compile a diary of the events concerned with the cultivation of the garden at 'The Wakes'– the *Garden Kalender* – and he was almost certainly observing the local wildlife at this time. On the death of his father in 1758 he became responsible for the family home. Due to the strange introverted nature of his father, Gilbert had been running the household for some time, yet it was not until the death of his uncle five years later that he actually inherited the house which became his base for the remainder of his life.

From 1765 his interest in the garden began to decline, to be replaced by natural history, and the following year he began to compile a *Flora Selborniensis*, which was sadly never completed. Perhaps because his main interest seemed now to be birds.

The Natural History of Selborne

The book for which Gilbert White is so well known consists of letters about the natural history of the parish of Selborne and its immediate surrounding area. Of the subject matter in the contents list, birds form by far the greatest part.

It was sometime during his stay in London in April 1767 that White made the acquaintance of Thomas Pennant, probably through his publisher brother Benjamin, who was responsible for producing some of Pennant's work. As a result of this meeting the correspondence began that was to become the basis of the first part of the *Natural History*. Richard Mabey (1986), White's most recent biographer, pointed out that with so little organised communication, since many scientific societies were in their infancy, the only means of contact between interested scientists was via this sort of correspondence.

To begin with, White was clearly in awe of Pennant, whose reputation in the subject was well established. White was one of number of Pennant's correspondents, and although he used Pennant as a sounding board for much of his own work, he seems to have received few, if any, original observations from Pennant in return. At any rate, if he did receive anything, it does not appear in the *Natural History*. It is clear that White recognised the potential of his own letters, since he went to the trouble of copying them. As the correspondence proceeded White gathered confidence, until there came a point at which the usefulness of the correspondence for both parties was waning; this was probably due, at least in part, to White's fear of travel sickness and his consequent reluctance to travel to Lancashire to visit Pennant.

Propitiously, via his brother Benjamin, he received in 1767 the printed forms for a 'Naturalists Journal', which was the idea of Daines Barrington. Barrington was a Fellow of the Royal Society and like Pennant he was a man who enjoyed a reputation as a competent scientist. White wrote to Barrington to thank him, and the second of the two correspondences in the *Natural History* was established. Mabey has suggested that some parts of letters, or indeed whole letters, were added by White to the *Natural History* without ever having existed as actual letters, particularly among those towards the end of the book.

The Natural History of Selborne was first published in 1789, and has such an enduring quality that ever since it has been re-issued time and again with versions and commentaries by many of this country's leading ornithologists, including, in recent times, James Fisher.

In the history of ornithology in Britain there can be few people who have 'discovered' new species by observing birds in their home village, yet in separating the leaf warblers (Fig. 55) – chiffchaff, wood warbler and willow warbler – Gilbert White was able to do just this:

> *I make no doubt but that there are three species of willow-wrens; two I know perfectly, but have not been able yet to procure the third. No two birds can differ more in their notes, for the one has a joyous, easy, laughing note, the other a harsh loud chirp ... the songster [willow warbler] is one-fifth heavier than the chirper [chiffchaff]. The chirper,, being the first summer bird of passage that is heard, begins his two notes in the middle of March, and continues them through the spring and summer till the end of August, as appears in my journals. The legs of the larger of these two are flesh-coloured; of the less black.*

FIG 55. Chiffchaff, from F. O. Morris's *History of British Birds* (4th edition, 1896). A good portrait, especially since most books up to the late nineteenth century had very poor illustrations of leaf warblers – which are, in all fairness, difficult to depict accurately.

Then White separated the wood warbler, based first on morphological features and secondly on the differing song:

I have now, past dispute, made out three distinct species of willow-wrens which constantly and invariably use distinct notes ... The yellowest bird [wood warbler] is considerably the largest, and has its quill-feathers and secondary feathers tipped with white, which the others have not. This last haunts only the tops of trees in high beechen woods, and makes a sibilous grasshopper-like noise, now and then, at short intervals, shivering a little with its wings when it sings; and is, I make no doubt now, the regulus non cristatus of Ray ... yet this great ornithologist never suspected that there were three species.

It is surprising, compared with today's distribution, to discover that black grouse (Fig. 56) were to be found in Hampshire, and White records their loss from his area:

but there was a nobler species of game in this forest, now extinct, which I have heard old people say abounded much before shooting flying became so common, and that was the heath-cock, black-game or grouse. When I was a little boy I recollect one coming now and then to my father's table. The last pack remembered was killed about thirty-five years ago; and within these ten years one solitary grey hen was sprung by some beagles in beating for a hare.

In providing information of this kind White's work is of enormous value. Rather like the information from the Lincolnshire fenland from Pennant (see Chapter 5), this is one of very few instances in which we are given evidence of the local status of a species. For most birds, clear information on local status in Britain is virtually non-existent before the nineteenth century.

From the comparative ecology of hirundines emerged a conundrum which puzzled other ornithologists of his time, notably John Legg (see Chapter 7), and White muses 'how strange it is that the swift, which seems to live exactly the same life with the swallow and house-martin should leave us before the middle of August invariably!'

White noted the spring and autumn passage of ring ouzels (Fig. 57) and speculated on the origins and destinations of these birds. Like much of his observation, his study of ring ouzel movements took place over several successive years and his thoughts are gradually revealed with each succeeding observation. Within the section on the ring ouzel is a clear indication of a slight reprimand from Pennant as White became a little absorbed in surmise for which he had no

TAB . XXXI.

Urogallus five
Tetrao minor
The Black game
Heath cock or
Grows

FIG 56. Black grouse, from the Willughby/Ray *Ornithology* (1676). Presumably drawn from a bird left hanging to mature for the table, but the artist has made a rather incongruous attempt to make it appear to be standing one-legged on a rock!

Merula torquata.
The Ring Ouzell.

FIG 57. Ring ouzel, from the Willughby/Ray *Ornithology* (1676). This illustration is typical of the pose adopted by many artists for birds at this time.

evidence on which to base his theory – although, as we now know, White's theory was largely correct. This incident is important in that it illustrates just how far White and Pennant were involved in factual observation above all else, contrasting markedly with most ornithology before, and not a little after. First, White reported the presence of ring ouzels:

> *Some birds, haunting with the missel-thrushes, and feeding on the berries of the yew tree, which answered to the description of the Merula torquata, or ring-ousel, were lately seen in this neighbourhood. I employed some people to procure me a specimen, but without success.*

Next he noted the birds as migrants, hypothesising on their origins and destinations:

> *Last week a farmer, seeing a large flock, twenty or thirty, shot two cocks and two hens, and says, on recollection, that he remembers to have observed these birds again last*

spring, on their return to the north. Now perhaps these ousels are not the ousels of the
north of England, but belong to the more northern parts of Europe; and may retire
before the excessive rigour of the frost in those parts, and return to breed in the spring,
when the cold abates. If this be the case, here is discovered a new bird of winter passage,
concerning whose migrations the writers are silent; but if these birds should prove
the ousels of the north of England, then here is a migration disclosed within our own
kingdom never before remarked. It does not yet appear whether they retire beyond
the bounds of our island to the south; but it is most probable that they usually do,
or else one cannot suppose that they would have continued so long unnoticed in the
southern counties.

Pennant must have responded that he thought the origin of the ring ouzels
was, as White had suggested, northern Europe, and White reminded Pennant
that he had asked him to try to find out if they left the mountains in northern
Britain in winter, to which Pennant must have replied that they did not.
Here there seems to be some discrepancy with the situation today, since over-
wintering in Britain is now rare. Does this mean that Pennant *knew* that ring
ouzels overwintered? In which case there has been a change of habit. Or did
he simply take on trust information relayed to him by others who were not
competent in bird recognition, and who mistakenly thought they saw ring
ouzels in winter? At this point Pennant is quick to point out to White that he
(White) might be making an assumption about the direction of the autumn
migration, and White replies, 'you put a very shrewd question when you
ask me how I know that their autumn migration is southward ... common
ingenuousness obliges me to confess, not without some degree of shame, that
I only reasoned in that case through analogy.' Yet despite all this theorising
White was still in doubt about the true origins of the birds, as the next entry
shows, and the letters never reveal whether White discovered the source of
the birds: 'from whence then do our ring-ousels migrate so regularly every
September, and make their appearance again, as if in their return, every
April?'

White's notes on stone curlews amounted to a superb series of observations
concerning aspects of their ecology, particularly the use of camouflage:

The History of the stone-curlew, charadrius oedicnemus, is as follows. It lays its eggs,
usually two, never more than three, on the bare ground, without any nest, in the field,
so that the countryman, in stirring his fallows often destroys them. The young run
immediately from the egg like partridges, etc., and are withdrawn to some flinty field by
the dam, where they skulk among the stones, which are their best security; for their

feathers are so exactly of the colour of our grey spotted flints, that the most exact observer, unless he catches the eye of the young bird, may be eluded.

Two years later White reported some stone curlew findings from a correspondent in Sussex:

They live with us all spring and summer, and at the beginning of autumn prepare to take leave by getting together in flocks. They seem to me a bird of passage that may travel into some hilly country south of us, probably Spain, because of the abundance of sheep-walks in that country.

Another bird that White studied quite extensively was the nightjar (Fig. 58), with particular reference to the calls and sounds made by this most enigmatic of birds.

There is no bird whose manners I have studied more than that of the caprimulgus (the goat-sucker), I have always found that though sometimes it may chatter as it flies, in general it utters its jarring note sitting on a bough, and I have for many a half-hour watched it as it sat with its under mandible quivering. It appears to me past all doubt that its notes are formed by organic impulse, by the powers of the parts of its windpipe formed for sound just as cats pur ... This bird also sometimes makes a small squeak, repeated four or five times; and I have observed that to happen when the cock has been pursuing the hen in a toying way through the boughs of a tree.

He noted that the local chaffinch flocks consisted almost entirely of hen birds and considered it likely that they were migrants:

For many years past I have observed that towards Christmas vast flocks of chaffinches have appeared in the fields; many more, I used to think, than could be hatched in any one neighbourhood. But when I came to observe them more narrowly, I was amazed to find that they seemed to me to be almost all hens.

He also was one of the first observers to describe the lesser whitethroat:

A rare and I think a new, little bird frequents my garden, which I have great reason to think is the pettichaps: it is common in some parts of the kingdom; and I have received formerly several specimens from Gibraltar. This bird much resembles the White-throat, but has a more white or rather silvery breast and belly.

FIG 58. Nightjar by Archibald Thorburn, from Swaysland's *Familiar Wild Birds* (1883–8).

There is potential for confusion here. White describes the pettichaps (presumed to be the lesser whitethroat) and the greater pettichaps (presumed to be the garden warbler), yet migratory routes for the two, as revealed by ringing, show a difference: lesser whitethroats migrate through the eastern Mediterranean, and it would therefore be unlikely that White obtained specimens of lesser whitethroat from Gibraltar. It is also worth recording that the name 'pettichaps' or 'pettychaps' may have been used indiscriminately for warblers. The description from White, however, leaves little doubt that the bird he observed was the lesser whitethroat and not the garden warbler.

A final extract, from a letter dated 2 September 1774, contains among other matters a whole list of short sharp facts – rather suggesting that it was a 'letter' added afterwards:

> The grasshopper-lark [grasshopper warbler] chirps all night in the height of the summer. Swans turn white in the second year, and breed the third ... Sparrow-hawks sometimes breed in old crows' nests, and the kestril in churches and ruins ... Hen-harriers breed on the ground, and seem never to settle in trees ... Hedge-sparrows have a remarkable flirt with their wings in breeding-time; as soon as frosty mornings come they make a very piping plaintive noise ... Wrens sing all the winter through. Most birds drink sipping at intervals; but pigeons take a long continued draught, like quadrupeds.

These extracts illustrate the important ornithological discoveries of White: the separation of the three leaf warblers, the discovery of the spring and autumn migration of the ring ouzel, the finding that chaffinches flock by sex in winter and that stone curlew chicks and eggs have natural camouflage. His description of the lesser whitethroat was not in fact the first, since Linnaeus described it in 1758 – although it seems that White was unaware of this. White also provided the first sound ecological information on a number of species – nightjar and stone curlew, swift, swallow and the martins.

White spent the later part of his life almost exclusively at Selborne, and remained unmarried. He was often the host for friends and family and was assisted by members of the subsequent generation of Whites in much of his work. Mabey stated that White's formal scientific discoveries have often been overplayed, which may be true, but as an ornithologist he established a new approach to birds that transformed the 'identify and describe' technique that preceded him into a genuinely enquiring science.

About migration he remained ambivalent. He accepted that the ring ouzel made such regular seasonal movements, and even speculated about the origins of the birds; but he remained convinced that the hirundines, which he loved,

HIRVNDO VRBICA.— Page 6.

FIG 59. House martin, from Forster's *Observations on the Brumal Retreat of the Swallow* (1808) – one of the species White was unable to accept as a migrant.

did not (Fig. 59). Mabey has suggested that this was an emotional block and that White could not accept that birds which were so important to him and were such symbols of summer could desert his beloved Selborne – and therefore he liked to believe that they must spend the winter in the area in torpor.

The letters contain a wealth of original ornithological observations, and in that respect White is quite different from nearly all his predecessors in British ornithology, with the possible exception of Willughby.

A view of the relative merits of Pennant and White a few decades after their deaths is shown by their entries in the *British Cyclopedia* of 1838, where Pennant merited nearly three columns, in which he was described as a great naturalist, while White was summarised in a single paragraph of six lines as a clergyman who was born in 1720, wrote *The Natural History of Selborne*, and died in 1793. These descriptions, quite the reverse of what one would find today, show that at the time the significance of White's work was obviously not appreciated.

Daines Barrington

Of White's two correspondents, Pennant was in his day an extremely prestigious scientist, and his publications, together with those of Latham, were to be standard works for quite some time. Daines Barrington (1727–1800) was of lesser importance – ornithologically – though clearly he was something of an establishment figure. He was a lawyer educated at Oxford and the Inner Temple who became a judge in Wales in 1757 (at what today seems the remarkably early age of 30) and then was appointed Second Justice at Chester, a post he held up until 1785. He then retired back to London, living chiefly around the Inner Temple.

Like many a judge he seems to have been a man of firm opinion, except that in Barrington's case he was frequently wrong. His views on the parasitic nature of the cuckoo, expressed in an essay, are a good example: 'though it hath been so implicitly believed for centuries, that the cuckow neither hatches nor rears its young, I hope to be permitted to express my doubts, with regard to this most unnatural neglect in the parent bird being general.' Barrington followed this with a long discussion on the poor nature of the evidence that the cuckoo is parasitic, going back to Aristotle and stating that no one ever found a cuckoo egg in the nest of small birds. Barrington found it unbelievable that a dunnock would allow its eggs or young to be destroyed, and he argued that because a cuckoo's egg must be larger than a dunnock's and has entirely the wrong colouration, the dunnock must surely notice. These were all valid points, but, like others before him, Barrington made the mistake of arguing on the basis of logical thought as opposed to careful observation. He was not entirely gullible, however, and to his credit he further described the idea that the nightjar sucks milk from domestic animals as preposterous.

Barrington lambasted the Linnaean system and found Linnaeus a poor ornithologist – which in all honesty he probably was, but his pronouncement on Linnaeus's *Systema naturae* turned out to be most unfortunate: 'such is the system of Linnaeus: novelty made it please, and its obscurity rendered it admired; but it cannot be lasting.'

Barrington's role in the second half of the correspondence with White is unclear. He was undoubtedly responsible for sending White ideas for recording his observations (via Gilbert's brother Benjamin) but Walter Johnson, an early twentieth-century biographer of White (1928), considered Barrington's influence to be not entirely beneficial, describing him as a 'legal-minded dilettante, whose ill-founded speculations and hasty conclusions occasionally led White astray'. Johnson suggests that White may have been deliberately distancing himself from his correspondent when he described himself – in the very first letter to Barrington – as 'an out-door naturalist, one that takes his observations from the subject itself and not from the writings of others'.

So Barrington remains a very minor player in British ornithology but, despite his faults, not one to be ignored – if only for his catalytic role in encouraging the recording of observations by Gilbert White.

EDWARD JENNER'S CUCKOO STUDIES

The very opposite of the Barrington approach was used by Edward Jenner, who with a combination of careful observation and experimentation discovered the way in which the young cuckoo ensured the exclusive attentions of its foster-parents by ejecting the young of the host (Fig. 60).

Jenner was born in Berkeley, Gloucestershire, in 1749, the third son of the vicar of that parish. He went to school in Cirencester and even at that early age was interested in natural history. Later he studied pharmacy and surgery near Bristol before going to London and becoming a pupil of John Hunter at St George's Hospital. Despite many possible opportunities Jenner returned to Berkeley as a country doctor. He is well known as the discoverer of the principle of vaccination – perhaps less well known as an ornithologist.

Jenner's tutor, John Hunter, was also interested in natural history, and over the years he made various requests of his former pupil for, among other things, young blackbirds, fossils, eels and even a great bustard, all of which Jenner

FIG 60. A cuckoo at a meadow pipit's nest, from a curious book *The Pipits* by 'the author of Caw Caw', with illustrations by 'JBH', published in 1872. This book contains a rather childish poetic version of the story of the cuckoo's parasitism of a pair of meadow pipits.

appears to have obtained for him. Together they investigated the physiology of hibernation, using hedgehogs. The important finding concerning the cuckoo was stimulated by Hunter, who wished to know more about the life of the bird and may have had his curiosity raised by the attitude of Barrington.

Jenner's study began with the dates of arrival, before going on to say that cuckoos do not pair and that the female is often 'attended by two or three males, who seem to be earnestly contending for her favours'. He gave the first date of laying, stating that he was unable to find an egg until the middle of May. Next he listed the host species: dunnock, pied wagtail, meadow pipit, yellow-hammer and whinchat. He proceeded by detailing the laying of eggs by the host and the cuckoo, and began to hint at what was to come by stating that the young of the host are 'turned out' so that the young cuckoo has the nest to itself. Jenner pointed out that some cuckoos hatch after the parent birds have left in late summer, so that the adults could hardly be involved, and secondly that when emerging from the shell the newly hatched young cuckoo is not much bigger than a dunnock nestling, so smothering was out of the question. Before giving instances of his observations on the ejection of the hosts' young, Jenner was at pains to counter the view of Barrington, who did not believe even that cuckoos are raised by foster-parents. Jenner wrote 'I saw the old birds feed it [the young cuckoo] repeatedly, and, to satisfy myself that they were really titlarks, [meadow pipits] shot them both, and found them to be so.'

Then Jenner gave a detailed description of his observations of the actions of cuckoo nestlings (Fig. 61), which merits quoting at length:

> On inspecting the nest I found, that the bird had hatched this morning, and that every thing but the young Cuckoo was thrown out. Under the nest I found one of the young Hedge-sparrows dead, and one egg by the side of the nest ... on examining the egg, I found one end of the shell a little cracked, and could see that the sparrow contained was yet alive. It was then restored to the nest, but in a few minutes was thrown out. To see what would happen if the Cuckoo was removed I took out the Cuckoo and placed the egg containing the Hedge-sparrow in the nest in its stead. The old birds during this time, flew about the spot, shewing signs of great anxiety; but when I withdrew they quickly came to the nest again. On looking in a quarter of an hour later I found the young one completely hatched, warm and lively. The Hedge-sparrows were suffered to remain undisturbed with their new charge for three hours (during which time they paid every attention to it) when the Cuckoo was again put into the nest. The old sparrows had been so much disturbed by these intrusions, that for some time they shewed an unwillingness to come to it: however, at length they came, and on examining the nest

FIG 61. A drawing of the event described by Jenner, from *The Pipits* (see also Fig. 60).

*again in a few minutes, I found the young sparrow was tumbled out. It was a second
time restored, but again experienced the same fate.*

This is almost certainly the first example of an experiment being performed
in the field to show a particular form of behaviour. Jenner gave other instances,
including a very detailed description of the way in which the young cuckoo ejects
the young of the host:

*The little animal with the assistance of its rump and wings, contrived to get the
bird upon its back, and making a lodgement for the burden by elevating its elbows,
clambered backward with it up the side of the nest till it reached the top, where resting
for a moment, it threw off its load with a jerk, and quite disengaged it from the nest.*

Jenner then noted that the same process is used to eject an egg. He went on to
point out that if an unusually large nestling is introduced (another experiment)
the cuckoo continues to struggle to eject it despite the fact that the obvious
disparity of size makes ejection an impossibility. He further noted that the urge
to eject other occupants is strongest when the cuckoo is two or three days old,
waning thereafter up to about twelve days, when it no longer bothers – an early

example of a now accepted phenomenon that instinctive actions can be very time-limited, especially in newborn animals (imprinting, for example). He described the particular physical structure of the cuckoo nestling that assists the bird to perform its task:

> *The singularity of the shape is well adapted for these purposes; for different from other newly-hatched birds, its back from the scapulae downwards is very broad with a considerable depression in the middle. This depression seems formed by nature for the design of giving a more secure lodgement to the egg of the Hedge-sparrow, or its young one, when the young Cuckoo is employed in removing either of them from the nest.*

Jenner stated that the egg of the cuckoo is very small for so large a bird, although he also noted that cuckoos' eggs are often different in size and that the colouration is very varied.

Next he pointed out that cuckoos only parasitise the nests of small birds because the cuckoo fledgling would be less able to eject the young of larger species. He described an instance of two cuckoos laying in the same nest, leading to a gargantuan struggle between the two cuckoo fledglings which lasted a whole day until one of them prevailed.

Jenner attempted to discover why the cuckoo (Fig. 62), rather than raise its own young, should parasitise other birds, and he ended up concluding that since it stays for so short a time the only breeding strategy open to it is to leave its young to be raised by resident species (although the truth is likely the reverse – it stays only as long as it needs to ensure a future generation, and the time limitation is likely to be the availability of nests to parasitise within the time frame to allow a young cuckoo to mature in time to migrate). Jenner ended with notes on the diet of both the cuckoo and some of its foster-parents. An impressive piece of ecology.

Yet it was not a piece of science that impressed the Council of the Royal Society. Not for the last time, members of the establishment were not prepared to listen to theories that went against their long-held prejudices. Sir Joseph Banks, the President at the time, wrote to Jenner in July 1787 rejecting his paper, saying that the 'council thought it best to give you full scope for altering it' – a rather unsubtle way of saying that they did not believe it – followed with 'another year we shall be glad to receive it again, and print it.'

Despite this, Jenner's paper was eventually published in the *Philosophical Transactions of the Royal Society* in 1788, doubtless due to the insistence and reputation of John Hunter, its sponsor, and its conclusions were very gradually accepted.

FIG 62. Head of a cuckoo by J. M. W. Turner, from his *Ornithological Collection*. From Hill's *Turner's Birds* (1988).

JOHN BLACKWALL

The initial thrust into bird ecology had one more exponent, who lived in the northwest of England and north Wales. John Blackwall is a surprisingly overlooked ornithologist and although strictly speaking his output makes him a nineteenth-century figure it makes sense to include him in this chapter, for reasons that will become apparent.

Blackwall was born in Manchester on 20 January 1790, and after his education he joined his father in business as an importer of Irish linen. He was an all-round naturalist of some importance, known mainly for his work on arachnids – spiders – that culminated in the publication of *A History of the Spiders of Great Britain and Ireland* between 1861 and 1864. Blackwall was also one of the first ornithologists to speak out against the obsession with collections, although he was trying to stop the unstoppable tide. His ornithological studies predate the arachnid work, so presumably he began his interest in natural history by studying birds. He made some contributions to the early work on migration (see Chapter 7) but he also conducted some elegant experiments in field ornithology following the methodological approach of Jenner, with whose work he must have been familiar.

He began with a study of bird song (1822) to determine to what extent it was instinctive, and he traced his interest in the songs of birds to a paper by Barrington. Blackwall stated that Barrington's experiments were 'imperfect and unsatisfactory and the conclusions drawn from them, hasty, unwarranted, and contrary to common experience'. Outlining his own experimental approach to determine the origin of bird song, he explained that 'in order to ascertain whether nestlings when taken very young will or will not have the calls and songs of their species, they should be kept in situations where they have no opportunity of learning any sounds that they may substitute for them.' Blackwall took three nestling crossbills – grosbeaks he called them – a male and two females, approximately two days old, and raised them to maturity in isolation. Their songs and calls were those typical of the species. However, he realised that since these young had heard their parents call they might have copied them. Next, therefore, he swapped over the young of newly hatched robins and chaffinches and subsequently took them into isolation when ten days old (he left them in the nest this long because he recognised that he would be unable to raise them from hatching). The robins developed typical robin calls despite being exposed only to those of their chaffinch foster-parents, and vice versa. With difficulty he managed to keep alive until autumn only a male robin and a female chaffinch (Fig. 63). The male robin proceeded to sing the typical autumn

FIG 63. Chaffinch. Blackwall's chick-nuturing experiments to determine the possible influences on song went awry when the only chaffinch he reared turned out to be a female. (Photograph by Rebecca Nason)

song of its species. These were very sophisticated experiments for the time, although we now know that only the basis of bird song is innate, the essential ingredients of recognisable song being learned.

In 1824 he published his observations on the cuckoo, confirming everything that Jenner had said. While accepting the principle, alluded to by Montagu (see Chapter 8), that a female cuckoo can retain an egg in her oviduct, Blackwall opposed the idea that a cuckoo begins incubation in situ, pointing out that she always lays in a recently completed nest to ensure the correct incubation period for her egg, and that there would, therefore, be no advantage in advancing incubation within her oviduct. As with all those interested in this species, Blackwall hypothesised as to the reason behind the cuckoo's parasitic behaviour. He dismissed the suggestion that the bird is anatomically unsuited to brooding its young with the example of the similarly shaped nightjar; he ridiculed a view expressed by Buffon that it was to protect the eggs from the male; and, stating that many people thought that cuckoos were compelled to be parasitic breeders because of their short stay, he pointed out that the truth was most probably the reverse, that as parasitic breeders there was no reason to stay longer; and he used the opportunity to correct the views of Erasmus Darwin (not for the first time – Blackwall was not an admirer of the Doctor).

Blackwall continued by emphasising the role of instinct in cuckoo behaviour, in its call, in the laying behaviour of the female, and in the nature of the unguided migration of juveniles when the adults have preceded them. He gave a thumbnail sketch of the first year of life for a cuckoo, and declared that it proved the importance of instinct and countered the argument of acquired behaviour – an early example of the 'nature versus nurture' debate.

The final part of the paper concerned a letter sent to Blackwall which quoted an instance in which a young cuckoo was taken from a dunnock's nest and placed, in a cage, upon a pole in the experimenter's garden (a certain Captain Porter). Not only did the foster-parents feed the bird but a third dunnock joined them and even a passing spotted flycatcher fed the nestling, which Blackwall suggested showed the power of the instinctive response to a begging nestling (Fig. 64).

His next paper, 'On the instincts of birds' (1833), might well be the first paper on the subject. Blackwall repeated many of the statements and researches that appeared in his other papers, particularly his work on song. He gave examples of instinctive behaviour such as the nature of nest construction and the fact that like species breed with like, and he quoted the fact that ducks hatched under chickens rush to water and swim immediately despite the inability of the foster-parent to do so.

FIG 64. Pied wagtail feeding a cuckoo chick. Detail from John Gould's *Birds of Great Britain* (1862–73).

He used a piece of observation to illustrate an important feature of instinct, which was also possibly the first recorded observation of food caching, a behaviour prominent in corvids (Fig. 65):

> *Two Crows by the sea-shore [were] employed in removing some small fish from the edge of the flowing tide. They carried them one by one, just above high-water mark, and there deposited them under large stones or broken fragments of rocks, after having amply satisfied the immediate calls of hunger. Now it must be conceded that these birds were aware that the advancing flood would sweep away their prize unless they conveyed it beyond the limit of its usual rise, or their conduct is quite inexplicable. It is equally plain that this knowledge could be derived from observation and experience only; because if it originated in a blind instinct, it would be common to every individual of the species.*

Blackwall then pointed out that the act of hiding was, in itself, instinctive within certain species, particularly crows, magpies etc. He further suggested that the autumn gatherings of certain species were mainly for protection from predators and that sometimes within such flocks some birds acted as sentinels. Blackwall suspected this to be instinctive but admitted that it would be hard to prove.

There were other papers: on pied flycatcher breeding behaviour, based on observations in the Lake District; on the recognition that Bewick's swan was a separate species (which Blackwall claimed to have discovered before Yarrell published his book – see Chapter 8); on the notorious topic of the nudity of the

FIG 65. Carrion crow. A rather sinister woodcut from Eric Fitch Daglish's *Birds of the British Isles* (1948).

head of the rook, which Blackwall suggested was caused by some physiological occurrence rather than by the mechanics of sticking its head into soil, as some people suggested.

Finally in *Remarks on the Diving of Aquatic Birds* he dismissed the idea propounded by Montagu that the webbed feet were used to propel birds upwards and stated that they were used to propel the bird downwards against its natural buoyancy.

Blackwall was a much more perceptive and original scientist than is generally recognised within the literature.

The great pioneering work of White, Jenner and Blackwall ought to have been the impetus for a flowering of this area of study, but it was not. With a very few exceptions the main area of interest moved back to the publication of the great avifaunal works and the study of classification, much as outlined by Blackwall in the quotation at the head of this chapter. Ecological ornithology became dormant for a hundred years.

CHAPTER 7

Early studies of migration: Legg, Jenner and others

The stork in the heaven knoweth her appointed times; and the turtle and the crane and the swallow observe the time of their coming.

Jeremiah 8.7

THE FACTS OF migration took a long time to be generally accepted. As with the breeding biology of the Cuckoo, there were observers who stubbornly preferred to believe in the accepted wisdom, in this case hibernation. By the late eighteenth century, however, the principle of migration had been investigated thoroughly by a number of observers, including the painstaking Edward Jenner, and the concept was incorporated into the writings of the mainstream ornithologists such as Pennant. One small book from a most extraordinary and neglected ornithologist stands out.

In 1780 a 45-page booklet was published with a title page that summarised the contents thus:

A discourse on the emigration of British Birds, or this question at last solv'd, Whence come the stork and the turtle, the crane and the swallow, when they know and observe the time of their coming. Containing a curious particular and circumstantial account of the respective retreats of all those Birds of Passage which visit our island at the commencement of spring, and depart at the approach of winter; as, the cuckow, turtle, stork, crane, quail, goatsucker, the swallow tribe, nightingale, black-cap, wheat-ear, stone-chat, whin-chat, willow wren, white-throat, etotoli, fly-catcher &c &c. Also a copious entertaining and satisfactory relation of Winter Birds of Passage, among which are the woodcock, snipe, fieldfare, redwing, royston crow, dotterel, &c.; shewing the different countries to which they retire, the places where they breed, and how they perform their Annual Emigrations, &c., with a short account of those Birds that migrate occasionally, or only shift their quarters at certain seasons of the year. To which are added Reflections on that truly admirable and wonderful instinct, the Annual Migration of Birds! By a Naturalist.

No author's name was printed. The third edition carried the name George Edwards, and thus Swainson in his *Biographies of Zoologists* (1840) reviewed the work under the heading Edwards with the words, 'not having seen this work, we know not whether it is by the George Edwards.' Sixty years later, there was still doubt about the authorship. Alfred Newton, Professor of Zoology at Cambridge University in the late nineteenth century, wrote in his copy of Swainson's book, in pencil,

1st Ed 1780? this ed. has no author's name. On the title page my copy has written on it 'George Evans' but the edn of 1814 which only differs in the title page from that of 1795 names George Edwards as the author – but it can hardly have been the naturalist of that name.

So who was this mysterious naturalist? Newton, aware of the importance of the book, was motivated to discover who the author might be and followed the first clue provided by the address on the inside page – Market Lavington in Wiltshire. He contacted an acquaintance, Reverend A. C. Smith, author of the *Birds of Wiltshire*, and asked him to investigate. After considerable tribulation and failure Smith, via an advertisement in the local newspaper, discovered that the author was a man named John Legg.

Legg was an amazingly advanced ornithologist. The summary of the book alone contains nearly all the features that one might look for in a description of migration. The importance of this work is that at the time the general view of the disappearance of certain species of bird in winter, particularly swallows and martins (Fig. 66), was that they either hibernated or lay submerged in the bottom of ponds. Sir Thomas Browne and Gilbert White had obviously begun to guess at the truth, but Legg was almost certainly the first to expound a theory of migration in detail and, as we now know, with considerable accuracy.

Of Legg's early life there is little to tell. He lived and died a bachelor. He seems to have supported himself from the income of his estate, at Townsend near Market Lavington in Wiltshire. He devoted his time to various pursuits: the study of natural history, writing (he wrote for the *Lady's Magazine* and even began a novel), also spending time in experimentation and investigation. As well as the booklet on migration he wrote a *Treatise of the Art of Grafting and*

HIRVNDO RVSTICA.—Page 3.

FIG 66. Swallow, from Forster's *Observations on the Brumal Retreat of the Swallow* (1808).

Innoculation, also published in 1780, and his family testified that he spent a great deal of time practising the art in his garden. He produced a booklet with the maudlin title of *Meditations and Reflections on the Most Important Subjects or Serious Soliloquies on Life, Death, Judgement, and Immortality*, which was published in 1789. This latter booklet had the initials JL after the title, and those initials were the only evidence that Smith had, to find the name of the author of the migration book.

There must have been contemporary interest in Legg's work on migration, since the booklet was reprinted in the year of publication, again in 1795, and again in 1814, as described by Alfred Newton (above). In the booklet is a statement suggesting that Legg was engaged in writing another book on British birds. He described this more ambitious and wide-ranging work as follows:

A curious, particular and accurate account is given of every bird found in Great Britain, whether aquatic, migratory, or local; and every thing relating to the nature of birds in general, is treated of in as entertaining a manner as the nature of the subject would allow. In short, we think we may style it A new and complete system of British Ornithology.

Sadly this later work never saw publication. An attempt was made by Smith to find the manuscript, but he seems to have failed, and Hugh Gladstone, the twentieth-century ornithological historian, confirmed in 1928 that it was never traced. If that book had been of the quality of the migration booklet it would have been a landmark publication.

Smith discovered that Legg had been an eccentric man, and in his later years he is said to have become virtually a recluse, never leaving his house and gardens. His depressive nature was revealed when he confessed that he was 'long afflicted with a violent nervous disorder, attended with lowness of spirits and great weakness of body ... which gradually debilitated my constitution'. He died in 1802, aged only 47.

JOHN LEGG'S *DISCOURSE ON THE EMIGRATION OF BIRDS*

Legg's booklet was an extraordinary piece of work, both for the time in which it was published and also for the conclusions that he drew from so little hard evidence. The book began by discussing summer migrants, starting with 'the swallow tribe'. Legg stated the theories that had been used to explain the absence of these birds in winter (Fig. 67), and having stated them he waded into each one,

FIG 67. Swallows apparently being hauled ashore by fishermen. From Olaus Magnus, *Historia de gentibus septentrionalibus* (1555). The existence of this kind of illustration was taken as proof of the event.

becoming more vitriolic with each attack. On the theory that they lay up in the bottom of ponds etc.:

> *Inconsistent as it may appear to a serious and considerate reader: unnatural and unreasonable as the supposition is, credit has actually been given to the submersion of swallows, even by our own countrymen. What superstitious presumption, erroneous assertion indeed. How incompatible with reason – how monstrous to thought. We cannot think on it without smiling at the folly, at the simplicity of the authors ... not the smallest reason is given how they preserve themselves or remain without decaying in such a cold and turbulent element, which must be very unnatural to so weak and delicate a bird.*

On the theory that birds hibernated:

> *Notwithstanding the authority of Aristotle, Pliny, Klein, Pennant, Achard and others we cannot assent to the above circumstances viz that swallows lie torpid in caverns of rocks hollow trees &c. The innumerable testimonies of an opposite nature, which continually crowd in upon us, sufficiently convince us that this conjecture, which so many have adhered to and which has for so long been maintained, is in reality only a superfluous error ... we do not deny but that there are undeniable instances of a few being found in a dormant state at the beginning of winter; but in all probability they were only stragglers, which were hatched too late to join the general migration.*

On the curious theory that they flew to the moon:

> *The notion of flying to the moon &c is, I think, too extravagent to require any confutation.*

This theory had been propounded in a book published in 1703, whose title page was remarkably similar to Legg's: *An essay towards the Probable Solution OF THIS QUESTION. WHENCE come the Stork and the Turtle, the Crane and the Swallow, when they Know and Observe the appointed Time of their coming. OR WHERE those Birds do probably make their Recess and Abode, which are absent from our Climate at some certain Times and Seasons of the year. By a Person of Learning and Piety.* Perhaps Legg consciously used and adapted this title in mockery of the 'Person of Learning and Piety'; a more likely explanation, however, is that it was simply a fashionable title for works on the topic, with its heavy emphasis on the quote from the biblical Book of Jeremiah. Hugh Gladstone discovered that the 'Person of Learning and Piety' was a man named Charles Morton (1627–98), a cleric who, having been ejected by the Act of Uniformity, became a teacher and eventually emigrated to America in 1685. The book therefore must have been published posthumously. His early career at Wadham College Oxford brought him into academic contact with John Wilkins, Wadham's Warden. Wilkins too was a subscriber to the idea of migration to the moon and wrote a book called *The Discovery of a World in the Moone* in 1640, the third edition of which discussed the possibility of a passage to the moon. Wilkins quoted from a book of 1638 by Francis Godwin, Bishop of Hereford, which described the passage of one Domingo Gonsales to the moon in 1601 by means of harnessing trained swans (Fig. 68). Godwin, however, described his book honestly as 'an essay of fancy', something that Wilkins and Morton seem to have overlooked!

Having disposed of these theories, Legg went on to state that migratory birds flew to hot countries, mentioning Egypt and Ethiopia as two possible destinations. He reported sailors having seen swallows crossing the oceans in large numbers and stated that he had watched swallows gathering before heading out to sea, adding that when he returned later to the same spot there was no sign of them.

As further evidence, he asked if swallows hibernated why did they not emerge during occasional unseasonably warm weather, such as in February and March 1760? Furthermore, he pointed out that the regularity of their arrival and departure dates could only be explained by migration; he gave the dates for Wiltshire for the years 1774 to 1779, when first arrival occurred between 3 and 10 April and final departure between 9 and 23 October.

Legg posed a question about the timing of the departure of swifts:

> *The swift constantly disappears about the middle of August. We cannot pretend to determine the cause why it leaves us so early; want of food cannot drive it from our climate, as insects are then very plentiful in our island, neither can the severity of the season compel it to quit this country, as the weather is usually very warm when it departs. Perhaps it may feed on a particular species of insect, which may be very common in the first summer months and vanish in the autumn.*

Next came a fundamental question about orientation. Having first noted that swallows came back to the same place and used the same nest (although he produced no firm evidence to back this statement), he asked:

> *How they can steer their unerring course to their native countries, after such a long and distant migration cannot easily be conceived; unless we will suppose that they are guided and impelled as it were, by a certain quality of air. If this be the case, at first*

FIG 68. Domingo Gonsales on his way to the moon. From *The Man in the Moone: or a Discourse of a Voyage Thither by Domingo Gonsales,* by Francis Godwin (1638). From Gladstone, *British Birds* (1928a).

setting out they must soar aloft and after meeting with a particular atmosphere, congenial to their natures, they follow the same aerial tract, which brings them safe to their respective countries at which they are wont to arrive. But if we allow this supposition, we must grant that a providential instinct is the compass by which they are guided.

This is almost certainly the first mention of a compass in connection with migration; indeed it is virtually the first time in British ornithology that anyone broached so obvious a question. It is also worth noting that experiments conducted by Papi and his colleagues (1982) on the possible use of olfactory clues in navigation have suggested that there may be some use of this sense in pigeons, though not on the scale that Legg envisaged.

Legg went on to suggest that wing morphology could be directly related to migratory distance, and he made the observation that 'in all probability the innate knowledge which prompts them to make these yearly excursions directs them to the narrowest part of the channel and shun the passing over the wider seas.' The wing morphology observation and supposition prove to be correct, and modern ringing recoveries show that Legg's assessment of the strategy used by most passerine migrants to get to and from the Continent is remarkably accurate. Legg's reference to 'innate knowledge' has also subsequently been proved correct, with Peter Berthold's recent work (2001) revealing that in many species direction and duration of migratory activity are genetically controlled, i.e. that the individual bird is pre-programmed for its migratory flight.

Legg then turned his attention to the times of arrival and departure. Having discussed this with regard to the swallow, he pointed out that

Next to the cuckow, the swift is the first that disappears in the summer. In the beginning of September the nightingale retires and is seen no more till the latter end of April, or the beginning of May. The black-cap, the white-throat, the wheat-ear, the fly-catcher and the stone-chat depart about the same time, but the two latter are among the foremost in species frequently appearing about the middle of March. Next come the willow-wren and the red-start, the whin-chat and the tit-lark, to proclaim the approach of spring.

It seems strange that so accurate an observer as Legg could make the mistake of thinking that the flycatchers return at the end of March, Wheatear *are* seen from the end of March, but not flycatchers, unless of course there has been a dramatic change in the habits of flycatchers.

FIG 69. Redstart, from George Graves's *British Ornithology* (1811–21) – recognised as a migrant by John Legg.

There was a note on the migration of quails, suggesting that 'like cranes' they fly in pairs at night choosing a north wind, 'the south being detrimental as it retards their flight by moistening their plumage'.

Next Legg turned his attention to partial migrants, noting that chaffinches although resident in Britain are migratory in other countries: strangely, he mentioned America, a country not known for its population of chaffinches! This general observation was encapsulated in a further comment, which began with as good a definition of migration as you might find:

> Birds of passage are generally understood to be those which are compelled annually to take long and distant excursions but in reality, almost every British bird is a bird of passage, though they may not journey to places so remote. Small birds usually remove at some seasons of the year, either from one country or district to another, or towards the shore from more inland provinces ... Larks, which are settled inhabitants here, are birds of passage in the north, deserting that region in winter to return with the returning spring.

Legg described the geographical origins of winter migrants with uncanny accuracy, explaining that fieldfare (Fig. 70) and redwing (Fig. 71) come from Sweden, Norway and neighbouring countries and that they are 'tempted here by the berries'. He then suggested (wrongly) that the thrushes in Prussia and Russia do not migrate, though why he should think this is not stated. He noted that winter thrushes do not arrive in France until the beginning of December and was utterly perplexed as to why these birds feel the need to return to Scandinavia

FIG 70. Fieldfare, from F. O. Morris's *History of British Birds* (4th edition, 1896).

FIG 71. Redwing by Archibald Thorburn, from Swaysland's *Familiar Wild Birds* (1883–8).

to breed. He gave the reason for their visiting Britain, explaining that 'they take their flight to more moderate climes, where the earth is open, penetrable, and adapted to their way of feeding.' His observation that woodcock bred is significant, since up to this date commentators stated that the woodcock was a winter visitor only. In addition Legg stated that woodcock were known to winter further south than Britain, and he mentioned Smyrna and Aleppo, even Egypt. He also noted the snipe as a winter visitor.

This more or less concluded the book, except to repeat his assertions about the phenomenon in general, to pour a little more scorn on those who believed the previous explanations, and to link the process with the wonderful works of the creator by including some biblical quotations.

Legg's work was reported in the 1920s by Hugh Gladstone, who obtained more than one copy, including one that had formerly been the property of Pennant. This copy contained, on the flyleaf, the comment: 'Mostly formed from my works and in other parts very erroneous. T.P.' Not the first time that an opinionated scientist got it wrong (on both counts)! Strangely, this wonderful work seems to have disappeared from the radar of many of the more recent writers on the subject, surprisingly including James Fisher.

THOMAS FORSTER'S *OBSERVATIONS ON THE BRUMAL RETREAT OF THE SWALLOW*

Despite the work of John Legg the interest in explaining migration continued. In this context Thomas Forster published his small book about swallows in 1808.

Forster restated the case for migration (as opposed to hibernation etc.). In evidence he cited the experiences of people travelling by ship who had seen swallows off the coast of Senegal on 6 October. He stated that Latham, Pennant and White had all favoured migration but that they had all thought that some individual birds might remain behind in a torpid state. He made no mention of John Legg, and judging by his writing he was probably unaware of Legg's book.

Forster included detailed descriptions of the various species of swallow recognised at the time – including the swift (Fig. 72) – but the most useful part of his paper was the inclusion of a suggested table of observations with the following headings:

HIRVNDO APVS.—Page 9.

FIG 72. Swift, from Forster's *Observations on the Brumal Retreat of the Swallow* (1808).

Species of bird
Day of appearance
Direction and force of wind
Previous and supervening currents
The state of the thermometer
The state of the barometer
Weather and clouds
Place of observation

JOHN GOUGH'S REMARKS ON THE SUMMER BIRDS OF PASSAGE AND ON MIGRATION IN GENERAL

This 1812 paper was largely based on Forster's book, but it contained some interesting information such as the proposition that 'the swallow is known to winter in different parts of Africa; and in all probability, future observers will discover the southern retreat of the other migrating species partly on the same continent, and partly in the warmer countries of Europe or in the corresponding districts of Asia.' Among the scientific information was a list that showed the northward spread of spring via the dates of plants coming into flower. The earliest singing of the nightingale was included:

Athens (Greece): 24 March
Stratton (England): 22 April
Uppsala (Sweden): 15 May

Gough used this table to suggest that it was temperature that triggered migration
– a notion that was dismissed by another Manchester man, John Blackwall.

JOHN BLACKWALL'S MIGRATION PAPERS

Blackwall gave his first paper on the subject of migration in 1822, entitled
'Tables of the various species of periodical birds observed in the neighbourhood
of Manchester'. In it he stated his agreement with the principle of migration
and provided dates for the arrival and departure of most migratory species,
although he rather rejected Gough's idea of temperature being the driving force
for migration. This publication contained little that was fundamentally original
but there were some pieces of novel evidence in favour of migration, including
experiments he had undertaken to try to persuade cuckoos to become torpid –
which met with no success.

Blackwall's biological approach to ornithology yielded one significant piece
of evidence in favour of migration, 'that several species of periodical summer
birds moult during the interval which elapses between their departure and
reappearance.' Blackwall argued that if this fact had been generally known to
ornithologists it would have been used as one of the most conclusive arguments
in support of migration. He pointed out that 'perhaps no part of the animal
economy of the feathered tribes has been so greatly neglected by natural
historians as their moulting. That swallows, swifts, cuckoos, redstarts, and
spotted flycatchers moult during their absence scarcely admits of a doubt'
(Fig. 73). Indeed, Blackwall suggested that moulting could be a strong reason
why summer visitors migrate to Africa in winter and added that moult 'seems
to be regulated in a great measure by the cessation of their parental cares, and
not by temperature solely.'

This was undoubtedly the first time that the significance of moult had
been mentioned; indeed it seems to have been the first reference by any writer
to moult in a biological context. Furthermore, Blackwall suggested that the
end of breeding was a significant factor in determining migration timing –
although, in a slight contradiction, when Jenner (see below) hypothesised that
the urge to migrate in autumn was due to physiological changes in the adults
(such as the reduction in size of the sexual glands) causing the breeding urge
to decline, Blackwall questioned this argument, citing particularly the example
of the cuckoo, which continues to lay right up to the time of its departure.
A good argument, but the choice of species hardly represents a typical
migrant.

FIG 73. Spotted flycatcher, a species that Blackwall mistakenly thought moulted in its winter quarters. (Photograph by Jim Lawrence)

Blackwall described his torpor experiments in another paper on the 'Capability of the periodical birds to become torpid' (1824). He took young birds from the nest, mostly cuckoos but some hirundines, and kept them in aviaries into the winter, whereupon he provided suitable apertures in which they might hibernate. None of the birds showed the slightest interest in torpidity. This contrasted with experiments he conducted on animals such as hedgehogs and dormice, which readily went into hibernation in captivity.

In his paper 'Remarks on the swallow tribe' (1834) he stated that hirundines frequently desert half-grown young in the nest in order to migrate (as was also noted by Jenner). Blackwall stated that this was a demonstration of the overwhelming power of the urge to migrate, since leaving their young required them to overcome an equally powerful basic instinct. He then quoted many instances of the parental instinct in which birds continued to feed young in nests that had been transported from their natural position, even into houses.

EDWARD JENNER'S MIGRATION PAPER

Jenner also wrote a paper on migration, which was published posthumously in 1824. It is apparent that even forty years after Legg's booklet there was still a large body of opinion that remained unconvinced by the theory of migration and preferred to cling to the idea of hibernation.

The first part of Jenner's paper was very much an echo of the Legg treatise, but the main, novel, suggestion was that physiological changes preparing the bird for breeding, the enlargement of the testes and ovaries, played a part in stimulating migration.

Jenner also pointed out that the staggered arrival of migrants may be allied to their varied reproductive state, and he noted that they only arrive in large numbers when the insects are increasing, while the converse happens in autumn. Without offering an explanation he also noted that the young of some species such as cuckoo must make their migration without any guidance. Jenner stated that winter migrants such as fieldfare and redwing do not feed exclusively on berries but that the majority of their diet is of earthworms and other invertebrate material – information he discovered by dissecting large numbers of these species. He described the woodpigeon and stock dove as arriving in large numbers in winter and surprisingly suggested that the stock dove did not breed in England. He was possibly the first person to remark on hard-weather movements, commenting that fieldfare, redwing and some other winter birds disappear during a long continued frost. He cited an occasion when a friend shot some fieldfares during a cold spell, and the contents of their stomachs revealed food items that showed that they must have flown in from some unfrosted area.

Jenner left such a contribution to the medical world through his work on inoculation that it can hardly be surprising if his observations of birds have been under-exposed. Through his use of simple experimentation in the case of the cuckoo, and by his thorough dissection of specimens in the case of the fieldfare, he used scientific and medical techniques to a degree that had probably not been tried before in ornithology.

By the 1820s only the most stubborn ornithologists denied the truth about migration. The work of Legg, Forster, Blackwall and Jenner had provided clear evidence of the mechanism, and also many ideas of the detail, which, although conjectural at the time, were for the most part subsequently shown to be correct. In fact, a combination of the writings of these four people would provide a very good grounding in the study of migration today. However, as in the area of ecology, migration was much neglected through the later part of the nineteenth century.

CHAPTER 8

A Dictionary and Two Histories

In 1837 two works entitled History of the Birds of Britain began to appear simultaneously. One was in five volumes, written by the imaginative and temperamental MacGillivray; the other was in three volumes by the conventional William Yarrell.

Erwin Stresemann, *Ornithology* (1951)

SUPERFICIALLY THE nineteenth century began in much the same way that the eighteenth ended, with a country gentleman, Montagu, watching birds, collecting specimens and cataloguing the characteristics of both their physical appearance and their behaviour in the field. There was, however, a significant difference in the quality of the work that was published. Previously work of the standard of Pennant, White and Jenner was exceptional, not mirrored by most publications on the birds of Britain, which were largely derivative. Almost as soon as the century turned, poorer-quality general publications became the minority, replaced by an altogether higher standard – and the work of George Montagu (Fig. 74) is the first example of this.

GEORGE MONTAGU'S ORNITHOLOGICAL DICTIONARY

Montagu's *Ornithological Dictionary* (1802) combined all facets of ornithological knowledge: behaviour as well as anatomy, status and distribution as well as plumage descriptions.

Born into a relatively aristocratic family in Wiltshire in 1753, very little is known about Montagu's childhood. Indeed, accounts of his life are often at

FIG 74. George Montagu: a miniature portrait. (Linnean Society)

variance. It seems that like many a younger son he was compelled to find his own way in the world, and he left home to join the army at the age of seventeen. At eighteen he married Anne Courtney, a niece of the former Prime Minister, the Earl of Bute, and there is a suggestion that they eloped to Gretna Green. After only a few months, in which they made trips to Scotland and Ireland visiting relations, Montagu's regiment was sent to America, where Montagu began to collect specimens of the American avifauna, ostensibly to present to his wife on his return to England. Having been promoted to Captain, Montagu remained in America only a couple of years before returning home and leaving the army altogether. He then joined the Wiltshire County Militia, in which he ultimately achieved the rank of Lieutenant Colonel before being court-martialled late in 1799, largely due to the machinations of his junior officers. Three or four years previously he had met Elizabeth (Eliza) Dorville. Despite both parties being already married, Montagu set up home with Eliza. The liaison undoubtedly played a significant part in the subsequent events in Montagu's life.

The death of George Montagu's elder brother in 1797 led to a downturn in family fortunes. By living with Eliza, George had virtually disinherited himself, and the family property, including the estate in Wiltshire, was left not to George but to his eldest son. Within a year George and Eliza moved to Knowle House, near Kingsbridge in Devon, but due to the profligacy of his son the financial situation deteriorated, with a legal battle between father and son and matters ending in Chancery.

Montagu remained at Knowle for the rest of his life. Disappointed by the deteriorating relationship with his oldest son, he also suffered the loss of his three younger sons in the Napoleonic Wars. In June 1815 Montagu trod upon a rusty nail and as a result contracted tetanus, from which he died.

As an ornithologist Montagu was meticulous, and because of it he earned a reputation as a rather dull man, whose grammar and punctuation were highly idiosyncratic. Yet, as a scientist, being meticulous was a priceless characteristic, and his work was more reliable than anything that had been published previously. Like Gilbert White he recognised the subtle differences between certain species and as a result added three new species to the British List: the cirl bunting, the roseate tern and the harrier that bears his name. Montagu wrote two letters to Gilbert White (the year after *The Natural History of Selborne* was published) and the content shows Montagu working to clarify the anomalies of the identification of the birds that White had described. Sadly we have no knowledge of the reply that Montagu received to his first letter, in which he enquired about 'the weight and descriptions of the two uncommon willow wrens'. In the letter Montagu also included a list of birds that he was anxious to obtain for his collection:

> *The hawks and the owls are difficult to get. Of the former I want all except sparrow, kestrel and common buzzard; of the latter all the eared and the little owl. The great butcher bird and wood chat, goatsucker, crossbill, aberdevene, siskin and spotted gallinule with many cloven and webfooted water birds together with any of their eggs.*

And Montagu went on to give typically precise instructions for the preservation of specimens. The reference to 'aberdevine' and 'siskin' is puzzling, as these names had previously been used for the same species, the modern siskin (Fig. 75), and quite what Montagu meant by the two names is not clear.

The second letter discussed the discovery of a third species of 'willow wren' and tried to identify a hawk described by White: 'I am at a loss for your blue pigeon hawk especially as you say its female is brown. The hobby that I want has been called the blue hawk by some. Its eggs I should be glad of and are no doubt to be found in your extensive woodlands; they are scarce with us.' The blue pigeon hawk was almost certainly the merlin. Although it might seem strange to call that small bird of prey a 'pigeon hawk', this is the name it was once known by in North America.

FIG 75. Siskin. (Photograph by Rebecca Nason)

These two letters give a very fair account of the way in which Montagu went about collecting information on birds, their eggs, nests, habits, distribution and nomenclature – all of which went into his *Ornithological Dictionary*.

The *Ornithological Dictionary* was published in two volumes in 1802 with a supplement in 1813. The book consisted of species accounts in alphabetical order, dealing with birds which were mostly, but not all, British. It began with an introduction dealing with the physiology of birds, but got rather bogged down in the details of the breeding cycle of the cuckoo, in particular in the results of Jenner's research. Among other subjects tackled were the problems associated with trying to separate species by plumage alone, and Montagu pointed out that many previously supposed species were in fact simply birds of a single species but in an unfamiliar plumage. The introduction mentioned migration, and the views expressed were not dissimilar to those expressed by Legg, although he made no mention of Legg's booklet.

Each species had a comprehensive entry, with cross-references where necessary (e.g. 'Puttock: see buzzard'), and Montagu was nothing if not comprehensive in the information he gave on nomenclature. A helpful innovation was that he supplied an overview of the essential anatomical features of each genus. For example, in the case of the phalaropes: 'Bill straight. Nostrils minute. Body and legs in every respect like a sandpiper. Toes furnished with broad and generally scalloped membranes.' For each species this was followed by a list of the nomenclature used in previous publications and the sources such as Latham, Brisson, Buffon, Pennant etc. Then there was a physical description, presumably taken from a dead specimen.

Next came a section that could be summarised under the heading 'habits', followed by the geographical distribution. These sections varied in length according to the species since the state of knowledge was often still rather sparse in the 1800s. For example, for the grey phalarope Montagu reported that it 'is said to inhabit the northern parts of Europe and to congregate about the borders of the Caspian Sea'. Given the time at which the *Ornithological Dictionary* was written, this was probably as much as was known. I have chosen the grey phalarope as an example because the entry was comparatively short.

The supplement published in 1813 contained many entries which were longer than in the original, showing that Montagu continued to collect information after the initial publication of the *Dictionary*. In addition, a number of issues were clarified. For example, a bird which had appeared in the earlier publication under the name Greenwich sandpiper turned out, on inspection of a specimen, to be a ruff in winter plumage – an example of just the sort of problem with plumage variation that Montagu had alluded to in his original introduction.

In the introduction to the supplement he also broached a subject that remains topical to this day:

> We know that some species have been placed in collections of British Birds, which are not to be found in this work, but without authentic information upon the subject we are not justified in recording such upon the bare authority of a catalogue. We should be happy to obtain sufficient authority for giving such addition to the fauna of Great Britain; at the same time caution is required in the admission of subjects, without the fullest evidence of their having been killed at large in the kingdom. It is well known that several species of bird have been captured within these realms, that can have no claim to originality, nor even to migratory accident; such circumstances therefore must be attributed to their escape from confinement.

This sounds very much like the forerunner of the policy adopted by those later responsible for the British List (see Chapter 19), and here Montagu was well ahead of his time, for this appears to be the first time that such a sentiment was expressed – and it was not repeated for a hundred years or more.

Besides the *Dictionary*, Montagu published papers on birds, mammals and marine life. The first of his papers, published in 1798, was entitled 'Descriptions of three rare species of British birds'. It contained descriptions of the 'Wood Wren, the Phayrelarn Sandpiper and the Rock Lark', better known to us as the wood warbler (already described by Gilbert White, which Montagu readily acknowledged), the purple sandpiper (previously described by Walcott), and the rock pipit (previously described by Lewin and previously called 'the dusky lark' by Montagu himself). Once again the nomenclature is extremely confusing.

In 1807, following publication of the *Dictionary*, Montagu wrote his paper on the harriers. It contained two extremely important facts. The first was that 'the ringtail', previously considered to be a species in its own right and given the scientific name *pygargus*, was in fact the female hen harrier, scientific name *cyaneus*. In typical measured way Montagu described how, through a friend, he discovered a nest of three hen harriers still in downy plumage, which he was able to take into captivity in order to observe the maturation of their plumage. Although one died, of the remaining two one became a male and the other a ringtail (female). Montagu waited for the development of the full plumage in the male, which was not achieved until the middle of October. The second major contribution made in the paper was a description of a bird Montagu called the ash-coloured falcon. Among the features he noted were

> *secondary quills cinereous-brown above, pale beneath, with three remarkable dusky-black bars across them, nearly in parallel lines, each half an inch in breadth; one only of which is to be seen on the upper side of the wing the others being hid by the coverts ...*
> *It is probable that this species may be indigenous to us, and that it has frequently been mistaken for a variety of the Hen Harrier.*

The bird in question was the species we now know as Montagu's harrier. Montagu declared that he did not know if it was a migrant but since the bird he dissected was shot on 10 August he felt that it was unlikely to have been a winter visitor – though he went on to say that the previous specimen he had seen had been shot in November, suggesting that this second bird was a winter visitor. It is a typical piece of Montagu's thoroughness – a presentation of the facts and his hypothesis, even when the two are contradictory.

The paper continued with further notes on the Dartford warbler (Fig. 76). Having already given a paper on this bird and mentioned that it remained in Devon in winter, he went on to give an instance of breeding in Cornwall, a subsequent discovery of a nest by himself and details of the breeding behaviour of this bird in considerable depth. Montagu completed the paper with reports

FIG 76. Dartford warbler by
J. G. Keulemans, from
Lilford's *Coloured Figures of
the Birds of the British Islands*
(1885–97).

of four birds 'newly discovered in Great Britain' – the 'Little White Heron'
(cattle egret), the 'Green Ibis', which he correctly stated might well be a form
of the glossy ibis, the 'red-breasted snipe' (short-billed dowitcher), and the
'Austrian pratincole' (collared pratincole).

Montagu's last paper, about a black stork record, was published
posthumously in 1817:

> This bird was captured by means of a slight shot-wound in the wing, without breaking
> a bone, and is now in my possession in excellent health. To my scientific friend, Mr
> Austin of Bridgewater, naturalists in general, and myself in particular, are indebted for
> this addition to the British Fauna, he having rescued it from plebian hands, where in
> all probability the circumstance would have consigned it to oblivion. It was shot in
> West Sedgemoor, adjoining the parish of Stoke St. Gregory, Somersetshire, on the 13th
> of May 1814; and what is remarkable another very rare bird, the White Spoonbill, was
> shot on the same moor, by the very same person, in November of the preceding year.

Montagu went on to describe the food and behaviour of the black stork, which he kept captive. The only other paper he wrote on birds was concerned with the anatomical structure of the gannet (1811). These examples of his work undoubtedly justify the impression that he left after his death, of being an accurate and meticulous observer.

For the last ten years of his life Montagu maintained a correspondence with a friend, Robert Anstice, which has recently been edited and published by Peter Dance (2003). The letters give much insight into the way in which Montagu went about his observations through the use of specimens:

> I have lately received from a Yorkshire friend two or three rare birds for my museum: the Pied Flycatcher, Horned or Sclavonian [sic] Grebe, and Solitary Thrush [this turned out to be a juvenile starling!] ... The Eared Grebe I for the first time obtained from a friend in Cornwall in the spring and I am now clear that the Eared and the Horned Grebes are species perfectly distinct.

The enthusiasm and amateur spirit of Montagu may have been a legacy of the eighteenth century, but his careful methods of study were very much those of the nineteenth, and set the standard for subsequent observers. The *Dictionary* remained the standard authority on birds in Britain for many years, until the work of Yarrell. But north of the border a very different man was to make his mark, with similar professionalism but a different style – William MacGillivray.

WILLIAM MACGILLIVRAY – THE FIRST PROFESSIONAL ORNITHOLOGIST?

MacGillivray came from a very different background to the British ornithologists who preceded him. Not being a man of independent means, he had to support himself and, once he was married, his wife and children also. For MacGillivray, work was his source of funds for living. Yet what better way to work than to be paid for what you would do for free, as an ornithologist?

William MacGillivray (Fig. 77) was born in Aberdeen in 1796, the son of an army surgeon. At the age of three he was dispatched to the Hebridean island of Harris to live with two of his uncles and to be educated in the local school. From his own account it is clear that this period of childhood shaped the subsequent man as he explored the coves and streams and became acquainted with their wildlife. He returned to Aberdeen as an eleven-year-old and eventually attended a course at King's College leading to an MA. Around 1814–15 he started a course in

FIG 77. William MacGillivray, from an engraving in Harvie-Brown and Buckley's *Vertebrate Fauna of the Outer Hebrides* (1888).

medicine and began to study the works of Pennant and Linnaeus, and thus drifted into zoology. Holidays were taken back on Harris, and as his only means of transport was to walk he took the opportunity to acquaint himself with the flora and fauna along the way. On Harris he occasionally taught at the local school (about flora and fauna) and on the mainland he expanded his specimen hunting to wider horizons, although still within Scotland. After five years of studying medicine he changed direction and became a naturalist. Following a new interest in mineralogy, MacGillivray went to Edinburgh for research and there attended the lectures of the Professor of Natural History, Professor Jamieson. On the next trip to Harris 'hammering gneiss rocks' was added to his list of pursuits – 'gathering gulls eggs and shooting birds'.

Marriage in 1820 (to Marion MacGaskill of Harris) drove him to seek employment, and so he returned to Edinburgh to work as Jamieson's assistant, although not much is known about this period of his life.

In 1830 he published what could be described as a field guide to British plants, when he updated the volumes of Withering's *Systematic Arrangement of British Plants*. MacGillivray compressed the information into a single book suitable for taking into the field. The book was sufficiently successful for eight editions to be published, but as Robert Ralph pointed out in his 1993 biography of MacGillivray, he seems (surprisingly) to have made no money from it.

MacGillivray's big break came when he was put in charge of the Edinburgh Natural History Museum. When the exhibits were moved into a new building in 1831, MacGillivray seized the opportunity to reorganise, and to give him some ideas he travelled to other museums in Britain. His journal entries give an idea of their relative merits and introduce his pithy style. At Glasgow he found 'a collection of British birds, very clean and neat, but generally in bad attitudes'. At Liverpool he found the birds badly stuffed and 'not one specimen in a characteristic attitude'. The British Museum had 'Montagu's collection of British birds, which is fine on account of its extent, but does not contain ten well-stuffed specimens. When are we to see some improvement in this art?'

At this time he was already working with Audubon, writing the text for the *Ornithological Biography* which came out in 1831 (see Chapter 9). When Audubon chose MacGillivray as his collaborator the two families lived close by and were as involved socially as they were professionally. Lucy Audubon wrote to one of her children, 'Mr MacGillivray breakfasts at nine each morning, attending the Museum four days a week, has several works on hand besides ours, and is, moreover, engaged as a lecturer in a new seminary on botany and natural history. His own work progresses slowly but surely.' The working relationship between the two men was excellent. Their disparate characters were complementary and they had a mutual respect for each other. Audubon acknowledged his debt to MacGillivray in the various volumes of the *Ornithological Biography*. Looking at the finished product, complete with typically detailed anatomical drawings by the Scotsman, it seems clear that MacGillivray should have been a co-author.

MacGillivray had hardly been inactive on his own account. He had contributed the entry on ornithology in the *Encyclopaedia Britannica*, edited the *Edinburgh Journal of Natural History and Physical Science* from 1835 to 1840, and written a *History of British Quadrupeds* for Jardine's *Naturalist's Library*. But his unique contribution of this period was the first specialised bird book in Britain – his *Descriptions of the Rapacious Birds of Great Britain*, published in 1836. This book, which covered 26 species of British raptors, was somewhat sparsely illustrated with some anatomical drawings at the front and a single detail of the head of some, but by no means all, species. The foreword reflects the author's poor view of previous publications, not without justification, but seemingly rather arrogant:

> An apology for offering a new book on birds to those who may be pleased to accept it, is quite unnecessary. It is evident that none which has yet appeared contains perfect descriptions and it is probable that the best of which we can boast will at no distant period be looked upon in many respects extremely childish.

MacGillivray gave a potted autobiography to offer his credentials as the author. He also stated his views on the difficulty of finding a satisfactory method of classification and commended Linnaean nomenclature, stating that Linnaeus's specific names should be 'inviolable'.

The text began with a general introduction before dealing with the birds species by species. Inevitably those species with which MacGillivray was most familiar had the longest entries – 37 pages on the white-tailed eagle, 23 on the golden eagle (Fig. 78), 22 on the peregrine, compared with six on the gyr falcon and a mere three on the hobby. For certain species he drew heavily on information provided by his friend 'Mr Audubon', for example quoting the American's observations that the configuration of an opsrey's feet made it very difficult for the bird to walk. The book contained considerable anatomical and plumage description and was punctuated with the personal experiences so typical of MacGillivray's work.

A year later saw the publication of the first volume of MacGillivray's *tour de force*, the *History of British Birds*. The book was based on observational information, written in a very personal style, and the early volumes were particularly innovative and entertaining. That the final parts were less so was largely due to MacGillivray's deteriorating health. Superficially the *History* used the same information as Montagu's *Dictionary* but the content, or perhaps its presentation, was markedly different. MacGillivray began with a short introduction in which he addressed the problem of classification with characteristic clarity of mind:

FIG 78. Head of golden eagle, drawn by MacGillivray, from *Descriptions of the Rapacious Birds of Great Britain* (1836).

It is extremely difficult to separate [birds] into groups distinguishable from each other by well marked characters ... No two writers have adopted the same divisions and that while in the system of one there are only four great sections, there are no fewer than thirty-eight in that of another ... No Classification of birds has ever been generally adopted; and none has stood for twenty years. And why? No ornithologist will ever arrange the ten thousand species which probably exist in the world in an order conformable to the plan of their creation.

Having explained that to find a system of classification was virtually impossible, he had to find a method of presentation for his *History*. He eschewed the alphabetical approach of Montagu (his innovative mind being repelled by imitation) and organised his book on a classification system based on the digestive organs, which led him to propose four groups of birds. MacGillivray proceeded to describe the anatomical structure of birds, and in this section were the first of a collection of illustrations of incredible detail and great beauty (Fig. 79).

He began by giving general points on each genus (as Montagu had done) before presenting the information species by species. For the grey phalarope MacGillivray stated that the distribution was 'as far northward as Melville Peninsula, and [it] is said to be abundant in the eastern part of the north of Europe.' Not exactly informative but, as with Montagu, probably the extent of knowledge at the time. There followed a discussion on habits, including an

FIG 79. Head of a skylark, drawn by MacGillivray, from his *History of British Birds* (1837–52).

account (presumably the result of a discussion with Audubon) of how they 'swam beautifully, played about, picked up substances floating on the water, now dispersed, and again came close together'.

MacGillivray was not afraid to use the testimony of others when his own knowledge fell short. Where he had no personal experience or trustworthy testimony of a species, he said so.

The *History of British Birds* had a unique additional feature. Every so often the text broke off for a 'practical ornithology lesson'. The second of these lessons, for example, began with a summary of its contents: 'Winter excursion during a snow-storm from Edinburgh to Peebles. Birds observed. Bat hunting in Nidpath Castle. The valley of the Tweed. Birds found around Edinburgh in winter. Snow-storm in the outer Hebrides viewed from the summit of Clisheim. Birds found there in winter.' These 'lessons' were very varied in content. Some sections were purely descriptive, others contained a wealth of factual ornithology. Lesson seven was primarily concerned with the structure and function of the tongue of the green woodpecker, with several highly detailed drawings, and it took up five pages. Volume three (1840) began with a walk in the country described by the author thus: 'A walk into the fields cannot fail to refresh our feelings, enliven our sympathies, and prepare us for the task, not altogether one of unmixed delight, of composing or perusing eight hundred pages of ornithology.'

At the end of volume three was an appendix that contained further information on the species in volumes one and two. It seems that MacGillivray intended that his book would be illustrated with colour plates, and to this end he painted some himself, of which 122 survive in the Natural History Museum Library (Fig. 80). Inevitably, without the private income of many of his contemporaries, publication of the illustrations within the *History* would have been unaffordable.

MacGillivray's work with Audubon ended in 1839, and in 1841 he was appointed Professor of Natural History at Marischal College, Aberdeen. At Aberdeen he was an inspirational teacher, bringing into the classroom his enthusiasm and experience of natural history. He was also able to resume his wanderings, taking some of his students with him. His lectures attracted students from other courses, not to mention the Professor of Humanity, who subsequently enrolled as one of MacGillivray's students.

In his eleven years at Aberdeen MacGillivray built up a substantial collection of zoological specimens, which eventually formed the basis of a new museum. In 1843 he published a work on molluscs of northeast Scotland and did much preparation for *The Natural History of Deeside and Braemar*. But by Christmas 1850

FIG 80. Common gull: unpublished painting by William MacGillivray, from the collection in the Natural History Museum.

he was ill and exhausted. The following autumn, having shown no signs of sustained recovery, he went with his daughter to stay in Torquay. Then in February 1852, while he was still in Torquay, his wife died, an event which, together with his own declining health, convinced MacGillivray that time was running out. The following month the fourth volume of the *History of British Birds* came out and the preface betrayed MacGillivray's sense of foreboding when he wrote 'as the wounded bird seeks some quiet retreat where it may pass the time of its anguish in forgetfulness of the world so have I, assailed by disease, betaken myself to a sheltered nook.' The final volume, the fifth, followed in the same year. MacGillivray noted that 'with death apparently not distant before my eyes, I am pleased to think I have not countenanced error through fear or favour.' And indeed he had not. These last two volumes, published twelve years after the third, sadly do not contain any of the diverting material, being confined entirely to the species-by-species descriptions. Without the 'lessons' or the 'walks' these two volumes certainly seem more serious, yet the overall impression today is of a very readable and scholarly work – no wonder his pupils loved him. MacGillivray was an exceptional ornithologist. In the same year that the final volume was published MacGillivray returned to Aberdeen, where he died in September 1852.

William MacGillivray's contemporaries had not recognised him as the genius he undoubtedly was, perhaps because he did not live and work in London, which was the focus of all scientific work at the time, or perhaps, even more likely, because he was so outspoken. Fifty years after his death Alfred Newton had no doubt about his merit, saying, 'I may perhaps be excused for repeating the opinion that, after Willughby, MacGillivray was the greatest and most original [ornithological] genius that this island has produced.' MacGillivray was perhaps best described by the American ornithologist Elliott Coues:

> MacGillivray appears to have been of an irritable, highly sensitised temperament, fired with enthusiasm and ambition, yet contending, for some time at least, with poverty; ill-health and a perhaps not well-founded, though therefore not the less-acutely felt, sense of neglect; thus ceaselessly nerved to accomplish yet as continually haunted with the dread of failure ... This author was undoubtedly unwise in his frankness; but diplomacy is a stranger to such characters ... he never hesitated to differ sharply with anyone, or to express his own views pointedly – if he scarcely disguised his contempt for triflers, blockheads, pedants, compilers and theorisers he was nevertheless a lover of Nature, an original thinker, a hard student, and finally an ornithologist of large practical experience, who wrote down what he knew or believed to be true with great regard for accuracy of statement and in a very agreeable manner.

The fact remains that his work faded rapidly, for two reasons. First, his magnum opus the *History of British Birds* contained the information that MacGillivray wished to put before the public rather than the information the public wished to receive. His detailed anatomical descriptions and drawings fell on stony ground, and the more serious nature of the final two volumes went some way to negate the obvious difference between the first parts of his book and Montagu's *Dictionary*. Second, and more fundamental to his failure to achieve the posterity he deserved, was that in London another publication with the same title appeared coincidentally at exactly the same time. This was the work of William Yarrell, who set out to do the opposite of MacGillivray – to provide the public with what they wanted to know. Yarrell's book eclipsed that of MacGillivray in popularity and (updated and revised several times) became the 'standard' work on British birds.

WILLIAM YARRELL'S *HISTORY OF BRITISH BIRDS*

William Yarrell (Fig. 81) was born in London in 1784, the son of a newspaper agent. He was educated at Ealing and at the age of eighteen he became a bank clerk at Herries, Farquar & Co. This occupation lasted only a short time before he joined his father in the newspaper trade. He began to go off on shooting and fishing trips and it seems that it was on these expeditions that he developed an awareness of the countryside and became interested in zoology. Unlike Montagu, he seems not to have been a fanatical field ornithologist; unlike MacGillivray, he was not a scientist; he was, if anything, the first of a breed, commoner today, of collectors of occurrence records – something of a list maker. It was in 1823 that he began to note the records of rare and interesting birds. Living in London, he was very much at the hub of the scientific establishment: for example by 1825 he was a Fellow of the Linnean Society, and he was also a founder member of the Zoological Society.

Yarrell's great works began to appear ten years later. First came the *History of British Fishes* in 1836, to be followed a year later by the first volume (published

FIG 81. William Yarrell. (National Portrait Gallery)

in parts) of the *History of British Birds*. Volumes two and three followed, the work being completed in 1843 with a supplement in 1845. The work was an immediate success for Yarrell, who had hit on the requirements for a standard ornithological work. As Alfred Newton recounted, Yarrell 'well knew that the British public in a Book of Birds not only did not want a series of anatomical treatises, but would even resent their introduction. He had the art to conceal his art, and his work was therefore a success while the other [MacGillivray's] was unhappily a failure.' The second edition was published in 1845, only two years after the last volume of the first, and a third edition appeared in 1856, two years after the author's death. The popularity of the book is shown by the fact that despite the demise of its author a fourth edition in four volumes, considerably edited by Alfred Newton (Vols 1 & 2) and Howard Saunders (Vols 3 & 4), appeared between 1871 and 1885. Then in 1889 Saunders produced a condensed version as a single volume under the title *An Illustrated Manual of British Birds*, with a second edition ten years later. So, in one form or another, Yarrell's *British Birds* was in production for nearly sixty years, a record equalled only in the second half of the twentieth century by the groundbreaking identification guide to European birds known to all as Peterson, Mountfort & Hollom.

Yarrell's *British Birds* lacked both the heavy methodological approach of Montagu and the idiosyncratic style of MacGillivray. It was a precise account, well presented, written in straightforward terms, if somewhat lacking in character, drawing on the major publications of the time for information with additions from the personal communications of fellow ornithologists. Yarrell, like Pennant before him, seems to have been a repository for information.

There was no complicated explanation of the system of classification employed – indeed there was no explanation at all, and therefore it required no justification. Volume one launched into its subject immediately with species-by-species accounts. The illustrations, wood engravings by Fussell and Thompson, were not very inspiring; some were tolerably good, most were less so, especially in contrast with the Bewick woodcuts (see Chapter 9) or MacGillivray's drawings. The birds were portrayed with rather unnatural stilted poses (presumably the subjects were stuffed and mounted), and some birds had strange proportions – in the case of the waterfowl the head was frequently far too small for the body (Fig. 82). But the little vignettes to be found now and then at the end of an entry were quite delightful (Fig. 83), giving the impression of an artist who was good at his art but not so good at depicting birds.

Each entry began by quoting other authors, followed (again using the example of the grey phalarope) by a short description of the generic characteristics of phalaropes and a succinct specific description – red in summer, grey in winter.

FIG 82. Wigeon, from Yarrell's *History of British Birds* (1837–43). An example of the poor proportions of the wildfowl.

FIG 83. A typical vignette 'end piece' from Yarrell's *History of British Birds* (1837–43).

Next came a section on the status of the species in Britain, which was something of a Yarrell speciality and undoubtedly a big selling point:

> *Though formerly a rare bird in this country, since Pennant says that he only knew of two instances in which it had occurred in his time, they are now more common, and generally appear in the autumn, when on the way to their southern winter quarters. They are also for the most part young birds of the year, in various stages of change towards the pure and delicate grey colour of the plumage of winter.*

There followed sections on feeding ecology, breeding distribution and habits, with a section on geographical distribution far more informative than either Montagu's or MacGillivray's:

> *The United States, where it performs periodic migrations north and south similar to those observed in Europe. According to Pennant, this species is found in the eastern parts of the North of Europe; is abundant in Siberia, and about the large lakes of Asia to the Caspian Sea. It is occasionally found in Holland and Germany but is considered a rare bird in France, Switzerland and Italy.*

Finally the account devoted about a page to the plumage characteristics. Here, once again, the descriptions were geared much more to the layman than those provided by either Montagu or MacGillivray (Fig. 84).

Yarrell's aim to attract a particular audience succeeded better than probably even he ever imagined. Comparison with the works of Montagu and MacGillivray shows that Yarrell reduced his text to the kind of entry commonly found in the handbooks of the twentieth century. One area in which Yarrell had great influence, consciously or unconsciously, was in the use of English names. Probably because his book became the preferred text, so his preferred English names became the basis for the first British Ornithologists' Union List in 1883.

As a result of his success Yarrell became a senior figure in the British ornithological sphere, consulted by many. He was also an enthusiastic member of the learned societies of his day, being Secretary of the Zoological Society from 1836 to 1838, a founder member of the Entomological Society in 1833 and its Treasurer from 1834 to 1852. His committee work made him a considerable force in the world of the scientific establishment: those who were recommended by Yarrell usually got the job! He died in September 1856 and is buried at Bayford in Hertfordshire.

The *History* made Yarrell not only famous but rich. He is said to have made four thousand pounds from it, a considerable sum of money in the early

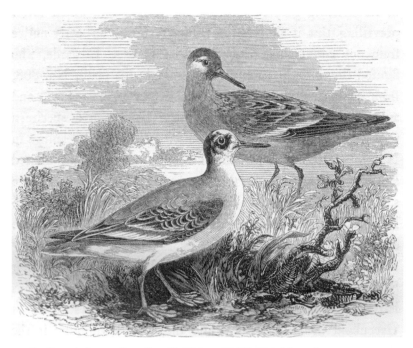

FIG 84. Grey phalarope, from Yarrell's *History of British Birds* (1837–43).

nineteenth century. Newton's view was 'whatever may have been done by the generation of British ornithologists now becoming advanced in life, he educated them to do it; nay his influence even extends to a younger generation still, though they may be hardly aware of it.'

The books of Montagu, MacGillivray and Yarrell were one half of the plethora of works on British birds that began to emerge in the early nineteenth century. The other half consisted of avifaunas which were less scientific but much more artistic – which is hardly surprising, since they were produced by men who were first and foremost artists.

CHAPTER 9

The Artists and Their Avifaunas

It was becoming commercially viable to produce large illustrated bird books [and] there were considerable scientific advances throughout the eighteenth century which provided the stimulus for ornithological publications.

A. M. Lysaght, 1975

B Y THE BEGINNING of the nineteenth century there was a growing market for books on natural history. Many of the works prior to this period were written by ornithologists with drawings or paintings as illustrations, but as time passed more books by artist-birdwatchers, who were not ornithologists in the true sense, began to appear. For text they quoted from the works of others, Latham or Pennant especially. The most well known today are the works of Thomas Bewick, whose woodcuts are still often used as illustrations, Audubon's *Birds of America*, and latterly the books of John Gould, who employed a number of artists to produce the many paintings that made up the avifaunas that he produced.

BEWICK'S *HISTORY OF BRITISH BIRDS*

Of the illustrated publications of this era by far the most influential was that of Thomas Bewick, whose *History of British Birds* was an instant success, mostly because of the quality of the woodcuts that illustrated it (Figs 85–8).

Bewick was born at Cherry Burn, Ovingham, Northumberland, in 1753. His father was a farmer and colliery owner. His education was unexceptional but he enjoyed drawing from an early age. At the age of fourteen he was apprenticed to

FIG 85. Woodcut of grey wagtail by Thomas Bewick. This and the next three figures are all from his *History of British Birds* (1797). With the wheatear Bewick slightly missed the characteristic upright pose, and the hooked bill is rather misleading, as it is on the stonechat.

FIG 86. Woodcut of wheatear by Thomas Bewick.

FIG 87. Woodcut of pied flycatcher by Thomas Bewick.

FIG 88. Woodcut of stonechat by Thomas Bewick.

an engraver, Ralph Beilby, in Newcastle, where he rapidly picked up the skills of the trade. When Beilby received work that required woodcuts, disliking that part of the business, he invariably delegated to Bewick the task of producing the blocks, and Bewick's skill at it soon became apparent. In 1774 Bewick finished his apprenticeship and worked more or less freelance for a while before travelling to both Scotland and London. On his return to Newcastle in 1777 he went into partnership with Beilby and for several years merely carried out the work as it accrued. In 1779 he was awarded the Medal of the Society of Arts for his woodcuts illustrating Saint's edition of *Gay's Fables*. In 1785, having been critical of the standard of illustration in children's books, he set out to produce a series of woodcuts that gave more accurate representation of the subjects, beginning with the dromedary. These woodcuts formed the basis of the *History of Quadrupeds* (1790), the text of which was written by Beilby. Yet Beilby, possibly seeing the future success of the book, felt that only his name should be on the cover – and although Bewick succeeded in restraining him (their names appeared together) this disagreement eventually caused the severing of their partnership.

The success of the *Quadrupeds* book led to the *History of British Birds*. Bewick studied the texts of the past, particularly Pennant, Willughby/Ray, Gesner, Belon and Albin, and was invited to visit the collection of (dead) birds at Wycliffe, where he spent two months drawing – but he soon realised that these specimens were less lifelike than the recently killed birds brought to him. In 1797 the first volume (*Land Birds*) appeared, with the text jointly written by Beilby and Bewick, and the second volume (*Water Birds*) was published in 1804. The success of these books is demonstrated by the fact that before he died in 1828 no fewer than six editions had been published. Newton attributed the considerable interest in birds in this country in the nineteenth century to Bewick's two volumes: 'the existence of these two works explains the widely-spread taste for Ornithology in this country, which is to foreigners so puzzling'.

Bewick's illustrations remain in use today, frequently to be seen illustrating articles, where, although simple, they remain both ornithologically and artistically pleasing. Bewick's focus was on birds as the subject of his art, and his use of the old division into land birds and water birds shows his lack of concern for the science of ornithology. The illustrations that were from life were of the highest quality, those drawn from skins less so, particularly where Bewick was unfamiliar with the species in the wild. Some early editions lacked the skilled printing necessary to do justice to the woodcuts, and by the time the printing techniques had been improved sufficiently the cuts themselves had been used so much that they had deteriorated, so that very few editions show them at their best.

He received handsome tributes from both ornithologists and non-specialists alike. Jardine later wrote, 'the number of blocks he engraved is almost incredible. At his bench he worked and whistled with the most perfect good humour from morn to night ... he was fond of early rising, walking, and indulging in all the rustic and athletic sports so prevalent in the north of England. He did not mix much with the world [and] possessed a singular and most independent mind.'

Bewick's was undoubtedly the best of his kind of avifauna, but it was not alone. Other artists tried to follow his success. Less well known but good enough to be a rival of a kind to Bewick are the three volumes of George Graves's *British Ornithology* published in 1811, 1813 and 1821. Graves's illustrations perhaps lacked the lifelike impression of Bewick's and the backgrounds were rather stark, as against the detailed backgrounds of Bewick. Graves's work was, however, hand-coloured. Most of the engravings have a very agreeable sense of composition, but some remain rather crude compared with those of the master (Fig. 89).

FIG 89. Starling by George Graves, from his *British Ornithology* (1811–21).

The understandable tendency to publish works in parts – for convenience of working, to spread the cost, and to start generating income – inevitably led to some works being unfinished for one reason or another: lack of funds, or even the death of the artist. One such was John Hunt's *British Ornithology* of 1815–22. The three volumes that saw the light of day contained illustrations and descriptions of raptors, wildfowl, waders, rails and passerines such as thrushes, crows, woodpeckers, warblers and tits. The standard of the illustrations was highly variable: some, such as the peregrine, were exceedingly good, some were poor, and the majority were mediocre. The text was said by Newton (from a note in his copy) to have been written by Richard Charles Coxe, later Archbishop of Lindisfarne. Hugh Gladstone (1919) later dismissed that idea and seemed convinced that Hunt was both author and illustrator. Gladstone pointed out that Hunt's book was the first to describe the red-crested pochard as a British bird, and that the sedge warbler plate was in fact an aquatic warbler and therefore possibly the first record of that species too. Furthermore some illustrations, the white-tailed eagle for one, are taken directly from Bewick but portrayed in reverse – although at the time such copying was not considered as unreasonable as it would be today, and in fact many illustrations in different books show remarkable similarity one with another. Hunt presented the birds in a classification that was almost slavishly Linnaean, and the text seemed largely to be compiled from the works of Montagu, Latham, Pennant and Buffon. It included all the known names, both scientific and English, and made an attempt to describe the world distribution of each species. The descriptions were fairly sparse and the information, where it was not derivative, was mainly anecdotal.

Hunt was born in 1777, a native of Norwich. Facts about his life are scarce, but he seems to have had many different forms of employment including work as a taxidermist. He was a collector of bird skins in a small way and probably used specimens that passed through his hands as models for his illustrations. He was responsible for a list of Norfolk birds published in Stacey's *General History of Norfolk* of 1829. In August 1834 he sailed for New York and subsequently lived in America. From a letter quoted by Gladstone it seems clear that the subscribers to his books had not been very good at coming up with the money, and Hunt reportedly said he was glad to be rid of them, so we must assume that the reason the work was not completed was because he was not paid. Gladstone reported finding only eleven copies in any way complete and those he found were variable in their completeness, so clearly the work is very rare. Hunt died in America, probably New York, in 1842.

THE WORKS OF SELBY AND JARDINE

Selby's *Illustrations of British Ornithology* might be described as the English equivalent of Audubon's *Birds of America* but of an inferior quality. The work consisted of 218 plates in folio and most illustrations were life-size, drawn by Selby from his own collection and from that of his brother-in-law (Admiral Mitford). They were engraved by Lizars at Edinburgh and it was Lizars' treatment of Selby's work which subsequently persuaded Audubon that Lizars was the man to do the engraving for *The Birds of America*. They were issued, with a text, in two separate volumes in 1825 and 1833 (Fig. 90). As in Bewick's books, the birds were classified under the old land birds/water birds system, recognising four orders: *Raptores, Incessores, Grallatores* and *Natatores*. The plates were impressive and usually of a high quality. The poses were somewhat typical of the period, yet the body shapes and general appearance were very accurate – very imposing when seen in folio. Swanson described it as 'the most splendid and costly work yet published on the birds of Great Britain. Most of the figures are of natural size ... one of the best works extant on our native ornithology.'

Prideaux John Selby was born in Alnwick, Northumberland, in 1788, educated at Durham Grammar School and at University College Oxford. As a country gentleman he had the time required to pursue his interest in collecting bird skins; his friend and fellow naturalist Leonard Jenyns recorded that 'his fine collection of British birds – if I remember right stuffed by his own butler – was arranged in a spacious hall.' Selby was able to devote his time to drawing, and was an all-round naturalist. He published several papers on British ornithology, principally concerned with birds in Northumberland. He was a member of the Linnean Society and a prominent naturalist in the north of England. As well as the *Illustrations of British Ornithology* Selby collaborated with Sir William Jardine in a series *Illustrations of Ornithology*, the first part of which was published in 1827, with others being issued irregularly until the last in 1843 brought the total to 203 plates. These illustrations were principally of non-British birds, mostly exotics from Australia and South America. The quality of the plates was good, the colours accurate and the postures generally lifelike, although one or two were a little unnatural; but the production on the whole was much inferior to Selby's British illustrations. The plates took up the majority of the book, there being only a small amount of text at the end. This was devoted, not to the habits of those birds depicted but to information concerning the source of the specimens. Selby, whose life has been recorded in detail by Christine Jackson (1992), died at his home in 1867 and was buried nearby at Bamborough.

FIG 90. Plate from Selby's *Illustrations of British Ornithology* (1825–33). Alfred Newton's copy has this plate coloured, while the other plates are in black and white.

Selby's collaborator William Jardine was a Scotsman born in 1800 at Edinburgh, where he grew up before being sent to York, in his own words, 'to learn English'. He then studied medicine at both Edinburgh and Paris before succeeding to the family title, becoming the seventh baronet in 1821, whereupon he moved into the family home, Jardine Hall in Dumfries.

Jardine's ornithological works were linked with Selby's, and judging by Leonard Jenyns's account the two men were frequently to be found staying at each other's houses. Jardine's first published ornithological work was a biography of the eminent Scottish/American ornithologist Alexander Wilson in 1832, but his magnum opus was the impressive *Naturalist's Library*, which consisted of forty volumes devoted to mammals, birds etc. without geographical restrictions. The volumes devoted to birds contained coloured drawings with black and white backgrounds and several pages of text. Visually they were very pleasing, and the factual content was well presented. Since much of it referred to exotic birds it was probably not in competition with other such books. In the volume devoted to parrots (written by Selby) the illustrations were provided by Edward Lear and were usually of a very high quality. Both Jardine and Selby used the quinary system of classification (see Chapter 11). Each volume of the *Naturalist's Library* commenced with a biography of a famous naturalist: among the ornithologists were Willughby in volume five, Pennant in volume seven and Bewick in volume ten.

Jardine alone was responsible for *Contributions to Ornithology*, the five volumes of which he produced between 1848 and 1852. He also produced *Illustrations of the Duck Tribe* and many papers. He was editor of the English edition of Wilson's *American Ornithology*. Jardine was a Fellow of both the Royal Society and the Royal Society of Edinburgh, and in 1841 he was made Deputy-Lieutenant of the county of Dumfries.

There can be no doubt that Selby, and especially Jardine, were genuine ornithologists and not simply illustrators like the others in this chapter.

AUDUBON'S BIRDS OF AMERICA

Although, like Linnaeus, Audubon was neither British nor made any real study of the birds of Britain, he warrants inclusion because it was his presence in this country that led to the initial publication of *The Birds of America*, and because of the interest his illustrations aroused.

John James Audubon's life has been thoroughly documented (Chancellor, 1978), so it will suffice to give the barest details. He was born in 1785 on the island of Hispaniola (Haiti), the illegitimate son of a French sea captain and a creole beauty – at least that is the most likely version of his origin; others, often fruits of his own imagination, were more romantic or even sensational, including the story that he was the Dauphin, son of the guillotined King Louis XVI of France. His mother having died at the hands of revolutionaries in Haiti, his father took him to France, where he lived with the Captain's legitimate wife.

When Audubon was eighteen his father sent him to oversee one of his properties near Philadelphia, with the additional aim that Audubon might learn English. He was not successful at either, the property going downhill fast, and his mastery of English being no better than rudimentary. The father made several attempts to involve his son in the world of commerce but from a very early age John James's interest lay elsewhere. The young Audubon was fascinated by natural things and particularly birds. He collected eggs and nests and from his teens, shot and skinned the local avifauna, and soon began to draw his victims.

In April 1808 he married Lucy Bakewell, the daughter of a wealthy neighbour, and they went to live in Louisville, Kentucky, where Audubon now had a partnership in a shop. He tried to maintain an interest in business and keep his drawing and collecting as a hobby but it is clear that this proved almost impossible, his enthusiasm constantly getting the better of him.

Sometime in 1810 he was visited in his shop by the American ornithologist Alexander Wilson, who tried to sign him up as a subscriber to his *American Ornithology*. Although Audubon was tempted, his business partner pointed out that his own drawings were of a much finer quality than those of Wilson (Fig. 91). He realised that his skill with the brush was more likely to support him and his family and, remembering the project that Wilson had undertaken, he decided that he could do the same – so he tramped around America collecting skins and painting.

After unsuccessful attempts to have his work published in the United States, Audubon sailed for Liverpool with his work and numerous letters of introduction in 1826. His plan was to get the paintings engraved and published, life size, in a single work which he hoped would rival that of Wilson. He was advised by the family with whom he stayed in Liverpool to go to Edinburgh, and there he met William Lizars, the engraver of Selby's work on British birds. Lizars offered to print the first part of *The Birds of America*, and in November 1826 Audubon was shown the proof of the first plate, with which he was delighted. He was well received in Edinburgh, as he reported home: 'my success in Edinburgh borders on the miraculous. I am feted, feasted, elected honorary member of societies [and] making money by my exhibition and my paintings.'

Audubon met Thomas Bewick in Newcastle, and the two men expressed

FIG 91. Mallard: detail from the painting by John James Audubon from his *Birds of America* (1836). Audubon's distinctive style was either liked or disliked. Most of the detail and colouring was very accurate, but the postures were often strange: look for example at the angle of the head of the male bird here.

admiration for each other's skill and technique. He was elected a Fellow of the Royal Society of Edinburgh and settled down to preparing a prospectus for his work. He promised eighty parts (there were eventually 87) of five plates to be spread over fourteen years. Unfortunately Lizars had problems keeping to schedule and the project ground to a halt due to a strike of the colourists.

Audubon then engaged Robert Havell of London to undertake the engraving, and this partnership proved itself over the period of the entire publication. In order to be close at hand Audubon moved to London, where he worked hard at building up a list of subscribers, and, in order to pay for the publication, he returned to his painting, mostly portraits.

One of the potential subscribers he approached was Baron Rothschild. Audubon went to the banking house with his letter of introduction. The Baron declared that he would never sign his name to any subscription list, adding 'but you may send in your work and I will pay for a copy of it.' The work was duly sent and about a year later an account came to the bank. When the Baron saw the account – a hundred pounds – he exploded and offered 'five pounds and not a farthing more'. The work was repossessed and Audubon was able to comment later that 'I kept the work, and sold it afterwards to a man with less money, but a nobler heart.' A copy of the same work sold in 2000 for $8.8 million – so that particular member of the Rothschild family lost a great opportunity for an investment.

Audubon found himself on a treadmill, servicing both the engraver and the subscribers, and for such a man life became rather tedious, so it was hardly surprising that he befriended the equally unconventional William Swainson. At that time Swainson was an illustrator and writer for various magazines, often responsible for the reviews. The manner of their meeting says much of them both. As a reviewer Swainson wrote to ask Audubon for a copy of *The Birds of America* at cost price, a device he frequently tried with writers, to which Audubon replied that cost price was considerably in excess of the charge to the subscribers! However, he offered a reduced price, and got a good review – though whether there was any connection between these two facts is not recorded.

In 1829 Audubon returned to America to gather more birds and drawings, and also to see his family after a gap of three years. When he returned to Britain he began work on a production of both the drawings and text which eventually became the five-volume *Ornithological Biography*. Audubon sought a suitable person who 'would undertake to correct my ungrammatical manuscript and assist me in arranging the more scientific part of the *Biography of Birds*'. His first choice was Swainson but Swainson was quite unprepared to be involved in a form of editing, more particularly since the name on the book would be that of Audubon. Audubon was then referred to MacGillivray, and it is obvious that whatever scientific content there is in the work was the result of this happy union. Audubon worked incessantly at his book but MacGillivray kept ahead of him and Lucy Audubon rewrote the entire manuscript to send to America so as to secure copyright there. The first volume was published in 1831. Swainson, who had been generous about *The Birds of America*, savaged the *Ornithological Biography* – maybe partly because he was not the author.

In 1838 *The Birds of America* was finished, and the *Ornithological Biography* was completed the following year. Audubon returned finally to America and began work on *Quadrupeds of America*, which sadly remained unfinished. His physical condition, particularly his eyesight, began to decline, then his mental state deteriorated, and on 27 January 1851 he died.

His later years were spent mostly selling his work and making appearances at social and scientific gatherings. Audubon had his detractors, chief among whom in England was Charles Waterton. This was because Waterton's American correspondent, George Ord, had been inspired by Alexander Wilson, and Ord and Waterton formed an alliance to promote Wilson and demote Audubon. Much of their acidity wounded Audubon and undoubtedly sapped some of the pleasure from the fame that accompanied his later life.

During his time in England Audubon had met two young men who impressed him with their interest in illustration, Edward Lear and John Gould. Gould may have been influenced by Audubon's books, and he was a man destined to see the financial opportunity presented by lavish avifaunas.

THE AVIFAUNAS OF JOHN GOULD

John Gould (Fig. 92) was born in 1804, the son of a gardener who was subsequently employed in the royal gardens at Windsor, and initially he followed in his father's footsteps. Very soon, however, he became proficient in the art of taxidermy, which led him away from plants and into zoology. His taxidermic skills came to the attention of King George IV and Gould was given several royal taxidermy commissions, which he seems to have discharged with credit, leading to his name being mentioned in the right circles.

Gould's work in the bird world began in 1828 in the infant Zoological Society of London, where he was employed as keeper and taxidermist by the secretary, Nicholas Vigors, who taught Gould exotic ornithology.

Either by accident or by design, Gould found himself in an almost unique position. This was the age of expeditions, and most of the expeditionaries used societies such as the Zoological to pay a part of their costs. The society's return on the investment was always that the specimens collected would come to the society. This in turn led to the specimens being examined, and those that were new to science were given extensive descriptions and named, with the results published in the various journals. Gould became the main point of receipt of

FIG 92. John Gould. (Natural History Museum)

collections of birds sent to the Zoological Society, and he soon took advantage of the opportunities this presented. He became the person who undertook the process of describing and naming birds new to science, at which he developed considerable expertise. But there were two important consequences of being the right person in the right place at the right time. First, Gould developed quite a reputation as an ornithologist, as his name began to appear regularly in the literature; second, he discovered that there was a ready market for any book that would illustrate these new discoveries.

Among the people who had wandered into the Zoological Society collections was a young Edward Lear, who was working on drawings for his *Illustrations of the Family of Psittacidae, or Parrots* (Fig. 93). Lear's work was issued in parts, beginning in 1831, and Gould, always alert to an opportunity, recognised the skill of Lear and the potential of lithography, which Lear proposed to use to publish his work. Both of these Gould subsequently employed – and took the credit for. Gould persuaded Lear to teach his wife Elizabeth Gould how to do the drawings on stone that were the essential ingredient of the lithographic technique.

In 1830 Gould took the ornithological community by surprise with the issue of the first part of *A Century of Birds from the Himalaya Mountains*. The lithographed illustrations were largely by Elizabeth Gould, from John Gould's sketches, and Vigors wrote the text. Gould's ornithological prowess was clear, and Vigors made him Superintendent of the Ornithological Collection in 1833.

Gould began to learn a great deal about the birds he drew, and he travelled widely on the Continent, visiting zoological collections and museums. He took Edward Lear with him. Lear's *Parrots*, despite great critical acclaim, had not been a commercial success and Lear, in need of work, was soon to become the artist for one of Gould's great works – *The Birds of Europe*, which began to appear in 1832, the five volumes being completed in 1837. In 1833 Gould began to issue his monograph on toucans, illustrated by Lear, followed in 1836 by a monograph on

FIG 93. Bay-headed parrot by Edward Lear, from his *Illustrations of the Family of Psittacidae* (1832).

trogons. From the start Gould used all his connections to obtain a substantial and prestigious list of subscribers, and as his productions became well known so his list expanded.

In 1836 Gould was the natural person to be approached by Darwin to work on the bird specimens brought back from the voyage of the *Beagle*. It was Gould who first realised that what to Darwin had seemed a diverse collection of species from the Galapagos Islands were in fact a series of ground finches which formed an entirely new group containing twelve species. For Gould this provided another opportunity to publish the discovery of species new to science; for Darwin it was part of the evidence that propelled him towards his theory of evolution. Gould agreed to be responsible for the plates of the birds to be published in Darwin's journal of the *Beagle* expedition.

By this time, despite his humble background, Gould was becoming an established figure in England. It may have been this same background that drove him forward in a ceaseless round of production. Gould, considered by many contemporaries to be a great ornithologist, was in fact a ruthless entrepreneur, managing his business with little regard to his workforce, including his wife, in the sole pursuit of the financial rewards that his books provided. This was never more evident than in his association with Darwin. Isabella Tree, in her biography of Gould, points out that Darwin began to frequent the Zoological Gardens to talk through his ideas with Gould, but that the latter, clearly aware that there was little further to be gained financially from the association, made himself less and less available. Furthermore, when Darwin published *The Origin of Species* in 1859 Gould was uncharacteristically reticent about his role, for fear of being drawn into the controversy and thus antagonising some of his subscribers, many of whom would have been shocked by what were seen as blasphemous suggestions. Gould's desire to disassociate himself from Darwin's idea was noted at the time by Alfred Newton in one of his letters to his brother, Edward, with considerable amusement.

Gould's *Birds of Australia*

The project for which Gould may be best remembered was *The Birds of Australia*. The undertaking was such that he resigned his position with the Zoological Society to concentrate on the project. After the first two volumes were finished he realised that to do justice to the work he needed to visit Australia, so in May 1838 he sailed off around the world, arriving at Hobart in Tasmania in September. In the course of the voyage Gould took the opportunity to gather specimens of many and various pelagic species, giving further opportunity for new descriptions of his discoveries. Once in Australia it did not take Gould long to realise the inadequacy of the Australian avifauna project to date, so when he returned to Britain he cancelled the previous work and began again. Gould spent the best part of two years in Australia, accompanied by his wife, who set to work on illustrations almost immediately. Gould travelled in Tasmania, New South Wales and South Australia while his assistant John Gilbert was sent to Western Australia. In all, Gould and Gilbert gathered so much material that *The Birds of Australia* made up eight volumes, seven up to 1848 with five supplementary parts making up the eighth published between 1851 and 1869. When Gould returned to England he left Gilbert behind in Australia to continue the work of collecting. Gilbert provided Gould with many specimens of new species, all of which Gould described without any reference to his assistant. Gilbert subsequently perished during the ill-fated expedition to cross Australia led by the strange and ultimately discredited Ludwig Leichhardt – Gilbert having been literally deserted by Gould, who was not prepared to wait for him to cross from the west to get to the boat for England. It was in Australia that Gould made his most significant contributions to science, and he is often revered as the father of Australian ornithology.

Gould's *Hummingbirds*

The saga of the hummingbirds is another example of Gould in action. These small highly attractive birds were an obvious and early subject not just to Gould but to Victorian society as a whole. Gould began building up a significant collection, and set out to publish a monograph on the family. He commissioned collectors in South America and obtained specimens from far and wide, including many from Europe, where they were imported in large numbers to furnish the drawing rooms of the wealthy. In 1849 Gould published the first part of his monograph, which eventually comprised five volumes, the last being published in 1861. The work attracted much scientific praise, but in a letter he boasted of attracting the custom of most of the crowned heads of Europe, adding 'for whom the work is specially adapted' – once again showing where his priorities lay.

Controversy arose from Gould's use of gold leaf to portray the iridescence of the hummingbirds' plumage. He was taught the technique by an American by the name of Baily, who sent Gould an illustration to demonstrate it, only to have Gould exhibit it as his own, subsequently claiming that his method was different from Baily's. Gould's financial acumen, already showing a profit on these tiny creatures, then moved into action for a second bite at the cherry. The Great Exhibition of 1851 prompted the idea that the hummingbirds should become an exhibition item at the Zoological Society, and he arranged that a building should be erected in the grounds to house the collection, for which he would bear the cost but receive the money charged for entry. The Society agreed and Gould cleaned up, making an income of £1,500 in one summer!

Other works by Gould

Among Gould's other publications were the five volumes of *The Birds of Great Britain*, published between 1862 and 1873. He intended this to be his grandest work, and he employed one of the most skilled of all bird artists, Joseph Wolf. Wolf was never overlooked in the way that Lear had been. Due credit was more forthcoming from Gould, probably since Wolf was already known throughout British naturalist circles as a painter of unrivalled talent. But Wolf was no more immune to Gould's activities than anyone else – a specimen of Wolf's somehow got into Gould's box and never found its way out! Wolf did a large number of the paintings for the book, but many others seem to have been largely finished by Henry Constantine Richter (the son of a famous painter) from conceptions by Gould. In general the illustrations in *The Birds of Great Britain* were of a higher quality than much of what had gone before, perhaps not just because of Wolf's contribution but because Gould and Richter had perfected their art through experience (Figs 94, 95).

Gould himself was not an artist of any quality, and from the beginning

FIG 94. Dotterel, from Gould's *Birds of Great Britain* (1862–73). A rather wooden painting typical of the Gould stable; even the background is unaccomplished.

FIG 95. Long-tailed tits in juvenile plumage, from Gould's *Birds of Great Britain* (1862–73). It was unusual at the time to portray birds in this sort of picturesque way.

he was entirely reliant on the talent of others: firstly his wife, then Lear, then Wolf. After his wife's death he used Richter and William Hart as artists and colourists to lithograph the basic sketches much as Elizabeth Gould had done (Hart also did illustrations for Dresser and for the *Catalogue of Birds*: see Chapter 11). Regardless of the real artist, however, Gould nearly always appended his own name to the plates: to say that he was never keen to distribute the credit is an understatement.

What Gould was good at was business. He was probably the most commercially minded of any ornithologist in this country, at any time. He had an eye for what the public would find attractive, and he produced the books at a price that people would pay. Whenever he was faced with the choice between science and financial advantage he chose the latter. Of the paintings themselves Newton praised those by Wolf, and of the others he wrote that 'there is, it is true, a smoothness and finish about them not seen elsewhere; but, as though to avoid the exaggerations of Audubon, Gould usually adopted the tamest of attitudes in which to represent his subjects, whereby expression as well as vivacity is wanting.'

Gould was elected a Fellow of the Royal Society in 1843, largely as a result of his Australian expedition, and was considered in his day to be a great ornithologist, which, within the narrow confines of the collecting period, he must have seemed. His lasting testament lies partly in the naming of so many new bird species, partly in his initiation of Australian ornithology, but ironically today he is largely remembered for the artistic books that he produced – whose illustrations were almost entirely the work of others.

THE ILLUSTRATORS – EDWARD LEAR AND JOSEPH WOLF

Of the two principal artists employed by Gould, Edward Lear and Joseph Wolf, Lear is, of course, better known for his nonsense verse. Born in 1812, he was the penultimate child from a family of twenty-one and by all accounts a fragile child, and he suffered from epilepsy. When he was fifteen the family lost all its money and the only form of work open to Lear was to paint. He painted and/or drew any subject that commanded a price until, at the age of only seventeen, his first big commission arrived – to paint the illustrations for at least one of the Jardine *Naturalist's Library*. The success of this venture encouraged him to produce his own work, and he chose to draw parrots, live specimens of which he found conveniently close by at the gardens of the Zoological Society. His book *Illustrations of the Family Psittacidae*, which began publication in 1830, was a great success technically, but Lear soon tired of the tedious business side of publication and in 1832 he abandoned the project with two parts remaining. However, Gould had seen his work and soon engaged him for his *Birds of Europe*. Lear worked for Gould for about six years, but commented that 'he was one I never liked really, for in spite of a certain jollity and bonhomie, he was a harsh and violent man ... In his earliest phase of bird-drawing he owed everything to his excellent wife, and to myself – without whose help in drawing he had done nothing.' Following his disentanglement from Gould, Lear seems to have ceased to draw birds. Instead he became a landscape painter and of course a poet. The *Psittacidae* paintings were undoubtedly of a quality never previously seen. Of his other work, his worst is better than many previous painters' best.

Wolf was a peasant's son from Morz, Germany, who was, like Audubon, a passionate bird artist. From an early age he pursued his subjects, shooting or netting them in order to capture their likenesses (Fig. 96). He had no formal drawing education. His work came to the attention of the German ornithologist Eduard Rüppell (of Rüppell's warbler fame), who engaged him to illustrate his book on the birds of North Africa – a commission that led to Wolf's abilities

FIG 96. Hobby by Joseph Wolf, from Gould's *Birds of Great Britain* (1862–73). Apart from Thorburn and Lear, Wolf was in a class of his own as a bird and animal painter, especially of raptors, as this picture shows.

FIG 97. Marsh warbler, from Gould's *Birds of Great Britain* (1862–73). Finished by Richter from a Gould sketch or possibly entirely Richter's conception.

being recognised Europe-wide. After travelling on the Continent carrying out commissions he came to England in 1848, where he had a picture hung in the Royal Academy, and more significantly made the acquaintance of John Gould. Unlike Gould's other artists, Wolf worked outside his commitment to Gould and illustrated articles in journals such as *The Ibis* and the *Transactions of the Zoological Society.*

In 1861 Wolf published paintings of the animals in the zoological garden under the title *Zoological Sketches,* and a second series appeared in 1868. One of Wolf's biggest fans, Alfred Newton, waxed lyrical: 'Though a comparatively small number of species of birds are figured in this magnificent work ... their likenesses are so admirably executed as to place it in regard to ornithological portraiture at the head of all others. There is not a single plate that is unworthy of the greatest of all animal painters.'

Wolf contributed to other books such as Elliot's *Monograph of Pheasants* (1872) and *Birds of Paradise* (1873), and for Gould he painted many of the illustrations in the *Birds of Great Britain*. As a painter of birds of prey he was, and possibly remains, unequalled. Artistically Lear and Wolf seem to have been entirely independent of Gould, working to their own designs. For the rest Gould seems to have sketched the outline of the birds, sometimes the background composition as well. These he gave to whoever was working for him at the time – Elizabeth, Hart, or Richter – who worked them into the finished article. As with other artists, there is no doubt that with time the standard rose, and some of the plates for the *Birds of Great Britain* are illustrative of that improvement (Fig. 97).

Finally, in this review of the bird art of the nineteenth century, a series of masterful paintings from an unexpected source. The great landscape painter J. M. W. Turner was a frequent visitor at Farnley Hall in Yorkshire, the home of the Fawkes family, and while there he painted a small number of bird portraits, including a red grouse hanging in a pantry (see Fig. 183) and the heads of a number of species including cuckoo (see Fig. 62), barn owl (see Fig. 116), marsh harrier (see Fig. 182) and peacock (Fig. 98) (Hill, 1988). These studies are very

FIG 98. Peacock from J. M. W. Turner's *Ornithological Collection*. From Hill's *Turner's Birds* 1988.

much a combination of Turner's style and a handbook-like pictorial representation. Those drawn from specimens are of a high quality, but where Turner attempted to present birds in a lifelike pose the result was less successful, with the birds looking a little stiff and unnatural.

Perhaps it was due to a move towards a more scientific approach to ornithology, or even because the age of discovery was drawing to a close, but whatever the cause, or causes, Gould's great works were essentially the last of their kind. By the beginning of the twentieth century the appetite was virtually exhausted and with a very few minor exceptions there were no more of these kind of books.

CHAPTER 10

Alfred Newton and the Founding of the British Ornithologists' Union

In those streets of Cambridge which lie between Magdalene College and the University Museum a tall, bent figure with two sticks and a tall stove-pipe hat, with white hair and white whiskers was often seen in the early years of this century. This was Alfred Newton, the University Professor of Zoology, and one of the last great figures at the end of the age of great figures. There is nobody like Newton today in ornithology. There are many without doubt, with his ability, there is none with his individuality or his character ... his clothes were old-fashioned, his manners were old-fashioned and his speech was old-fashioned (he called matches Vesuvians years after they had ceased to go off like volcanos). But he was a progressive, for such are all true scientists.

James Fisher, 1966

T HERE WAS LITTLE change in ornithology in the second half of the nineteenth century: internationally and nationally it continued to be dominated by the study of faunistics, the birds of this place or that, and the consequent systematics – where these newly described birds fitted into the classified system. This preoccupation seemed to choke the life out of field ornithology and there was little interest in ecological studies or studies of basic bird biology. In Britain, one man – Alfred Newton – touched on aspects of birds beyond classification, being interested in subjects as varied as great auks, dodos, bird protection, and mechanisms of migration. Newton (Fig. 99) was the first Professor of Zoology at Cambridge, and through his obsession with scientific observation and statements drawn from facts he guided ornithology along a straight and narrow path. Happily he was a productive correspondent, and in

FIG 99. Alfred Newton as a young man. From *The Ibis* Jubilee supplement (1908).

addition to his crisp, precise and often pithy scientific writing he left a legacy of letters which display both the depth of his interest in birds and often his sense of amusement at the events that surrounded him, making him something of a chronicler of the ornithology of his time.

Newton was born in 1829, the fifth son of a family whose estate at Elveden on the Suffolk/Norfolk border was said to provide the finest partridge shooting in England. Alfred, having suffered an accident as an infant, was slightly lame. He became interested in natural history at an early age and was soon quite proficient in the arts of identification and all the techniques required to collect and prepare specimens. By the time he went to Cambridge University in 1848 he had already written his first ornithological paper. At Cambridge he was a student at Magdalene, the beginning of a lifelong association with that college. He later reported that he had not found the curriculum very interesting, preferring to be involved in practical natural history – which his parents discouraged, since they could see no way in which he could make any kind of living from it. During this time Newton built up correspondences with some of the figures of the day such as Yarrell, Gould and Jardine. He formed a friendship with a fellow undergraduate, John Wolley, who was widely travelled and as a result amassed an important collection, particularly of eggs. Having taken his BA in 1853, Newton was elected to a Travelling Fellowship at Magdalene and for the next few years, often in the company of Wolley, he set about exploring distant places. He visited Lapland, and in 1857 he went to the West Indies, where his family had estates. He was delighted by the hummingbirds (Fig. 100) that he saw:

> *No pen can describe and no pencil depict the suddenness with which the little fairy appears before you, the rapidity with which, on wings whining like a cotton mill, he visits flower after flower, and then when you least expect it, away he shoots in pursuit of a rival. All this while (about thirty seconds) you are holding your breath for fear of blowing him away.*

He travelled on to the United States, where he was taken ill, but this did not prevent him from making the acquaintance of some of the prominent American ornithologists such as Agassiz and Baird.

In the spring of 1858 Newton and Wolley travelled to Iceland, hoping to find relics of the great auk (Fig. 101), or garefowl as Newton called it (he almost invariably adhered to old English names for birds). Newton and Wolley

FIG 100. Rufous hummingbirds by John James Audubon, from his *Birds of America* (1836).

FIG 101. Great auk by William MacGillivray. (Natural History Museum)

considered it possible that the great auk might have survived in some small pocket somewhere, and although they found no evidence of this they were very successful in collecting first-hand accounts of the bird from witnesses. Tragically Wolley, still a young man, died the following year, but that trip to Iceland marked the beginning of Newton's interest firstly in the great auk and subsequently in all extinct birds. He began to draw up a list of all great auk specimens in Britain and tried to find, and if possible purchase, those remaining eggs not already in collections. He reported his first success to his friend Henry Tristram in a letter in 1860:

In going about London this day I have picked up the greatest prize an English Oologist can meet with. The long and the short of it is that I have today purchased a Great Auk's egg, one whose existence was previously unknown to me and I am glad to say her antecedents are likely to prove extremely interesting.

His next discovery, made at Surgeon's Hall, was described in a letter to his brother Edward in 1861: 'to cut it short there were ten nearly all in excellent preservation. How they came there I don't know but expect to make out. No doubt they are [from] Iceland.'

His work on the great auk resulted in a number of publications over a 37-year period, and he was always considering aspects of the bird's biology, as is evident from a letter to his friend Feilden 1885:

I can't satisfy myself as to the way in which the Garefowl's flightlessness was produced, and I suppose I never shall. I can only conjecture that he found wings fit for flight articles too expensive for him to indulge in. In the air a wing must be very good to be good for anything. If not it's better not to fly at all, natural selection would soon weed out animals with moderate wings and leave those that had the best or the worst. On land I take it that the Great Auk had practically no enemies till man.

Other ornithologists of the period scarcely, if ever, hypothesised in this way. Even as late as 1894 Newton was still hoping to put together a book on the subject. Around the time of his interest in the great auk he became equally interested in the birds of the Mascarene Islands, particularly the dodo and the Rodrigues solitaire. How much this interest was fired by his brother, Sir Edward Newton (who was Colonial Secretary of Mauritius for a time) is not clear, but the interest was shared, and Edward was able to obtain the bones of specimens that could be used for anatomical analysis. Newton exhorted visitors to the Mascerene Islands to seek out relics of the dodo and solitaire and was able to build a collection for the Cambridge Museum.

Newton's interest in extinct birds led him to consider the fate of the great bustard in Britain – particularly since the last individuals had lived so close to his home in the Brecklands around Thetford (Fig. 102). Much as he had with the great auk, he collected information on the great bustard in Britain, again with the aim of writing a book on the subject. Sadly neither book (on great auk or great bustard) was completed. When Wolley died in 1859, he bequeathed his collection to Newton. It was delivered to Elveden in twenty-four packages, weighing a ton, and filling a railway truck. It spawned a book from Newton, the

FIG 102. Great bustard by Archibald Thorburn, from his *British Birds* (1915–18).

Ootheca Wolleyana, the first part of which was published in 1864, the remaining parts nearly forty years later.

THE BRITISH ORNITHOLOGISTS' UNION

It is scarcely surprising that by the seventeenth century those interested in science began to realise that they needed to meet together to discuss their work and discoveries. It was these meetings, often held in London, that led in 1660 to the formation of the Royal Society of London. Among the first Fellows of the Society was Christopher Merrett, author of the first list of British birds, and one of the earliest secretaries was Robert Plot, the writer of the early county avifaunas of Oxfordshire and Staffordshire (Lyons, 1944). As a scientific forum the Royal Society had two significant limiting factors. First it had a limited membership, and second it embraced all scientific subjects, so that the time available for each individual subject, such as ornithology, was very small. As the interest in science increased and the needs of subject groups expanded it was inevitable that other, more specialised organisations would emerge, such as the Botanical Society in 1721 and the Aurelian Society (devoted to entomology) in 1745. Almost certainly due to a lack of proper organisation, interest in both these societies waned. Yet the demand for outlets for publication of results of the study of natural history remained, and it was met, initially, by the formation of the Linnean Society in 1788. From the beginning the Linnean Society began to build up a library and collection of specimens, and more importantly the members also met regularly for the sole purpose of reading papers. Eventually, however, the increasing interest in the separate branches of scientific natural history led to the development of separate sections within the Linnean Society, and in 1823 a zoological section was formed. Yet the great need of the day was for a more effective vehicle of publication than the *Transactions of the Linnean Society*, and this problem remained unsolved. In truth the zoologists had outgrown the Linnean Society long before the zoological section was formed and, rather to the chagrin of the Linnean establishment, in 1826 they formed their own Society – the Zoological Society.

In 1830 the Zoological Society began the regular scientific meetings that led to the publication of the proceedings, which at last provided a specialist outlet for zoologists to publish their work. While there is little doubt that the emergence of the Zoological Society went some way towards fulfilling the needs of ornithologists, there seems to have been a strong undercurrent from the start that they needed to push ahead with their own society, a need that grew with a slow but unstoppable momentum. In the end the prime mover and inspiration was Alfred Newton, and the regular meetings held in his rooms at Magdalene College, usually on a Sunday evening, provided the impetus. Most of the prominent ornithologists of the day would occasionally, or regularly, travel to Cambridge to attend these meetings, and it seems that their most important outcome was the proposal for the publication of a journal – as described in the first issue of *The Ibis* (Figs 103, 104):

For some years past a few gentlemen attached to the study of Ornithology, most of them more or less intimately connected with the University of Cambridge, had been in the habit of meeting together, once a-year, or oftener, to exhibit to one another the various objects of interest that had occurred to them, and to talk over both former and future plans of adding to their knowledge of this branch of Natural History.

In November 1858 the annual assemblage took place at Cambridge and those present [agreed] that a Quarterly Magazine of General ornithology should be established, that a limited subscription should be entered into to provide a fund for that purpose and that the subscribers should form an 'Ornithological Union' their number at present not to exceed twenty.

FIG 103. Front cover of the first edition of *The Ibis* (1858).

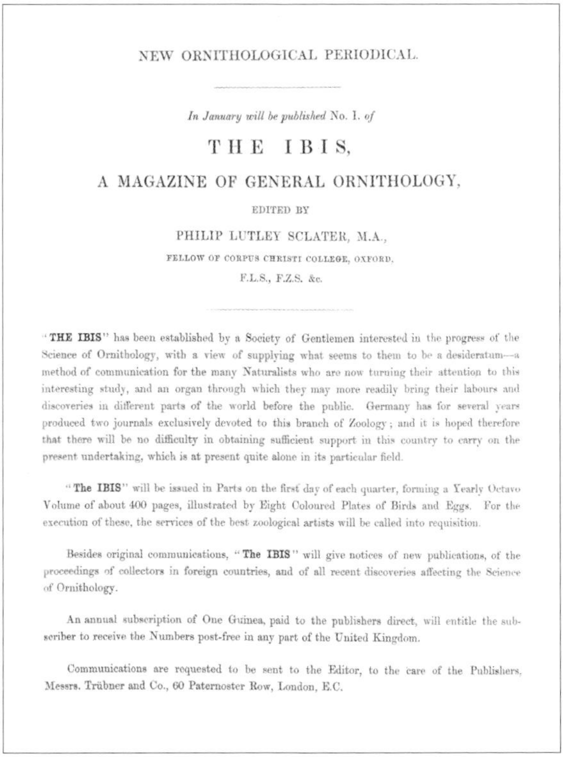

NEW ORNITHOLOGICAL PERIODICAL.

In January will be published No. 1. *of*

THE IBIS,

A MAGAZINE OF GENERAL ORNITHOLOGY,

EDITED BY

PHILIP LUTLEY SCLATER, M.A.,

FELLOW OF CORPUS CHRISTI COLLEGE, OXFORD,

F.L.S., F.Z.S. &c.

"**THE IBIS**" has been established by a Society of Gentlemen interested in the progress of the Science of Ornithology, with a view of supplying what seems to them to be a desideratum—a method of communication for the many Naturalists who are now turning their attention to this interesting study, and an organ through which they may more readily bring their labours and discoveries in different parts of the world before the public. Germany has for several years produced two journals exclusively devoted to this branch of Zoology; and it is hoped therefore that there will be no difficulty in obtaining sufficient support in this country to carry on the present undertaking, which is at present quite alone in its particular field.

"**The IBIS**" will be issued in Parts on the first day of each quarter, forming a Yearly Octavo Volume of about 400 pages, illustrated by Eight Coloured Plates of Birds and Eggs. For the execution of these, the services of the best zoological artists will be called into requisition.

Besides original communications, "**The IBIS**" will give notices of new publications, of the proceedings of collectors in foreign countries, and of all recent discoveries affecting the Science of Ornithology.

An annual subscription of One Guinea, paid to the publishers direct, will entitle the subscriber to receive the Numbers post-free in any part of the United Kingdom.

Communications are requested to be sent to the Editor, to the care of the Publishers, Messrs. Trübner and Co., 60 Paternoster Row, London, E.C.

FIG 104. Advertisement for the forthcoming new ornithological journal, *The Ibis*. Placed in the very front of the first issue of the journal, this advertisement was followed by a form to enable readers to subscribe.

Among the twenty founder members were Alfred Newton and his brother Edward, Philip Sclater, the brothers Fred and Percy Godman, Osbert Salvin, John Wolley, Henry Tristram, Lord Lilford and John Henry Gurney. Newton wrote that he considered the founders to be 'Drummond, Tristram, Newtons 2, Salvin and Godmans 2'; the rest (including Sclater, Gurney and Wolley) were, he stated, asked to join.

Newton stated that there had been a problem with Wolley concerning the name of the journal, which the founders wanted to call *Aves*. According to Newton, it was the printer who came up with the name *Ibis* – possibly because he misheard, or misread, the word *Aves*! Wolley disliked the name *Ibis* and threatened to withdraw from the foundation membership but Newton persuaded him to remain, writing to Tristram, 'as for the name itself I don't think it signifies twopence and *Ibis* is as good as any other'. An alternative explanation is that the ibis was chosen as the name of the journal since the bird represented the Egyptian god of wisdom. At all events the name stuck.

The members of the original BOU were largely from the educated upper class, men with private income. They shared ornithological interests that, although varied, were largely centred on their collections. Most of them wrote a treatise on classification, most were responsible for the publication of a major avifaunal work, and towards the end of the period most of them contributed to the monumental *Catalogue of Birds* (see Chapter 11). Some of the original members faded into obscurity, to be replaced by the likes of Howard Saunders, Henry Dresser and Henry Seebohm.

The majority of the BOU members were interested in the naming and status of birds, and they seemed to divide the world into portions, each concentrating on a specific geographical area. Philip Sclater (1828–1913), for example, having begun his collection as an undergraduate at Oxford, intended, with youthful optimism, to collect every bird known to man – but by the time he matured he realised that he should specialise, and since little was known of some families of South and Central American birds he set out to collect passerines, woodpeckers and parrots from that region. Osbert Salvin (1835–98) (Fig. 105) and Frederick Godman (1834–1919) also studied the birds of Central America. Salvin's interest was fired when, having graduated from Cambridge, he travelled to Guatemala in 1857. He returned twice, once with Godman, and they became experts on the birds of Central America. They published over a hundred papers on the subject

FIG 105. Osbert Salvin. From *The Ibis* Jubilee supplement (1908).

FIG 106. Henry Baker Tristram. From *The Ibis* Jubilee supplement (1908).

and their collaboration led to the 63-volume *Biologia Centrali-Americana*, which, not restricted to birds, was published over a 37-year period, describing over 50,000 species, 19,000 for the first time. Fred Godman also produced two books of his own, the *Natural History of the Azores* (1870) and the *Monograph of the Petrels* (1907–10).

Newton's great friend Canon Henry Tristram (1822–1906) was an expert on the birds of Palestine and parts of North Africa and was the author of *The Great Sahara* (1860). For over twenty years Tristram (Fig. 106) made journeys to Palestine, Jordan, and once into Syria. He wrote *The Natural History of the Bible* (1867), which was a very popular book running into several editions, but his *Flora and Fauna of Palestine*, published in 1884, was a more academic offering and became a standard work on the area. Tristram published well over seventy papers on the birds of Palestine and his name has been given to several of them such as Tristram's grackle, which he discovered near the Dead Sea in 1864. Tristram spent most of his life in England in the northeast. Born in Northumberland, the son of a clergyman, he was educated at Durham School and Oxford and worked most of his life as a priest in the Northumberland/Durham area. In 1868 he was elected a Fellow of the Royal Society and in 1873 he was appointed a resident canon of Durham Cathedral. His collection, in which he specialised in the birds of remote oceanic islands, ended up in the Free Public Museums of Liverpool in 1896, comprising some 20,000 skins. In this context it may seem ironic today that Tristram was a great supporter of bird protection and chaired the British Association 'Close Time' Committee as well as becoming a Vice-President of the RSPB. He was described as being a controversial figure, outspoken, restless, tenacious and uncompromising in his views.

Of the other founder members Thomas Powys (later Lord Lilford) (1833–96) was initially interested in the Mediterranean region and devoted two years to collecting in the countries that border the Mediterranean. Among his triumphs was the rediscovery of Audouin's gull – thought at the time to be extinct. Much of his journey is recorded in letters to Newton, and his letter from Turin, dated October 1858, ended with a splendidly archetypal piece of Englishman to Englishman:

> Let me hear from you every scrap of ornithological knowledge. I am only waiting for the arrival of some English powder to start for Sardinia. Your objections to Spain are, I think, groundless. Garlic certainly exists, but the consumption of it is by no means compulsory.

NEWTON AND DARWINIAN THEORY

Despite his considerable dislike of change in the world about him, as witnessed by his refusal to countenance some of the contemporary English names of birds, Newton was progressive about his science. He was among the first to espouse the theory of evolution expounded by Darwin and Wallace, and unlike others he never swayed from complete adherence to it despite what must have been a certain antipathy within the conservative cloisters of the university.

In the course of their sojourn in Iceland Newton and Wolley had come to the firm conclusion that some species were so similar in their plumage, habits and so on that the idea of them being created individually 'could not fit the facts'. Furthermore, Newton was intrigued by the specimens Tristram had brought back from the deserts of North Africa, where each species of lark and chat differed only slightly one from another. Shortly after a visit to Tristram, Newton returned home and found that a copy of the *Journal of the Linnean Society* had been delivered, whereupon he sat down to read it and discovered the paper by Darwin and Wallace explaining the evolution of species. He was delighted, writing 'herein was contained a perfectly simple solution of all the difficulties which had been troubling me for months past. I hardly know whether I at first felt more vexed at the solution not having occurred to me than pleased that it had been found at all.'

To his surprise, not everyone embraced the evolution of species. 'I lost no time in drawing the attention of my friends to the discovery of Mr Darwin and Mr Wallace and I must acknowledge that I was somewhat disappointed to find that they did not so readily as I had hoped approve of the new theory.'

Newton did influence his friend Tristram, who in his paper on the ornithology of North Africa (1859) stated 'it is hardly possible, I should think, to illustrate this [evolution] theory better than by the Larks and Chats of North Africa.' When in 1859 the *Origin of Species* was published Newton wrote, 'now I began to see that Natural History possessed an interest far beyond that which it had entered my mind to perceive.'

Newton was a prominent Darwin supporter at the famous meeting of the British Association for the Advancement for Science at Oxford in 1860, where the matter of Darwinian theory was discussed. By this time Tristram, possibly as a result of feeling his ecclesiastical position was in danger of being compromised, rejected Darwinism. When Newton wrote to him after the Oxford meeting, stating that 'I am developed into pure unmitigated Darwinism', Tristram replied negatively, saying, 'many sane men have their monomania. It's my hope yours is a transitory one.'

By 1863 Newton was publishing work as illustrations of Darwinian principles, and when reviewing Darwin's book *Animals and Birds under Domestication* (1868) he praised Darwin's section on the pigeon. Darwin wrote to thank Newton for his unqualified support, and this marked the beginning of a friendship between the two men.

Newton was equally interested, later in his life, in Wallace's 1876 publication *The Geographical Distribution of Animals*. Newton proposed that the geographical zooregions should be modified, with the Palearctic and Nearctic regions amalgamated into a Holarctic region, a view that gradually became accepted.

THE ORNITHOLOGICAL 'ESTABLISHMENT'

With the formation of the BOU came an ornithological 'establishment', men who were intimately involved in the organisation and administration of the BOU and other British scientific societies. Pre-eminent was Philip Sclater (Fig. 107), born into a family of landed gentry, educated at Winchester and Oxford. From an early love of natural history and the countryside he was able to devote his spare time at Oxford to birds, and in particular to the exceptional collection of books on

FIG 107. Philip Lutley Sclater. From *The Ibis* Jubilee supplement (1908).

natural history in the Radcliffe Library. While at Oxford he met Hugh Strickland, who gave him instruction in scientific ornithology. Sclater's earliest scientific communication dates from this period (1845). In 1851 he began his formal training in the law, so that by 1855 he was active on the Western Circuit as well as a Fellow of his old college. In the following year he set out on a trip around the United States of America before taking up his life as a barrister, living in London and devoting his spare time to the study of birds.

While Sclater was a very active ornithologist, as an administrator he was almost without parallel. He had become a Fellow of the Zoological Society in 1850, beginning an association that was to last half a century; by 1857 he was on the council, becoming Secretary in 1859. As Secretary, Sclater soon showed his skill in administration and set about a fundamental reorganisation of all aspects of the society. The Zoological Gardens were rearranged, and the publications (*Transactions* and *Proceedings*) were brought up to date, having been running in arrears for some time. By 1861 he was a Fellow of the Royal Society. Although in 1874 he served as private secretary to his brother, who was a member of Disraeli's Government, he turned down an offer to become a member of the civil service in order to continue his work at the Zoological Society. He increased the membership from 1,700 to 3,000 and the income from £14,000 to £30,000 per annum, as well as repaying a loan of £14,000 to the bank. He saw that a library was purchased and a librarian (Richard Sharpe) installed, and he began the *Zoological Record*. In 1876 he was elected General Secretary (one of two) of the British Association. In 1880 he became a Life Fellow of the Royal Geographical Society, taking a leading part in its administration for several years and helping to organise many expeditions to all parts of the world, no doubt with strict instructions to the participants concerning the collecting of bird skins. Many of the skins collected on those expeditions were written up by him and published in ornithological journals. Indeed the greater part of his output concerned bird specimens. On ornithology alone he published 582 papers. In 1892 he embraced Richard Sharpe's idea for a British Ornithologists' Club with great enthusiasm, and became its first chairman. By this time he was undoubtedly, with Newton, the established voice of British ornithology until the century turned, when his influence waned. In 1903 he resigned as Secretary of the Zoological Society, a post he had held for 44 years. Even then, though living in Hampshire, he continued to travel regularly to London to visit the libraries of the Zoological Society and the British Museum – and of course the Bird Room – until his death in 1913.

Fred Godman and Osbert Salvin – immortalised by the BOU in the Godman–Salvin Medal – were also public-school and Cambridge educated. Salvin edited *The Ibis* from 1871 until 1882, partly alone and partly with Sclater. In 1877 he took up the post of curator of the Strickland collection at Cambridge. Salvin was also a Fellow of the usual societies – the Royal, the Linnean, the Zoological and the Entomological –and served on the councils of all the last three. He was Secretary of the BOU at the time of his death in 1898. Godman seems to have been even closer to the heart of the establishment. He was a Fellow of the Royal, the Linnean, the Geographical, the Royal Geographical and the Entomological Societies, being President of the latter for a few years; he was also a Fellow of the Society of Antiquaries, a Member of the Royal Institution and a Trustee of the British Museum. He served as Secretary and President of the BOU and was a member of the committee that produced the BOC *List of British Birds* in 1883. Fred Godman outlived his friend by twenty years and was the penultimate survivor of the twenty founders of the BOU, outlasted only by his brother Percy. He was a lover of all outdoor pursuits and his ornithological collection was his pride and joy; when he handed it over to the British Museum (including Salvin's) it comprised a remarkable 520,000 items.

CONTRIBUTIONS ON BRITISH BIRDS

The founders of the BOU turned out to be British ornithologists, rather than ornithologists of Britain. Sclater, Salvin, Godman and Tristram made little direct scientific contribution to British ornithology. However, Lilford and Gurney were exceptions. Lilford was perhaps one of the last true amateurs in British ornithology. His publications were largely concerned with the birds of his home county, Northamptonshire, with the exception of his magnum opus *Coloured Figures of the Birds of the British Islands* (1885–97). For this work he employed the finest artists of the time. He had previously employed Joseph Wolf to paint panels of raptors in his study, and now, with Archibald Thorburn as his chief artist, backed by J. G. Keulemans, and with one or two contributions from George Lodge and William Foster, he produced what is arguably the last of the 'grand' Victorian books. Lilford was born in Mayfair and brought up in the ancestral home at Lilford Hall, Northamptonshire, and educated at Harrow and Oxford. He kept badgers in his room, snakes also. A friend who travelled with him across London recounted that with them on the journey, on the roof of the cab, was a cage containing an eagle owl (Fig. 108), and within the cab were two armadillos – which subsequently ate the landlady's cat. He inherited the Lilford title in 1861, and with it came the opportunity to house the collection of live birds and animals that he had begun at Harrow (where he kept a pair of bitterns in a locker!). He encouraged falconry and even employed a falconer at Lilford Hall. In 1896 his health deteriorated and he died in June of that year.

An even more English ornithologist, indeed a Norfolk ornithologist, was John Gurney (senior) (1819–90). Born into a well-known Norfolk banking family, Gurney was educated first by a private tutor and later at the Friends' School, Tottenham, where he met William Yarrell. He then entered the family business in Norwich. His interest in natural history began at a very early age: he sent his first specimen to Norwich Museum at the age of nine.

Gurney's contributions to the literature were invariably associated with the birds of his native county, the first dating from 1842. He was at the founding meeting of the BOU in Cambridge and paid for the coloured plates that appeared in the first series of *The Ibis*, making the proviso that they should be of raptors. He published many papers, over 140 in *The Ibis* alone, though most were very short. In time he became the accepted authority on hawks and owls. Gurney was unusual among the twenty BOU founders, being a businessman and not university-educated. He showed the zeal and devotion of the amateur to his science, channelling his available resources entirely into ornithology, and

FIG 108. Eagle owl by Archibald Thorburn, from his *British Birds* (1915–18).

particularly into his collections. A number of other businessmen showed similar characteristics.

One such was Howard Saunders (Fig. 109), whose published work began in 1866 with a paper on the birds of Walney, the Lakes and Farne Islands. In 1879 he wrote a paper on the geographical distribution of gulls and terns, which embraced the subject begun by Sclater, establishing Saunders as an expert on the Laridae.

Saunders (1835–1907) was a merchant banker, and in 1855 through his connections at the bank he had the chance to travel to South America. He journeyed to Brazil and Chile and in 1856 to Peru, where he remained for four years. He spent much of his time exploring the interior, looking for both birds

FIG 109. Howard Saunders. From *The Ibis* Jubilee supplement (1908).

and antiquities, and ended his stay by travelling across the Andes before returning to England in 1862. However, on his return he became absorbed with the avifauna of Spain and made many journeys to that country, becoming something of a world authority on its birdlife.

By the 1880s the previous editions of Yarrell's *History of British Birds* were out of date, and Saunders helped Alfred Newton to produce a new edition. Saunders subsequently took overall responsibility for volumes three and four, and these came out in 1884–5. This sparked other ideas, and in 1887 Saunders produced *A List of British Birds*, keeping up the tradition of Yarrell by listing the occurrences, and this list was updated in 1907. In 1889 he produced the book for which he remains well known, *An Illustrated Manual of British Birds*, a compressed version of Yarrell which was, in the crudest sense, the forerunner of the modern field guide, and many birdwatchers used it as an aid to identification. Saunders was also the editor of *The Ibis* for both the fifth and the seventh series.

Henry Seebohm's (1832–95) steel factory in Sheffield was so successful that in middle life he had enough money to allow him to pursue his hobby. Seebohm (Fig. 110) travelled widely around Europe, but it was his trips to Siberia in the 1870s that established his reputation, resulting in the works *Siberia in Europe* and *Siberia in Asia*. He studied migration with Gätke at Heligoland and visited southern Africa to see European birds in their wintering area, and wrote a monograph on plovers and an avifauna of Japan – even though he never visited the country. Seebohm produced yet another *History of British Birds* in 1883–5, compiled largely from his own observations. In 1893 he wrote a booklet developing his other main interest, geographical distribution, as it applied to British birds; but Seebohm was largely interested in his Siberian birds and in classification, and thus made little direct contribution to British ornithology.

An equally important businessman was Henry Dresser (1838–1915), who followed his father into the metal trade. After schooling Dresser (Fig. 111) settled into his father's firm and began travelling in connection with the business, and this gave him every opportunity to collect birds and their eggs. Dresser was one of the most obsessive collectors, described by Manson-Bahr in the centenary *Ibis* (1959) thus:

> *with demoniacal energy, boundless enthusiasm and immense application ... a striking appearance which was arresting in company ... heightened by a rather ill-fitting wig, because he was completely bald. He and his wife developed different interests. She moved in spiritual circles, while his interests were much more mundane in things ornithological, so that their mutual conversation was a matter of comment and at times entertainment to others.*

FIG 110. Henry Seebohm. (Norwich Museum)

FIG 111. Henry Dresser, a man of strange appearance made worse by his ill-fitting wig. Photograph from *British Birds* (1916).

FIG 112. Grey partridge, from Dresser's *History of the Birds of Europe* (1877). The artist is the relatively lesser known Edward Neale, whose work could be compared favourably with much other contemporary output but looks rather less accomplished when measured against Lear, Wolf, Keulemans or Thorburn.

Dresser published his first paper in 1865 and in the same year became a member of the BOU, from which point he became a regular contributor to *The Ibis*. In 1871 he began his famous book *A History of the Birds of Europe* (Fig. 112) with Richard Sharpe, who was soon after engaged by the British Museum to write the *Catalogue of Birds*. When Sharpe was compelled to withdraw from the *Birds of Europe* Dresser continued alone.

Dresser became an expert on two families, bee-eaters and rollers, and wrote monographs on both. His final great work was *Eggs of the Birds of Europe*, a companion to his major work published in 1910. Dresser was, as his obituary noted, 'one of the old order of systematic ornithologists who did not believe in subspecies or trinomials'.

ALFRED NEWTON AT CAMBRIDGE

Yet the work of these men was always overshadowed by the contribution of Alfred Newton. In 1863 Newton vacated his travelling fellowship, largely as a result of his decision not to go into the Church. It was generally accepted that the holder of the fellowship would take holy orders, and that had originally been Newton's intention; however as the day approached for his ordination by the Bishop of Ely in 1862 he changed his mind. One of his pupils, Shipley, later stated that 'the nearer he got to them [the holy orders] the less he liked the look of them and on the whole I am inclined to think that it made for peace in the established church.' When, in 1866, the Cambridge Chair of Anatomy was divided into a chair of human anatomy and a chair of zoology and comparative anatomy, Newton, to the surprise of many within the university, put himself forward as a candidate for the latter and was elected, due in no small part to the excellence of his testimonials. This appointment effectively put an end to his wanderings, and in 1877 he was elected to a Foundation Fellowship at Magdalene, where he based himself for the rest of his days.

Newton set about reorganising the zoology course, and in doing so attracted many new students. Giving lectures, however, was not a part of the job that he relished. Shipley reported that Newton's lectures were delivered verbatim from a manuscript, and Newton himself commented, 'if I could afford it I would tomorrow give up part of my salary to pay a lecturer who would be more competent than myself, I know that I am one of the worst of lecturers.' An area in which he was considerably more successful was in developing the Zoology Museum, which on his appointment amounted to a very small collection. He not only cajoled his friends and acquaintances from around the globe to send specimens to Cambridge, but, in addition, quite frequently paid for the purchase of collections from his own pocket. As well as the specimens of Strickland and Swainson, which the University had purchased in 1843, Newton added his own and John Wolley's (mostly eggs) to the museum. Nor was his interest in any way restricted to birds. He encouraged equally the collection of all zoological specimens. He gave his library also, and almost all of the library material has pencilled comments, often caustic, usually corrections either to the facts or the grammar, in the margin.

Newton's first publication, entitled 'Notes on the arrival of summer birds at Elveden and its vicinity', appeared in the *Zoologist* in 1844. In the 1860s he began to produce a flow of publications that slowed only at the turn of the century, between thirty and fifty every ten years. The subjects were many and varied: for example, 'On the possibility of taking an ornithological census' (1861), 'The rooks and London rookeries' (1878), 'Errors concerning the sanderling' (1892) (Fig. 113).

When he took up the chair in zoology Newton settled into the period of his life where he became the national ornithologist. Whenever there was any interest in birds or related topics Newton was called upon to comment or compose an explanatory article. When Albert Gunther began a *Review of Zoological Literature* in 1864, subsequently re-named the *Zoological Record*, Newton was immediately the principal ornithological contributor. In 1870 he was elected a Fellow of the Royal Society, but this was not before he had asked that his name should be removed

FIG 113. Sanderling. (Photograph by Rebecca Nason)

from the list of candidates in order to ensure the election of his friend Tristram first. His articles for the *Encyclopaedia Britannica* were fine examples of informative essays on topics such as the 'History of ornithology', 'Migration' and 'Geographical distribution', and his contributions on the anatomical aspects of birds were also of the highest quality. Newton was heavily influenced from an early age by the work of Gilbert White, admiring (and trying to copy) the simple style of writing and the accuracy of White's observations. Later he assisted Professor Thomas Bell in the preparation of his edition of *The Natural History of Selborne* (1877). He never failed to punish, either by word of mouth or more frequently by some written admonishment, those who in his view offended the memory of White with inaccuracies. Newton wrote the entry on White for the *Dictionary of National Biography*, enlisting the help of a descendant of the great naturalist and thus gaining access to information previously unpublished.

Newton's magnum opus was undoubtedly the 1,000-page *Dictionary of Birds*. Presented alphabetically to avoid any of the pitfalls of the various classification systems, the *Dictionary* provided information on the physiology and anatomy of birds, the names and their derivation, typical species within each genus, particularly the British birds, and long sections on those topics that Newton had researched: the dodo, the great auk, extermination, geographical distribution and migration. Every entry is readably factual. Newton used the introduction to provide a comprehensive history of ornithology which included a critique of the many and varied systems of classification. There can be little doubt that the *Dictionary* was the finest work of its kind to be published up to that time, and it remains one of the 'classics' of ornithological literature. Newton's obsession with factual accuracy made him the bane of publishers. Deadlines were more often missed than met, not because of indolence but because of the need to check and double-check everything. This led to the inevitable exchange of letters, with publishers complaining at the delay and the author explaining the importance of the manuscript being correct. The feeling of antipathy was mutual:

> *I have forgotten the particular incidents of the opening of the 6th Seal but I know there is somewhere an uncomfortable place mentioned in which there will no doubt be room for publishers, and bootmakers, who next to the former inflict the greatest misery on unoffending mortals.*

In 1899 Newton was awarded the Gold Medal of the Royal Society, the first ornithologist to receive such an honour. When making the award, Lord Lister stated that progress in ornithology in Britain was due to his 'critical, suggestive

and stimulating influence'. He was awarded the Gold Medal of the Linnean
Society the following year.

THE BRITISH ORNITHOLOGISTS' CLUB

It was Richard Sharpe's idea to form a club with regular meetings in London
for ornithologists to discuss matters of mutual interest. The inaugural meeting
was held at a hotel in Covent Garden in October 1892, with Philip Sclater in the
chair. Of the mainstream ornithologists Sharpe, Sclater, Seebohm and Saunders
were the only ones present. The group agreed to have meetings on the third
Wednesday in the months October to June, and that the proceedings would be
published in a new journal, the *Bulletin of the British Ornithologists' Club*. Sharpe
was appointed its editor. By the second meeting a membership of sixty was
announced. The general form of the meeting revolved around the systematic
and faunistic studies. Commonly, specimens were displayed and members such
as Sharpe and Ernst Hartert, the two principal systematists of the late nineteenth
and early twentieth century, presented proposals for the nomenclature of
previously undescribed species, as well as alterations to the nomenclature or
taxonomic position of previously described birds. Although it is fair to point out
that the Cambridge men were ageing, it is noticeable that they seemed to play
little part in the BOC, perhaps because the meetings were in London – but it is
conceivable that the BOC was formed in part to move the 'power base' away from
Cambridge and back to London. There is certainly an unwritten sense of a
possible rivalry with the BOU, and neither Sharpe nor Hartert was ever close
to the centre of the BOU.

NEWTON'S LATE YEARS

Newton's later years were productive, and the *Dictionary* did not appear until he
was well into his sixties. The death in 1897 of his brother Edward, however,
affected him profoundly and his friends testified to the change, noting that the
Professor suddenly became an old man (Fig. 114). His infirmity began to restrict
him more and more, and although he continued working to the end those last
ten years witnessed a gradual winding down. He continued, however, to sound
off: 'the lot of rubbishy naturalists we have about is very great and the worst of it
is that the people of this country like a low class of Natural History writing better
than a high one.' An unlikely newspaper story stating that an eagle had swept

FIG 114. Alfred Newton as an old man, from Wollaston's *Life of Alfred Newton* (1921).

down and carried off a child from its mother's arms elicited the response, 'I am so glad that eagles survive – a few girls and boys may well be spared or even an occasional bull, but there are not too many eagles in the world.'

His general dislike of change became a passion in later years. When hymns were introduced into Magdalene chapel he would snap the hymn book shut before the hymn had quite finished and sit down with a show of relief. One of his letters to Harvie-Brown, dated 1905, contains a short but succinct list of the four things he found least acceptable: 'trinomials, motor-cars, hymns and cats'. When he died in 1907, British ornithology lost its overseer. His former student Arthur Shipley summarised him:

> When once you were a friend of Newton's, you were always his friend. He was possessed of the old-fashioned courtesy of manner, and a certain leisureliness of habit, which made a visitor feel that he was not trespassing on the time of his host. Both in appearance and in character he had the finest attributes of the old race of English country gentleman, to which, by birth, he belonged. He was staunch in his friendship, firm in his opinions and he invariably followed with a dogged perseverance that which he held to be right.

Alfred Newton's contributions were many and varied. At a time when ornithologists were largely concerned with collections, the discovery of new species, and the definition of the avifaunas of previously undescribed parts of the world, Newton remained firmly interested in the birds of Britain, not just in their status but also in their conservation. Yet ultimately his importance lies in the fact that unlike many of his contemporaries he was a zoologist in the widest sense of the word and his interest in birds was the result of their biological interest – hence his excitement in, and instant acceptance of, Darwin's theory of evolution. As a scientist his obsession with accuracy, while the bane of many an editor or publisher, meant that his published work carried both authority and respect. His *Dictionary of Birds* was a masterpiece, so different from any other contemporary publication, and once again biologically based. Newton was perhaps the first person in Britain to study birds in the wider zoological or even biological context. Newton was also a visionary, seeing all too well the problems that would follow industrial and agricultural development, seeing how Darwinian theory could be applied to the ecology of birds – both areas that are the centre of study nearly a century later. In short, he was ahead of all the others – a great figure at the end of the age of great figures.

CHAPTER 11

Theories of Classification, the National Collection and the Catalogue of Birds

It is chiefly through the instinct to kill that man achieves intimacy with the life of nature.

Kenneth Clark, *The Faber Book of Aphorisms* (1964)

T HE VICTORIANS WERE passionate collectors, and the ornithologists of the nineteenth century were no exception. Beginning for some as early as their childhood, ornithology meant shooting and stuffing specimens – gathered initially from the vicinity in which they lived – and using the skins (and eggs) to begin a personal collection. The ornithologist of this period was also a traveller, visiting any part of the globe for the purpose of collecting the local avifauna and bringing the skins back to Britain to be catalogued and/or placed on display. Even the vaguest sense of science dictated that the catalogues and displays must be organised in a principled and defined manner, and thus each serious collector found himself drawn to classification.

THE SEARCH FOR A 'NATURAL' CLASSIFICATION

'New' classifications were published at regular intervals. The author typically began by condemning the various existing systems before presenting a variation of his own or, in the case of more thoughtful ornithologists, a completely new order based on some characteristic(s) hitherto not considered.

The obsession with systematics was by no means restricted to Britain. Indeed in many respects the path was blazed by Continental anatomists and ornithologists – none perhaps more so than the French anatomist Cuvier, whose classification system was widely used. The German Illiger also, according to Newton, produced a 'classification quite new, and made a step distinctly in advance of anything that had before appeared'. In order to avoid getting bogged down in technical anatomical detail I will resist the temptation to describe the various systems (for further information see Newton et al., 1896; Stresemann, 1975; Walters, 2003). As the nineteenth century progressed, a new generation of classifiers searched for the 'perfect' system. Needless to say, many of these systems were as eccentric as they were uninformed.

The Quinary system

Natural history has always attracted eccentrics, and never was this better demonstrated than in the proposals for the various geometrically based systems of classification. Charles Bonnet, a Swiss entomologist, suggested a ladder of progression, while others thought a system of interrelated circles or some other geometrical shape was the right approach. The idea of circles was originally put forward by W. S. MacLeay in 1819 in his *Horae entomologicae*, and it appealed sufficiently to Nicholas Vigors, Secretary of the Zoological Society, to persuade him to publish a treatise *Observations on the Natural Affinities That Connect the Orders and Families of Birds*. Vigors suggested that the natural characteristics of birds allowed a circular arrangement for classification; this became known first as the 'Circular system of affinities' and later, as it was based on the number five, with five groups of birds, five families per group, etc., it was dubbed by many the 'Quinary system'. This kind of thinking was given the overall name of natural philosophy, and among its keenest supporters was William Swainson, who took over the Quinary system and made it his own.

Swainson was born in 1789 and, being interested in natural history as a child, he collected and drew as many creatures as he could find. He left school in Liverpool at the age of fourteen and went with the army to Sicily from 1807 to 1809. During this time he published a booklet, *Instructions for Collecting and Preserving Subjects of Natural History and Botany*. When he returned to England he was chosen for an expedition to Brazil in 1816, and from Brazil he returned with many specimens, including 760 bird skins. He then 'worked' the Brazil specimens, describing some new species, and used his skills as a competent lithographer to produce illustrations of his subjects, resulting in publications such as *Zoological Illustrations* and *Ornithological Drawings*. He spent most of his later years living among the London zoological circle, expounding his theories and publishing criticisms on all topics ornithological, especially classification. His book *Taxidermy with the Biographies of Zoologists* provides us with his views on a range of ornithological publications, contemporary and past.

Swainson not only agreed with the Vigors system, but expanded it, producing circles within circles until an extremely complicated, hopelessly impractical diagrammatic system evolved (Fig. 115). Swainson, however, was convinced of the rightness of the scheme:

> we are upon safe and solid ground, although these principles are of very recent discovery … we become as much inclined to question the circular progress of the planets round the sun, as the circular development of the variation of forms in the animal and vegetable creation.

Swainson studied the external characteristics of birds, together with their habits, and did not consider internal structures to be of any significance. In 1836 he published a *Natural History and Classification of Birds*, which was the

FIG 115. Swainson's classification based on circles. From Swainson (1836–7).

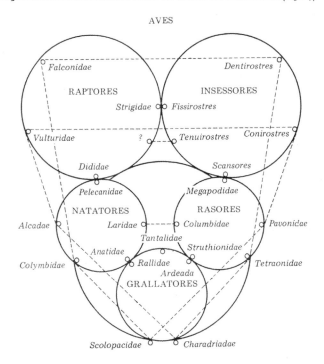

culmination of his ideas on the subject. One of Swainson's suggestions was that 'great leaders in the field of natural history' had the right to 'clean up' scientific nomenclature from time to time and 'choose' for a species from among good or bad names that which they deemed most appropriate. However, Swainson alienated many with the vigour and tenacity of his argument, and feeling somewhat unloved – probably justifiably – he emigrated in 1840 to New Zealand, where he died fifteen years later.

Among his difficulties, Swainson had a famous disagreement with Charles Waterton that was both petty and personal. Waterton, the owner of Walton Hall in Yorkshire, was a Roman Catholic, and was thus excluded by law from most of the usual pursuits open to his class, including the Army and Parliament. He was therefore sent to Demerara, in what is now Guyana, to manage a plantation belonging to his family. Waterton was famous in his day thanks to his book *Wanderings in South America*. The ornithological content was minimal, the book being about riding a cayman along the riverbank, wrestling with an anaconda, and battling alone barefoot through the jungle with vampire bats sucking blood from his toes – at best exaggerated, at worst made up. Despite the fiction, or perhaps because of it, the book sold well.

Waterton's publications were more popular than scientific, mostly appearing in the *Magazine of Natural History*, with titles such as 'The habits of the barn owl and the benefits it confers on man', and he produced a book, *Essays on Natural History, Chiefly Ornithology*, which was almost entirely a compendium of these articles. His work was generally sound, based on good ecological studies, yet on occasion so short of dispassionate assessment as to be entirely wrong.

In 1837 Waterton produced a privately printed polemic with the title *An Ornithological Letter to William Swainson*, a rambling and bitter attack of some fifteen pages. Swainson had for some reason taken it into his head to produce an avifauna of Demerara and had written to Waterton to pick his brain when Demerara, as far as Waterton was concerned, was his province. The letter attacked everything associated with Swainson: his *Classification* book, his methods of specimen preservation, and his support for Audubon's *Birds of America*. Waterton produced some memorable phrases including:

> *you have given us a series of Circles which would puzzle Sir Isaac Newton himself; and which will tend to scare nine-tenths of the votaries of ornithology clear out of the field. Your nomenclature has caused me jaw-ache.*

While Swainson was the possessor of a wonderfully innovative mind, Waterton, sadly, was not. Furthermore, Waterton was guilty of reacting critically to the work

FIG 116. Head of a barn owl, from J. M. W. Turner's *Ornithological Collection.* From Hill's *Turner's Birds* (1988).

of others without evidence, he was constantly sniping about Yarrell's *History of British Birds* in his letters to George Ord, an American ornithologist (Irwin, 1955), and he justified Swainson's criticism of him that he was unscientific by his dismissive criticism of Jenner's cuckoo studies.

Altogether it was an extraordinary broadside from an extraordinary man which may well have played a part in Swainson's subsequent decision to quit Britain. Swainson, who died ten years before Waterton, seems to have given no answer to the Waterton letter.

The Strickland rules

The Quinary system allowed for considerable invention. On the Continent, Johan Jakob Kaup produced a system in 1854 based on the five points of a star (Fig. 117). Small wonder that MacGillivray, for one, made fun of these geometrical ideas. But the one constant in the search was the idea that there was a 'natural' system, as if the birds themselves had a predetermined order and we hadn't figured it out.

The Englishman who began to attack these 'natural philosophers' was Hugh Strickland. He was determined to bring some order to the chaos, and he had no time for fanciful geometric shapes, relying instead on morphological features which could be seen to be constant in groups of birds. It was this reliance that led him to class the dodo as a flightless pigeon – as is now accepted – in contrast to other workers, who variously considered it to be anything from a sort of ostrich to a bird of prey.

Strickland was born in Yorkshire in 1811, and after studying natural sciences

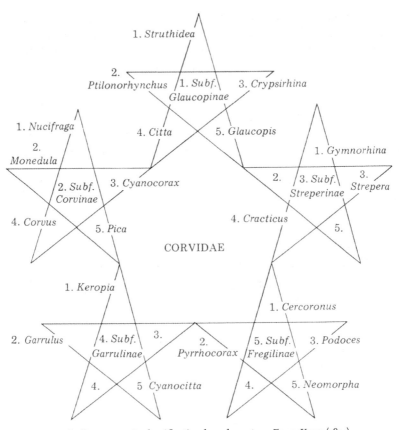

FIG 117. Kaup's diagrammatic classification based on stars. From Kaup (1854).

at Oxford and getting his MA in 1835 he travelled to the Near East on a scientific journey with the geologist W. J. Hamilton. In July 1845 he married the daughter of Sir William Jardine. His wife was a skilled painter, and they travelled quite extensively on the Continent after their marriage. Strickland was, however, primarily interested in geology and in 1850 he was appointed Reader in Geology at Oxford. His demise at the early age of 42 was due to a railway accident which has all the hallmarks of a Whitehall farce involving the absent-minded professor. He had been examining part of the geology of a railway cutting when he saw a goods train coming down the line. In order to avoid it he removed himself to the other line, where he was run over by a speeding passenger train that came around the corner in the opposite direction.

Strickland's collection of skins formed the basis of the collection now lodged in the Cambridge University Zoology Museum (he seems to have been unusual in that most of his collection was kept in drawers rather then mounted, an idea he is said to have copied from Swainson). His significance in ornithology is that he was the instigator of a committee appointed by the British Association to consider classification in the light of the controversies raging at the time. The terms of reference were clearly stated: 'a committee consisting of Mr C. Darwin, Professor Henslow, Rev. L. Jenyns, Mr W. Ogilby, Mr J. Phillips, Dr Richardson, Mr H. E. Strickland (reporter) and Mr J. O. Westwood be appointed to consider rules by which the Nomenclature of Zoology may be established on a uniform and permanent basis.'

The rules drawn up by the committee, intended to be used in all British zoological classification and nomenclature, were published in 1842, and became known as the Strickland Code. The Code was based on the twelfth edition of the *Systema naturae*, and allowed changes only when circumstances warranted, such as where the nomenclature was shown to be no longer appropriate, so that names could no longer be altered arbitrarily. One of Strickland's recommendations was that the specific name should not repeat the name of the genus (as in *Carduelis carduelis*, the present scientific name for goldfinch; Fig. 118).

FIG 118. Goldfinches, from John Gould's *Birds of Great Britain* (1862–73).

The Strickland Code was adopted in many countries, until the Americans in the 1890s wished to use other rules of their own making. At this time most British ornithologists rallied to its defence, not least because it had provided stability for more than fifty years.

THE NATIONAL COLLECTION – THE NATURAL HISTORY MUSEUM

The founding of the the Natural History Museum [originally the British Museum (Natural History)] can can be said to have taken place on the death of Sir Hans Sloane in 1753. Sloane was concerned that his collections should 'remain together' and be sited in London, 'where they may by the great confluence of people be most used.'

Over the first hundred years the museum suffered many ups and downs, depending on the competence and interest of the changing personnel (Stearn, 1981). As far as birds were concerned the significant event was the splitting of the Natural History section into three subsections – botany, zoology, geology and mineralogy – in 1835. John George Children, an entomologist who had been working on the antiquities, was appointed Keeper of Zoology. Children was not perhaps the most likely appointee, but it seems that he was, as is so often the case in these situations, chosen in order to prevent another person getting the job – in this case Swainson. Children was a hard worker, and he was undoubtedly instrumental in the rise to fame of both John James Audubon and John Edward Gray, who subsequently succeeded him as Keeper.

Gray was the first of the two influential characters involved with the natural history collection. Children engaged him to write a catalogue of the reptiles, and thus Gray began a distinguished career in the zoological sphere. His brother George (G. R.) Gray was responsible for the bird collection, and with it the first attempt at a comprehensive catalogue.

John Gray's aim was not only to make the collection under his care the finest in the world; he also wanted to make it available for study, and he set about a fundamental organisation of the material. His industry was subsequently rewarded by the decision of the Zoological Society to transfer its museum contents to the Natural History Museum collection in 1855. This example was a catalyst, and several other important collections were donated, to create a single impressive national zoological collection to rival those in the other major capitals of Europe. Thus the museum became the recognised national centre for zoological specimens.

The following year, 1856, saw the appointment of Richard Owen as the first Superintendent of the natural history departments. This appointment did not go down well with the keepers of the various departments, who were not pleased to have someone brought in above them. Owen was by training an anatomist and palaeontologist, but the antipathy towards his appointment was due largely to the reputation of his personality. He was a difficult man whose intellectual capacity seems to have been matched by an unsympathetic and autocratic style. Thomas Huxley described him as 'a queer fish both feared and hated', with 'a brilliant penetrating intellect linked to sly ways of attaining his ends'. Owen had been greatly influenced by the French anatomist Cuvier and he had employed Cuvierian principles to reconstruct long-extinct animals from just a few bones, the most famous ornithological example being the moa. Given a single femur, sent from New Zealand, Owen produced a paper describing the bird in great detail – which, naturally enough, was received with great scepticism. Yet as more and more discoveries were made about the moa it became clear that Owen was entirely correct.

Owen wasted no time in seeking better premises for the natural history collections. Using all his considerable connections, including Prime Minister Gladstone, Owen eventually, in 1863, secured House of Commons agreement that a new site should be purchased in South Kensington, and the process of design and building was begun.

While the planning process for the new museum site continued in the 1860s John Gray's health began to decline, yet he refused to retire; even a stroke in 1869 was surmounted. He finally retired in 1874 and died a year later, and Albert Gunther became Keeper of Zoology. In 1880 the natural history collections were moved to South Kensington and three years later, with the new museum still taking shape, Owen retired, to be replaced as Director by William Henry Flower – a change that marked the end of an era that had lasted fifty years. By the later part of the nineteenth century, thanks to the industry of John Gray and the political machinations of Richard Owen, the Natural History Museum was established as one of the prime centres in the world for the study of zoology in general, and of course ornithology in particular. The Bird Room was the hub of the activity, probably never more so than following the arrival of Gunther's new appointee as Keeper of Birds, Richard Bowdler Sharpe.

THOMAS HUXLEY'S CONTRIBUTION

The Strickland rules seem to have restrained the nomenclature and taxonomy problems for a while, but the publication of the theory of evolution by Darwin and Wallace in 1858 provided ornithologists with the opportunity, or perhaps the excuse, to reconsider systematics in the light of completely new criteria. One of the fundamental restrictions on pre-Darwinian classification was the belief that all creatures were created by God; that species, however apparently similar, were immutable and had no biological relationship one to another – and inevitably this had influenced the construction of systems of classification. The publications of the theories of Darwin and Wallace changed all that.

In the second half of the nineteenth century the systems of classification shed many of the previous eccentricities to reach a more solid scientific base, helped by the quality of the scientists working on the subject and influenced by the publication of the theory of evolution and natural selection. The main contribution came from Thomas Huxley (Fig. 119) – a follower of Darwin and

FIG 119. Thomas Huxley, from a Daguerreotype of 1846. The frontispiece to *The Life and Letters of Thomas Henry Huxley*, by Leonard Huxley (1900).

Wallace – whose celebrated paper 'On the classification of birds' was presented to the Zoological Society in April 1867. Huxley began with the statement that birds had so many structural similarities with reptiles that there must be some relationship between them. He proceeded to list fourteen shared anatomical features which justified his claim, but tempered these with eight characteristics in which birds differ from reptiles. The first bird to appear in Huxley's classification was *Archaeopteryx*, the oldest known bird at that time, whose fossil had been purchased by the British Museum in 1862. The chief principle that he used in his classification was the structure of the cranium, and his paper was richly illustrated with drawings showing the differing features. He divided birds into three groups: Saururae (*Archaeopteryx* alone), Ratitae (ostriches etc.) and Carinatae (all other birds). Huxley's work quite rapidly became a new standard which ornithologists worked to and adjusted, and much of his framework remains in use in modern classification. A year after his classification was published he produced the first genealogical tree for birds – something that has remained a common way of expressing the evolutionary connection between families of birds.

SCLATER'S VARIATION AND ZOOGEOGRAPHIC REGIONS

In 1877 Philip Sclater began work on the bird specimens from the *Challenger* round-the-world expedition, and it seems likely that it was this work which led him to enter the classification debate. In 1880 he presented his own classification for birds at the British Association for the Advancement of Science, stating that Cuvier's system had been 'broken down' by the new discoveries and something was needed in its place. Sclater's system was really the same as Huxley's, but presented the birds in reverse order, beginning at the top of the evolutionary scale and working down. Sclater said that he had been drawn into the classification debate out of necessity rather than inclination and, with one or two minor exceptions, mainly concerned with nomenclature, he avoided becoming embroiled in the argument.

The great contribution that Sclater made to ornithology was in the study of geographical distribution. Indeed, he was described as the originator of zoogeography. His first ornithological paper on the subject was published in 1858 and was a substantial opening contribution 'On the general geographical distribution of the members of the Class Aves'. In this paper Sclater delineated and named the zoogeographical regions that we know today, and which have

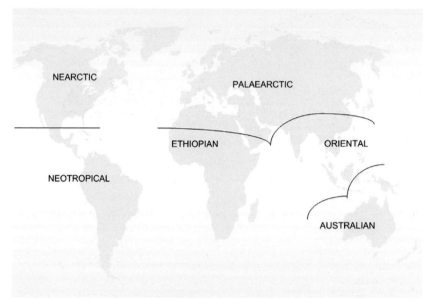

FIG 120. Zoogeographic regions proposed by Sclater, 1858.

stood the test of time (Fig. 120): Palaearctic, Aethiopian (later the Ethiopian and more recently the Afrotropical), Indian (later called Oriental), Australian (Huxley later called this Australasian), Nearctic and Neotropical. Nearctic and Palearctic were later amalgamated into Holarctic at the suggestion of Newton, although the original delineation is still in common usage, as in the modern handbook *The Birds of the Western Palearctic*. The whole area of zoogeography became another important factor in the consideration of classification, as the close geographical proximity of some species suggested a common ancestor and a close relationship. When, towards the end of the century, systematists began to study subspecies, they quickly realised that the most significant factor separating subspecies was geographical distribution.

NEWTON'S TAKE ON SYSTEMATICS

Given the topicality of classification, Alfred Newton could scarcely ignore the subject. Yet, while constantly interested in the many and varied new offerings for a system of classification, he shrank from offering his own, mainly because he knew that no system would ever satisfy him. He worked with both Sclater and

FIG 121. Head of whooper swan (elk), from the Willughby/Ray *Ornithology* (1676).

Huxley on their systems, and often wrote his views in letters, but nothing was ever published.

His views on nomenclature were not merely conservative but positively traditional. Trinomials (employed by the systematists working on subspecies) were given short shrift: 'all this new-fashioned stuff and nonsense about trinomials and nomenclature generally is begotten by self pride (or self-conceit) upon illiteracy, and a very pretty progeny is the consequence.' This attitude was combined with a slavish devotion to the twelfth edition of the *Systema naturae* (Strickland Code). His concern about nomenclature was also due to his great interest in language, particularly the Classics and Anglo-Saxon. Many of his letters contained explanations of the derivation of English and scientific names of birds, with considerable emphasis on the Anglo-Saxon or Norse origins. He was extensively consulted by Professor Skeat, the famous etymologist, and occasionally students at Cambridge were referred to him to be tutored in Anglo-Saxon. As we have already seen he was an adherent to the 'old' names. He always spelt cuckoo 'cuckow' and whooper (swan) as 'hooper', since Skeat assured him that the addition of the W was an affectation which began in the late fifteenth century with no etymological basis (Fig. 121).

THE BIRD ROOM, SHARPE AND
THE CATALOGUE OF BIRDS

What about the national ornithological collection? George Gray's work received a massive boost when Gunther appointed Richard Bowdler Sharpe (Fig. 122) to the Zoology Department just after Gray's death in 1872. Sharpe was undoubtedly one of the most important ornithologists of the nineteenth century. He was

FIG 122. Richard Sharpe. From *The Ibis* Jubilee supplement (1908).

born in London in 1847 – the son of Thomas Sharpe, publisher of *Sharpe's London Magazine* – and showed a keen interest in natural history. This interest was not encouraged by his worried parent, who, as William Pycraft later pointed out, was 'irritated at this marked fondness for what he regarded as an unprofitable subject boding no good for the future'.

So Sharpe went to work for W. H. Smith for a couple of years before moving on to work for Bernard Quaritch, a well-known bookseller, where he was able to study some of the finest ornithological literature of the day. During this time he began work on a kingfisher monograph; he spent every spare penny buying specimens of kingfishers, and every spare moment researching and writing.

His ornithological publications began in 1865 with a note on rare eggs. In 1867 he was appointed Librarian of the Zoological Society, and by 1871 he had completed his first book, the *Monograph of the Kingfishers*, with life-size illustrations by J. G. Keulemans (see below). In the same year he was elected to the British Ornithologists' Union. He proceeded to work with Henry Dresser on the *Birds of Europe* but had to abandon his part in the work when he was appointed Senior Assistant in the Department of Zoology at the British Museum.

From the moment of his arrival at the Bird Room Sharpe got to work on the *Catalogue of Birds*. The original aim of the *Catalogue* was to provide a list of the birds in the Museum's collection, effectively most of the species then known to exist, and to give some further basic anatomical information. In Sharpe's hands it became much more. Plumage variations were described, and for some species ecological data were added, and of course it was also a classification of the birds of the world. The work had been proposed by Gunther but he had probably never imagined that he would find a man so perfectly suited to the task. It took just two years for the first volume to appear, yet it comprised over 500 pages, a huge undertaking. Of the 27 volumes Sharpe wrote eleven himself. He also wrote parts of three others and edited the whole publication, as well as assisting in the various stages of production.

It was Sharpe's reputation that persuaded many ornithologists to donate or bequeath their collections to the British Museum in the certain knowledge that their specimens would be cared for and used scientifically. As if all this were not enough, he used his spare time to continue his own writing, producing several articles based on specimens, a monograph on swallows and several other books, including a four-volume *Hand-Book to the Birds of Great Britain*, a *Sketch-Book of British Birds* and *Wonders of the Bird World* (which was accompanied by lantern slides designed by the artist J. G. Keulemans). He also produced an edition of Gilbert White's *Natural History of Selborne*, and he completed several works begun by others but halted by their deaths, such as John Gould's *Birds of Asia* and *Birds of New Guinea*. He finished Henry Seebohm's *Coloured Figures of the Eggs of British Birds* and his monograph on thrushes. In all these works Sharpe stuck to the outlines of the original authors, even where he did not quite approve of them.

Sharpe was quite unlike most other prominent Victorian ornithologists in that he neither inherited nor attained private means, nor did he have a university education. As a consequence throughout his life he had little opportunity for travel apart from visits connected with his work, and since he was also productive in other fields – he produced ten daughters – he was under considerable financial pressure, which restricted his freedom to undertake tasks which carried no remuneration. He made one long trip to India to supervise the transportation of a collection containing 63,000 birds and 18,500 eggs which A. O. Hume of Simla donated to the Museum. During Sharpe's period in charge of birds (for despite his titular status that is what he was), the collection expanded from around 30,000 specimens to well over 400,000. He was clearly a very generous man, and was said to always respond to begging letters, frequently sending money he could ill afford to part with. His generosity even extended to purchasing collections for the Museum from his own purse if the need arose.

Sharpe was neither one of the founding fathers of the BOU nor a part of the main group running the Union, though he was both a supporter and a contributor. However, he was the founder of the British Ornithologists' Club (BOC). The monthly evening meetings of the BOC in the metropolis, mulling over specimens, nomenclature and systematics, all of it published in a *Bulletin*, were doubtless more suited to Sharpe.

It was inevitable that someone to be found at the heart of systematic ornithology should have clear views on the subject of classification, and Sharpe's address to the Second International Ornithological Conference at Budapest in 1891, *A Review of Recent Attempts to Classify Birds*, is probably the best exposition on the subject. This paper was subsequently published in a booklet, and it charts the various systems proposed after Huxley, including the schemes advanced by Newton, Sclater, Seebohm and of course Continental ornithologists, discussing most in some depth and finally adding some amendments of his own. Sharpe in his own inimitable style provided an ideal analogy:

> *The building-up of the Natural Classification of Birds resembles the construction of a building, to which each earnest labourer in the field of Ornithology contributes his quota. Sometimes the structure has to be altered and amended, but it is seldom that a labourer, whose soul is in his work, retires without having added something to the shape of useful materials … our difficulty in the present day lies in the fact that so many of our foundations are insecure, irretrievably buried in the sands of the past.*

Sharpe died on Christmas Day 1909 at the age of 62 – probably from exhaustion! All those who wrote about him after his death emphasised not just his energy and industry but his knowledge, which was considered unrivalled. One of his obituaries stated that of the estimated 18,000 species of birds in the world Sharpe could name almost any one on sight. Another bemoaned the fact that Sharpe took much of his knowledge with him to the grave, since he never found the time to write it all down.

Sharpe took the ornithological collections of the Natural History Museum into the twentieth century, and for the next thirty years the Bird Room became the unchallenged focus of establishment ornithology. And the professional occupants of that room were, by association, in the most prestigious positions in British ornithology.

The *Catalogue of Birds* (1874–98) was clearly a child of its time. Today we might admire the wealth of information, but the presentation – and indeed the information itself –has little appeal. Newton did not think highly of the *Catalogue*, as he explained to Tristram: 'you are easily pleased if you can find delight in B.M. Cats. as a whole a more useless litter was never kitted.'

THE ARTISTS – KEULEMANS AND THORBURN

In the late nineteenth century two artists began to find their work in demand. These were J. G. Keulemans and Archibald Thorburn. Keulemans was born in the Netherlands in 1842 and came to England at the age of 27, principally to work as an illustrator for Sharpe. Sharpe's daughters were colourists, and they did some of the colouring on Keuleman's work. Thereafter scarcely any reputable book on birds was published that did not have some of Keulemans' illustrations. Many of his paintings appeared in the *Catalogue of Birds*, and not infrequently *The Ibis* was able to afford to print an illustration or two. Judging by the standards of today is always harsh, but much of Keulemans' early output seems somewhat unsophisticated. Some of his later paintings, however, were exceptional – none more so than those in Lilford's *Coloured Figures of the Birds of the British Islands* (Fig. 123). Keulemans was twice married and had nine children to support, so it is

FIG 123. Stonechat by J. G. Keulemans, from Lilford's *Coloured Figures of the Birds of the British Islands* (1885–97).

hardly surprising that he was so productive in his artistic life. He was an ardent spiritualist – a fairly common Victorian interest – and apparently an excellent cellist. He died in 1912.

The early paintings of Archibald Thorburn also look very ordinary. He was born in 1860, and one of his first offerings was in the series *Familiar Wild Birds*, a popular general-interest series of books by Walter Swaysland published in the 1880s, where his work looks very amateur. From these somewhat unpromising beginnings, however, Thorburn blossomed into a bird artist beyond compare, and his illustrations for Lilford's *Coloured Figures* are consummate examples of his art. Keulemans was originally to be the artist, but when he fell ill Lilford engaged Thorburn, who ended up contributing over half the illustrations (Fig. 124). His style was a legacy of the great bird painters of the nineteenth century, but in the end he outdid them all, and some of his paintings were hung in the Royal Academy. In 1915–18 he produced his own book, *British Birds*, which contained portraits of those species considered to have occurred in Britain at that time, usually between two and five species on a page, with skilfully painted background. This book appeared in several editions, the last of which was published as recently as 1967 with a text by James Fisher. Thorburn was a great supporter of bird protection, and for many years he painted the illustration used on the RSPB's Christmas card. His work may have been equalled, but it has rarely been surpassed (Figs 125, 126). He died in 1935.

FIG 124. Grey plover by Archibald Thorburn, from Lilford's *Coloured Figures of the Birds of the British Islands* (1885–97).

TRINOMIALS

As the museum collections proliferated, some ornithologists felt that classification to species level was insufficient. Specimens from a range of sources could be seen to differ in definable ways, allowing ornithologists to identify birds down to the level of a subspecies, or, as it was sometimes called, a race. This additional level would be annotated by an additional scientific name, the 'trinomial', and where the third scientific name was identical to the second this race or subspecies was called the 'nominate'. For example, in the case of the yellow wagtail, *Motacilla flava*, the subspecies with which we are familiar in Britain is *Motacilla flava flavissima*, whereas the nominate form, *Motacilla flava flava*, is found in Continental Europe (see Fig. 230). In all classification, not just birds, the nominate form was always taken from the first specimen of the species to be described, or the 'type' as it became known – those specimens that people like Latham had described in the previous century and the ornithologists of the nineteenth century continued to discover.

For the generation who had formed the BOU the recognition of the a taxonomic subdivision below species was a bridge too far, as evidenced by Newton, who listed the trinomial among his four *bêtes noires*. Among the first proponents of the trinomial system was Henry Seebohm, who put forward his views in *The Classification of Birds* (1890). Seebohm, like Sclater, was interested in geography as well as ornithology, and this interest was reflected in the way he matched the two subjects, looking at geographical effects on birds. As a result of his work in Siberia he realised that geographical isolation was of vital importance in the differentiation of subspecies (and ultimately for the development of species), and that where subspecies overlapped they interbred. He produced this rule for the division of subspecies: 'whatever individual variation be found within the range of a species, if it be not capable of being defined geographically I do not regard it of subspecific value.' Seebohm became acquainted with Newton, who was mightily impressed by Seebohm's style and skill at lecturing, as well as by his collection and his exploits in Siberia. However, the Professor had a poor opinion of him as a scientist, noting that 'his writings show him not to be clear-headed or logical' – fatal flaws to Newton. Furthermore, when Newton tested Seebohm's identification skills on skins of British birds he found him wanting. Henry Seebohm thus did not quite pass the Newton test. Nevertheless Seebohm remained an influential figure and the one man of his generation who espoused the concept of subspecies and the use of trinomials.

FIG 125. Tawny owl by Archibald Thorburn: one of the better examples of his early work, from Swaysland's *Familiar Wild Birds* (1883–8).

At a meeting in the Natural History Museum in July 1884, attended by Elliott Coues, an emissary of the American Ornithologists' Union and one of the most influential ornithologists in the United States, Seebohm was the only person to take up the cudgels for the adoption of the American (trinomial) system. He went further in his book on the *Charadriidae* (1887) when he stated,

FIG 126. Tawny owl by Archibald Thorburn: a later painting, from his *British Birds* (1915–18). The comparison with Fig. 125 clearly shows the progression from competence to brilliance.

quite truthfully, that while British ornithologists accepted the Darwin/Wallace theory of evolution in principle, they ignored it in practice. Seebohm argued for the adoption of the trinomial system (genus, species, subspecies) to be used. When he died in 1895 the cause of the trinomial system was taken up in Britain by Ernst Hartert.

THE CONTRIBUTION OF ERNST HARTERT

Ernst Hartert (Fig. 127) was born in Hamburg in 1859. Like many contemporary ornithologists, he began by bird-nesting as a boy, moving into taxidermy and beginning a collection of bird skins, with the victims mostly collected locally with his gun. He also spent his spare time reading and consulting the standard works on birds. He travelled to Nigeria in 1885–6, and to southern Asia, including Sumatra, Perak and India, in 1887–9. In November 1889 he was commissioned to sort and catalogue the collection of birds in the Senckenberg Museum – over 10,000 mounted specimens which had been neglected for nearly forty years. He completed the task in less than ten months, and the resulting catalogue was published eight months later.

Yet this achievement failed to gain him employment in his native country and he was compelled to seek work in England, where, despite a letter of introduction to Sclater and a meeting with Sharpe, he was no more successful. He returned to Frankfurt, continued to write up his views on trinomials, and hoped for a change in fortune.

He did not have to wait long. Hartert and Sharpe had hit it off straight away. Hartert had felt uneasy in the formal stuffy atmosphere of the German methodologists, and Sharpe's boyish enthusiasm and sense of humour cemented their friendship at their very first meeting. It is hard to say how much this was due to both of them being 'outsiders' from the English governing class, but it seems a likely bond. Sharpe was by now involved in the writing of the *Catalogue of Birds*, and when one of the co-authors dropped out Sharpe was able to offer his post to Hartert. Thus Hartert came to England, having scooped up his fiancée and married her within a few days of Sharpe's offer of a temporary job, to write up nightjars and swifts for the sixteenth volume of the *Catalogue*. Hartert completed the task with customary zeal in eight months; and this time, rather than ending up out of work, he was introduced to Walter Rothschild, who had a private museum of zoology at Tring in Hertfordshire. Hartert persuaded Rothschild to finance a trip to South America so that he (Hartert) might collect birds and insects. Hartert, accompanied by his wife, was unable to land in Venezuela and spent a short time wandering the Caribbean until in August 1882 he received a telegram calling him back to England with the news that he was to be the Director of the Rothschild Museum.

From the moment of Hartert's arrival the reputation of the Rothschild Museum soared as he gathered together a huge collection of ornithologia and lepidoptera, which soon outstripped those of most Continental museums and

FIG 127. Ernst Hartert. From *British Birds* (1933–4).

began to approach the level of the Natural History Museum itself – where Sharpe worked ceaselessly to keep ahead. Erwin Stresemann (1975) later described this unofficial competition between Sharpe and Hartert:

> *The conservative and the radical reformer loved each other, resented each other, and competed against each other for the great travelling collectors and the most precious rarities, the more enthusiastically because triumph sweetened the prize. When Sharpe reached 400,000 birds and eggs in 1908, Hartert was already on his heels. He [Hartert] never quite recovered from the early death of his only congenial [Sharpe].*

Hartert persuaded Rothschild of the need to send collectors out into the unexplored regions of the world, to almost every little island, to gather new specimens, a process by which he hoped to gather material together to tackle the trinomial:

> *I agree with Seebohm, who views the subspecies as forms in the process of development. Seebohm wishes to have classed as species all forms that are not related by a series of intermediate forms. That this expresses the nature of subspecies in a scientific manner I do not doubt but I object to taking it as a definition ... I believe that it is right to regard as subspecies forms that differ only in a small variation in size, lighter or darker colouring, or small variations in pattern, even though one does not have intermediate*

forms at hand. This type of nomenclature shows the closeness of the relationship,
whereas the simple specific name gives no indication whether the species are poles apart
or very nearly related.

These words, written in 1891, set out the message that Hartert was to preach
his whole life. As with all other strongly held views on systematics it had its
supporters and its detractors. The whole of European ornithology, particularly
the German and English schools, continued to debate systematics in a strong
post-Darwinian atmosphere. At first this had pivoted around acceptance that
birds evolved and were not created. Those who found the Darwin/Wallace theory
unacceptable clung to previous classification; those who embraced the theory
constructed new classifications. Now another schism developed, with the
supporters of classification to species level (such as Sclater, Sharpe and Newton)
on one side and the radical reformers who wanted to adopt the trinomial system
(such as Seebohm and Hartert) on the other. Hartert proceeded in 1903 to
counter some of the criticism of the traditionalists by defining a subspecies in
his work *Die Vögel der Paläarktischen Fauna*:

> We describe as subspecies the geographically separate forms of one and the same type,
> which taken together make up a species. Therefore not just a small number of
> differences, but differences combined with geographic separation, permit us to determine
> a form as a subspecies, naturally when there is general agreement of the main
> characters.

This book was another of the many texts throughout the history of ornithology
bringing the world up to date with the state of ornithological knowledge, but
in Hartert's case it covered the birds of the whole Palearctic region. Hartert still
had two major hurdles to overcome in the shape of the (still in place) editor of
The Ibis, Sclater, and his old friend Sharpe. Sclater was implacably opposed to
this new idea and wrote that 'the author calls upon us virtually to give up the
binomial system which has been in universal use since its foundation by
Linnaeus.' Sharpe also felt compelled to try and stop the change, and showed
great percipience in his prophesy, as we shall see:

> As for trinomialism, I look upon the subject as destructive. I consider that the burden
> imposed upon the zoologists who follow this method for the naming of their specimens
> will become too heavy, and the system will fall by its own weight. That races or
> sub-species of birds exist in nature, no-one can deny, but to my mind, a binomial
> answers every purpose.

The argument swung, or was pushed, Hartert's way by the ornithologist who became the most influential British figure of the first half of the twentieth century. That man was Harry Witherby, the founder of the journal *British Birds*, which from its inception used the trinomial nomenclature. As a result, despite opposition from certain quarters, the habit spread so that in 1912 even *The Ibis* capitulated. Trinomialism (and Hartert) had triumphed.

GADOW'S CLASSIFICATION – THE END AT LAST?

A bringing together was expressed by the classification of Hans Gadow. Gadow, a German, came to England to work on the *Catalogue of Birds*, and in 1884 he succeeded Salvin as Strickland Curator at the Zoology Department in Cambridge, where he was first Lecturer, then Reader, in the Morphology of Vertebrates. In 1898 he produced *A Classification of Vertebrata*, a list of all vertebrate genera. Gadow's classification, like many others, drew from previous efforts, particularly that of his compatriot Fürbringer (1888), and was based on giving due consideration to a number of factors, internal structure being the most important (Fig. 128). Gadow surmised that as creatures evolved so their morphology

FIG 128. A sample portion of Fürbringer's classification, from Sharpe's *Review of Recent Attempts to Classify Birds* (1891).

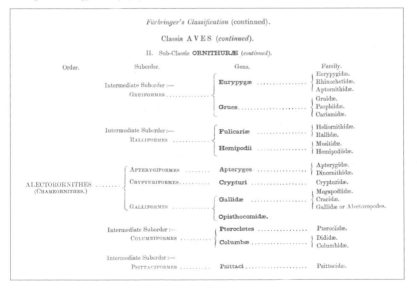

diverged, but mostly in subtleties, so that closely related species would appear similar, if not externally then internally. Gadow's scheme provided a relatively stable basis for the classification employed by ornithologists in the twentieth century, with variations such as Wetmore, Voous etc. adopting the framework of his organisation – until the arrival of molecular biology.

The obsession with faunistics, collections and trinomials spread over into the twentieth century, when it gradually became the subject of some hostility as the interests of the 'ornithologist in the street' moved away from this specialised area. The result was a war of words between the grass-roots membership of the BOU and the established hierarchy, leading eventually to a very different sort of ornithology.

CHAPTER 12

The Twentieth Century: Winds of Change

To-day in the twentieth century ... the classification and enumeration of the British species is so cut and dried, that the attention of the classifiers is now devoted entirely to subspecies, rather than species, or even to small populations of birds in restricted areas.
James Fisher, *The Birds of Britain* (1942)

T HE TWENTIETH CENTURY saw an incredible increase in the study of Britain's birds, so much so that it is impossible to cover anything more than the most significant events in this book. Happily the documenting of developments is extensive, and many sources of further information are available via the bibliography at the end of the book. We are fortunate that several ornithologists have published autobiographical accounts, such as H. G. Alexander's *Seventy Years of Bird Watching* and more recently Ian Wallace's *Beguiled by Birds*. Both give a wonderful flavour of the development of birdwatching, seen from the perspective of men whose lives were devoted to birds. Equally, the *Ibis* centenary edition in 1959 had a number of articles covering the first half of the twentieth century, many of them about academic ornithology. There is a great deal in which the interested reader can find more detail.

The first decade of the new century was marked by an immediate change in the leading ornithologists. Within a few years Alfred Newton, Howard Saunders, Philip Sclater and Richard Sharpe, the four 'giants' of the late Victorian era, were dead and a new generation of ornithologists was in place – Ernst Hartert, Harry Witherby, Francis Jourdain and the Ticehursts, Norman and Claud. One significant change that took almost immediate effect with the passing of the old men was that ornithology moved away from the mainstream administration of science. The global scientific revolution, most of which was laboratory-based, ploughed through the waves like the bow of a ship, leaving the comparatively simple studies of natural history, and particularly ornithology, in its wake – where, sadly, it remained until after World War II. This was due, in the main, to the tenacity with which the ornithologists in positions of power clung to the notion that ornithology was about nothing more than skins, eggs and cabinets, as we shall see (Fig. 129). But in the context of the development of science as a whole it is difficult to see how such studies can be considered to be in the same bracket as atomic physics, neurophysiology or chemistry, which were unlocking many of the secrets of life.

The study of birds in Britain continued to be dominated by men for whom it was a pastime, not by professionals or academics. Most of them were drawn from

FIG 129. An example of a collector's workshop, where bird skins were prepared. From James Harrison's *Bird Taxidermy* (1976) David and Charles Publishers.

the upper classes, educated at the public schools and the premier universities, and served in the army, navy or colonial administration, where they were ideally placed to travel the world and take advantage of golden opportunities for bird study, since many of these regions in Africa and Asia were devoid of any kind of systematic recording of the indigenous avifauna. With a gun and a 'bird boy' a dedicated worker could soon amass a collection of previously undescribed birds. These interests continued well into the new century, and *The Ibis* published many papers with titles such as 'On the birds collected by C. H. B. Grant at various localities in South Africa, April 1911'; 'A systematic list of the birds of Sierra Leone, April 1921'; or 'The birds of northern Nigeria, part III, April 1931'.

THE GREAT NOMENCLATURE CONTROVERSY

The growing knowledge of bird forms in all parts of the world revealed the extent of geographically based racial differences within a species, and inevitably this gave new impetus to press on with the subdivision of species. Empirical anatomical measurements and recognisable plumage variations enabled ornithologists to re-examine their specimens, and to name and determine the limits of the various subspecies. So the process of examination was expanded and the naming and labelling began all over again. Pre-eminent in this field was Ernst Hartert. His pronouncements appeared throughout the literature, and if he had any doubts about matters systematic he certainly did not betray them in his published work. When Sclater attacked Hartert in a review of *Die Vögel der Paläarktischen Fauna*, Hartert responded angrily:

> We cannot arrest the progress of science and nomenclature, and we must alter our views when we learn new facts and know better ... The study of these geographical representatives – or subspecies, as they are now, somewhat unfortunately, called – is scientifically of the same importance as that of widely different species.

Hartert's detailed rebuff of Sclater's criticisms occupied nine and a half pages of *The Ibis* in 1904, and marked the beginning of an open season on nomenclature which lasted well over thirty years. After this, Hartert contributed very little to *The Ibis*, but he worked tirelessly on the Rothschild collection, publishing papers with such regularity that his obituary contained a bibliography running to nearly twenty pages of small type. His *Die Vögel der Paläarktischen Fauna* was published in parts throughout the first twenty years of the century, being completed in 1922, and his contribution to ornithology was marked by the award of the Godman–Salvin Medal of the BOU.

The trinomial sparked endless arguments about nomenclature, sweeping away any last vestiges of adherence to the Strickland principles. Committees, each of a greater prestige than the last, met to 'decide' on both the English and scientific names to be used. On each occasion the aim was to provide names based on a clear and concise system of rules, yet after every committee had announced their findings some eminent ornithologist would find fault with them and thus ignore them, and the publications of the day remained consistently inconsistent in their use of nomenclature. Then there was also the problem of the 'other' English-speaking people across the Atlantic who were adopting vernacular names that differed from those of the mother country (Fig. 130). Furthermore there were transatlantic disagreements about the scientific nomenclature as well, which developed along predictable lines with the 'old guard' opposed to any change and the younger ornithologists favouring radicalism.

FIG 130. Black-throated diver, from a lantern slide by Oliver Pike. The divers of Britain are the loons of North America.

In Britain, and in the BOU in particular, even among the younger generation not everyone approved of all this chopping and changing of names. This was particularly the case among the grass-roots members, whose interests were less scientific. They tried (relatively unsuccessfully) both to halt the continual changes in nomenclature and, latterly, to move *The Ibis* away from the emphasis on publication of regional or national avifaunistic information. Robert Gurney was the author of the first shot across the bows, writing to *The Ibis* in February 1912:

> *I think that many such Members will agree with me in protesting against the changes which have been proposed in the nomenclature of British birds during the last few years ... Would it not be practicable for a Committee of the Union to draw up a list of European (or even only British) birds with Latin names appended, and let no generic or specific names but these be printed in 'The Ibis'? Surely Latin binomial or trinomial nomenclature should be regarded as an instrument of precise description, and not as a weapon of offence.*

The editors replied that they agreed with the remarks and pointed out that a new edition of the BOU 'List of British birds' (to replace that produced by Saunders in 1907) was in preparation; yet if they believed that the publication of the new 'List' would provide an authority for ornithological nomenclature they were greatly mistaken.

The new List appeared in 1915 but it did little to improve the situation. Largely this was because the 1915 list differed from the *Hand-List of British Birds* (Hartert *et al.*, 1912), and there was a question as to which was correct (if either). James Harting, by 1918 a member of the BOU for fifty years and by nature a conservative, put his views on the matter forcefully in a letter to *The Ibis* dated March 1918:

> *I do not like the way in which the journal is conducted on lines at variance with opinions expressed in 'The Ibis List of Birds' 1915. That volume of 430 pages cost a great deal of money and was intended to bring about greater uniformity in nomenclature. In this direction it has not succeeded. Neither the Editor nor the contributors to 'The Ibis' seem bound by it, and names recommended for use are disregarded.*

Harting then gave an instance of his objection, based on the divers. The American Ornithologists' Union gave divers the generic name *Colymbus*, and this was adopted in the Hand-List of 1912, but the BOU 1915 List stuck to the generic name *Gavia* and used the name *Colymbus* for grebes.

Harting went on to complain about changes made 'on the score of priority', and launched an attack on subspecies, changes of name and the use of the tenth edition of the *Systema naturae*:

> *I deplore the amount of time expended and valuable space wasted in describing so-called 'subspecies', based either on individual variation or on the most trivial differences, which are wholly insufficient to entitle them to recognition ... I object further to the bestowal of new names on old and well-known species on the pretext of their being 'British forms' or 'Continental forms'... I take up a number of 'The Ibis' and find birds that I have known all my life referred to by new and strange names, some of which I have never heard before ... But the practice to which I take the greatest exception, on the score of the inconvenience and confusion which it causes, is that of quoting the 10th edition of Linnaeus's 'Systema' (1758) instead of the 12th (1766), which was the last revised by him and published in his life-time. This is a direct violation of the Code of Rules for Zoological Nomenclature [The Strickland Code].*

Harting's letter served as a catalyst for a discussion at the BOU Annual General Meeting in March 1918. At that meeting Harting received little support for his views, which were regarded as reactionary. As a consequence, presumably feeling marginalised, he wrote an angry letter resigning from the Union. The editors of *The Ibis* took a strongly defensive line, explaining that progress meant change and thus the abandonment of the Strickland Code. They explained the need for cooperation with the 'great English-speaking nation across the Atlantic', but they did agree with Harting that the twelfth edition of the *Systema naturae* would be a more appropriate basis than the tenth – before defending the use of the tenth, as agreed by the International Zoological Congress in 1897. They continued by pointing to the significance of subspecies, while admitting that at times the concept was overused: 'we do not think any present-day worker in systematic ornithology can ignore subspecies or their true significance and utility.'

It was a measured response to the old man's criticism. Far less inhibited was the letter that followed from Francis Jourdain. Jourdain, a renowned oologist and one of the principal ornithologists of the first half of the twentieth century, attempted to show that Harting's opinion was scarcely worthy of consideration by listing several of Harting's errors (Fig. 131) from work published in *The Field* etc., including:

> *His discovery that the Ring-Ouzel is resident in the British Isles, and the publication of a 'Handbook of British Birds', in which full details of some 33 occurrences of the Great Black Woodpecker are given (not one of which is worthy of credit), certainly form*

FIG 131. Ring ouzel, from F. O. Morris's *History of British Birds* (4th edition, 1896) – quoted by Jourdain as a jibe at J. E. Harting, who had written that it was resident in Britain whereas in fact it is a migrant.

a remarkable record, but one which will scarcely give him the right to speak ex cathedra on ornithology.

Jourdain lived up to his binomial nickname of *Pastor pugnax* as he belittled the parochial approach of Harting, pointing out that ornithology was no longer the province of a collection of interested parties but a truly international science, and that ornithologists from all countries had every right to partake in the formation of a scientific nomenclature that would be universal. Jourdain's letter was considered by some to have been unjustifiably and unpleasantly cruel.

The controversy over subspecies and their accompanying nomenclature threatened to become so all-consuming that the editors of *The Ibis* sought to bring an abrupt halt to the acrimony with the customary printed line: no further correspondence on this subject will be accepted. But, as is often the case, such a device did nothing to stop the argument, since the argument was unstoppable. The combination of the recognition of subspecies, the consequent use of trinomials, the discovery of 'new' birds and the growth of international studies inevitably meant that the precision that had previously applied to nomenclature (the Strickland rules) and systematics (limited to the level of species) had disintegrated.

In 1920 serious criticism of the subspecies concept appeared in *The Ibis* under the heading 'The last phase of the subspecies', written by Leverett Mills Loomis, an American member of the Union. The substance of this letter was that the concept of subspecies had been exhausted, and that it was now being employed to ridiculous extremes. Loomis concluded with an analogy that echoed that of Sharpe:

> *Engineers tell us that the strength of a structure is primarily the strength of its foundation. The foundation of the subspecies is an unstable variation, and in consequence the structure is collapsing. Hasten the day when we shall view its ruins with the same complacency as we view the ruins of the Quinary System.*

This letter, in turn, provoked an ambivalent flow of opinions on the subject, many of which seemed to show some sympathy with Loomis's point of view yet drew back from condemning the subspecies idea *per se*.

In a commendable attempt to draw all these opinions together the President of the BOU, Henry Elwes, produced a paper in *The Ibis* of 1922 with the title 'Modern nomenclature and subspecies', in which he summarised the points made by critical writers and added some remarks of his own. Emphasising the confusion of the past, he pointed out that the Hartert Hand-List of 1912 had changed the names of no fewer than 226 out of 417 species, and that the BOU List of 1915 had changed a further 100 names. Elwes suggested that the previous system should be cast aside, that priority and editions of the *Systema naturae* should be discarded, and that

> *a list, catalogue, or book of comparatively recent date, [be] approved and sanctioned by a strong committee representing all shades of opinion in this country ... that no new names of species or subspecies should be recognised as binding and properly published, until they have been accepted and passed by the committee appointed for that purpose by a constituted authority such as the BOU.*

It was a methodical approach, but it was the same old sticking plaster for the same old wound, and it was no more successful than any previous attempt to impose a solution.

THE CONTENT OF *THE IBIS* – A REFLECTION OF ORNITHOLOGY?

In 1924 *The Ibis* contained a letter from a Captain J. N. Kennedy which made unfavourable comment about the content of the journal. Kennedy stated that when friends enquired about the BOU he would send them a copy of *The Ibis* to read, which, far from encouraging their interest, invariably only put them off. Kennedy complained that most papers consisted of a 'long list of skins, unaccompanied by field-notes upon the habits of the birds', which he stated were of little 'value for anyone'. This criticism was instantly dismissed. Claud Ticehurst and David Bannerman both wrote, the former somewhat stuffily, to defend the status quo, stating that ornithology was the documentation of the world's birds and patronisingly pointing out that *The Ibis* was a scientific journal. Neither Ticehurst nor Bannerman seemed to grasp the point that the journal had become exclusively devoted to one particular branch of the subject – faunistics, the listing of the birds found in a particular country or district. Indeed, as Ticehurst wittingly or unwittingly confirmed, the ornithological establishment had come to regard faunistics almost as the *only* form of ornithology.

In the same volume of *The Ibis* was a letter from a young Bill Thorpe, whose influence was later important in changing the direction of British ornithology and who was at the time newly elected to the Union. While agreeing the necessity for faunistic studies, Thorpe suggested that research on more biologically based topics was worthy of inclusion in the journal. It would take more than a decade for such suggestions to be taken on board.

NOMENCLATURE PROBLEMS RESURFACE

In 1930 a highly indignant W. Maitland Congreve wrote to complain that while writing a paper on the birds of Transylvania he had rigidly adhered to the recommendations of the BOU List Committee, the latest edicts of which had been published in 1923, yet he found in the same volume that Claud Ticehurst and Whistler, writing about the birds of Yugoslavia, had not. Ticehurst replied that nomenclature was still 'in a state of flux' and pointed out that there were no rules for the naming of new birds or for deciding 'what species shall be included in any one genus'. He further defended himself and Whistler on the ground that many members of the BOU Committee themselves ignored the List in their work! Despite all the efforts over a period of many years, when it came to published work authors exercised their prejudices at will. It was nothing short of anarchy.

One of the members of the committee whose nomenclature Ticehurst had quoted as differing from the List was Harry Witherby, and in 1931 he provided some much-needed clarity with the following pronouncement:

> The name for a bird does not become a nomenclatorial question until the author has decided on the taxonomic position of the bird. This involves, of course, a study of the bird itself and the group or groups to which it appears to belong. I have every intention of following all the Committee's rulings on nomenclature ... but to ask me, or any other ornithologist, to abide by majority decisions on taxonomic points is to ask us to relinquish the study of ornithology.

In 1934 the business emerged once again. This time the protest came from Richard Meinertzhagen (see Chapter 19). Sparked by the latest edict from the Committee on Nomenclature, Meinertzhagen wrote:

> Nomenclature in itself is not a science but an aid to science. As soon as it proves itself the reverse it becomes worse than useless, and I submit that the time has arrived when we should aim at stability in nomenclature.

As usual, the editor defended the committee, somewhat gently pointing out that the changes were due mainly to mistakes made in the original List of 1915.

In May 1935 Witherby once more employed his wisdom and common sense and at his instigation the BOU Nomenclature Committee was divided into two subcommittees, one for nomenclature and one for taxonomy. The idea was to try and overcome those nomenclatorial problems that emanated from taxonomic principles, as outlined by Witherby in his letter in 1931.

THE SALE OF THE ROTHSCHILD COLLECTION AND THE DEATH OF HARTERT

In 1930, due in the main to his deteriorating health, Hartert retired and returned to his native country, settling in Berlin, where he was allotted space in the museum for his work.

Walter Rothschild, however, found himself in financial difficulties resulting from an entanglement in his private life (it is said he was being blackmailed by a former lover – of which he allegedly had more than one). Needing to raise funds on the quiet, he found himself in the sad situation of having to offload his bird skins, and so in 1932, to his everlasting regret, he sold them to the American Museum of Natural History. In 1933 Hartert died after a short illness, thus robbing the taxonomic world of a man who was arguably (with Sharpe) the greatest of his kind. Rothschild recorded his gratitude to Hartert in an obituary in *The Ibis*, echoing what had been said of Sharpe in his lifetime, that 'Hartert knew more birds of the world probably than any other ornithologist.' The relationship between Hartert and Rothschild was delightfully described by Meinertzhagen in the centenary *Ibis*:

> *Though the Rothschild–Hartert association was close on forty years old, their relationship remained formal to the end. It was always 'Mr' or 'Lord Rothschild' and 'Dr Hartert'. Walter Rothschild could never resist large natural history specimens – cassowaries, giant tortoises etc. – and would often purchase such specimens without even enquiring the price. And, as often happened, when Hartert was anxious to purchase some valuable collection of birds from some remote district, he would find that no money was available, a bill having just come in for some large stuffed mammal. This always led to a heated discussion, doors were closed and both would break into German, which could be heard all over the Museum.*

WINDS OF CHANGE

The first signs of a new dawn came from the work of Reg Moreau. Moreau was fortunate in obtaining a 'colonial' posting as a civil servant, firstly to Egypt then to Tanganyika (now Tanzania). In the early days of his ornithological interest he concentrated largely on describing the avifauna of both these countries, but as time went by he became more and more interested in the ecology of birds, and particularly in migration. Although he was principally concerned with birds in Africa, and thus made little direct contribution to British ornithology, he played a part in the gradual move away from the concentration on systematics.

When books or papers by field ornithologists, such as Max Nicholson, David Lack and Eliot Howard, were published, they were reviewed with barely disguised contempt in *The Ibis*. Nicholson's book *The Art of Bird-Watching* (1931), for example, received a dismissive review:

We find some of the chapters, particularly that on equipment, rather elementary ... In spite of the author's assertion that too much reliance must not be placed on peculiarities of plumage, the watcher who knows museum specimens will find that this will carry him a long way ... A census of breeding birds over a limited area is no doubt feasible, though the resultant use is rather problematical ... The statement that no specimens should be collected merely because they may come in useful is surely not what the author meant to say. The whole National Collection has been formed in the belief, not entirely unfounded we think, that their specimens may be of use ... Sometimes it seems that elaborate plans and statistics are made to prove what is commonplace knowledge to the mere collector.

Reading this sixty years later it seems a sad reflection on the narrow-mindedness of the 'establishment' ornithologists of the time, since Max Nicholson's book was arguably responsible for the genesis of the field ornithology that prevails in Britain today (Fig. 132). The results of David Lack's research showing the changes in the bird community as the Breckland forest developed (1933a) were treated with similar disdain, panned on the basis that they were entirely predictable, the reviewer concluding, 'we find so little remarkable in this paper that we wonder whether the time spent on making these observations was not wasted.' Lack's work on nesting conditions and climate (1933b) was also savaged:

We should have thought it perfectly self-evident that birds will not breed unless nest-site factors are suitable ... the Author presumed, instead of finding out that the gonads of the birds in all three colonies were fully developed, a quite unwarranted assumption which greatly detracts from the value of the observations.

The reviewer was clearly indicating that the birds should have been shot so that their gonads might be examined. The only sympathetic response that Lack got from *The Ibis* was when the reviewer was Reg Moreau. A review of Howard's *Nature of a Bird's World* (1935) brought forth more concern about 'the state of the bird's gonads' and ended, 'in the present state of our knowledge the translation of behaviour into terms of psychology is merely to substitute one obscurity for another.'

However, close upon the outbreak of World War II, chinks of light were breaking through. There was a long review of census techniques and results by David Lack in the 1937 volume of *The Ibis*. This paper discussed such things as methodology, population problems, controlling factors, and the relation to bird numbers of food availability, predation, fecundity, disease, behaviour and territory.

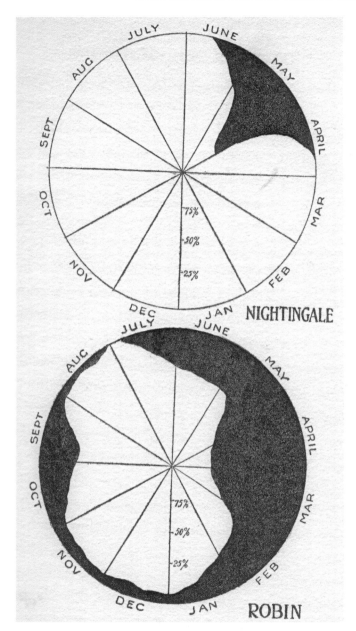

FIG 132. Figures to show the timing of the song of nightingale and robin. From Nicholson's *The Art of Bird-Watching* (1931).

In 1940 there were two significant events. The first was the publication in *The Ibis* of David Lack's robin studies, the first truly ecologically based large work to be published in the journal. There had been several other smaller offerings on subjects such as the food of the barn owl (Fig. 133), based on pellet analysis, but on the whole all such work was published in *British Birds*. The second important development was the proposal by the Trustees of the British Museum to move the bird collection out of London to Tring. This caused the faunists near apoplexy. The editor of *The Ibis* did not mince his words:

> *The removal of the National Collection – the finest collection in the world – to a small provincial town would be a retrograde step which would so hinder research that British ornithology, which has always held a premier place in the world, would be enormously handicapped.*

The editor intimated that the country's ornithologists were totally opposed to the idea. A voice in favour of the move was the maverick Meinertzhagen, who argued that the collection was not merely for local workers but open to the whole world, and that the conditions at Tring would be more spacious and better for

FIG 133. Barn owl. (Photograph by Rebecca Nason)

both the health of the collection and for the workers. He refuted the suggestion that all workers were against it, as based on only a number of the editor's acquaintances, and stated that the most important consideration was not the convenience of those who used it but the welfare of the collection itself. Bannerman backed the editor's view and added that the whole study of systematics, which had been carried out largely by the enthusiastic amateurs, would now fall into decline due to the relative inaccessibility of the collection at Tring.

THE DEATHS OF THE 'PRIME MOVERS'

Halfway through the twentieth century, quite suddenly the prime movers of the interwar years died. The grim reaping began in 1940 with the death of Jourdain. Francis Jourdain, the son of a clergyman, followed his father's calling, being ordained in 1890 after his university career at Oxford. Jourdain is primarily remembered for his contribution to *The Handbook of British Birds* (Witherby *et al.*, 1938–42), in which he wrote the sections on breeding, his fundamental ornithological interest. He was widely travelled within the Palearctic region. His chief love, or as Bernard Tucker, a fellow author of the *Handbook*, described it, his 'focal point', was his egg collection (Fig. 134). Jourdain was perhaps the last 'respectable' egg-collector and as such he was not always in tune with the move towards greater protection for birds. That he enjoyed the aesthetic qualities of his collection is beyond doubt, but unlike many supposed scientific collectors Jourdain was truly interested in the use of the eggs, as Tucker confirmed in an obituary in *British Birds*:

> his aim was not only to have well-authenticated eggs of all the species in the western Palearctic region, but that his collection should contain sufficient variety to illustrate the range of normal individual, and especially geographical variation in form, size and colouration, as well as show affinities or differences in specific or larger groups.

Jourdain's interest in avian breeding, however, did not stop at the eggs. He was keen to discover all he could concerning the nesting, incubation and fledging habits of birds. Jourdain was a contributor to, rather than an author of, great works. His contributions were many and varied, to such as Hartert's *Die Vögel der Paläarktischen Fauna* and to the Mullens and Swann bibliography – a two-volume work detailing the lives and publications of all of Britain's ornithologists. He was always a champion of subspecies and trinomials.

FIG 134. A classic plate of birds' eggs, from Swaysland's *Familiar Wild Birds* (1883–8).

Throughout his life he played an active part in local ornithology wherever he lived, and he was also very much involved with societies and journals, being assistant editor of both *British Birds* and *The Ibis*, and of course editor of *The Oologists' Record*. He was honoured by many ornithological societies in both Europe and the United States. His scientific persona was uncompromising. When he thought someone was in error he attacked them ruthlessly, as in the case of Harting, and his style was pithy and acerbic. Yet Tucker explained that

> *the belligerent qualities ... caused a certain amount of hostility and earned him a reputation for pugnacity which while not unjustified, gave many the wrong impression of his real character. Even when his criticisms were most caustic his own attitude was essentially impersonal and, paradoxical as some might think it, this formidable antagonist in ornithological disputes was in his personal relations one of the kindest and most sensitive of men.*

A year later Claud Ticehurst (Fig. 135) died. Claud was the younger brother of Norman Ticehurst, and his interest in ornithology began as a youth when visiting Norway with his father on a hunting/fishing holiday. After school at Tonbridge he went to Cambridge University to read medicine, where he came under the influence of Alfred Newton. Newton's strict adherence to verified fact was ingrained in the young Ticehurst.

FIG 135. Claud Ticehurst. From *The Ibis* (1941).

By 1910 he was working as a doctor in Lowestoft, Suffolk. In 1917, when World War I intervened, Ticehurst was sent to India, where he served for three years. During that time he was able to study birds in the province of Sind. When he returned to Lowestoft his increasing deafness, the result of an earlier accident, encouraged him to seek a less demanding practice and in 1923 he returned to his native Kent, where he spent the remainder of his life and married, rather late in life, the daughter of a local clergyman. In matters ornithological Ticehurst was intransigent. Using his mentor's standards, and utterly absorbed by the interests of his time, he pursued the birdlife of all the areas he visited to amass a large collection. He travelled widely on the Continent, visiting (among other places) Spain, Portugal, Albania, Yugoslavia, Holland and Egypt.

His writings were prodigious, most, but not all, on matters faunistic or systematic. His great contributions were as editor of *The Ibis* from 1931 until shortly before his death, and then in *The Birds of Suffolk* (1932) and his *Systematic Review of the Genus Phylloscopus* (leaf warblers), which was heralded as a masterwork when it was published in 1938. His reactions to inaccuracies, real or perceived, were often as fierce as those of Jourdain and seem, today, unjustifiably self-righteous. His reviews of the works of the ecologists show his lack of perception of the direction that ornithology was heading, and betray the thinking of the time – nowhere better illustrated than in his obituary by his friend Hugh Whistler, who, referring to Ticehurst's home in Lowestoft, commented, 'at Grove House I was first shown the aims and work of a scientific ornithologist' – the clear inference being that the tools of ornithology were to be found stuffed and mounted within a sitting room. The death of Claud Ticehurst in February 1941, aged only 59, came as a shock to his contemporaries. It also removed another bulwark of the systematic establishment.

THE APPOINTMENT OF A BIOLOGY EDITOR

The year after Ticehurst's death *The Ibis* contained a paper by William E. Glegg on the status of the hoopoe in Great Britain and Ireland over the period 1839–1938. This paper was the first to use graphic interpretation to display information (Fig. 136), although by today's standards the graphs appear primitive.

Also in 1942 Percy Lowe in his presidential address at the AGM explained that over the past year the number of non-faunistic contributions to *The Ibis* had increased, and he suggested that this trend should be encouraged. The BOU appointed a 'biology editor' for *The Ibis*, David Lack, who thus became assistant editor to Claude Grant (who had taken over the editorship of *The Ibis* at the age

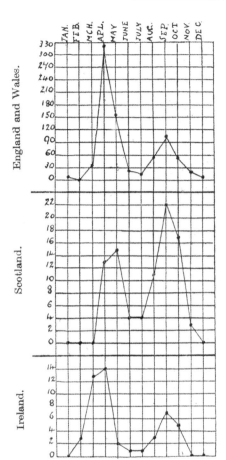

FIG 136. Graph showing the months in which the hoopoe was recorded in Britain and Ireland. From W. E. Glegg's paper on the status of the hoopoe in Britain, *The Ibis* (1942).

of 62 – the war having left few suitable candidates at home to replace Ticehurst). The appointment of a biology editor marked a watershed in the affairs both of the BOU and of *The Ibis*, for instead of the occasional non-faunistic paper almost every issue had at least one, and some had two or even more. After almost a hundred years it was clear that quite suddenly the collector–ornithologist was in decline. Like some huge gold mine that runs out of ore, the world had been worked out, and only a handful of birds lay undiscovered. Attitudes too were changing, as conservation gradually replaced the exploitation of resources. Last but not least, there was a new generation of ornithologists, weaned on the works of Edmund Selous, Julian Huxley and Eliot Howard (see Chapter 16), who were field biologists, interested in the whys and wherefores and not in the whats.

Thus, as in many other walks of life, World War II marked the end of an era in British ornithology. Things were never the same after the war.

The other important factor was that the study of racial variations had, for some, taken systematics beyond its scientifically reasonable limits – much as Harting had suspected and other ornithologists such as Meinertzhagen had feared. It was left to Julian Huxley to put the matter into scientific perspective.

THE NEW SYSTEMATICS

Julian Huxley's book *Evolution: the Modern Synthesis* (1942) expounded, among other things, the theory that the physical characteristics of races (in birds) were often not clear-cut, and that within a population there was a range of change, often very slight between geographically close individuals but gradually getting greater so that at the extremes the differences were clearly measurable. In the case of the blackbird, for example, he showed that wing length increased gradually with latitude, from France to Norway. This range Huxley called a 'cline', and he suggested that within certain very small and often isolated communities there existed 'micro-subspecies'.

This brought to an end the idea that subspecies could be defined with total precision and, in consequence, marked the death-knell for the conventional use of trinomials in scientific publications. This was recognised by Mackworth-Praed, who remarked in a letter to *The Ibis* that 'in Dr Huxley's view trinomialism can no longer express the facts of biological division in nature, as we now know them to be. What we call subspecific differences are really divisions of highly diverse natures and biological values.'

So Newton and Sclater's early scepticism was proved justified; Harting too, who had been the victim of Jourdain's savage attack. No one denied the existence of subspecies, no one denied the usefulness of trinomials – but it became clear that the division of subspecies was not as robust as had been suggested.

How did this leave the reputation of the champion of trinomialism, Ernst Hartert? After all, much of Hartert's work relied on the concept of subspecies, and few had campaigned harder for the acceptance of trinomials. In general his work stands. Hartert's use of trinomials was justified in the hands of such a meticulous systematist, but was brought into disrepute by less scrupulous practitioners. At the time of Huxley's book very little of this was mentioned. There was no comment from the systematic establishment.

Huxley's book did not deter work on subspecies, which continued, although the quantity of papers on the subject in *The Ibis* was much reduced. W. S. Bullough (1945) made a strong case for 'physiological races', stating that:

> *Unfortunately there is often a great reluctance on the part of many systematists to permit the creation of species, or even of subspecies, which are distinguished only by some peculiarity, however important, in physiology, although they will permit such a creation on any morphological grounds, however slight and unimportant.*

Bullough pointed out that physiological characteristics had been used to classify many animal phyla, and he quoted Huxley's 1940 book *The New Systematics*, which suggested new, wider-based, criteria for the definitions of species and subspecies. Bullough argued that birds with such slight morphological differences as the marsh tit and the willow tit were happily separated by systematists but British starlings, which could be described as physiologically different from the Continental race, were not (Fig. 137). Witherby, now in the autumn of his life, argued against physiological races, presumably because they were based on intangible (or invisible) criteria, and rather curiously (and illogically) he suggested that the Linnaean system and trinomialism were matters for systematists, not biologists, to which Bullough sensibly retorted, 'as though the study of systematics is an end in itself and not an integral and important part of biology'. Not for the first time, as an ornithologist got older he became as conservative as his predecessors.

FIG 137. Starling. (Photograph by Rebecca Nason)

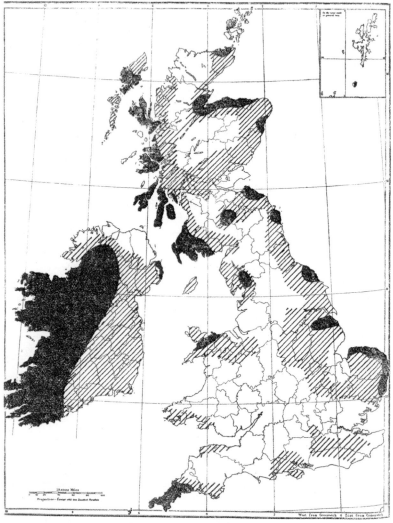

Woodcock in winter. Black shows areas containing estates where the average annual bag exceeds 50 ; hatching, where the average annual bag is 25–49.

FIG 138. Map showing the results of the woodcock enquiry. From Alexander (1945–7).

The content of *The Ibis* began to show real change. Papers in 1946 included a summary of the enquiry into the national status of the woodcock by W. B. Alexander (Fig. 138), as well as articles on the breeding habits of African birds and about clutch size. The biology subjects were subdivided for the first time into breeding biology; general behaviour; ecology and population; migration and dispersal; evolutionary problems; and finally physiology, genetics and morphology.

The policy of expanding the area of interest, however, allowed the publication of a paper by A. H. E. Mattingley on migratory navigation and orientation, which presumably escaped specialist scrutiny to slip into the October issue of 1946. Arthur Landsborough Thomson subsequently wrote to *The Ibis* and complained that Mattingley's paper, although appearing to be an original contribution, consisted largely of excerpts from an unnamed book by a certain Georges Lakhovsky. Thomson further exposed the dubious nature of the scientific content of both the paper and the book from which it was drawn, ending with a remark concerning the original author, Lakhovsky: 'in conclusion the scientific level displayed may be illustrated by a quotation "Among nocturnal birds, let us take the bat as an example."'

The following year, 1947, saw changes to the BOU Committee which reflected the movement away from systematics, with the membership including Landsborough Thomson (vice-president), H. N. Southern, Brian Roberts and Bill Thorpe, and the editorship of *The Ibis* passed to Reg Moreau. Finally, as an indication of the shape of things to come, the BOU organised its first ornithological conference; four days long, it was based in Edinburgh in June and was considered an 'unqualified success'.

CHANGES TO ENGLISH NAMES

In 1949 Max Nicholson suggested a small number of changes for greater simplicity, accuracy or convenience in the English names of birds. He pointed to changes in the past such as 'common bunting' to corn bunting and 'mistletoe thrush' to mistle thrush. His suggested changes were:

dunnock for hedge sparrow
pied woodpecker for great spotted woodpecker (Fig. 139)
barred woodpecker for lesser spotted woodpecker
sheldrake for shell-duck
Mauretanian shearwater for Balearic shearwater

FIG 139. Great spotted woodpecker (pied woodpecker of Nicholson's names). From George Graves's *British Ornithology* (1811–21). This portrait shows remarkable similarity to the woodcut of the same species by Thomas Bewick – an example of copying that was clearly not regarded as the sin it would be today.

Cory's shearwater for North Atlantic shearwater
great blackback for great black-backed gull
lesser blackback for lesser black-backed gull
mew gull for common gull
pomarine skua for pomatorhine skua

Some of these changes have come about, but others have not. Most seem to have
obvious merit and, as Nicholson pointed out, they are all shorter and would lead
to a saving of time and space. Nicholson's names elicited a letter from Professor
Maury Meiklejohn, who applauded the suggestions and pointed out other
possible changes with typical humour: 'we have a moustached warbler with no
very apparent moustache, a booted warbler with no boots, and a marsh warbler
with no excessive predilection for marshes.'

In 1950 *The Ibis* published a short, succinct paper by the German ornithologist Erwin Stresemann entitled 'The development of theories which affected the
taxonomy of birds'. This paper put all the controversies concerning systematics
of the past hundred years or so into perspective. Stresemann concluded, just
as MacGillivray and Newton had done long before, that no system could satisfy
all requirements.

COMPLAINT AGAINST COLLECTING

Possibly stimulated by Huxley's suggestion of micro-subspecies, one or two
workers continued to separate subspecies to even greater extremes. Of these the
most notable was Philip Clancey, who proposed various new races of birds based
on slight differences in plumage or other characteristics. Much of this work
related to racial differences between birds in Scotland and those in lowland
England.

The 1950 volume of *The Ibis* contained a letter which shows that the
protectionists were beginning to campaign against the systematists' desire for
specimens. In response to the twenty-first report of the List Committee naming,
or rejecting, various subspecies, a letter was published from G. R. H. Pye-Smith
complaining that of nineteen races suggested by Clancey only one had been
found acceptable and that 'a very large number of breeding birds have been
sacrificed for no ultimately valid reason, and I am not alone in feeling strongly
that the time has come to appeal to the Union to discourage this type of selfish
behaviour.' Clancey replied:

While I fully and sincerely sympathise with the humanitarian principles which presumably compelled the writing of the above letter, I feel it necessary to draw the attention of Mr Pye-Smith and his fellow critics to the fact that practically all comparative systematic work is carried out on composite series of specimens drawn from a variety of sources, public and private. My studies, which resulted in the naming of some nineteen new British races, were no exception, and Mr Pye-Smith's charge is in plain levelled against the whole complicated issue of collecting birds for research purposes in this country.

Having published so many 'short notes' on small racial differences in this species or that, Clancey had taken the study of racial forms to the very edge of (and, in the view of Pye-Smith and others, beyond) its limits. But the tide turned, and the study of birds became the subject of a new kind of bird-hunter, one with binoculars and telescopes – and ornithology moved back outside, where, by and large, it seems to belong.

CHAPTER 13

Recording the Avifauna of Britain

Oxford in those few years of recuperation immediately following the War also chanced to house an unusually serious and thoughtful crop of undergraduates. One of these was Bernard Tucker ... the other was E. M. Nicholson ... Between them they founded modern British field ornithology, to such effect and with so sure a touch that it continued to thrive basically unchanged and has gone on to influence many of its sister studies.

David Elliston Allen, *The Naturalist in Britain* (1976)

T HE PREVIOUS TWO chapters suggest that ornithology in Britain in the fifty years from 1890 to 1940 was about nothing other than systematics and faunistics. Yet this was not entirely the case. Away from this dominant interest, a few ornithologists were engaged in studies that, although unfashionable then, we would regard today as the mainstream of the subject. As the century progressed, a new generation of ornithologists emerged whose interest was not in skins and collections but in the study of live birds in the wild, particularly counting them, and keeping records and lists.

The earliest attempt to record the status of birds in Britain had begun in the late eighteenth century, and was given momentum in the early nineteenth century by the publications of Montagu and Yarrell. Yarrell was the first person to try to describe the national status of British birds and to list the occurrences of the various rarer species. Around the same period county avifaunas appeared: Cumberland (Heysham, 1794), Cambridgeshire (Jenyns, 1838), Norfolk (Gurney & Fisher, 1846; Stevenson, 1864), Middlesex (Harting, 1866), Berkshire & Buckinghamshire (Kennedy, 1868), Somerset (Smith, 1869), Northumberland (Hancock, 1874), Nottinghamshire (Sterland & Whitaker, 1879), Cornwall & Scilly

Isles (Rodd, 1880), Leicestershire (Macaulay, 1883), Lancashire (Mitchell, 1885), Suffolk (Babington, 1886; Tuck, 1891), Wiltshire (Smith, 1887), Oxfordshire (Aplin, 1889), Essex (Christy, 1890), Sussex (Borrer, 1891), Derbyshire (Whitlock, 1893), Devon (D'Urban & Mathews, 1895), Northamptonshire (Lilford, 1895) and Shropshire (Paddock, 1897).

At the turn of the twentieth century there had been a flood of lists, which were as much to do with defining nomenclature as with recording Britain's birds, but in 1920, mainly as a result of the spate of dubious records now known as the 'Hastings Rarities' (see Chapter 19), the BOU List Committee issued this statement:

> The Committee, having recently had under consideration the accounts of rare or hitherto unknown bird visitors to Great Britain, felt it very desirable that some means should be employed by which these reports might be investigated and stamped with the Authority of the Union before being generally accepted. They accordingly propose that the present committee which deals with the BOU List of British Birds should be enlarged and should in future deal with all cases of this nature, in addition to seeing that the List itself is kept up to date in every respect.

The AGM agreed, and the BOU began the process of scrutinising records to decide upon their acceptability. This was an important development, since it acknowledged that the production of a carcass to be identified was no longer sufficient to merit inclusion in the List. Furthermore, it paved the way for the new generation of birdwatchers who used field glasses – as binoculars were called – and left the bird where and how they found it instead of using a gun to take it away.

THE FOUNDING OF THE JOURNAL *BRITISH BIRDS*

It was the growing interest in the living birds of Britain that led to the founding of the journal *British Birds* by Harry Witherby in 1907 (Fig. 140). *British Birds* began in response to a need for a journal devoted entirely to British ornithology. The first paper in the first number of the first volume was by Howard Saunders, entitled 'Additions to the List of British birds since 1899'. This paper gave immediate direction to the journal, a direction that it not only maintains to this day but one that has now become the overriding interest of both the journal and its readers. There was also an article by Hartert making use of subspecific features to describe certain 'British' birds, and a section of short notes describing

FIG 140. Front cover of the first issue of the journal *British Birds*, 1907.

and cataloguing new species occurrences, usually in the context of counties but also nationally novel occurrences (and among them a large number of reports from the Kent/Sussex coastal border!).

This successful formula continued for many years, with a blend of scientific contributions, mainly from Witherby himself (status of British birds) or from Hartert (nomenclature and trinomials), and also accounts more in the style of magazine articles, which would be considered highly anecdotal today. For example, the articles by Frederick Selous concerning the nesting habits of various species rare in Britain were little more than a recollection of various bird-nesting trips, and Charles Alford's offering on diving ducks in 1920 opened with the remark that 'in all the wonderland of Ornithology there is, perhaps, no study more fascinating than the habits of Diving Ducks.' This type of article became less common as the years went by, and by 1930 the journal was heading towards the more scientific base it subsequently attained, with papers presenting analysis of data gathered by various surveys, including a paper by Arnold Boyd summarising the results of greenfinch ringing and an announcement of a great crested grebe inquiry.

A significant proportion of each volume was devoted to the updating of both national and county avifaunas, particularly in the section 'Notes', which featured occurrences such as Pallas's sandgrouse in England, red-footed falcon in Norfolk, purple heron in Caithness and glossy ibis (Fig. 141) in Northumberland. These notes varied in length from a descriptive paragraph to a sentence that was nothing more than a statement of the event.

FIG 141. Glossy ibises in flight. (Photograph by Rebecca Nason)

By the mid-1930s the journal was established with a breadth of topics that remained its style for years to come. 'Breeding habits of the corn bunting', 'Territory in the Dartford warbler', and 'A census of water-birds on the Highgate and Kenwood Ponds' are a sample of the contents of that time.

THE ROLE OF HARRY WITHERBY

Throughout the first half of the twentieth century Harry Forbes Witherby played the role previously occupied by Newton, and because of the breadth of his ornithological interest an account of his life could be placed, equally appropriately, in any of the other chapters covering the period. Bernard Tucker, his natural successor, described him as having come to 'represent and almost personify British ornithology'.

Witherby was born in 1873 into a family of publishers. He married the daughter of a clergyman in 1904 and had five children, a significant fact only because the contentment of his family environment was a most important factor in his life. Witherby, like his contemporaries, began as a collector and travelled quite widely, in Egypt, Sudan and Iran, as well as closer to home in Lapland, Spain and Morocco. He served in Naval Intelligence during World War I under the command of his friend and fellow ornithologist, Admiral Hubert Lynes.

Like Newton before him, Witherby was productive in many areas of ornithology, but beyond doubt his greatest contribution at this time was the founding, development and consistent support of *British Birds*.

Witherby was a member of the 1912 (Hartert) List Committee, and this led almost directly to *A Practical Handbook of British Birds*, prepared with Hartert, Jourdain and Norman Ticehurst with assistance from Annie Jackson and Charles Oldham, and published between 1920 and 1924 (Fig. 142). The *Practical Handbook* was the natural, and more scholarly, successor to Yarrell. Witherby, as well as being a major contributor, was the editor and production manager – a huge task, especially considering that at the same time he was doing the same jobs for *British Birds*. The *Practical Handbook* was very successful and sold so well that when it went out of print requests were constantly being received for a new edition.

That new edition became an advanced version: the landmark *Handbook of British Birds* (1938–42), of which Witherby was also the director of operations. All the time he was also running the family publishing business, or at least until 1938 when he retired, only to go back to work when World War II required him to. Of the *Handbook* it can confidently be said that no publication before or since

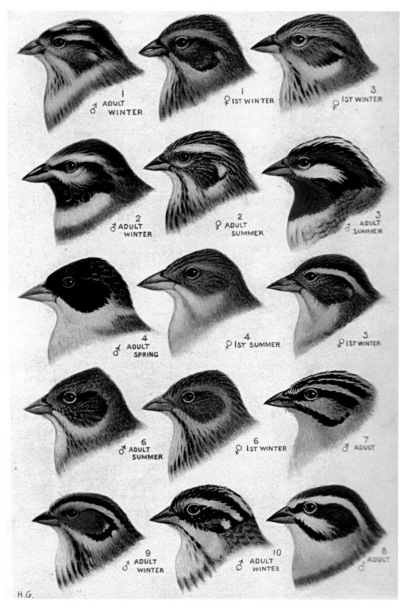

FIG 142. European buntings' heads by Henrik Gronvold, from *A Practical Handbook of British Birds* (1920–4).

has provided such an authoritative overview of the birds of these islands.

From 1909 Witherby was also the focal point of the *British Birds* ringing scheme (Fig. 143). He wrote up the results and the reports, until Elsie Leach arrived in 1930, and the records were kept in the firm's office until in 1937 the scheme was passed onto the BTO.

Witherby's personal ornithological interests began by looking at plumage, particularly plumage progressions and moult, an understudied subject. As time went by he also became interested in geographical distribution and migration. But for most of his life his interest centred on British birds, and particularly the occurrences. He played a central role in the early investigations into the Hastings Rarities, of which he was highly sceptical. At the time of his death Landsborough Thomson, whose ornithological activities ran parallel with Witherby's, explained that:

All that he did, whether in his own work or for the aid of others, was marked by
unstinted care and critical accuracy. His modest and charming personality made him
as deeply liked as he was greatly respected. His was a life inspired by the love of nature

FIG 143. On a trip to Heligoland to study migration and bird ringing, c.1930. L to R: Harry Witherby, Bernard Tucker, Mrs Meiklejohn, Elsie Leach, Wilfred Alexander. Presumably the photographer was Professor Maury Meiklejohn. (BTO collection)

and by zeal for scientific truth – a life rich in sympathetic human contacts, full of service, culminating in leadership.

Witherby was always at the helm. Membership of the major societies was enhanced by his serving as Secretary and Treasurer of the BOC from 1904 until 1914. He was Chairman of the BOC in the 1920s and President of the BOU in the 1930s, and was presented with the Godman–Salvin Medal by the latter in 1938. Scarcely anything significant that happened in British ornithology, between the early 1900s and his death in 1943, did not find Witherby's hand on, or near, the tiller. Yet for all that Witherby was no self-publicist and particularly disliked speaking in public. He did his work in the background with quiet but persistent diplomacy. At Witherby's death there was an ideal replacement in Bernard Tucker, but what should have been the Tucker period was, as we shall discover, not to be.

THE BEGINNING OF SYSTEMATIC BIRD COUNTING

One of the most interesting – and subsequently significant – early papers in *British Birds* was by C. J. and H. G. Alexander (1909), entitled 'On a plan of mapping migratory birds in their nesting areas' (Fig. 144). The authors came to the conclusion that in many species each pair inhabits a definite area, into which other pairs do not intrude. This acknowledgement of the existence of territory allowed them, by mapping these exclusive areas, to obtain an estimate of the breeding population. The paper provided data from two years' survey around Tunbridge Wells, and showed changes in population. In addition to the recognition of the exclusive territory it provided an excellent example of the way in which valuable information could be gathered by amateurs – and was in every respect a common birds census, long before that of the BTO.

Another significant event was the use of *British Birds* as the organ of information to organise a census of heronries, largely the idea of a young Max Nicholson. In scientific terms this pioneering work resulted in both the first national count of heron nests in 1928 – a count that provided a base for future censuses – and the most comprehensive report on the status of a single species ever published in this country up to that time. Nicholson summarised his view in the introduction:

The want of satisfactory data regarding the numbers of animals in relation to space and time is an obstacle of which biology is becoming acutely aware. It is clear that until

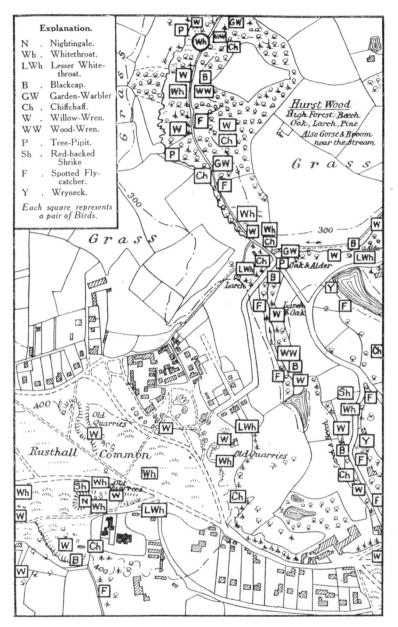

FIG 144. The map resulting from the Alexander brothers' survey, from *British Birds* (1909).

accurate statistics are secured on a sufficient scale research must be restricted, if not actually held up, at a great many points. The small number of observers who are available for any such task, and the obvious difficulties in practice, make it essential at this stage for the object of any national census to be large, conspicuous and easily identified. For such a purpose the Common Heron Ardea cinerea cinerea *is very nearly ideal.*

FIG 145. The distribution and number of nests at heronries. From Nicholson, *British Birds* (1929).

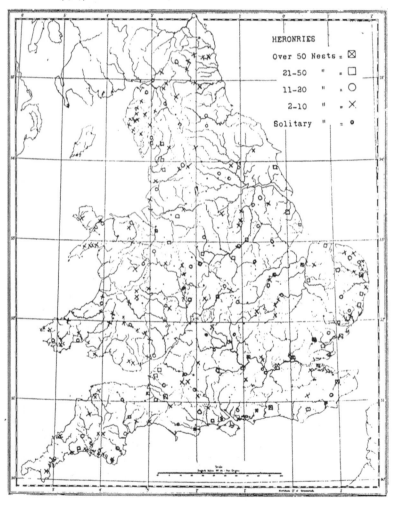

As well as containing the results of the census (Fig. 145), the report examined the relation between herons and humans, and the future prospects for the species, taking into consideration factors such as persecution. It was a very advanced piece of work.

But Nicholson achieved much more than a breeding census of the heron in Britain. His enterprise and organisation demonstrated the practicability of the concept of national censuses undertaken by amateurs. Using the success of the heron results he was able to add substance to his call for an organisation to undertake the regular counting of Britain's birds.

FORMATION OF THE BRITISH TRUST FOR ORNITHOLOGY

When the British Trust for Ornithology first publicised its 1987 appeal for new premises it described the prospective buildings as a 'National Centre for Ornithology'. It seems an entirely appropriate title since when the BTO was founded in the early 1930s it was intended to be a 'clearing-house and centre for the use of field ornithologists in this country'. Yet although the final impetus for the formation of the BTO was provided by the success of the heron census, the initial idea for the formation of the Trust was very much Witherby's. Back in 1907, part of the editorial in the first issue of *British Birds* contained a statement of intent that could well have been a constitution for the BTO:

> We hope, with the co-operation of our readers, to embark upon a series of more systematic investigations than have hitherto been attempted, with regard to matters concerning birds of this country. Our plan is to make organised enquiries into such questions as the extension or diminution of the breeding range of certain species, the exact status and distribution of some birds, the effects of protection in certain areas and on different species, the nature of the food of particular birds, and many kindred subjects.

For various reasons, not least the effects of World War I, this ideal was never pursued until Max Nicholson gave it new impetus, and above all showed that it could work. When he went up to Oxford in 1926 Nicholson organised an 'Oxford Bird Census' in order further to demonstrate the practicability of his ideas. Nicholson used the Oxford experience to persuade Witherby that he could organise a national heron census, and it was the success of this which persuaded others of the viability of a national centre. In order to obtain funding from

FIG 146. Rook. (Photograph by Rebecca Nason)

government it seemed sensible to stress the possible importance of birds in the control of agricultural pests. Thus was born the idea of 'economic ornithology'. In 1929 Nicholson organised a census of rooks (Fig. 146) around Oxford and used the results to show that the predation of invertebrate pests by rooks was substantial, given the food requirements of the species. Using that pretext it was possible, in 1930, to persuade both Oxford University and the Ministry of Agriculture to provide space and funds respectively for a research officer (W. B. Alexander) to work on the economic aspects of birds.

The next stage was to expand the Oxford Census into a national enquiry and to provide a 'directive centre for all kinds of ornithological field work in the United Kingdom', as Nicholson described it, and to have 'a chain of organised bird-watchers throughout the British Isles, in order to undertake co-ordinated research on a long-term plan'. The final structures required were premises and a solid financial base, and to this latter end it was agreed to raise money by appeal. In spring 1932 Nicholson, Bernard Tucker and W. B. Alexander discussed the project and Nicholson produced the name – the British Trust for Ornithology. The appeal was launched, signed by most of the prominent ornithologists of the time including Lord Grey of Fallodon (the former Prime Minister), Witherby, David Bannerman, the Duchess of Bedford, T. A. Coward, Eliot Howard, Julian Huxley, Jourdain, Tucker and Nicholson. Thus the idea became reality with the formation of the Trust in 1933.

The Council of the BTO, in direct contrast to that of the early RSPB, which was peopled by the great and the good, had a very strong contingent of ornithologists.

The Chairman was Lord Scone MP, the Vice-Chairman was Harry Witherby, the Secretary was Max Nicholson, the Treasurer was Bernard Tucker, and making up the numbers, if you could call it that, were Julian Huxley and Guy Charteris.

The initial home of the BTO was in Oxford. Despite enthusiastic support from the then Chancellor of the University, the birdwatching Lord Grey, the set-up was not entirely a success, and Nicholson commented that 'history shows clearly that the twinning of the embryonic BTO with Oxford University was from the first unpopular and difficult to implement.' The university was understandably not keen to play host to an organisation over which it had no jurisdiction, and the situation was further complicated a few years later by the founding of the Edward Grey Institute of Field Ornithology (the EGI) in memory of Lord Grey, who had died in 1933. The embryonic BTO and EGI lived, literally, in each other's shadows, since they shared premises.

The work of the BTO, however, now began in earnest. Wilfred Alexander continued the Oxford Census investigation into the bird populations of an Oxford farm, which eventually blossomed into the Common Birds Census, David Lack led a team investigating the bird populations of heath and moorland, Arnold Boyd organised an inquiry on swallow broods, there was the woodcock inquiry later written up by Alexander (Fig. 147), an investigation into the food of little owls, and a Woodland Bird Inquiry.

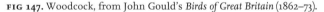

FIG 147. Woodcock, from John Gould's *Birds of Great Britain* (1862–73).

For the BTO the first real challenge was a political one over bird protection. This was at the time when the controversy over egg-collecting was at its height. The Trust, challenged to state its position in 1935, did so by refusing to make 'general pronouncements upon controversial issues' – in other words, its position was not to have a position. Inevitably some people interpreted this as meaning that the BTO supported egg-collecting. Thus in 1936 the Council of the Trust felt compelled to point out that the BTO's aim was the collection of scientific information, and it further clarified the position by explaining that it had no opinion on matters concerning bird protection – a position that came to be respected.

Another advance was in natural-history broadcasting. In 1936 the BTO was allowed three twenty-minute slots to broadcast its aims and in the same year, in response to requests from local bird clubs, the Trust highlighted three species for study: little owl, grey wagtail and lesser redpoll.

The ringing of birds in Britain (see Chapter 14) had begun with two separate schemes, one organised by Arthur Landsborough Thomson and the other by Harry Witherby (Fig. 148). These schemes were subsequently amalgamated, and results published by *British Birds* in the form of an annual report. One of the most significant events for the BTO came in 1937 when the Trust was given responsibility for the national ringing scheme, for which it appointed a committee under

FIG 148. A photograph that could be a depiction of Witherby's life: a bluethroat, having been ringed, is held in front of the second volume of the *Handbook*. (BTO collection)

the chairmanship of Landsborough Thomson, and the scheme was allotted its own secretary, Miss E. P. Leach, whose name appeared at the bottom of the annual report for many years.

In 1939 the BTO was incorporated by a licence from the Board of Trade. This welcome bureaucratic advance was counterbalanced by the fact that, unsurprisingly in the wartime climate, the Trust was barely able to survive financially, although this did not deter the progress of the work. As the war progressed the membership passed the thousand mark and the finances, against all odds, became more stable. Investigations into the status of rook and woodpigeon were conducted for the Agricultural Research Council and use was made of wartime photographs – taken by Coastal Command – to examine the outlying sea cliffs and stacks for breeding seabirds. However, the problems of space and identity within the framework at Oxford remained. Not long after the war ended the EGI was moved away from the city of Oxford to nearby Wytham and a new director was appointed – David Lack. This move meant that the Trust was virtually homeless, since there was no room for it at Wytham, forcing the Council to address the problem of long-term accommodation, a problem that was not finally solved until the 1960s.

Around this time the bird observatories asked the BTO to set up a committee to oversee their work (see Chapter 14) and in 1948 a full-time Secretary of the BTO, Bruce Campbell, was appointed – and the membership subscription was doubled to pay for him! The first regional representatives (unpaid) were appointed and investigations such as the hatching and fledging inquiry (later to become the Nest Records Scheme) and the black redstart inquiry began. In short, the Trust's development continued steadily so that by 1950 it was, in many ways, the basis of the BTO we know today.

SCOTTISH ORNITHOLOGY

At the beginning of the twentieth century Scottish local ornithology began to bloom, largely due to John Harvie-Brown (1844–1916), the most prominent Scottish ornithologist of his time. After attending Murchison College and Edinburgh University, he went to Cambridge, where he met Alfred Newton, with whom he 'remained on intimate terms' for the remainder of Newton's life. Harvie-Brown never married nor followed any profession, and devoted his life to the study of natural history, particularly vertebrates and more particularly birds. He had a small yacht on which he sailed in summer with friends around the remoter parts of Scotland, gathering information that eventually saw publication in the various faunas published between 1887 and 1911. These were among the first such reference works for a neglected country, a birds of Shetland (Saxby) having been published in 1874 and Berwickshire (Muirhead) in the 1880s.

Like his contemporaries, Harvie-Brown (Fig. 149) was involved in the societies of the day, although residing in Scotland probably made him less accessible. He was founder editor and owner of the *Annals of Scottish Natural History* until it became the *Scottish Naturalist*. And one great innovation introduced by Harvie-Brown was the use of square brackets around a record to indicate a sense of probability rather than certainty. In later life he became more sedentary, partly due to his size: his obituary records that shortly before his death he weighed as much as 27 stone.

By 1936 Scotland had its own Ornithologists' Club, a descendant of the Inverleith Field Club founded by George Waterston when he was a schoolboy. Waterston bestrode Scottish ornithology and conservation, starting with the heron census of 1928. The Misses Rintoul and Baxter, also prominent in

FIG 149. John Harvie-Brown. From *British Birds* (1916).

Scottish ornithology at this time, became the joint Presidents, and their studies culminated in the masterwork *The Birds of Scotland*, published in 1953.

In the 1930s the Scottish Ornithologists' Club (SOC) developed branches in the two main cities of Glasgow and Edinburgh, and after the war in Aberdeen. As the membership expanded some professional help was needed, so in 1955 George Waterston became part-time Secretary, as well as being the RSPB's representative in Scotland at a time when the ospreys returned. When in 1959 Waterston became the RSPB Director for Scotland, his wife took over the job of Secretary of the SOC. The SOC developed a library, and following the demise of *Scottish Naturalist* in 1957 founded the journal *Scottish Birds*, with Maury Meiklejohn as its first editor. Like the BTO, or perhaps alongside the BTO, the SOC developed a whole sequence of investigations and has continued to publish work on the avifauna of Scotland.

BRITISH COUNTIES

The 1920s saw the formation of societies recording birds at a county level. This was almost certainly encouraged by a second round of county avifaunas published from the turn of the century: Cheshire (Coward & Oldham, 1900), Surrey (Bucknill, 1900), Cornwall (Clarke, 1902), Hampshire (Kelsall & Munn, 1905), Kent (Davis, 1907; Ticehurst, 1909), Yorkshire (Nelson *et al.*, 1907), Dumfries (Gladstone, 1910), Northumberland (Bolam, 1912), Hertfordshire (Hartert & Jourdain, 1920), Essex (Glegg, 1929), Ayrshire (Paton & Pike, 1929) and Norfolk (Riviere, 1930), with several more in the early 1930s. Local ornithological societies (bird clubs) began to emerge: first Oxford, formed in 1924, followed closely by Cambridge in 1928. These clubs differed from the more stuffy natural history societies in being peopled largely by the new generation of ornithologists such as Tucker, Lack and Thorpe, and the local bird clubs began to publish the first county annual reports. Again Oxford led the way, with a 1924 report on the birds of Oxfordshire, Berkshire and Buckinghamshire; Cambridge followed in 1927; and by 1932 Devon, Dorset, Hertfordshire, London and Somerset were also producing county bird reports.

COWARD'S *BIRDS OF THE BRITISH ISLES*

In 1920 Thomas Alfred Coward produced the first edition of his famous book *Birds of the British Isles*. This genuine pocket-book was written following in the Yarrell tradition: lots of facts, often drawn from correspondents, presented in a

FIG 150. A page of small birds' eggs, from Coward's *Birds of the British Isles and Their Eggs* (1920). Most of the illustrations in the book were the familiar ones by Thorburn, but there were several pages of eggs – which considering the date of publication were probably greatly used by readers.

concise manner with a limited number of illustrations, some paintings from Thorburn's portfolio and some photographs (Fig. 150). Sandwiched between the *Practical Handbook* and the *Handbook*, and appealing to the man in the street or the young person with limited starting knowledge, Coward's book was a great success. Charles Oldham described the book as 'simply-written but authoritative ... it has had a larger circulation and [has done] more to promote an interest in ornithology than any book of our time.' Coward was a man of Cheshire, a businessman by inheritance who was no businessman by instinct, in the family firm of bleachers. When the business was bought out Coward took early retirement, probably with a great sense of relief, since it allowed him to follow his interests. He died in 1933 at the age of 66, but his book ran into three editions. Pocket-sized though it was, it did not provide a great deal of information on the problems of identification. Oldham described Coward as 'essentially a field man ... squabbles and inflexibilities of nomenclators perturbed him as little as hair-splitting niceties of taxonomists ... he was a bird protectionist – albeit a sane one.' This final remark shows that, to many of the collectors, bird protectionists were seen as a destructive force (see Chapter 15). Coward produced articles for local journals and magazines and gave lectures on a variety of natural-history topics but remained outside the established order of British ornithology. His book, however, was an inspiration for many a young birdwatcher in the early twentieth century.

PICTORIAL AND SOUND RECORDING

Following the deaths of the nineteenth-century artist giants, Lear, Wolf, Keulemans and Thorburn, there was a surprising dearth of quality painters. Alan Seaby, George Lodge, Roland Green and others produced some good work, but their best was not comparable with those who had gone before, being neither as pictorially representative nor as artistically meritorious as the work of say, Thorburn. Towards the middle of the century, however, Charles Tunnicliffe began to emerge as a painter of quality. Tunnicliffe proved a worthy successor, but his best work did not become known until after World War II, when Britain saw a general revival of the artistic skill of the bird painters – and the standard then soared to such an extent that we have become accustomed to very high-quality illustrations as an integral part of ornithological publishing, perhaps making judgements of past work seem harsh.

From the beginning of the twentieth century more and more publishers used photographs to illustrate books, journals and magazine articles, and at the same time artwork became less popular. The first bird photographs were very primitive, often vast swathes of tree or meadow with a small image of a bird in the middle. Soon, however, would-be photographers realised that there was benefit in being hidden from their quarry, so they used hides and concentrated on photographing birds at the nest. In fact, almost all bird photography in the period between the two world wars, and not a little afterwards, took place at nest sites. This was one of the reasons that bird photographers came to discover quite a lot about breeding behaviour. Among the main exponents were the Kearton brothers, Cherry and Richard, noted for the ingenuity of their hides. One such was a dummy cow, with holes in suitable places, in which the photographer lay to photograph the unsuspecting subject, with the cow moved a little closer to the nest with every passing day.

Perhaps one of the best-known of the pioneers was Oliver Pike. Born in 1877, Pike bought his first camera at the age of thirteen and ten years later published his first book, *In Bird-Land with Field Glasses and Camera*. He went on to write 24 more books, and built a quarter-plate camera that was much lighter than the standard, to be portable for bird photography, which was subsequently produced commercially. Pike was made a Fellow of the Royal Photographic Society in 1907 and went on to develop cinephotography, including making a scientifically significant film showing the process of a cuckoo laying in a meadow pipit's nest. By the time he died in 1963 he was among a handful of bird photographers with the highest reputation (Fig. 151).

G. K. Yeates was some thirty years younger than Pike, born in 1910. He achieved a reputation for photography that was highly skilled. Yeates was educated at Oxford and after taking his degree he taught at Sherborne from 1933 until the war, when he served in the Army. His *Life of the Rook* (1934) was a combination of a study of the breeding ecology and the photographs that Yeates had taken. In the book Yeates referred to the work of Edmund Selous and its influence on him, and there is a most unusual dedication 'to the George and Dragon at Fordwich and all its inmates in gratitude for all their kindnesses to me.' After the war Yeates produced a book on bird photography, and then two volumes on bird haunts, covering northern and southern England. He died in 1996. Ferguson-Lees described Yeates as an ornithologist who took photographs of birds, rather than the reverse.

Beyond all doubt the doyen of bird photographers was Eric Hosking. Born in 1909, his name became synonymous with the highest-quality photographs, more often than not with the subject full-screen in pin-sharpness. He bought his first Box Brownie at the age of eight and even then used it for commercial purposes. His images became the standard, and as familiar in the twentieth century as

FIG 151. Little tern at the nest: a hand-coloured lantern slide by Oliver Pike, c.1930. (BTO collection)

Bewick's drawings had been in the nineteenth: the barn owl with a rat hanging from its bill, the tawny owl slipping in between the crack of a tree, the Montagu's harrier descending into a reedbed, the hawfinches drinking from a water pool, as well as many lesser-known photographs such as the female shoveler on the nest (Fig. 152). All these images are examples of Hosking's supreme skill in marrying pictorial representation and artistic merit.

How much these photographers brought to ornithology *per se* it is difficult to assess. Most of their published work centred on the photographs, and very little of it contained any concrete discoveries. The photographers did, however, provide a new medium – the lantern slide show, bringing birds to the masses before the age of television and film – and Hosking in particular supplemented his income by lecturing, using his images as the basis for his talks well into the 1960s.

The first known sound recordings of British birds were the song thrush and the nightingale, recorded by Cherry Kearton around 1900. The person credited with the very first bird recording was Ludwig Koch who, aged eight, recorded a captive common shama in 1889. Early recordings were made onto wax cylinders, later wax discs; magnetic tape was not used before the late 1940s. Ludwig Koch

FIG 152. Shoveler, by Eric Hosking, 1941. (Reproduced by kind permission of David Hosking)

became synonymous with sound recordings of birds. German by birth, he came to England to escape Hitler's persecution of the Jews in the 1930s. Max Nicholson, who befriended him, stated that Koch was not at all knowledgeable about birds at that time, and Nicholson acted as his tutor and mentor. They published two books, with accompanying recordings: *Songs of Wild Birds* (1936) and *More Songs of Wild Birds* (1937). After the war Koch was frequently to be heard on the BBC radio describing and playing his recordings, all introduced with his heavy German accent. The quality of the recordings was amazing considering the technological limitations of the time. Nicholson told a delightful story concerning an attempt to record a curlew early in the morning. He and Koch stayed at a little hotel in Woking but Koch, concerned that Nicholson would oversleep, sought him out in the early hours, bursting into the room proclaiming in his accented voice, 'come, it is time'. Unfortunately he had got the wrong room, and found himself speaking to a startled young lady!

With the development of the reel-to-reel tape recorder people such as John Kirby and Vic Lewis began to make recordings, and in 1954 Myles North and Eric Simms produced *Witherby's Sound Guide to British Birds*, featuring 195 species. Inevitably the BBC were very interested in using material for radio programmes and as with other forms of sound broadcasting they created a library of bird song. From an ornithological perspective this archive material has gradually revealed complexities such as dialect, and recordings have been used in taxonomic studies worldwide.

BRITISH BIRDS UP TO THE 1950S

In direct contrast to *The Ibis*, *British Birds* was a constant source of information on the birds of Britain, and by the 1930s the journal was publishing the results of detailed field studies. Examples of this sort include H. G. Alexander's chart of bird song (1935) and a paper analysing the lapwing population in Britain, the results of a BTO survey, which was immediately followed by M. D. Lister's account of the lapwing population on a Surrey farm (1939) (Fig. 153). Almost all

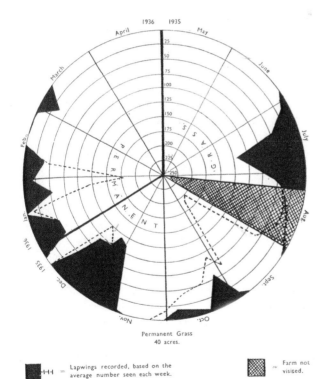

Permanent Grass
40 acres.

= Lapwings recorded, based on the average number seen each week.

Total number of Lapwings recorded on the farm.

Farm not visited.

FIG 153. Diagram of lapwing occurrence on permanent grass, from Lister's paper in *British Birds* (1939).

these papers were the result of the work of informed amateurs, but no less scientific for that. *British Birds* was also responsible for the continual updating of records on the occurrences and distributions of British birds.

THE HANDBOOK OF BRITISH BIRDS

The nineteenth century had been littered with books on the birds of Britain. Some, like Yarrell's, proved durable, while others gathered dust. Yet the twentieth century saw very few attempts to encapsulate all the information on Britain's birds in volumes of grand design. The *Practical Handbook* was probably so good that it deterred any others, and even that was eclipsed by its successor, the *Handbook*. Witherby, Jourdain, Ticehurst and Tucker produced a definitive series of five volumes between 1938 and 1942, all illustrated with colour paintings. Wilfred Alexander chipped in to the final volume after the death of Jourdain, and the acknowledgements for each volume read like a who's who of British ornithology of the first half of the twentieth century. Each species entry provided information on habitat, field characteristics and general habits, voice, display and posturing, breeding, food, distribution, migrations, distribution abroad, description (both adults and juveniles, and even nestlings) and characters (and allied forms). Even truly rare birds such as the Eskimo curlew rated two pages. The Eurasian curlew took up six pages – a measure of the success of the authors in compressing the entries for the commoner birds. Jourdain wrote the sections on food, breeding and distribution abroad, Norman Ticehurst provided the section on migration, Witherby wrote the section on distribution in Britain and edited or wrote the section of description, but it was Bernard Tucker who contributed most. Habitat, field notes, habits, voice and displays were all covered by him. The illustrations provided for the first time a view of each species in different plumage forms so as to cover all the possible identification variations – where space allowed (Figs 154, 155). They weren't quite field-guide standard, but they far exceeded anything before them.

Those readers brought up on the modern *Birds of the Western Palearctic* might be surprised to see the standard of the *Handbook*. Its only problem was that it was published just at the dawn of the age of field ornithology in Britain, and in a matter of a decade or two, knowledge had advanced a long way, leaving the *Handbook* behind.

1st winter f.   2nd winter f. (upper)   Juv. m.
COMMON GULL (*ca.* ⅟₁₀)

2nd winter f.   Juv. f.   2nd summer m.
HERRING-GULL (*ca.* ⅟₁₀)

Ad. f. summer   Ad. m. summer   Ad. f. winter
COMMON GULL (*ca.* ⅟₁₀)

Ad. m. winter   Ad. m. and f. summer
HERRING-GULL (*ca.* ⅟₁₀)

FIG 154. Common and herring gull plumage types, from the *Handbook of British Birds*.

FIG 155. Young of some wader species, by Henrik Gronvold, from the *Handbook of British Birds.*

THE DEATH OF BERNARD TUCKER

The death of Witherby in 1943 had left a gaping hole in British ornithology, but at least he had a full life. Not so Bernard Tucker, who died at the age of 49. Tucker had become the focus of field ornithology, and his early death was perhaps a greater blow than the loss of any other ornithologist in the twentieth century, since his most productive years would surely have been ahead of him.

Bernard Tucker was born in 1901 and spent his boyhood in Somerset. He was educated at Harrow and Oxford, where he came under the influence of Jourdain. He began to collect eggs, a phase that lasted but a short time. In 1925 he was appointed to a Demonstratorship in Zoology at Cambridge, where it was anticipated that he would replace Hans Gadow; but Gadow hung on and Tucker returned to Oxford, where he took a post first as Demonstrator then as Lecturer in Zoology and Comparative Anatomy.

Tucker was a contributor. His standalone output remained small, but his influence and behind-the-scenes work on committees was immense. He could be considered a pioneer of modern identification techniques. Of his contribution to the *Handbook of British Birds*, of which he was assistant editor, Lack stated that 'Tucker's notes on field characters have had a very great influence in raising standards of identification throughout the country', and others have commented that it was Tucker's contributions that raised the *Handbook* above the level of the previous *Practical Handbook* (Fig. 156).

In local ornithology he played a unique role: he was present at the founding of the Oxford Ornithological Society, of which he was the first Honorary Secretary, and he was also a founder member of the Cambridge Ornithological Club (now the Cambridgeshire Bird Club). Local bird recording remained a very important part of his contribution, and he was editor of the Oxfordshire, Berks and Bucks report for twenty years. He was also involved in setting up the Oxford Census, which was largely responsible for the formation of the Edward Grey Institute, and of course he worked tirelessly for the BTO, where he was the first Honorary Treasurer and a regular member of the Council. At Oxford he supported the EGI through thick and thin, as Lack described:

> It may be recalled that because of their relative uniform morphology, birds had been effectively banished from the Animal Kingdom by orthodox zoologists for some thirty years. It was a bold step for a British University to recognise Field ornithology, which zoologists tended to regard as the domain of the dilettante amateur. That this recognition no longer seems absurd is largely due to the Oxford example, and hence to Tucker.

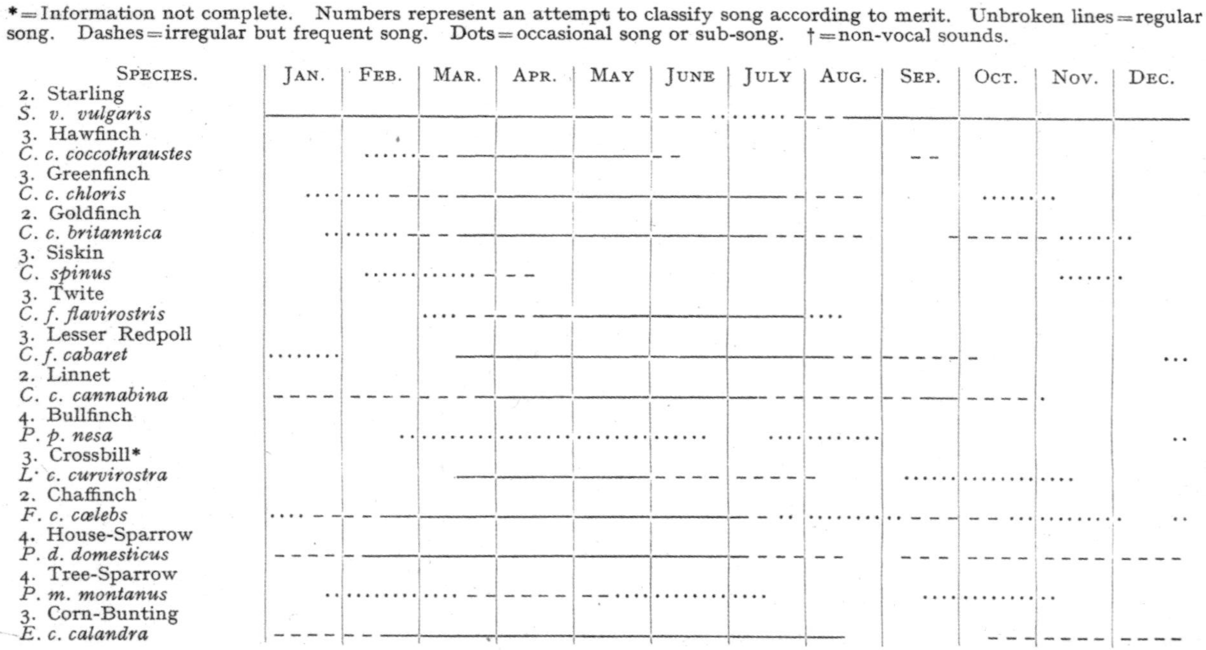

* = Information not complete. Numbers represent an attempt to classify song according to merit. Unbroken lines = regular song. Dashes = irregular but frequent song. Dots = occasional song or sub-song. † = non-vocal sounds.

SPECIES.	JAN.	FEB.	MAR.	APR.	MAY	JUNE	JULY	AUG.	SEP.	OCT.	NOV.	DEC.
2. Starling / S. v. vulgaris												
3. Hawfinch / C. c. coccothraustes												
3. Greenfinch / C. c. chloris												
2. Goldfinch / C. c. britannica												
3. Siskin / C. spinus												
3. Twite / C. f. flavirostris												
3. Lesser Redpoll / C. f. cabaret												
2. Linnet / C. c. cannabina												
4. Bullfinch / P. p. nesa												
3. Crossbill* / L. c. curvirostra												
2. Chaffinch / F. c. cælebs												
4. House-Sparrow / P. d. domesticus												
4. Tree-Sparrow / P. m. montanus												
3. Corn-Bunting / E. c. calandra												

FIG. 156. A chart of the song periods of common birds, an appendix in the *Handbook of British Birds*.

By the time Tucker became involved with *British Birds*, first as assistant editor and then as editor, the job was quite arduous, and it is not surprising that his personal output was limited. However, he continued to make contributions to the journal, including his last paper 'Species and subspecies' (1949), in which he explained that he proposed to jettison trinomials except for those subspecies that could be distinguished in the field. He contributed information on European birds to Bent's *Life Histories of North American Birds* and continued to publish notes on local avifauna in local journals and reports. In 1946 he was appointed a Reader in Ornithology in the University of Oxford, but sadly the illness which ultimately claimed his life set in soon after. Nevertheless he continued to work, even when confined to a hospital bed, although the true nature of his illness was kept from him. An obituary described him as:

> Slight in build and stature, gentle and unassuming in manner, mistrustful of unqualified statements and of snap judgements, Bernard Tucker by no means conveyed to a stranger an adequate impression of the vigour, the clear, firm judgement, the understanding of people and the all-round capacity which his achievements show him to have possessed.

The present-day interest in rarities and minute identification in the field, and the structured approach to recording Britain's birds, was undoubtedly begun by Harry Witherby, but it was brought to the state where it could flourish by the skills and enthusiasm of Bernard Tucker.

So from a haphazard and largely ad hoc culture of recording Britain's birds at the beginning of the century, by the 1950s everything was in place to bring a sense of order not just to recording birds but also, more importantly, to monitoring their status. In the second half of the twentieth century that is just what happened.

CHAPTER 14

Migration: the Scientific Studies Begin

In our own time the migration of birds has become a subject of scientific investigation. It is of concern not only to ornithologists and bird lovers, but is of much interest to general biologists as an outstanding example of animal behaviour.

A. Landsborough Thomson, 1936

B Y THE NINETEENTH century, although ornithologists accepted that birds moved from place to place on a seasonal basis, very little was known about the mechanisms involved, or indeed where birds that summered or wintered in Britain spent the other season, beyond a rather general idea of Africa and northern Europe respectively. And it was still not clear which species were involved, beyond the obvious summer and winter visitors.

Systematic studies attempting to fill some of the gaps in our knowledge began at the end of the nineteenth century. In part this was a response to, or continuation of, the work of Gätke on Heligoland, but it was also due to an increasing interest in the subject on the part of Alfred Newton, who, as in other areas of ornithology, encouraged the development of more formal study. In the late nineteenth and early twentieth centuries two large-scale studies were undertaken, using different sources of information, both with the aim of describing the substantial movements of birds over the North Sea and across Britain.

In 1880 the British Association for the Advancement of Science appointed a Committee on Migration, resulting in the first comprehensive study of the subject. Observations were derived from lightships and lighthouses, largely the idea of Harvie-Brown and John Cordeaux. Cordeaux, a keen correspondent of

Gätke's, had attempted to find out if Britain was as much a part of the migration pathway as Heligoland. Using personal observations and data collected from Flamborough, Spurn and Teesmouth, he produced a short migration paper in the *Zoologist* in 1877. Harvie-Brown attempted the same thing in Scotland, and by the late 1870s, realising that there was a need for coordinated observations, the two men united and sent out questionnaires to over a hundred lightships and lighthouses. It was almost certainly Newton who pressed for the British Association to take over the project. For eight years data were collected, showing both the patterns of movement and the species involved. The final report was published in 1896, written by William Eagle Clarke.

In 1905 the British Ornithologists' Club pursued its own migration study. In a precursor of the BTO surveys, the BOC used observers across the country, looking at a selected number of species – but the study came to a close with the beginning of World War I.

CLARKE'S *STUDIES IN BIRD MIGRATION*

William Eagle Clarke (1853–1938) was born in Leeds and studied at the university there before going into an engineering firm. In 1884 he became Curator of the Leeds Museum and four years later he was appointed Assistant in the Natural History Department of the Royal Scottish Museum in Edinburgh, which was the beginning of his long association with Scotland.

Published in 1912, *Studies in Bird Migration* was a comprehensive review of migration as it related to British birds in particular, and much of it was the result of Clarke's personal research. It began with a short summary of the views of the ancients before plunging into a review of the publications on migration of modern ornithologists, who were largely working abroad – such as Gätke. Yet for Clarke Britain was the most obvious place in which to study migration:

> *No country in the world is more favourably situated than our own for witnessing the movements of migratory birds ... [The British Isles] lie in the direct course of vast multitudes of migrants which for weeks during each season of migration rush – northwards in spring and southwards in autumn along our shores.*

Clarke included a complete list of those species that migrate through Britain, their probable origins and destinations, with a comprehensive explanation of the flyways and a detailed analysis of events in each season, as well as the influence of weather conditions. The bulk of the remainder of the first volume contained

FIG 157. 'White' wagtail, one of the species given detailed coverage by Clarke. From Birchley's *British Birds* (1909).

chapters on migration of individual species: swallow, fieldfare, 'white' wagtail (Fig. 157), song thrush, skylark, lapwing, starling and rook.

Volume one ended with a description of the observations Clarke made from the Eddystone lighthouse, and these observations are as interesting to read today as they doubtless were then. On the night of 12–13 October 1901:

> *Soon after midnight a great increase in the emigrants was observed and the movement assumed the character of a great rush southwards. Song Thrushes, Redwings, Mistle Thrushes, Blackbirds, Starlings and Skylarks then appeared in vast numbers, and were followed by Chaffinches, Grey Wagtails, Goldcrests, Fieldfares, White Wagtails, Meadow Pipits, and Curlews. At 5 AM the movement was again intensified by a fresh arrival of most of the species named and of others, including a Grasshopper Warbler, which struck the lantern, while a small party of Herons passed close over the dome, calling loudly as they flew by.*

In all Clarke spent a month on the lighthouse, and he considered it a satisfying experience despite the tribulations:

*Life on a rock station has, of course, its little trials. There was one feature in the life on
the Eddystone which was decidedly trying to an amateur, namely, the firing, every three
minutes during fog or haze, of a charge of tonite, an explosive producing a terrific report
which can be heard some 15 miles or more. The keepers were able to sleep peacefully
during these operations – an accomplishment I did not succeed in acquiring.*

The second volume was devoted to analysis of the migration at specific locations:
the Kentish Knock lighthouse (where Clarke also spent a month), Fair Isle (where
he spent a whole year), St Kilda, the Flannan Islands, Sule Skerry, Ushant and
Alderney. These two volumes were based entirely on observational analysis, and
considering that there were no ringing data they are remarkably accurate in their
conclusions. Clarke enthusiastically recreated the sense of immense excitement
as each wave of migrants was recorded. To Clarke must go the credit for the
discovery of the unique importance of Fair Isle as a recipient of the most
interesting and often unlikely species (Figs 158, 159). He reported the following,
among many other snippets, in *The Ibis* (1908):

> *I have just returned from a five week residence on Fair Isle, where, in the course of my
> interest, I witnessed the passage movements of no less than 82 species of migrating*

FIG 158. Ortolan bunting
on Fair Isle, a site for
migration revealed by
Clarke. (Photograph by
Rebecca Nason)

FIG 159. Lapland bunting, mentioned by Clarke as one of the rare birds seen on Fair Isle. From Donovan's *Natural History of British Birds* (1794–1819).

> *birds. Among the species observed were several of special interest … the Black-throated*
> *Chat (*Saxicola occidentalis*), Black-headed Bunting (*Emberiza melanocephala*),*
> *Grey-headed Wagtail (*Motacilla viridis*), Red-breasted flycatcher (*Muscicapa parva*),*
> *Greater Redpoll (*Acanthis rostrata*), Ortolan Bunting (*Emberiza hortulana*),*
> *Lapland Bunting (*Calcarius lapponicus*) and the Hoopoe (*Upupa epops*).*

Despite the publication of Clarke's detailed observations, and the excellent summary in *Studies in Bird Migration*, there were obvious limits to the amount of information that could be gathered using purely observational data. A technique to follow birds unseen was required.

THE DEVELOPMENT OF BIRD RINGING

As far back as Gilbert White and Edward Jenner, ornithologists had appreciated the value of marking birds. White placed a cotton 'ring' around the leg of a swallow, and Jenner cut the claws of swifts, in attempts to establish that individual birds returned to the same site to nest in following years – but ringing as we know it today, using metal bands, was started in Denmark by Hans

Christian Mortensen in 1899, and several European countries had schemes which preceded those in Britain. One of the earliest was in Rossitten, Germany, as recorded in *The Ibis* (1904):

> We are requested by the Director of the Ornithological station at Rossitten, on the Baltic coast of East Prussia, to call the attention of British ornithologists to an experiment, as regards the migration of birds, which it is proposed to carry on there. Every year during the migration seasons hundreds, and, in some years, thousands of Crows (Corvus corone and Corvus frugilegus) are caught alive in nets by the fowlers at Rossitten. These birds are liberated, each with a small metal ring bearing a number and date attached to one foot. Persons who capture or identify any of these marked birds are requested to return the foot and ring to the Vogel-warte Rossitten, East Prussia sending with them an exact note of the date and place at which the bird was shot or captured.

In 1907 *The Ibis* reported a letter from H. Thornicroft, Fort Jameson, Rhodesia, stating that he had found a stork 'shot in the gardens of the native village near by'. This bird had been ringed at Rossitten. Then in 1908 Arthur Landsborough Thomson wrote a report in *The Ibis* summarising the marking of birds by ornithologists at Rossitten.

Although the large rings used at Rossitten on birds such as crows and gulls carried an address, those used on small birds did not. Small wonder that no information on smaller birds was forthcoming. Large birds, however, were shown to move within Europe, usually east–west or vice versa depending on the season, and the ringing of storks soon revealed their African wintering areas.

In Britain ringing took ten further years to develop, and then, coincidentally, two schemes were launched. One was organised through *British Birds* by Harry Witherby and the other through the University of Aberdeen by Landsborough Thomson. Witherby's scheme subsequently absorbed Landsborough Thomson's, and the whole enterprise was handed over to the BTO to administer in 1937, to become the national scheme that runs today. At the beginning many birds were ringed as nestlings, but full-grown birds were also caught, using a variety of trapping methods (Figs 160–162).

Initially Landsborough Thomson used his scheme to greater immediate effect, making use of the results to expand on the work of Eagle Clarke. By the 1920s he had gathered together enough information to compile his book *Problems of Bird Migration*, which appeared in 1926.

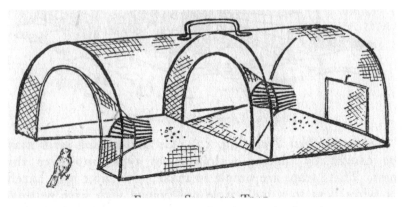

FIG 160. Sparrow trap, from Lockley & Russell, *Bird-Ringing* (1953), Reading University.

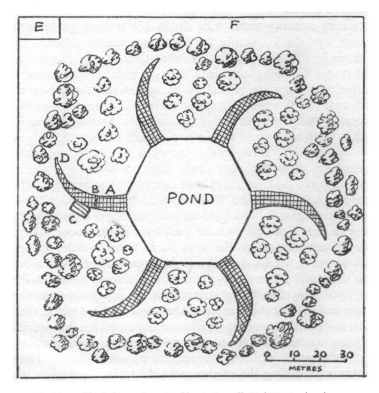

FIG 161. Plan of duck decoy, from Lockley & Russell, *Bird-Ringing* (1953), Reading University.

FIG 162. 'Leashing', a curious catching method for bird ringers involving a net held over a bush while someone beats the bush from the opposite side. (BTO collection, undated)

LANDSBOROUGH THOMSON'S *PROBLEMS OF BIRD MIGRATION*

Although only fourteen years elapsed between Eagle Clarke's magnum opus and Landsborough Thomson's, there was a great deal of progress as a result of bird ringing. Furthermore, Thomson's book, while similar in parts to Clarke's, had a more scientific approach.

Thomson began by quoting from John Legg's instructions for students of migration before proceeding to discuss migration of all fauna. The book was then divided into three parts: an overview of bird migration, special studies, and a finally a look at the evolutionary and ecological aspects. The first part described the behaviour of birds on migration, the routes taken, the effects of weather and 'irregular migration phenomena', mostly irruptions and the like. In the second part, like Eagle Clarke, Landsborough Thomson dealt with certain species individually, but by incorporating the results of the ringing schemes, and drawing on Witherby's publication of results, he was able to shed much new light. Discussing the swallow, lapwing, starling, mallard, pintail (Fig. 163) and gulls, he showed something of the routes taken by each of these species and the

FIG 163. Pintail by Archibald Thorburn, from Lilford's *Coloured Figures of the Birds of the British Isles* (1885–97).

areas of origin, and confirmed, scientifically, that individuals returned to their natal area.

Landsborough Thomson quoted Witherby's finding that British swallows wintered in the Cape of South Africa (Fig. 164). He showed that many Scottish-bred lapwing wintered in Ireland and Iberia. He demonstrated the geographical origins of starling and mallard wintering in Britain, and completed the second part of the book by considering individual case histories of many other species for which there was insufficient accumulated evidence.

The third part of the book was perhaps the most interesting. It discussed the theory of why birds migrate, summarised as follows:

> *Bird-migration is an example of behaviour for which the capacity is inherited. It is an expensive custom and would not survive if it did not serve some useful ends: the advantages of the custom, however, are in part obvious. But the presence of advantages is not in itself a causative force. The ultimate cause and origin of the racial custom must be sought in the past history of migratory species. Granted a useful end, an originating cause and a releasing stimulus – the modus operandi of migration still remains unexplained.*

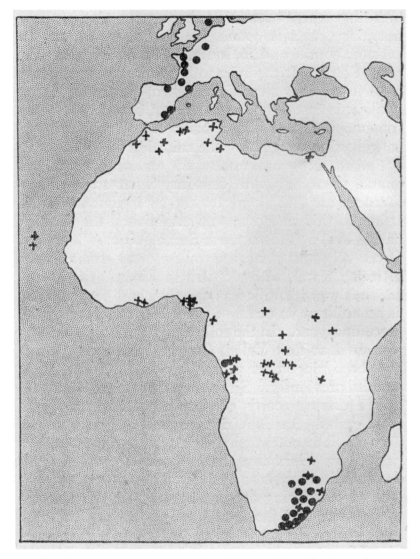

FIG 164. Recoveries of British-ringed swallows, from Landsborough Thomson's *Bird Migration* (1936).

Thomson considered all these ecological and evolutionary factors, together with the 'wider biological implications', based largely on the possible physiological mechanisms that could be involved in the many aspects of migration. He ended by pointing out that 'bird migration offered a biologist the chance to study an especially interesting example of instinctive behaviour', and that 'the general biological issues raised are much wider than the immediate problems of bird migration.' There was an appendix on the economic implications of bird-migration studies, which at that time was becoming a fashionable topic. Thomson suggested that birds play a large part in the control of insect numbers and that without the summer migrants agriculture could suffer. He also quoted the work of Stockman and Garnett (1923), which suggested that migrating birds could be vectors of the foot and mouth virus.

This last part differed markedly from any previous work on migration in the way in which Landsborough Thomson widened the interest in the subject beyond ornithology and took it into the realms of fundamental biological enquiry. Unfortunately most of the subsequent British interest in migration reverted to the basics, and only abroad was a more biological approach pursued.

Arthur Landsborough Thomson was born in Edinburgh in 1890. His father, J. Arthur Thomson, was Regius Professor of Natural History at the University of Aberdeen. His first published note appeared in the first volume of *British Birds* in 1907 and his last paper, concerning a reassessment of the migration of the gannet, 67 years later in 1974. Thomson was an administrator in what ultimately became the Medical Research Council, and his work was recognised with the award of a knighthood in 1953.

From the moment he was involved in the ringing of birds, despite the administrative changes to the scheme, Landsborough Thomson followed its every path, serving for many years on the Ringing Committee, for a long period as Chairman and, one suspects, its main driving force. Certainly his prime motivation was the scientific results.

As the years passed, Thomson's ability as an administrator was utilised by almost every ornithological organisation. He was Secretary and Chairman of the BOC in the mid-1930s. He was Vice-Chairman and then Chairman of the BTO during the difficult period of the 1940s, including the war years. He was Vice-President of the BOU from 1945 to 1947 and then President from 1948 to 1955, and he was personally responsible for two expeditions mounted in celebration of the Union's centenary, as well as for the publication of a book very loosely based on Newton's famous *Dictionary of Birds* entitled *A New Dictionary of Birds* (1964). In addition he served on committees many and various, and from 1967 to 1969 he was Chairman of the Trustees of the Natural History Museum. In 1959

he was awarded both the Godman–Salvin Medal of the BOU and the Tucker
Medal of the BTO, and in 1962 he was awarded the Buchanan Medal of the Royal
Society. He died in 1977. Max Nicholson wrote of him:

> Landsborough, as he was usually called, was a pillar of British ornithology during its
> years of most rapid advance and expansion. He was the most unfailingly reliable and
> readiest with wise counsel and practical aid in all sorts of difficulties. He had guts,
> integrity, a quiet humour, an ability to get on with different kinds of people and a
> terrific capacity for work. Such was his contribution that one was sometimes almost
> tempted to forget that behind it lay a warm, generous and rare human being.

In the mid-1920s Harry Witherby began to publish the results of the *British
Birds* ringing scheme within the journal and subsequently, with the help of
Elsie Leach, this report became a regular feature of the journal (Fig. 165) – and
the general structure still forms the basis of today's BTO ringing reports.

It is noticeable that migration studies received greater scientific priority
on the Continent. By the 1930s the Germans, in particular, led the field in the
investigation of the biological mechanisms involved such as orientation and
duration of flight – much as they do today in looking at the genetics of
migration.

In Britain coordinated information, beyond the reports of Witherby and
Leach, was largely restricted to reviews of the information for some individual
species or families. In 1936, however, Landsborough Thomson wrote a substantial
review article in *The Ibis*, in which he summarised the international advances in
the ten years since the publication of his *Problems of Bird Migration*. The review
showed the enormous inter- and intraspecific variation, for example how in
some species of duck migrating males outnumbered migrating females, how the
age structure of migrating aggregations varied, and so on.

Among other theories, Thomson reviewed those of Ackworth (1930), whose
strange writings suggested that migrating birds aimed for a 'fixed although
unseen location' determined by some 'inherent power', and that during their
journeys birds could easily be affected by crosswinds so that they journeyed in
a curve and ended up in an entirely different location, something he referred
to as 'drift' – a view that Thomson dismissed.

In the theoretical part of the review Thomson considered the purpose and
origin of migration and the factors that might initiate it in each season. He
quoted the laboratory-based experimental studies of two Americans, Kendeigh
and Rowan, who had investigated the physiological effects of temperature and
photoperiod (Fig. 166). Rowan clock-shifted his birds (kept them in conditions

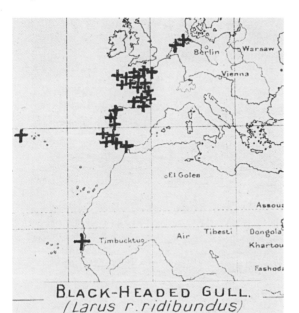

FIG 165. Maps to show (a) destinations of black-headed gulls ringed in Britain as nestlings and (b) origins of black-headed gulls wintering in Britain. From Witherby and Leach, *British Birds* (1931). (Original lantern slides in BTO collection)

BLACK-HEADED GULL.
(Larus r. ridibundus)
Map to show recovery positions abroad of birds ringed in Great Britain as nestlings.

BLACK-HEADED GULL.
(Larus r. ridibundus)
Map to show origin of winter visitors to the British Isles.
+ Recovered here. Ringed in England in February ● ③ Ringed here as young or breeding. Recovered in British Isles between August & March (4 April. 3 May. 1 June).

FIG 166. House sparrow, the subject of Kendeigh's studies on the physiology of migratory birds. (Photograph by Rebecca Nason)

where the amount of light/dark was artificially manipulated to create a false idea of time) so that they mistook autumn for spring and thus on release in November proceeded to migrate north instead of south. Thomson was wise enough to treat these (and other experiments into the mechanisms that trigger migration) with caution, suggesting that:

> The interrelated reproductive and migration cycles may both be expressions of a periodicity reflecting the influence of all the external conditions governing the bird's life: the phases of these cycles may be induced by environmental stimuli of different kinds, or may occur to some extent without extrinsic stimulus by virtue of an inherent rhythm.

This last statement has been recently shown to be true, at least in the case of the garden warbler, by the work of the German migration scientist Erwin Gwinner and his colleagues, who demonstrated that these small birds have an innate body clock which functions to impel migration, then breeding, then moult, then migration, and that the environmental clues are used to 'fine-tune' the innate clock.

One interesting paper reviewed by Thomson was by another German, a physiologist called H. O. Wagner who had undertaken experiments on biological rhythyms based on the migratory restlessness of captive birds. Thomson warned that 'it would appear dangerous, however, to base too much analogy between the restlessness of caged birds – which can probably be induced in various ways – and that which may be observed in the field in birds about to migrate.' However, he was wrong to be dismissive, since much valuable work has subsequently been done using this technique, and this line of research has significantly expanded our knowledge of migratory mechanisms.

Finally Thomson's paper summarised the experiments on orientation which were conducted by removing birds to locations far away and observing their capacity to return, in effect measuring their homing ability. Starlings were shown to return to their nesting area regardless of the direction in which they were taken. Young storks which had been prevented from migrating until all other storks had departed seemed to follow the usual pathway. Most interesting was the finding that mallards taken to Finland from England as eggs behaved exactly as if they were native Finnish birds and migrated in the same direction as the native birds in the autumn. All except the mallard results suggested a strong genetic component to migratory mechanisms.

Throughout the period between the wars Landsborough Thomson was undoubtedly the leading bird-migration scientist in Britain, amateur or professional. Yet as early as 1921 he suggested that our knowledge of many common species was now so complete that perhaps the time had come for ringing to be more directed, and he proposed that there should be a limit on the ringing of some species and a concentrated effort on others. This suggestion, based as it was on the need for scientific direction of the ringing scheme, seems to have had no effect, and the ringers were resistant to any direction that might restrict their activities – a situation that, to a degree, persists today.

BIRD OBSERVATORIES

The concept of a strategically placed (coastal) field station, an observatory, from which to watch migration was given reality just before World War II, largely due to Ronald Lockley's example at Skokholm in 1933. Skokholm was followed by the Isle of May and then Spurn Point, and after 1945 many more were established, most notably on Fair Isle, where Kenneth Williamson was appointed warden. The principle was to keep records of visual migration, augmented by a concerted effort to catch and ring as many birds as possible using the now standard 'Heligoland' traps (Fig. 167). These huge traps were built over and around areas of scrub in a tube of decreasing size. Birds were caught by people 'driving' them

FIG 167. Heligoland trap on the Isle of May, c.1930. (BTO collection)

into the large mouth of the trap and on until they reached the constricted end of the funnel, where there was a 'collecting box'.

Kenneth Williamson's work at Fair Isle set new standards for the observatories. Instead of being merely ringed and released, the birds were systematically examined and biometrics such as wing, tarsus, bill and tail measurements were collected, as well as the birds being weighed (Fig. 168). They were also frequently subjected to parasite hunts. Using Williamson's techniques, such information became an essential part of the identification diagnosis.

Many of the observatories in action in 1960 remain so to this day: Isle of May, Spurn, Lundy, Fair Isle, Gibraltar Point, Cley & Blakeney, Monk's House Seahouses, Jersey, Great Saltee (Ireland), Dungeness, Bardsey, Portland Bill, Copeland (Northern Ireland); to these might be added Sandwich Bay, which in 1960 was a ringing station only.

This period also saw the original ageing and sexing guide, appropriately called *The Bird in the Hand* (Cornwallis & Smith, 1960), which was an accumulation of biometrics specifically for use by the ringer, and this, together with the launch of the journal *Bird Migration*, of which Ken Williamson was editor, helped to put ringing on a more scientific base.

The observatories played their part in furthering the techniques of field taxonomy and helped in the process of making field sight records acceptable, but in the long term the information gathered added little to that of Williamson

FIG 168. A group studying birds in the hand at the Observatories Conference at Dungeness, October 1954. L to R: Eric Ennion, Kate Barham, A. N. Other, Barbara Snow, Richard Richardson, Bob Spencer (with pipe), E. R. Parrinder and (head down) W. D. Campbell. (Photograph by John Burton, from the BTO collection)

himself. The apparent failure to deliver the expected results is reflected in the relatively short life of the journal *Bird Migration,* and in the fact that when Williamson's contract as Migration Officer with the BTO ended and he moved to population studies, no one replaced him (see below).

The post-war period saw advances in migration studies, due mainly to technological developments. One very significant technical advance came with the gradual introduction and availability of mist nets, which enabled ringers both to catch larger numbers of birds and to catch species not easily trapped by the wood and wire-netting cages, particularly species such as warblers. But perhaps the most dramatic immediate post-war development was the use of radar to study bird movements, largely as a result of David Lack's involvement with the development of radar for its use in warfare (see below).

KENNETH WILLIAMSON'S CONTRIBUTION

Kenneth Williamson began life as a journalist, but he soon became convinced that ornithology had more to offer. He went to the Manx Museum, where he was tutored in the traditional pre-war arts of the subject. He was fortunate to spend much of the war in the Faeroe Islands and used his spare time, much as Lack had done, studying birds. After the war he returned to museum work, this time at York, before being appointed the first Director of the Bird Observatory on Fair Isle. There he combined his knowledge and skill from museum training with field identification, leading to new standards in the scientific examination of birds caught for ringing.

On Fair Isle Williamson had observed the 'falls' of migrants at first hand. Now, as Migration Officer at the BTO, he was appointed to analyse the information gathered by the observatories. He immediately set about standardising recording and getting information routinely placed on microfilm, and he gathered together the biometric information on the warblers (Fig. 169) to produce three comprehensive guides to identification for use by ringers (Williamson, 1960, 1962, 1964).

Williamson's first line of enquiry concerned the question of drift. In simple terms, if a bird sets off to migrate in a given direction and meets a persistent crosswind, without constant readjustment it will end up drifting away from its intended destination. The principle is simple, but in practice weather conditions can be highly variable along the migration route, leading to variable effects on migrating birds. Williamson soon began to put together a whole series of ideas on the effects of weather on migrating birds, particularly with regard to drift.

FIG 169. Blackcap, one of the species covered in Williamson's guide to the genus *Sylvia*. (Photograph by Rebecca Nason)

The concept of drift had first been mooted by Rintoul and Baxter (1918) as a result of a study of migration on the Isle of May. Williamson explored the effects of drift on the occurrence of certain species on Fair Isle, using his taxonomic skills to determine by plumage or size the race and thus the origin of each migrant caught for ringing. He hypothesised that as well as crosswind drift there was also what he called 'downwind drift':

> A migrant makes frequent and regular halts for recuperation, and a bird which finds itself wind-drifted over any inhospitable zone must continue flying until it reaches a habitat at where it is able to rest and feed. Even if the bird possessed an innate faculty of orientation independent of the sun and visual cues it is in the interests of survival to make a down-wind drift, for by doing so the bird adds wind speed to its own flight speed, covering the longest distance in the shortest time and with the least deterioration of its limited physical resources.

This hypothesis remains unproven. Despite the radar studies (below), downwind drift has not been universally accepted and only large-scale use of satellite tracking will enable us to trace the detailed movements of most migrating birds from origin to destination.

Williamson subsequently moved on to take charge of the Common Birds Census, and ultimately became head of the Populations Section of the BTO. He was awarded the Union Medal of the BOU in 1976, and he died in 1977 – coincidentally just a month or so after Landsborough Thomson.

RADAR STUDIES

The development and use of radar for military purposes during World War II revealed the presence of so called 'angels', initially unidentified but subsequently discovered to be caused by birds. This was first noted in the spring of 1940, when a passage of gulls caused unidentified echoes. The following year there were a number of incidents around the British coasts. Lack pointed out that:

> During the war, only large birds were usually detected though a big roost of starlings, repeatedly disturbed by V1 bombs passing over it, caused a scare that the enemy had invented a new form of radio-jamming. Thereafter the ornithological problem was allowed to languish for more than a decade, though in the latter part of this time, both in Bntain and the USA, radar equipment much stronger in power than those used during the war were regularly plotting bird-migration, unknown both to the operators

and to the investigating scientists who assigned the echoes in question to unidentified meteorological phenomena ('angels').

By the late 1950s it was well established that 'angels' were migrating birds. Radar allowed ornithologists to follow the unseen element of bird migratory movement, and it was most illuminating. Among the many discoveries made by Lack and others using this technique were that:

- Visible migration by day was unrepresentative of what was passing overhead.
- Night migrants found grounded represented a variable fraction of those that passed through, anything from a small to a significant proportion. In other words, what was found on the ground could not be used to determine what had passed overhead.
- Movements on a large scale often involve birds moving in more than one direction (Fig. 170).

Radar allowed detailed study of known migratory events. Off the coast of East Anglia, for example, Lack found the winter visitors that emigrated in spring peaked at night between 2100 and 2200 hours and in daytime within an hour after sunrise. Highest numbers were noted during warm weather with clear

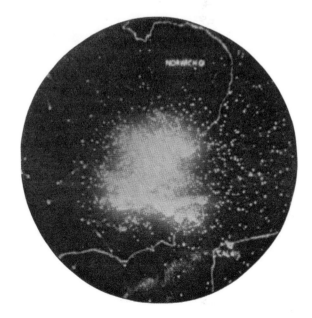

FIG 170. Lapwing movement into Britain along the line of the Thames. From Eric Eastwood's *Radar Ornithology* (1967).

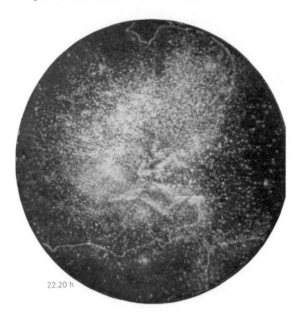

FIG 171. Swifts rising into the atmosphere after dusk, 22 June 1959. From Eastwood's *Radar Ornithology* (1967).

22.20 h

skies and light winds, lowest numbers during periods of rain or high winds and when it was cold. When conditions were suitable, movement took place all day and all night on a broad front. The tracks that the birds took were normally the result of the birds' heading and the wind direction. Lack noted episodes of drift and reported instances of birds migrating into bad weather and becoming disorientated – indeed, the radar studies suggested that on occasions birds that had drifted might return to their original leaving point to start again.

One extraordinary discovery confirmed that male swifts often take off after dusk and spend the night in the higher atmosphere, seemingly feeding or sleeping (Eastwood, 1963) (Fig. 171). The phenomenon of male swifts soaring at night had been reported by P. W. Masson in *British Birds* in 1930, and had first been noted in *The Naturalist* by H. B. Booth as long ago as 1907, but both these reports were of birds leaving at dusk and not after.

The sum total of these observations was that drift, reorientation, dispersal, irruption and reverse migration were all witnessed, sometimes occurring simultaneously, and the interpretation of all these data was often no more than surmise.

ORIENTATION AND NAVIGATION

The bulk of work on the mechanisms by which birds navigate was carried out on the Continent, but in Britain Geoffrey Matthews was the main investigator of the phenomenon. Matthews's work centred predominantly on homing pigeons, but he also studied Manx shearwaters, gulls and mallards.

Shortly after World War II the German migration scientist Gustav Kramer developed a cage suitable for studying the preferred orientation of birds during periods of migratory restlessness, and the study of orientation was thus moving into the laboratory. But most studies of orientation and navigation were undertaken in the open, with captured birds transported and released, or held captive temporarily and released at the point of capture. Data were collected by simply checking the initial direction of departure of released birds or the directional heading of the birds at the point at which they were last in view. This sort of information was used in conjunction with ringing recovery data to estimate their final destination. Matthews was among the pioneers who discovered the relative importance of clues in avian navigation: the way in which birds use pointers such as the position of the sun, the stars and the use of landmarks.

These early discoveries made up the content of Matthews's book *Bird Navigation*, the first edition of which appeared in 1955 when such work was at its height. A second edition in 1968 was virtually rewritten to bring the work up to date and included much work on Matthews's other interest, so-called 'nonsense' orientation. Nonsense orientation, revealed by a number of species but particularly by ducks, was shown when released birds always flew off uniformly in a single compass heading regardless of any alteration in the release conditions. Matthews used mallards in his experiments and discovered that his birds at Slimbridge showed:

> *well marked orientation within a few seconds to the NW, in a largely nonmigratory population. The orientation was consistent no matter which direction or how far from home they were taken for release, regardless of sex, age or previous experience; the topography of the release point or the direction of the wind; the time of day or night or the season of the year; yet the direction was not maintained for more than 20 minutes and most ducks had landed or broken away from the original direction within 10 miles. Subsequent recoveries were scattered at random.*

The functional significance of this behaviour is hard to determine, but knowing the extent to which some species are genetically programmed with information on direction and duration of flight (Berthold, 2001) it seems possible that this innate direction is a throwback to some ancestral migratory function.

AFRICAN STUDIES

One area of neglect had been studies of British breeding birds wintering in Africa. The one man who studied the migration systems of Europe to Africa was Reg Moreau, whose final work was the masterly book *The Palaearctic–African Bird Migration Systems*, published posthumously in 1972. The book summarised all the collected information on migrating birds from an African perspective, with detailed habitat and distribution information. For many British ornithologists this book was responsible for a new perspective on 'our' birds. Until relatively recently, studies of the factors that affect bird populations have concentrated on changes to the British countryside. Now we know that habitat changes in sub-Saharan Africa can have dire consequences for populations of birds that summer and breed in Britain, as revealed in the dramatic fall in whitethroat numbers that occurred in 1969 (Winstanley *et al.*, 1974).

Finally, a word must be said about *the* British ringer, the ginger- (later white-) bearded colossus whose distinctive voice was so familiar to so many (ringers especially), Chris Mead. He was a man whose enthusiasm and knowledge, and above all his ability to communicate, personified the ringing scheme. His book *Bird Migration* (1983) was an example of what Mead did best, compressing large amounts of information into readable and informative text, and the *Migration Atlas* (Wernham *et al.*, 2003) was just one of many recipients of his overwiewing eye. He contributed the sections on sand martin (Fig. 172) and swallow, and it seems safe to say that no one has ever handled as many of the former as Mead.

To join in a Mead ringing session was to experience incessant physical and mental exercise, to be part of a continual analysis and debate, often derived from a single feature on a single bird. Mead joined the BTO ringing office in 1961 and bought with him a love of mathematics, which combined with the weight of data provided him with all he required. He was instrumental in the acquisition of the BTO's first computer and convinced of the potential for computerising records. He stayed in the ringing office for thirty years, being the supremo for a period of that time, although the detailed day-to-day running of the scheme was a discipline that eluded his free-thinking personality.

Though it might have seemed heretical to Mead, it is likely that bird ringing

FIG 172. Sand martin premigratory roost, from Gould's *Birds of Great Britain* (1862–73).

has revealed all that it is capable of revealing about the pathways and timing of normal migration. New technologies are required to enable us to unravel the remainder of the detail. Nevertheless, ringing has provided a vast pool of knowledge over the course of the twentieth century. Consider how little they knew in 1907 and how much we know in 2007.

CHAPTER 15

Plumage, Cages, Eggs and Shooting: the History of Bird Protection

Gone are the glass cases with musty corpses, a rare bird is front-page news and the traffic is held up by a policeman should a Mallard decide to take her brood across Hyde Park Corner.

Phyllis Barclay-Smith, 1959

B IRD PROTECTION MAY appear to be a modern phenomenon, but the roots go back a long way. The Society for the Protection of Birds, now the Royal Society for the Protection of Birds (RSPB), was founded in 1889, but the beginning stemmed from the formation of the Royal Society for the Prevention of Cruelty to Animals (RSPCA) in 1824, and through the nineteenth century there were some, like Alfred Newton, who preached the message of conservation with some success, so that a number of Acts of Parliament covering bird protection were passed before the RSPB came into existence.

BIRD PROTECTION BEFORE 1889

James Fisher cited the sanctuary created on Inner Farne by St Cuthbert in 676 as the first act of bird protection. In 1843 Charles Waterton set up a sanctuary at his home, Walton Hall, Yorkshire, and there may have been other landowners of a similar persuasion who set land aside for wildlife. Equally, some of the properties belonging to religious foundations may have been partially or wholly devoted to the protection of birds (and animals), but we have little indication of where or when.

As the nineteenth century progressed the law was used to protect birds so that they could be shot – at the right time by the right people! There had been attempts to provide protection for 'game' for a long time before the first comprehensive Act of Parliament in 1831. This Act was devoted entirely to game, specified as black grouse, bustard, grouse, partridge (Fig. 173) and pheasant. It defined close seasons and introduced controls for the selling and possession of these birds. A further Act in 1860 added the requirement for a licence for hunting game.

Among the figures of the nineteenth century no one was more committed than Alfred Newton. He recognised that the social changes taking place in Britain were affecting the countryside and thus the bird populations, and he set about getting the statutory authorities to provide some legal protection. In a paper given at the British Association meeting in 1867 Newton lambasted the game fraternity for their persecution of birds of prey, stating that there was no relation between the population levels of raptors and game birds and pointing out that birds of prey have a selective influence over populations by removing the least fit birds. He railed against the wilful destruction of 'sea fowls' during the breeding season, stating that he did not believe that seabirds deprived people of a living,

FIG 173. Grey partridge by Archibald Thorburn, from his book *British Birds* (1915–18).

and that when adults were shot the nestlings starved to death. He condemned the slaughter of gulls, which was taking place so that their feathers could be used in ladies' hats. The final part of the paper was devoted to a summary of the game laws of the various parts of the Empire and other countries, and he stated a principle that many today might aspire to:

> As a zoologist, I entirely deprecate showing favour to one species rather than another – all should be put on the same footing. It should be as penal to shoot a Hawk or Sea Gull out of season, as a Pheasant or a Grouse. Each has its proper and useful function.

All this was very much in contradiction to the general trend for shooting at that time, but Newton ended with a statement that must be seen as truly prophetic, especially bearing in mind that it was written nearly 150 years ago:

> With all our boasted knowledge we know little of the workings of nature, and we cannot pretend to foresee the results on existing species of the progress of agriculture and manufactures. But if the present state of things goes on much longer, it requires no prophetic faculty to predict that many changes must come to pass as regard our fauna.

Newton's was a powerful voice addressing a powerful audience and, as with all subjects on which he held strong views, his language was uncompromising. There is little doubt that his choice of venue to deliver his polemic was calculated. This led to the formation of the Committee for Close Time, of which Newton was a prominent member and sometime chairman, and the Act for the Preservation of Sea-Birds followed in 1869, establishing a close season between 1 April and 1 August and prohibiting boats, nets, guns etc. from being used for killing seafowl (which included grebes and the chough). A second Act (1872) was designed to provide protection for wildfowl. The cause was taken up by an MP – a Mr Herbert – and this led to the protection of an additional 76 species, but unhappily as a result of Herbert's misguided assistance the Act prescribed a penalty for the guilty that was derisory. This was because at the discussion of the Bill someone pointed out that, with many common birds included, the penalty should be such that a small boy who killed a robin could pay it. With such an insignificant sum as its penalty the Act was widely flouted. Newton commented angrily on 'amateur' legislation – and this 'amateur' legislation was such that four years later a further Act had to be introduced, aimed specifically at the protection of wildfowl, with a close season between 15 February and 10 July laid down for 36 species.

Newton never lost his interest in bird protection, and he took a prominent role as the Society for the Protection of Birds became established. In the late 1890s, however, he resisted the notion of protection for birds' eggs – his own fond memories of collecting were too strong, and his collection too precious. But Newton supported moves to have areas designated where the taking of eggs was prohibited, and he was a strong advocate of the protection of habitats rather than specific species. One Sunday evening, when in the middle of a discourse on the fate of the (extinct) moa an earnest young man asked, 'Why do birds become extinct?' Newton replied, 'Because people don't observe the Game Laws: see Deuteronomy 22 verse 6.' The verse reads, 'if a bird's nest chance to be before thee ... whether they be young ones or eggs, and the dam sitting upon young, or upon the eggs, thou shalt not take the dam with the young.'

In 1880 all the previous Acts were replaced by a Wild Birds Protection Act which established a close season for all wild birds between 1 March and 1 August, yet the 1880 Act was so complicated that in 1881 a further Act was passed to 'explain' it, and there were two more amending acts in 1894 and 1896. The Act of 1894 gave local authorities the power to apply for the protection of both certain areas and certain species. Yet this did not prevent the wholesale destruction of some species, hounded to extinction in this country by egg-collectors and so-called sportsmen. The worst case was the osprey (Fig. 174), the last Scottish pairs of which were shot out boastfully by a man named Charles St John.

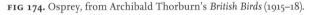

FIG 174. Osprey, from Archibald Thorburn's *British Birds* (1915–18).

THE SOCIETY FOR THE PROTECTION OF BIRDS

Like many charities, the Society for the Protection of Birds was formed to fight a specific issue: in this case the use of bird plumes as decorations for hats. Newton had brought the issue to the public's attention in a letter to *The Times* in 1876, decrying the use of the plumes of egrets, birds of paradise and the like and pointing out the huge loss of birds that resulted. Because of its target, the original membership was largely made up of, and aimed at, women. The first financial contribution, a guinea, came from Newton, although because of his view 'that people will gush and be sentimental' he remained slightly distanced from the Society, restricting his activities to advice. One of Newton's friends, Harvie-Brown, gave ten pounds, which allowed the treasurer to open a bank account.

The history of the RSPB has been documented (Samstag, 1988) and there seems little point in giving it in detail once again. The original members were drawn from the upper echelons of Victorian society and the organisation was run by a small group of what Samstag described as 'formidable women', including the Duchess of Portland as President, Mrs Frank Lemon (Fig. 175) as the first Honorary Secretary and Mrs Edward Phillips. The Society was founded at Didbury, Manchester, in February 1889, although there was already in existence a 'Plumage League' founded in London. The two organisations amalgamated, and the message that they preached was taken up so effectively that by 1898 they had 20,000 members and 152 branches. Of this burgeoning society Mrs Lemon was well and truly in charge, although from 1904 her husband was nominally Honorary Secretary.

The role of Mrs Lemon cannot be understated. It is probably sufficient to record here that her formidability was such that on one occasion when the Director of the Natural History Museum was told that she was on her way to see him to discuss some matter on which he did not feel too confident, he simply slipped out via the back stairs to the basement in order to avoid her. If Mrs Lemon was the martinet, the unsung heroine of the Society at that time was Linda Gardiner, who was employed as Mrs Lemon's assistant in 1900. She began the Society's magazine, *Bird Notes and News*, and she was largely responsible for the high profile of education in the Society's work. The early efforts were directed against the plumage trade, which had reached a peak in the period between 1900 and 1910. The campaign was sufficiently effective for the trade to decline rapidly in the 1920s, aided by an Act of Parliament stopping the flow of dead birds into the country, and by 1930 it had virtually ceased. In 1904 the

FIG 175. Mrs Lemon in her younger days. From Samstag's *For Love of Birds* (1988).

Society was incorporated by Royal Charter, and thus took the title by which it is known today.

An integral part of the success of the RSPB in its early days was both the popularisation of birds and the quality of the publicity that its work received, particularly through the writing of articles in magazines and journals. In this endeavour no one was more indefatigable than William Henry (W. H.) Hudson (Fig. 176). While unlikely to appear in a list of the great ornithologists of Britain, Hudson was an acute observer of birds and used his gift for prose to convey the atmosphere and beauty of the countryside in general, and birds in particular. As a wholehearted supporter of the RSPB, he never failed to include the case for conservation, and it was due to his writings that many people became interested in birds.

Hudson was born in 1841 and raised in Argentina, arriving in England aged 33. He continued to do in England what he had done in Argentina, which was to study the countryside and its occupants, with a special interest in birds. For the first 25 years or so in England he suffered from a lack of money, to which he was largely indifferent except that it restricted his opportunities. But gradually his position improved, thanks to his writing, especially the book *Nature in Downland* (1900), and a civil pension obtained for him by Lord Grey, so that in time he

FIG 176. W. H. Hudson, bird-nesting. (BTO collection)

became a more wealthy man. He served on the RSPB Committee with a fervour. Hudson was all too aware of the effects of collectors, as documented in a letter to Mrs Phillips in September 1897 in which he told her that ten marsh harriers had been shot in the area of the Norfolk Broads, complaining:

> If these Norfolk bird lovers would openly denounce by name the wealthy private collectors who pay for rare birds that are killed a change would take place. But they are afraid they are great men and they can't afford to make enemies of them.

Hudson went on to berate the 'framers of the Bird-protection Order' for not including a more realistic 'close time'. When Hudson died in 1922, he left the majority of his estate to the RSPB.

THE BOU, BIRD RESERVES AND THE SPNR

The BOU membership gradually espoused the cause of bird protection. In 1903 a note in *The Ibis* stated support for the Society for the Protection of Birds – though members' collecting activities could be construed as contradictory. An attempt to control the activities of the few led the 1908 AGM to pass a motion for a new rule which would allow the Committee to remove from the membership anyone involved in the taking of birds or eggs in Britain of a number of listed rare species.

At the turn of the twentieth century ornithologists knew of, and frequently visited, favoured bird sites. Being aware of the growing need for land for other uses, they feared that such sites might easily become vulnerable, and so they wanted to protect them. While this seems to be the core activity of the RSPB today, it was not so a hundred years ago. The desire for the protection of sites was reflected in the formation of the Society for the Promotion of Nature Reserves (SPNR) in 1912, by Charles Rothschild, a member of the famous banking family, and William Ogilvie-Grant, a prominent ornithologist. The aim of the SPNR was to purchase and manage land for the protection of the wildlife – not restricted to this country, but with the whole of the Empire included. Sadly, World War I interfered with the development of the Society, and although they were able to publish a list of important sites in 1916 both the atmosphere after the Great War and the attitude of government meant that the ambitions of the SPNR were largely unrealised at that time. By the late 1920s the Society was short on both members and funds. Opportunities for purchase, such as St Kilda for £3,000 in 1927, were missed and the Society had difficulty managing the sites it had bought. Much of this was doubtless due to a lack of dynamic leadership and direction following the death of Charles Rothschild in 1923.

The RSPB was able to give sites a minimal form of protection by the employment of 'watchers' who kept an eye on a site, and in 1905 a Watchers' Committee was formed. Yet it was not until 1929 that the first piece of land (at Dungeness/Romney Marsh) was purchased as a sanctuary/reserve. In 1932 East Wood, Stalybridge (Cheshire) was added. The watchers monitored sites such as Sandwich Bay, Radipole Lake and the Welsh islands of Ramsey, Skokholm and Skomer.

CHANGES TO THE LAW

In 1904 two Acts were passed. One made the use of pole traps illegal and the other gave special protection to the island of St Kilda. The general bird protection law, in the form of the 1880 Act and its amendments, remained so unsatisfactory that in 1913 a Departmental Committee was appointed to consider what was required to provide proper statutory protection for birds. Although the Committee consisted partly of civil servants from both the Home Office and the Board of Agriculture it included ornithologists such as Ogilvie-Grant, Meade-Waldo and Hugh Gladstone. The Committee's report was used as a framework for more Acts of Parliament in the 1920s, largely failing in their aims and followed by amendments in 1925, 1928, 1933 and 1937, and one in 1939 giving greater protection to wildfowl. Much of this legislation was piecemeal, dealing each time with a specific issue.

Within the RSPB, topics such as the morality of caging wild birds and the shooting of game birds were aired, and the Society appears to have taken a more dogmatic line then, especially on shooting, than its present-day position. Keeping birds, particularly songbirds such as finches, had long been a tradition, especially in London (Fig. 177). Caught in nets or, worse, by liming branches, many birds died in the process of capture; others were sold to take part in singing competitions, for which they were often blinded to 'improve' their songs. In 1933 an Act of Parliament prohibited the sale of certain species of British birds and the RSPB, in an attempt to put a stop to the shooting of game, bought up shooting rights to prevent sportsmen making use of them.

One aspect of protection that remained untouched by the 1880 Act and its amendments was the question of egg-collecting. The failure to legislate against the collection of eggs began to leave its mark, particularly on common birds, as is evident from a postscript to a famous paper on the breeding ecology of the corn bunting (Ryves & Ryves, 1934):

> In spite of it being so obvious the information this article present[s] to ornithology could not have been secured had egg-collectors been working in the district. While fully admitting the value of the knowledge obtained through eggs in the past, that phase of usefulness is now surely past so far as this country is concerned. Indeed the wholesale taking of eggs is in direct opposition to the advance of ornithology, because it cuts short further observation under natural conditions, and in the case of the scarcer species it seriously limits the number of birds that can be so observed.

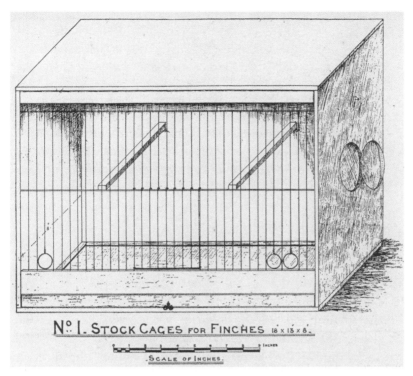

Nº I. STOCK CAGES FOR FINCHES 18 × 13 × 8.

SCALE OF INCHES.

FIG 177. Cage for finches. From Birchley's *British Birds* (1909) – a book for aviculturalists.

Egg-collecting, it seems, was so rife that in order to carry out a systematic study of a particular species you had to find an area where the collectors would not affect your results. Among the collectors of ornithologia the oologists were perhaps the most persistent. They were in the habit of meeting annually for a dinner, after which there was the opportunity to display their latest acquisitions. In 1922, after Lord Buxton had criticised the action of oologists at the RSPB AGM, the BOU felt sufficiently pressured to restate its position with regard to the protection of birds. A letter appeared in *The Ibis* signed by both the President, Elwes, and the Secretary, Stuart Baker, which firstly disassociated the Union from the activities of the oologists (ironic, since Stuart Baker was one of the principal exhibitors at oological dinners) and secondly declared that the Union supported 'the protection of rare birds in England in every way possible'. This letter was followed by a statement from the Committee which exhorted the membership to refrain from collecting eggs or skins except where there was a scientific justification to do so – but it also suggested that given the likely circumstances the Committee would find it hard to 'act as judge and jury in such cases'. This situation, in which words and deeds were at variance, was scarcely surprising, given that much of the published ornithology, as we have seen, relied on the collection of eggs and skins. Yet if the BOU supposed that they could maintain this ambivalence they were mistaken. Within just four years they found themselves in the embarrassing situation of having to accept the resignation of a member whose work was of a high quality and is still widely quoted today.

In 1926, Edgar Chance, whose studies of the cuckoo were classics of their time, was prosecuted under the Wild Birds Protection Act of 1894 for aiding and abetting Albert Wyatt, a farm bailiff, in the taking of eggs of crossbills (Fig. 178) in Norfolk. Chance was found guilty and fined. The BOU Committee accepted his resignation. Yet the case was complicated since Chance's defence lawyers argued that the eggs had been taken for a scientific purpose and that they were to be housed in Reading Museum. The curator of Reading Museum wrote to *The Ibis* to disclaim all knowledge of this, but a Reverend Bird then pointed out that in the course of a conversation with the person responsible for the collection of eggs at Reading Museum he had rather gathered that some crossbill eggs would be a welcome addition – whereupon it appears that he imparted this information to his friend Edgar Chance, who appears to have set the collecting

FIG 178. Crossbill. (Photograph by Rebecca Nason)

of the eggs in motion. So it seems possible that a genuine misunderstanding was responsible for Chance's conviction. Nevertheless it no doubt served to discourage similar acts.

There was also the question of international trading in birds. At a 1927 meeting of the British Ornithologists' Club David Bannerman drew attention to 'the scandalous manner in which live animals especially birds are often treated during their transit in ships from the tropics and elsewhere to English and Continental ports'. This provoked the Council of the Zoological Society to appoint a committee of enquiry. But little, if anything, changed.

TROUBLES AT THE RSPB

Despite, or perhaps because of, its initial success, the RSPB continued to be run in the same seemingly successful vein by the same group of people until the mid-1930s. Then the inability of those in authority to foresee and accept the sort of natural evolution, sometimes painful, that all societies need to undergo led, as it so often does, to an almighty row. In the background young men were emerging whose views were different and 'modern', none more so than Max Nicholson. In his book *Birds in England* (1926), Nicholson pointed out that the problems of bird protection required a coordinated approach, something that was patently lacking in the RSPB. Branch secretaries frequently advocated actions which were at odds with the views of Council, and there was by this stage a distinct lack of leadership. This was in no small part due to Hudson, who, though a redoubtable publicist, lacked the administrative and leadership qualities that his role as Chairman required. When he resigned Mrs Lemon considered it to be the best thing he had done for the Society! Nothing happened immediately but the retirement of Linda Gardiner in 1935 proved to be a pivotal point for change. The Assistant Secretaries (Phyllis Barclay-Smith and Beatrice Solly) asked that they might be regarded as of equal status to the new Secretary and threatened to resign if their wishes were not met. Mrs Lemon, never someone to challenge, accepted their resignations and wrote the briefest note about them in *Bird Notes and News*. Her autocratic action was not well received by the membership and was the catalyst for a subsequent campaign of criticism.

Events came to a head in 1936 (Fig. 179). At the AGM, with a membership now down to around 4,000, a Captain Hopkins took the opportunity to question the Council on such matters as inaction over cagebirds, land speculation, unreasonably high administrative expenses, and the excessive age of many of the organisers. The response was to appoint a Committee of Enquiry under the

The Royal Society for the Protection of Birds

FOUNDED FEBRUARY, 1889.

Incorporated under Royal Charter, November, 1904.

Forty-sixth Annual Report

JANUARY 1ST TO DECEMBER 31ST, 1936,

With Proceedings of Annual Meeting, 1937

Fellows and Members who have not paid their
subscriptions for the current year are requested
kindly to do so upon receiving this Report

PRICE ONE SHILLING

FIG 179. The stylish cover of the RSPB Report for 1936.

chairmanship of Julian Huxley. The suggestions of this committee were largely enacted and a new Secretary, Robert Donaldson, was appointed. Although World War II soon intervened there were some signs of innovation in the next few years, such as the founding of a section aimed at children – the Junior Bird Recorders' Club.

WORLD WAR II AND AFTER – THE COUNTY TRUSTS AND THE NATURE CONSERVANCY

In 1942 the SPNR was approached by the government, which was already looking ahead to the post-war development of the country and was keen to embrace nature conservation. As a result a Nature Reserves Investigation Committee (NRIC) was set up with the primary purpose of recommending the selection, acquisition and management of reserves. The NRIC established county subcommittees to provide local information, such as lists of sites worthy of protection, and these were subsequently used as the basis for the Sites of Special Scientific Interest. These subcommittee groups drew together naturalists from which the County Trusts subsequently emerged. Norfolk had led the way, forming a Naturalists' Trust in 1927 with the aim of protecting the marshes at Cley, and the Norfolk Trust model was adopted by many other counties.

By the late 1950s the SPNR had lost its way, but it was given new impetus by the need of the County Trusts for an umbrella organisation. The established trusts gradually became integrated into the SPNR structure, and the SPNR encouraged the formation of trusts in counties which did not have them. It was a process of slow development, and it took a great deal of time to become a truly homogeneous organisation. Over time, however, the movement has gelled into a not inconsiderable force under the generic name of the Wildlife Trusts, and the SPNR has been subsumed.

The work of the NRIC also led to a realisation within government that some agency would be required to oversee conservation on a national scale, and this resulted in the setting up of the Nature Conservancy in 1949. Once again one of the prime movers was Max Nicholson, who subsequently became its Director. The Conservancy, while being responsible for practical conservation on the ground through a series of National Nature Reserves, acted as a catalyst for a great deal of the research work that has been carried out. For example, research on the peregrine by Derek Ratcliffe – which ironically came about because pigeon fanciers wished to see peregrines culled – first highlighted the organochlorine poisoning of birds on farmland. But the Conservancy's biggest role was in sponsoring research, through both ideas and grants. Much of the BTO work was only possible as a result of financial assistance from the Conservancy and its successors, and the Common Birds Census, the Breeding Atlas and the ringing scheme have all been beneficiaries.

PETER SCOTT AND THE SEVERN WILDFOWL TRUST

The name that the post-war British public associated most with conservation was that of Peter Scott, only son of the Antarctic explorer, Robert Falcon Scott. Peter Scott had been a wildfowler in his young days, but there was something about ducks and geese that for him created an almost spiritual attraction, and he set about their conservation. In 1946 Scott established the Severn Wildfowl Trust, as it was originally called, leasing a few acres on the Severn at Slimbridge where a flock of several thousand white-fronted geese regularly wintered. The Wildfowl Trust rapidly established a substantial collection of captive wildfowl to study, as well as developing the potential of the land for wintering birds, and it was particularly noted for its work with the nene, or Hawaiian goose, which was at the time seriously threatened with extinction. The Trust collected a small group of birds and began a captive breeding programme, so that in time it was possible to start returning birds to the wild – one of the earliest examples of this sort of conservation technique. In 1948 the Trust already had over a thousand members, and by 1951 it was operating a wildfowl ringing programme at Borough Fen Decoy in Lincolnshire and at Slimbridge (Fig. 180). This, together with the Iceland and Greenland expeditions organised by Scott, led to a considerable increase in our knowledge of the origins and movements of wildfowl wintering in Britain.

By 1950 the Trust had already employed a research biologist – Hugh Boyd – and together with a warden the staff began to grow steadily. By 1960 there was a whole team of people involved on two different fronts: on the one hand a research team looking at all aspects of wildfowl ecology and behaviour, and on the other a team concerned with captive breeding and the international collection. The grounds also became an attraction for visitors, including many school parties.

A great part of the success, undeniably, lay in Peter Scott's skill at attracting the support of influential people as well as that of ornithologists and conservationists. He used his connections wisely, and royal visits to Slimbridge were common. As early as 1953 Scott realised the potential of lectures both for education and for raising revenue, and in that year he filled the Westminster

FIG 180. Peter Scott at Slimbridge constructing one of the original decoy tunnels. Fox photos from the second Annual Report of the Severn Wildfowl Trust (1948–9).

Hall with his illustrated lecture about the Iceland expedition to ring geese.

In 1954 the Wildfowl Trust (it had dropped the Severn prefix) assumed responsibility for the national Wildfowl Counts (which continue to this day), and also for decoy ringing at Abberton Reservoir in Essex. In 1957 it began a period of increasing its land-holding by setting up a second collection at Peakirk, near Peterborough, largely to help finance the decoy at nearby Borough Fen, and by this time the membership had topped 5,000. In 1964 the Slimbridge headquarters were augmented with a purpose-built research centre, and in 1967 the Trust acquired its first piece of land at Welney on the Ouse Washes to protect wintering Bewick's and whooper swans. In 1970 Caerlaverock, a wintering ground for barnacle geese, was added, and in 1973 Martin Mere in Lancashire, Arundel in Sussex and Washington in Durham. In recent times the Trust has altered its name to the Wildfowl and Wetlands Trust.

RSPB POST-WAR SUCCESS

World War II accidentally provided the RSPB with both its most famous site and its most famous success. The flooding of the area below Dunwich Heath in Suffolk as a part of coastal defences (the tank traps on the beach remain to this day) led to the incidental creation of the wetland that today makes up the bigger part of the reserve at Minsmere. In addition the accidental flooding of Havergate Island, due to a stray shell hitting the sluice, provided ideal conditions for avocets to breed (Fig. 181). These two events were instrumental in the RSPB being able to develop techniques for the management of wetlands which are now world-renowned.

A little later, in 1952, a pair of ospreys attempted to breed in Scotland, but the attempt failed because of the activities of egg-collectors. The RSPB then took a rather revolutionary step, and went public. Thus, rather as the Apollo mission that went wrong heightened interest in space exploration, the unfortunate fate of the ospreys drew the nation's attention to their existence and their need for protection. What helped most was that this was just at a time when broadcasting was increasing the public's knowledge of, and interest in, natural history.

The success of both ospreys and avocets played a huge part in providing a positive public image for the RSPB. What also raised the profile was that finally, after so many piecemeal attempts, a truly comprehensive piece of legislation passed onto the statute book. The 1954 Protection of Birds Act at last achieved all-embracing legislation giving protection to almost every bird species in this country, and to their eggs. Egg-collecting could be continued under licence, and in the case of the commoner species it was not an offence – in order to prevent the small schoolboy from appearing in court. The RSPB was in a good position

FIG 181. Avocet, a species whose success has mirrored that of the RSPB. From John Gould's *Birds of Great Britain* (1862–73).

to expand, and its membership, which had been below 4,000 at the start of the war, climbed to over 8,000 by the end of 1959.

At this time the RSPB offices were in London, and the first issue was to find a suitable place in the country where, with some adjoining land, the Society could expand. An ideal place was found at The Lodge at Sandy in Bedfordshire, and the move took place in 1961. Philip Brown, who had overseen the first part of the development, gave way to Peter Conder as Secretary (ultimately Director). Conder, a competent ornithologist, had a simple management technique, which was to delegate issues to those best equipped to deal with them. The role he played himself was that of an enabler, and he began the second phase of the Society's development by employing specialists to carry out the different tasks that the expanding organisation required: reserves manager, research biologist, education officer, etc. – and above all a film unit. The RSPB Film Unit was an integral part of the Society's success. Making films about many aspects of birds, but always very accessible to children and non-birdwatchers, and always with a high standard of photography, the RSPB utilised Scott's idea and launched nationwide film shows. Those annual travelling shows brought quality wildlife films to almost every major city and town, and the sale of tickets was guaranteed. The films had a dual purpose, education as well as revenue, and the foyer of the venue was used as an ideal recruitment opportunity. Together with the output of the BBC Natural History Unit and the ITV Survival team, these films stimulated an interest in birds in a whole new way, and among whole new strata of society. It was as much due to the films and television programmes as anything else that by the end of 1966 the membership had risen to nearly 32,000, quadrupling in just seven years.

Land acquisition now became a core activity of the RSPB. The vision of the 1920s protectionists that land would be under pressure was becoming reality. The RSPB began to acquire sites with high avian interest, among the earliest of which were Combes Valley in 1963, Leighton Moss in 1964, parts of the Ouse Washes in 1965, and ownership of many other sites dates from this period. The directorship of Peter Conder saw the RSPB expand into the truly influential national conservation organisation that we know today.

The success of the species protection programme and the provision of suitable habitat encouraged the return of many raptors. Among the first was the marsh harrier (Fig. 182), which had been persecuted so relentlessly that only a handful of pairs remained by the middle of the twentieth century.

When Peter Conder retired, his place was taken by Ian Prestt, who had been working as an ornithologist in the Nature Conservancy. Prestt carried the legacy forward, overseeing a further expansion in the staff and the activities of the RSPB.

FIG 182. Head of
female marsh harrier,
painted by J. M. W.
Turner, *c.*1830. One
of the paintings from
his stay at Farnley
Hall, from his
*Ornithological
Collection*. From Hill's
Turner's Birds (1988).

Under his Directorship the RSPB purchased its hundredth reserve (Wood of Cree)
and in 1997, under Barbara Young, the Society hit what would have seemed an
impossible target only a decade or two before, a membership of one million, far
greater than any political party could muster.

RE-INTRODUCTIONS AND RE-CREATIONS

In the final decades of the twentieth century conservation shed its beards-
and-sandals reputation, to be replaced by suits and lobbyists. The size of the
membership, not just of the RSPB but also of other organisations such as the
Wildlife Trusts and the National Trust, gave the movement a voice of political
significance. That voice has been heard.

Among the more recent developments are the programmes to reintroduce
species that we know have been part of Britain's avifauna in the past. Most
successful of these is the reintroduction of the red kite. From the beginnings
in the Chilterns these majestic birds have spread across much of the British
countryside. In Scotland the success of the reintroduced white-tailed eagles in
recolonising their ancient heartland has brought not just pleasure but eco-
tourism. Other reintroductions are now planned, and indeed recently the ospreys
reintroduced at Rutland have begun to breed. If there has been a debate about
the justification of this sort of activity it has been settled by the notion that *re*-
introduction is allowable, but introduction is not.

One of the great myths of the past was that it would not prove possible to
interfere with land in such a way as to recreate the kind of wildlife habitats that
had evolved over centuries. Deliberate re-creation might be said to have begun

when Bert Axell created 'the scrape' at Minsmere in 1962: a series of shallow
lagoons with brackish water that attracted large numbers of waders and wildfowl
and arguably made the reserve's reputation. More recently a Fenland farmer,
unencumbered by the accepted wisdom, has turned part of his land alongside the
River Cam into a wetland reserve that has attracted a mouth-watering list of birds
in just a few years (Tomkins, 1998). The RSPB has also taken the plunge, creating
a whole new wetland reserve at Lakenheath on the Suffolk/Norfolk boundary with
a more calculated approach, including the planting of reeds by hand. And other
organisations are looking to return whole blocks of land in the fenland basin to
wetland/grassland reserves. Doubtless more such schemes will follow in other
parts of the country, all adhering to Alfred Newton's expressed view that the
preservation, or in this case re-creation, of habitats is as vital as the protection
of species.

THE MORAL DILEMMA

Conservation has also had to consider the vital role that private landowners
can make. Were it not for grouse moors, or indeed game shooting, much of the
wilder countryside might well have already become housing, as has happened to
several tracts of heathland. Game preservation has always caused a conflict with
conservation, largely due to the gamekeepers' desire to control the predators.
But apart from the effects of gamekeepers on raptors, many ground-nesting
birds have almost certainly benefited from such predator control, and bird
conservation faces a considerable moral dilemma when corvids or birds of prey
take the eggs or young of nationally rare birds – as happened when kestrels
predated the chicks of little terns. Failure to protect our rare birds would have
prevented the public's support for the RSPB, but success has created its own
problems.

Doubtless the three ladies who led the crusade against the feather fashion
would be astounded by what was achieved in the century that followed their
founding of the Society, Alfred Newton too. This has been achieved not just by
the work of the RSPB but also through tireless lobbying within the corridors of
power by people such as Nicholson. However, the uncertainty of climate change
and the problems that have resulted from conservation's successes will continue
to exercise those responsible for the movement in the future.

CHAPTER 16

Behavioural and Ecological Studies

The only way to attain a right knowledge of the habits and actions of our feathered world is to carefully watch each movement, plumage, and haunt, allowing an impression to be made on the mind of what is seen.

Anon., *Birds and Bird Keeping* (late 19th century)

F OLLOWING THE DEATH of Blackwall in 1881 little or nothing by way of field studies was published in Britain until the turn of the twentieth century, when the books of Edmund Selous began to appear, together with the results of the first significant piece of applied ecology.

GROUSE DISEASE

The pioneering piece of twentieth-century bird ecology was the work not of a single scientist but of a committee, and the subject was the red grouse (Fig. 183). By the Victorian era game shooting was big business – estimated at a million pounds (even then) on grouse shooting alone. It became clear that despite all the attention of gamekeepers red grouse were susceptible to a sporadic mortality of epidemic proportions. This mortality was described by the catch-all name of 'grouse disease'. The observers of the phenomenon provided many and varied explanations as to the cause, including overstocking of the moors with sheep and pneumonia due to wet or cold spells in winter. With red grouse having so high an economic value the Ministry of Agriculture set up a committee in 1904 to oversee a scientific investigation into the cause of 'grouse disease', in the hope of finding some way of controlling or even eradicating it. The committee was

FIG 183. Red grouse hanging by J. M. W. Turner, from his *Ornithological Collection.* From Hill's *Turner's Birds* (1988).

chaired by Lord Lovat, a moor owner; A. S. Leslie was the secretary, and the other members were Drs Seligman, Shipley and Hammond Smith, plus E. A. Wilson and the Reverend E. A. W. Peacock, who were to be the eyes and ears on the ground. Wilson, who later accompanied Scott's expedition to the Antarctic, also made many paintings, which were used as illustrations. The product of the investigation was a two-volume report which concluded that the adult birds were killed by a parasitic worm, *Trichostrongylus pergracilis.* Although present in most birds, this would reproduce to so great an extent that at times it would simply overwhelm the health of the birds. The mortality of chicks was found to be the result of coccidiosis caused by an organism called *Eimeria avium.* The report formed the basis for a book (Leslie & Shipley, 1912) presenting a comprehensive review of the life history, classification, plumage variations, food and causes of mortality of the red grouse, as well as a section giving advice on the best way to manage a grouse moor – in effect a monograph on the species.

Elsewhere *British Birds* reported the results of behavioural research on ducks by H. Wormald (1910), who described the various ritualistic poses that characterise the courtship of the mallard – poses that were later given as examples of so-called 'fixed action patterns' by the Austrian ethologist and Nobel prize-winner Konrad Lorenz. The principle was that these were inherited (fixed) patterns of action that were specific. So, for example, the head-bobbing courtship signal (action) is used by many species of duck but the detail (pattern) varies, sometimes only very slightly, from species to species.

At this time only a handful of men were interested in observational research on birds. Apart from Julian Huxley almost all were amateurs, and this small group of dedicated men were responsible for work that has become a part of the classical literature of ornithology.

BEHAVIOURAL STUDIES – EDMUND SELOUS AND CONWY LLOYD MORGAN

Edmund Selous (1857–1934) was already studying the behaviour of birds at the end of the nineteenth century, and publishing his work in journals such as *The Zoologist* with titles such as 'Observational diary of the habits of nightjars, mostly of a sitting pair' (1899). Similar papers dealt with great plover (stone curlew), great-crested grebe, peewit (lapwing), great spotted woodpecker, blackcock (black grouse), ruff, red-throated diver and carrion crow – a wide-ranging collection of species (Fig. 184). These studies were all published in the first ten years of the twentieth century.

Most of Selous's work was written and published in book form, with titles such as *Bird Watching* (1901), *Bird Life Glimpses* (1905) and *The Bird Watcher in the Shetlands* (1905). After a period of silence he re-emerged with three more books, *Realities of Bird Life* (1927), the curiously titled *Thought-Transference (or What?) in Birds* (1931), in which he examined the phenomenon by which birds appear to act spontaneously in unison, an action that Selous attributed to a supersense, and *Evolution of Habit in Birds* (1933). Selous's style of writing was highly individual. Part of the content, particularly in the early books, had echoes of Gilbert White; but the subject matter was by no means limited to ornithology, frequently lapsing into rambling philosophical discourse – for example, 'Do we become more, or less, sympathetic as we get more civilised?' This was inspired by a passage wondering whether guillemots (Fig. 185) were 'concerned' about the

NIGHTJAR, GOATSUCKER, OR FERN-OWL.
Caprimulgus europœus, Linn.

FIG 184. Nightjar, one of the species studied by Selous. From Lilford's *Coloured Figures of the Birds of the British Islands* (1885–97), painted by J. G. Keulemans.

FIG 185. Common guillemot.
(Photograph by Rebecca Nason)

demise of their chicks at the hands (beaks) of predators, and the passage formed
the introduction to a discussion of the comparative emotions of men and
guillemots which occupied the next three pages! He also quoted widely from
English literature.

Selous was a Darwinian, and frequently compared his observations to
Darwinian principles, especially where they turned out to exemplify Darwin's
theories, particularly on 'sexual selection'. Equally, Selous drew the reader's
attention to observations that in his view contradicted Darwinian theory – such
as 'it is certain that the hen bird does sometimes court the cock and fight for him
with rival hens, even in cases where the cock alone is beautiful.' Selous went on to
ask what might be the evolutionary purpose for the male to be visibly attractive
where the role of the sexes seems to be reversed. Selous's skill as an observer and
his capacity to analyse his observations is well illustrated throughout his books,
such as in this example on why marine birds bathe:

> A land-bird bathes in water with the express object of cleaning itself, and therefore the
> energy which it expends in doing so is both guided and regulated. It is confined within
> a certain channel which it does not leave. But when this same bird takes to the water –
> for I assume all aquatic birds to have been land-birds once – bathing as a special
> activity, is not so necessary. Being always in the bath it needs not to specially bathe. It
> finds itself, however, with an inherited habit which it is impelled to continue.

For the time at which it was written this was an example of considerable depth
of thinking, as was his suggestion that 'the zoologist of the future should be a
different kind of man altogether: the present one is not worthy of the name. He
should go out with glasses and notebook prepared to see and think ... Every man
has his ambition. To make a naturalist who shall use neither a gun nor a cabinet
is mine'. This ambition is all the more extraordinary since his elder brother,
Frederick, who died in World War I and was by all accounts a larger-than-life
character, lived by the gun as a big-game hunter in Africa and was an assiduous
egg-collector. It was very much an indication of the relative priorities of the
times that Frederick Selous was deemed worthy of obituary in the ornithological
journals (and as a hunter and collector he is described in glowing terms), but
the death of Edmund, an observer of birds, was not reported. Indeed, the only
obituary published after his death was in the French ornithological journal
Alauda. Nowadays of course the roles are reversed. No one seriously mentions
Frederick as an ornithologist (though his name is immortalised in the Selous
Game Reserve in Tanzania) while many of today's ornithologists acknowledge
the pioneering work of Edmund.

The life of Selous remains something of a mystery. He seems not to have been part of any ornithological or scientific community, and there are few biographical details available. This was probably for several reasons: his self-confessed solitary nature, his lack of clubbability and, by no means least, the unfashionable nature of his subject. Selous had been an undergraduate at Pembroke College, Cambridge, and was later called to the bar, but by the time he moved his family to Mildenhall in the Breckland on the Suffolk/Norfolk boundary, he had given up law and was studying birds. He appears thereafter to have survived on a very limited income. Lack quoted a former reader for Selous's publisher who described Selous as 'odd, withdrawn, shy and solitary in type and a man of marked idiosyncrasy'. Lack remained convinced of the value of much of Selous's work: 'though neglected by ornithologists in his lifetime Selous may be regarded as the founder of the modern studies of behaviour, since he was the first to make intensive observations on individual birds and to theorise on what he saw.' This was a view shared by Julian Huxley:

> In ethology the real pioneer was Edmund Selous, one of the most indefatigable observers of bird habits that the world has seen. In particular, his observations on bird display paved the way for the inclusion of the results of bird-watching within the framework of scientific biology.

It is worth remembering that Selous achieved such detailed observation before the technique of bird ringing allowed recognition of individuals in the field.

At the same time as Selous was making his detailed observations in the field, an academic scientist with a background in engineering was using laboratory-based studies of birds, probably for the first time, to investigate behaviour. Conwy Lloyd Morgan (1852–1936) received little attention from the ornithologists of his day and is not always accorded mention today, probably because he was not an ornithologist *per se*. The son of a solicitor, he was educated at the Royal Grammar School, Guildford, and then trained at the Royal School of Mines as a mining engineer. A short time after that he came under the influence of T. H. Huxley and was given a copy of Darwin's *Voyage of the Beagle* to read, which further inspired him. He went on a tour of North America and Brazil and by the time he returned to England was determined to pursue a career in zoology, studying first with Huxley at South Kensington and then, in 1878, accepting the post of Lecturer in the Diocesan College, Rondebosch, South Africa. In 1883 he returned to England and secured the post of Lecturer in Zoology and Geology at University College Bristol, where he remained for his academic career, becoming temporary Principal in 1887. His interest strayed into psychology and thus, naturally enough, into the psychology of animals.

Lloyd Morgan's work was wide-ranging, and by the late nineteenth century he was studying the role of instinct in behaviour, using birds in laboratory conditions. These birds – chicks, ducklings and young moorhens (Fig. 186) – were 'hatched in an incubator and isolated from possible parental and other tuition', and 'their behaviour under precise experimental conditions was observed, recorded, and finally explained with a minimum of anthropomorphic interpretation.'

This work provided the basis for his book *Habit and Instinct* (1896), in which he concluded that much behaviour, such as the newly hatched chick's habit of pecking at anything, was inherited and not learned. But Lloyd Morgan also postulated that there were mechanisms that dampened or altered instinctive behaviour when appropriate – an example being that if a chick, whose early instinct is to peck at any object, pecked a bee and got stung it would learn not to peck at one again. In other words the instinct to peck is essential for life but the instinct has to be tapered down by learning so that a bird learns what to peck and what not to peck. Furthermore, Lloyd Morgan appreciated that instinctive behaviour could be changed by mutation, stating that evolution, while being a steady continuous process, can be altered more dramatically by the emergence of something new.

FIG 186. Moorhens with young, from John Gould's *Birds of Great Britain* (1862–73).

In 1901 Lloyd Morgan was appointed Professor of Psychology and Education, and in 1909 he became the first Vice-Chancellor of the newly established University of Bristol. His book *Instinct and Experience* was published in 1911. In 1923, retired, he gave a series of Gifford Lectures in Edinburgh which were published under the titles *Emergent Evolution* (1923), *Life, Mind, and Spirit* (1926), *Mind at the Crossways* (1929), *The Animal Mind* (1930) and *The Emergence of Novelty* (1933). In his Royal Society obituary notice he was described as:

> *a born teacher – a fluent lecturer, yet meticulously accurate in all his statements. Teaching must, in fact, have been almost a mania with him, for the present writer once came upon him in the open air on Clifton Down lecturing to whoever wished to hear him on the somewhat remote subject of atolls!*

In his later life, Lloyd Morgan became a great friend of, and influence on, the man who in his spare time studied the nature and existence of bird territories – Eliot Howard.

ELIOT HOWARD (TERRITORY) AND EDGAR CHANCE (CUCKOOS)

Henry Eliot Howard, born in 1873, was a businessman who, like Seebohm before him, used his financial security (he was a director of Stewart and Lloyds) to allow him to indulge his interest. He was by no means the first person to realise that birds held discrete territories, for as far back as the 1830s J. F. M. Dovaston had used a contraption he called an 'ornithotrophe' to feed birds, including robins, which he caught and marked, showing that they were territorial and attempting to map the territories. But Dovaston's work failed to penetrate the mainstream ornithological publications, and to Howard must go the credit for the elucidation of the functional importance of territory. Howard's contribution can be gauged by the titles of his books: *British Warblers* (1907–14), the seminal *Territory in Bird Life* (1920) (Fig. 187), *An Introduction to the Study of Bird Behaviour* (1929), *The Nature of a Bird's World* (1935) and *A Waterhen's World* (1940). The style of writing, it has to be said, was rather stilted and, sadly, parts of some of the books are quite heavy going, though ultimately rewarding. Yet the essentials of his work are clearly indicative of a man who not only documented his observations with great care but hypothesised about them in terms that although familiar today were quite new at the time. In Howard's obituary in *The Ibis*, Percy Lowe remarked:

The outstanding feature which characterised these books was their originality. The observations on which they were based, and the philosophical and physiological deductions drawn from them, were of such a close and purposive nature that it may well be said that no such observations and deductions have ever been known to approach before in any field ornithology. How many of us before Eliot Howard had expounded the matter had been conscious of bird-territory, the part it plays in a bird's pattern of life, and the neurally-linked pattern of events and reactions within it? – How obvious it is now!

FIG 187. Two pairs of pied wagtails fighting in defence of their territories. From Eliot Howard's *Territory in Bird Life* (1920).

Although he was not quite as solitary as Selous (he was a member of the BOU for 45 years, on the Committee and later Vice-President), Howard remained somewhat isolated, if not aloof. Lack later reported that Howard's service on the BOU Committee was of an inconspicuous nature and that he was so little seen and known that he had a book dedicated to his memory a dozen years before he died in 1940! Lack also recorded that Howard's only real scientific contact was Lloyd Morgan, until late in his life when Julian Huxley made contact with him. Howard did not receive the acclaim he deserved. The reviews in *The Ibis* were, if not scathing, often dismissive (see Chapter 12). Yet Percy Lowe, a systematic ornithologist, clearly recognised their worth:

> *He had the mind of a philosopher, a sufficient knowledge of physiology, and great powers of analysis and interpretation. Such characteristics are in other fields of research and discovery generally associated with genius. Eliot Howard was to my mind also a pioneer – and pioneers are so desperately few compared with followers.*

While Selous had ranged widely in his observations, from the Brecks to the Shetlands and from stone curlews to auks, Howard had been more specialised, seeking facts to fulfil his particular interests in territory and song. Edgar Chance, the third of these pioneers, was a monographer of that most interesting bird, the cuckoo (Fig. 188). His work consisted of the most careful observation of the whole business of parasitism. He recognised that each female cuckoo laid an egg of a certain size, shape or marking pattern that with practice could be recognised – something he had discovered originally from the eggs of red-backed shrikes.

With knowledge he was able to determine which nest had been parasitised by which female (Fig. 189). He watched as the females observed their hosts, and established beyond doubt that the female laid the egg in the host's nest and did not carry it in her bill pre-laid and deposit it in the nest – a view that was held by some ornithologists at the time and endorsed by no lesser authority than Jourdain (which is ironic, considering the way Jourdain lambasted Harting's failings: see Chapter 12). Chance's work was published in two books, *The Cuckoo's Secret* (1922) and an improved and expanded version entitled *The Truth about the Cuckoo* (1940).

Though also a businessman, in character Chance was the antithesis of Howard. He was blunt, shrewd and clearly a more clubbable man. He belonged to the BOU but was forced to resign in 1926, as described in Chapter 15. His death in 1955 was barely marked by the ornithological world, most likely because of his tarnished reputation. In Britain, however, Chance was probably the first ornithologist to devote his study to a single species.

FIG 188. Cuckoo by Archibald Thorburn, from his book *British Birds* (1915–18).

JULIAN HUXLEY'S STUDIES OF COURTSHIP DISPLAYS

Selous, Howard and Chance compressed years of observations into their books.
By contrast, Julian Huxley's classic study of the courtship of the great crested
grebe (1914) was the result of work undertaken at Tring Reservoir during a
fortnight's holiday. Huxley had been inspired first by his biology master at Eton
but secondly by reading the early books of Selous. His interest in courtship
behaviour began on a visit to Cardigan Bay in the spring of 1911, where observations of redshanks (Fig. 190) showed him that the female had the 'power' to
accept or reject the advances of an individual male, and thus he confirmed the
view expressed by Selous that mate selection, while fitting the general theory
propounded by Darwin, could be determined by the female.

Studying the great crested grebe, Huxley went further and showed that there
were three stages of courtship/breeding behaviour, each accompanied by a

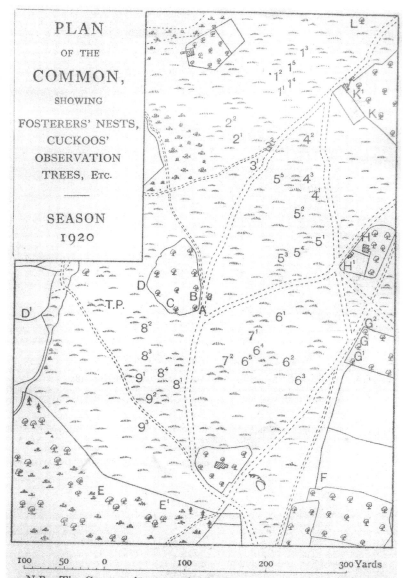

PLAN

OF THE

COMMON,

SHOWING

FOSTERERS' NESTS,
CUCKOOS'
OBSERVATION
TREES, ETC.

———

SEASON
1920

100   50   0   100   200   300 Yards

N.B.—The Common is surrounded by forest on three sides, north, west,
and south, from a point near tree L round to a point near the 100-yard mark
on the scale.

FIG 189. Map showing the egg deposition in nests of meadow pipits, from Chance's
The Cuckoo's Secret (1922).

particular display: firstly those that were associated with pairing, secondly those that were associated with coition, and thirdly those that were part of pair-bonding or pair-reinforcing. Huxley also noticed that, in amongst the various displays, there were actions that were hardly appropriate, such as feather preening. These acts, which he considered had been employed out of context, he described as 'pleasurable rituals' – a term which has subsequently become part of behavioural language to cover these curious acts – which seem by some evolutionary process to have become dissociated from their original purpose (just like the bathing ritual reported by Selous).

Julian Huxley conducted very little research on birds after his courtship studies. In an amazingly full life, he went on to be a professor of zoology both in this country and in the USA, Secretary of the Zoological Society of London, and later of UNESCO. He was knighted in 1958, and among his many other honours were the Darwin Medal of the Royal Society (1956), the Gold Medal of the World Wildlife Fund (1970) and the Godman–Salvin Medal of the BOU (1971). He wrote many books and was one of the original and lasting members of the BBC Brains Trust. He conducted basic zoological research on topics such as embryology and heredity, yet throughout his life birds remained a passion, and his books of essays rarely appeared without at least one chapter devoted to the subject. In *Essays in Popular Science* (1926) he described with admiration the work of Eliot Howard, and his essay on Howard's territory book is a masterful six-page précis

FIG 190. Redshank. (Photograph by Rebecca Nason)

FIG 191. An exceptional picture of the eye of a gannet, the subject of the Oscar-winning film by Huxley and Lockley. (Photograph by Rebecca Nason)

of the findings which Howard stretched to a whole book. Even as late as 1964, in his book *Essays of a Humanist*, he found space for a chapter called 'Birds and science'. These essays show his skill at popularising science, an ability too often derided by mainstream scientists.

That Julian Huxley was the recipient of an Oscar seems surprising today, but the film *The Private Life of Gannets*, made in 1934 in collaboration with Ronald Lockley, was the forerunner of the sort of films that we enjoy each week on television, and it was awarded the 1938 Academy Award for 'Best Short Subject, One-reel' (Fig. 191). Bill Thorpe used it as a teaching aid, and stated that 'although I have seen it scores of times its appeal has never waned.' Huxley was a zoologist with an interest in birds who realised that a good birdwatcher could make a fundamental contribution to biological knowledge.

OTHER CONTRIBUTIONS

There were of course other workers, mostly amateurs, involved in behavioural studies. Henry Boase, for example, wrote several papers on the courtship behaviour of fulmar, goldeneye, eider, teal, tufted duck, pied wagtail, shelduck, great crested grebe and mallard. And there was Frederick Kirkman, whose studies

of the Black-headed gull led to his book *Bird Behaviour* (1937). During the 1940s
there were works such as those of the two clergymen, Edward Armstrong, whose
book *Bird Display* was originally published in 1942, and Peter Hartley, whose
studies of song thrushes carried on the tradition of amateur interest in
behaviour. The work of all these men laid the foundation for behavioural
studies, although many other individuals contributed bits and pieces. The next
era in which the subject blossomed was after the war, with Bill Thorpe's study
of bird song.

ECOLOGICAL STUDIES – J. P. BURKITT'S ROBIN STUDIES

A less well-known character (both then and today) was J. P. Burkitt, who in the
1920s pioneered the use of ringing for field studies, studying robins (Fig. 192) in
County Fermanagh. Each robin in his garden was ringed with a metal ring of a
different pattern (he couldn't use colours since he was colour-blind). Using this
technique he established the facts of robin territorial behaviour and proved that
the females sang in winter to defend their territories. He was among the first to
realise the significance of threat-display and was the pioneer of the technique
of using ringing returns to estimate average age. His began his robin study at
the age of 37 without any ornithological background, and after it he published
almost nothing more. Lack described Burkitt as 'a deeply religious, extremely
humble and intellectually able man who spent his declining years reading his
Bible and working in his garden'. Yet Burkitt must be seen as a pioneer in the
world of British bird ecology, both for his technical innovation and for his
study of robins.

British Birds gradually included more and more studies undertaken by the
new generation of ornithologists, though the names of workers such as John
Dewar, Walter Collinge and J. H. Owen are largely unknown today. Dewar
from around 1910 to 1940 presented results from his studies of oystercatchers,
with particular reference to their feeding habits. Collinge, based first at the
University of St Andrews and later at the Yorkshire Museum, was one of the
first to be involved in the so-called 'economic ornithology', looking at the
dynamics of birds in agricultural production. He wrote a whole series of papers
on the feeding habits of various species, including bullfinch, rook, blackbird
and pheasant, but his work was almost entirely published in professional
journals such as the *Journal of the Ministry of Agriculture* and is not as well known
as it might be in ornithological circles. These studies were combined in a book,

FIG 192. Robins, from John Gould's *Birds of Great Britain* (1862–73). A typical example of late work by Richter, with a rather romantic composition.

The Food of Some British Wild Birds, which appeared first in 1913 with a second edition in 1924–7. J. H. Owen was a schoolmaster at Felsted in Essex who in his spare time carried out the work that culminated in a series of papers published between 1926 and 1936 in *British Birds* covering almost the whole ecology of the sparrowhawk. When he retired in 1939 he continued to study birds, and made several observations on the red-backed shrike. His obituary in *British Birds* described him as 'a first-rate observer rather than a scientific ornithologist ... essentially a field worker [who] relied little upon books ... his papers and lectures were always based solely upon his own observations.'

While these students of bird behaviour and ecology are relatively little known, the same cannot be said of the man who came to prominence as the main worker in this field after World War II – David Lack. Together with Thorpe and Tinbergen, Lack revitalised ornithology in this country, and their work spawned a whole generation of scientific ornithologists.

CHAPTER 17

After the War

She laments sir ... her husband goes this morning a-birding.
William Shakespeare, *The Merry Wives of Windsor*, quoted in the 1954
Field Guide to the Birds of Britain and Europe by Peterson, Mountfort and
Hollom under the dedication 'To our long-suffering wives'

THE IMMEDIATE PROSPECTS for British ornithology after the war seemed good. Although the country had lost some of the older generation, Jourdain, Witherby and Claud Ticehurst in particular, none of the promising ornithologists had been killed in the conflict. David Lack and Bill Thorpe (see Chapter 18) had both worked on the war effort using academic skills, Max Nicholson had been in the Ministry of War Transport helping to organise the traffic of vital supplies across the Atlantic, and Bernard Tucker had continued to work as an academic in Oxford. Tucker's early death in 1951 (see Chapter 13) was a body blow to British ornithology; if he had lived an average lifespan he would have survived into the 1970s and even beyond, and who knows what he might have achieved. But the impact of his demise was lessened by the organisational industry of Max Nicholson (Fig. 193).

THE INFLUENCE OF MAX NICHOLSON

Nicholson, a contemporary of Bernard Tucker, now played a pivotal role in the change of direction in British ornithology. His post-war achievements, many unseen in the background, cover almost every sphere of ornithology. When Tucker died the most immediate crisis was the editorial work for *British Birds*.

FIG 193. Max Nicholson: a portrait by Bruce Foreman, reproduced by permission of Derek Ratcliffe.

Nicholson, with his customary organisational skill, introduced a board of editors, of which he became Chairman, and shared out the load that Tucker had undertaken alone. He helped to take the journal forward into the more scientific era without ever losing the unique features that had defined it, and he remained a member of the board into the 1970s. While Nicholson was Senior Editor there were two important events concerning *British Birds*. The first was the regularisation of sight records from 1959 through committee scrutiny and the second was the examination of the infamous Hastings Rarities (see Chapter 19). Further developments saw the appointment of an Executive Editor, James Ferguson-Lees, and a Photographic Editor, G. K. Yeates. This latter appointment was a farsighted step, resulting in the journal's extensive use of high-quality photographs, black and white at first but subsequently in colour. These photographs have been much more than decorative interludes, especially when employed as illustrative aids to identification articles.

In 1952 Nicholson was appointed Director General of the Nature Conservancy, an organisation that combined science with conservation. It was a post he held until 1966. Nicholson loved birds with a boyish enthusiasm; they were a fundamental part of his life. His primary concern was the likely effects that increasing post-war industrialisation and resulting land use would have on wildlife populations. The fact that he walked (and talked) in the corridors of power gave him the opportunity to influence decision making at the highest level, an opportunity he undoubtedly made use of – and not without success.

Nicholson had been involved in the national reconstruction planning as the war drew to a close, including the establishment of National Parks in 1949. Like Newton fifty years before, he recognised that the best way to conserve wildlife was to protect the habitats. The National Parks, through their statutory control of the planning process and restrictions on development, offered some respite to species under threat from the march of industrialisation. The Nature Conservancy set about the business of establishing National Nature Reserves, in which Nicholson was personally involved. He also offered assistance to Peter Scott in setting up the Wildfowl Trust, and in 1961 he was, with Scott, a prime mover in the founding of the World Wildlife Fund. In addition, he gave what help he could to the then small but locally effective county wildlife trusts, many of which were founded during the immediate post-war period with precious few resources. Despite all this, Nicholson was not too busy for ornithology. He was the first Chairman of the Board of Editors of the authoritative *Birds of the Western Palearctic* (BWP) and he wrote the habitats section in all volumes and the voice section in many. Norman Moore, who himself served with great distinction in the Nature Conservancy, described Nicholson as having a distinguished but stormy career in the civil service – 'not an easy boss but such an inspiring leader that, over the years, respect and admiration grew into affection.'

THE BTO POST-WAR

In common with the other ornithological organisations the BTO began the process of slow but inexorable expansion after the end of World War II. In 1951 the membership passed 2,000, due in part to the enthusiastic reception of James Fisher's Pelican books (see below). In 1953 the first outside financial support was obtained from the Nature Conservancy to cover the permanent investigations (nest records, ringing and the heron census) (Fig. 194), leading to the appointment of an Assistant Secretary, John Burton. Finance was provided for a Ringing Officer, Elsie Leach, who, with Witherby, had already been responsible for the ringing reports for many years. The ringing office remained, however, in the British Museum in London. Arthur Landsborough Thomson subsequently sought and achieved funding for an officer devoted to migration studies, Kenneth Williamson.

By far the most significant development was the realisation that the Trust needed its own journal in which to publish the results of the various studies.

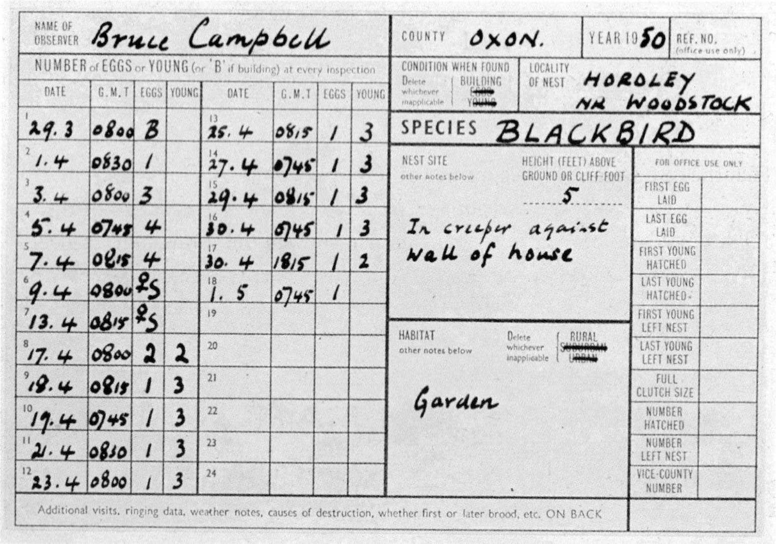

NAME OF OBSERVER *Bruce Campbell*   **COUNTY** *OXON.*   YEAR 19*50*   REF. NO. *(office use only)*

NUMBER of EGGS or YOUNG (or 'B' if building) at every inspection   CONDITION WHEN FOUND: Delete whichever inapplicable Building/Young   LOCALITY OF NEST *HOROLEY NR WOODSTOCK*

DATE	G.M.T	EGGS	YOUNG	DATE	G.M.T	EGGS	YOUNG
29.3	0800	B		25.4	0815	1	3
1.4	0830	1		27.4	0745	1	3
3.4	0800	3		29.4	0815	1	3
5.4	0745	4		30.4	0745	1	3
7.4	0815	4		30.4	1815	1	2
9.4	0800	5		1.5	0745	1	
13.4	0815	5					
17.4	0800	2	2				
19.4	0815	1	3				
19.4	0745	1	3				
21.4	0810	1	3				
23.4	0800	1	3				

SPECIES *BLACKBIRD*

NEST SITE other notes below — HEIGHT (FEET) ABOVE GROUND OR CLIFF: FOOT ...5...

In creeper against wall of house

HABITAT other notes below — Delete whichever inapplicable RURAL

Garden

FOR OFFICE USE ONLY: FIRST EGG LAID / LAST EGG LAID / FIRST YOUNG HATCHED / LAST YOUNG HATCHED / FIRST YOUNG LEFT NEST / LAST YOUNG LEFT NEST / FULL CLUTCH SIZE / NUMBER HATCHED / NUMBER LEFT NEST / VICE-COUNTY NUMBER

Additional visits, ringing data, weather notes, causes of destruction, whether first or later brood, etc. ON BACK

FIG 194. Nest record card from 1950. (BTO Collection)

Like the fledgling *British Birds* half a century earlier, *Bird Study* (Fig. 195) took a little time to settle into its stride, a process amusingly described by Bob Spencer (1983a): 'suffice to say there were those who desired nothing but serious science and those, contrariwise, who when confronted with such serious science in the form of graphs and equations saw it as unnecessarily complicated!' Also in 1954 the BTO held the first of its annual conferences, originally restricted to the regional representatives.

The 1960s saw the BTO establish the framework in which it has continued since. The first and most important logistical development was the departure from Oxford (in the case of the ringing office, from London) to Tring, where at Beech Grove the increasing numbers of professional staff were able to work under the same roof. There was also the appointment of the first Director, David Snow, and the commencement of that most essential feature of the Trust's subsequent work, the Common Birds Census (CBC). The catalyst for this was largely the findings of the peregrine survey: the deterioration in the numbers of peregrines, investigated by Derek Ratcliffe (1965) and subsequently discovered to be due to the cumulative effects of organochlorine pesticides in the birds on which peregrines preyed, led to a more general concern that farmland birds might be in decline as a direct result of pesticide use. The Nature Conservancy became very much involved in the ways in which these chemicals were affecting the environment, and one result of the investigations (Moore, 1987) was a clear indication that birds were an excellent 'early warning system' for detecting environmental pollution. It was realised that there was a need for a meaningful census, and thus in 1960 the Nature Conservancy asked for a census to be organised.

That the CBC began in the summer of 1961 proved providential, since it enabled the BTO to monitor the population crash of common birds following the appalling winter of 1962–3. The census also showed the subsequent recovery of bird numbers, demonstrating how 'fast' breeders such as wren (Fig. 196)

BIRD STUDY

THE JOURNAL OF
THE BRITISH TRUST FOR ORNITHOLOGY

VOLUME ONE   MDCCCCLIV

FIG 195. The front cover of the first issue of Bird Study, March 1954.

FIG 196. Wren. (Photograph by Rebecca Nason)

could recover their population level within a season or two whereas 'slow' breeders such as crows took several years. The main discovery that gradually emerged from the CBC, however, was the decline in the populations of farmland birds as a consequence of the agricultural revolution of the second half of the twentieth century, as documented by O'Connor and Shrubb (1986) and Marchant *et al.* (1990).

Nicholson and others were responsible for the support funding for the CBC, but the fieldworkers needed an advisor and motivator, and Ken Williamson was that man. From 1964 until his death in 1977 he worked as head of the Populations Section of the BTO and established the international reputation of the CBC. Over time the number of volunteers declined slightly – a methodology that required a minimum of four site visits per year proved demanding to sustain – and advancing standards of rigour meant that the analyses came under increasing pressure from scientific scrutiny. Two particular weaknesses emerged over time: first that the chosen sites were not randomly selected, and second that too many of them were in southern England, giving the results a regional bias. These and other factors eventually combined to see the BTO devise a new monitoring scheme, the Breeding Birds Survey (BBS), which uses randomised 1 km transects as its basis and has become the main method for population change monitoring.

The 1960s also saw the beginning of the Birds of Estuaries Enquiry, a joint project with the RSPB and the Wildfowl Trust whereby the birds on coastal estuaries were counted. The data collected were published, and eventually a book edited by Tony Prater (1981) summarised the status of estuarine birds. The information formed a benchmark against which any future estuary surveys could be compared. This aim, to conduct fieldwork with specific targets of interest and to publish the results to form a benchmark, became a common theme, the backbone of the BTO's work.

The most ambitious project was the national Breeding Atlas. The great success of the Atlas was not restricted to its scientific achievement: it also produced a surge of interest and practical enthusiasm for the concept of the BTO surveys. A later assessment suggested that the atlas methodology was too simplistic (it was changed for the 'new' Breeding Atlas in the 1990s) but by the time of its completion in 1972 there was an active army of surveyors across the nation. The BTO, intent on making use of the potential of this enthusiastic human resource, responded with the Register of Ornithological Sites (a doomsday book, as it was known by some people), and this resulted in a book on the bird habitats of Britain by Rob Fuller (1982).

Yet, despite the successes on the ground, with the core work of recording the nation's birds, the financial state of the BTO remained parlous. Following an investigation by consultants the post of Secretary was dispensed with, and in 1970 David Wilson, who had held the post for twelve years, was made redundant. Jim Flegg, who had become Director in the mid-1960s, returned to his previous research and the Trust engaged Raymond O'Connor as its new Director in 1978 – the very year that with help from the Nature Conservancy Council it also purchased its first computer. Sadly, the previous year had seen the death of Kenneth Williamson, who had been part of the engine room of the BTO since he first arrived back on the mainland in the fifties. Despite the financial tribulations the Trust continued to grow, both in membership and in staff.

The national ringing scheme continued to expand, mainly as a result of the proliferation of mist nets, and the 1960s and 70s saw the formation of a number of ringing groups, such as the Wash Wader Group and those based at Rye Meads and Wicken Fen. These groups combined experience and enthusiasm in a concentration of ringers, who were able collectively to achieve far greater coverage of specific sites than any individual could. This subsequently led to information being gathered on aspects of bird population changes and site usage, as well as the background migration studies. The importance of the Trust's dataset on ringed birds is nowhere better illustrated than in the recent *Migration Atlas*.

In 1973 the Nature Conservancy dropped its research council role and became the Nature Conservancy Council (NCC) within the Department of the

Environment, and by the various Wildlife and Countryside Acts of the early 1980s it was given certain responsibilities, including the protection of bird species. This responsibility was undertaken through the continuation of contracts to the BTO and the Wildfowl Trust, covering several core activities such as the CBC. In 1973 Ken Williamson organised a Waterways Bird Survey (WBS), designed to count the birds of riparian habitats, which were not covered by the CBC. When the WBS was introduced Williamson found funding for it, and did the analyses himself, until the NCC finally gave it financial backing. Since that time it has run at around 100 sites nationwide.

More recently the BTO outgrew the space at Beech Grove in Tring. After a number of possibilities the Nunnery at Thetford in Norfolk turned out to be the chosen spot. The move to Thetford in the early 1990s has enabled the organisation finally to achieve its initial goal and truly to establish a 'National Centre for Ornithology'.

SINGLE-SPECIES STUDIES

The 1950s and 1960s saw the publication of the results of a number of studies of the status and biology of British birds. The study of the redstart by John Buxton (1950) was one of the first of its kind after Chance's cuckoo studies; much of the fieldwork had been undertaken while Buxton was a prisoner of war in Germany. Norman Moore's study of buzzards (1957) showed a correlation between buzzard breeding distribution and the density of gamekeeping. Derek Ratcliffe's study of peregrines (1963, 1965) brought to light the effects of organochlorine pesticides, and there were specialist monographs on, for example, yellow wagtail (Smith, 1950), swift (Lack, 1956), hawfinch (Mountfort, 1957), blackbird (Snow, 1958) and woodpigeon (Murton, 1965) – all the results of long-term studies, and forerunners of the many single-species studies that have followed. Another valuable contribution was made by a series of books that covered families such as finches (Newton, 1972) (Fig. 197), birds of prey (Brown, 1976), thrushes (Simms, 1978), tits (Perrins, 1979), warblers (Simms, 1985) and waders (Hale, 1980) – all focusing on the British representatives of those families.

These high-quality books were almost like mini-handbooks. Probably the most significant publishing event around this time was the emergence of a new specialist publisher of ornithology, Trevor Poyser, who with his wife Anna established the imprint of T. & A. D. Poyser. The Poyser brand name was responsible for many of the seminal texts of the post-war period of British ornithology, particularly those resulting from the BTO surveys, the atlases, the

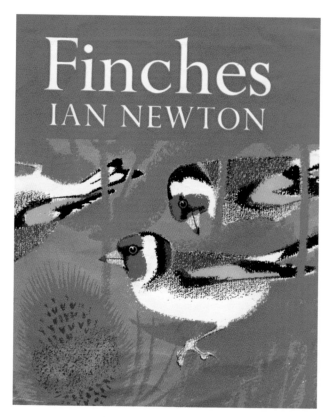

FIG 197. Front cover of Ian Newton's *Finches* (1972), one of the detailed studies published in the New Naturalist series.

register of sites, the estuaries enquiry, and so on. It is difficult to imagine a British ornithologist whose bookshelf does not contain more than one of the beautifully produced books with their distinctive white dust covers.

THE LANDMARK PUBLICATIONS

Of the texts of the post-war period three stand out as landmarks. The first was the identification guide, *A Field Guide to the Birds of Britain and Europe*, published in 1954. Up until that time the only forms of identification guidance were paintings of birds, usually in natural surroundings, and in the case of the *Handbook* showing some of the plumage variants by age or sex. Photographs, like paintings, showed the birds in natural surroundings, and were often spectacular – but while they could be used to get some idea of the appearance of a species they offered only gross clues for identification of a bird seen in the field. In the USA Roger Tory Peterson, a bird artist and ornithologist, had produced a novel identification guide using slightly simplified portraits and a system of pointers, straight lines that ran to the diagnostic features of the bird. The same system was used by Peterson to produce the first true field guide to the birds of Europe (Fig. 198), in collaboration with Guy Mountfort, who wrote much of the text, and Philip Hollom, who was responsible for the distribution maps. Peterson, Mountfort and Hollom's *Field Guide* was the first of its kind, and although it was equalled by other guides twenty or thirty years later it has only recently been bettered. 'Peterson', as it became known, was a bible. Tattered copies lived in overcoat pockets, and many a birdwatcher in the 1970s was on his second or third copy, the previous ones having fallen apart. One of the features of Peterson was the list of birds at the front, the so-called check list, with space beside to tick if seen, leading to the generic term of 'tickers' for rarity-hunters – now called 'twitchers'.

The second landmark text was the BTO's *Atlas of Breeding Birds in Britain and Ireland*. Previous efforts to define the distribution of breeding birds in Britain had relied on the lumping of data from a variety of sources, data that were often not concurrent, a high proportion of which were estimated, with little, if any, scientific standing. The *Atlas* was published in 1976 and edited initially by Ken Williamson. The text was written by a team of BTO staff and stalwarts and was finally put together by the project's organiser, Tim Sharrock. It was the culmination of fieldwork from 1968 to 1972, based not just on the presence or absence of each species in 10 km squares, but using three grades: present, possibly breeding, or proven breeding, depending on a series of predetermined criteria. The maps of breeding distribution had different-sized circles based on the three grades (Fig. 199), and there were overlay transparencies of various geographical and habitat features, enabling the reader to see correlations between the overlay feature and a bird's distribution.

Other atlases followed, the 'winter atlas' of 1986 and the subsequent 'new breeding atlas' of 1993, but they did not achieve the impact of the first breeding atlas, which was responsible for recruiting a large number of new fieldworkers.

Finally the third landmark publication began to appear in 1977 when the first volume of the much-awaited *Handbook of the Birds of Europe, the Middle East and North Africa*, subtitled *The Birds of the Western Palearctic* and abbreviated to BWP, was published. Once again Max Nicholson was the instigator, and he initially took the role of planning coordinator of what was both in conception and in reality a huge undertaking. When the project was close to becoming a reality the leading role went to Stanley Cramp.

FIG 198. Illustration of woodpeckers by Roger Tory Peterson, showing his straight-line method for diagnostic identification features. From *A Field Guide to the Birds of Britain and Europe* (1954).

BARN OWL

FIG 199. Breeding distribution of the barn owl, from the *Atlas of the Breeding Birds of Britain and Ireland* (Sharrock, 1976), Poyser and A & C Black Publishers.

There was no preamble. The first volume began with a short series of definitions such as the precise geographical area of the work, the proposed taxonomy, nomenclature etc., and some detailed explanation of what to expect under each heading. The book then launched into the systematic list of birds. Most species merited a minimum of four pages, and species that were most familiar, especially to the British ornithologists, were often spread over seven or eight. Illustration plates covered every species, often with many, if not all, plumage variations (Fig. 200). It became the work to which every ornithologist in Britain would turn for a definitive answer. But it proved to be a difficult undertaking, requiring considerable energy and stamina from its editors, particularly Cramp.

Stanley Cramp (Fig. 201) had been a birdwatcher before the war. He lapsed, but in 1943 he took up his hobby again, this time with determination and ambition. Professionally he worked in Customs and Excise, and after the war he moved to London, where both his profession and his hobby must have brought him in touch with Max Nicholson. Cramp threw himself into the London Natural History Society and then both the BTO and the RSPB in the late 1950s. He was involved in the toxic chemical issue with the former, and in the development of the RSPB through serving on its Council, being Chairman at the time of its considerable expansion under Peter Conder's directorship. He joined the editorial board of British Birds in 1960 and was Senior Editor from 1963 until his death in August 1987. His personal commitment to BWP was demonstrated when he took retirement from the civil service to be the major-domo of the project, not just in effecting the production but also in managing the financial and logistical side of the publication, which Cramp did with a skill that surprised some. Ken Simmons, his co-editor, described the process of the production of BWP as more difficult, demanding and costly than any of the production team had ever imagined, leaving Cramp an unending sequence of crises to overcome – using his characteristics as a 'hard, unsentimental, even ruthless realist'. Cramp saw the first four volumes to bed and was halfway through the fifth when he died.

The task took a huge toll of this 'obsessively secret man' who was not beyond 'promoting himself at the expense of others', according to Simmons. Nevertheless it seems hardly an overstatement to say that in the end it killed him. Cramp's death caused yet another crisis, but the role of supremo as far as the work was concerned was taken by David Snow and subsequently by the then Director of the EGI, Chris Perrins. For the business and logistics Sir William Wilkinson, an ornithologist who was also a banker, stepped into the breach and rescued the project from a probable premature end. Overall, nine volumes

PLATE 56. *Phasianus colchicus* Pheasant (p. 504): 1–2 ad ♂ hybrid showing variability, 3 ad ♀ hybrid, 4 ad ♂ melanistic hybrid '*tenebrosus*', 5 ad ♀ '*tenebrosus*', 6 ad ♂ *talischensis*, 7 juv, 8–9 downy young showing variability. (PJH)

PLATE 57. *Chrysolophus pictus* Golden Pheasant (p. 515): 1 ad ♂, 2 ad ♀, 3 juv, 4 downy young. *Chrysolophus amherstiae* Lady Amherst's Pheasant (p. 519): 5 ad ♂, 6 ad ♀, 7 juv, 8 downy young. (PJH)

FIG 200. Pheasant species and plumage variations by Peter Hayman. From *The Birds of the Western Palearctic*, vol. 3 (Cramp and Simmons, 1983), Oxford University Press.

FIG 201. Stanley Cramp. From *Ibis* (1989).

made up the set. The final volume appeared in 1994 and appropriately began with a foreword by Max Nicholson giving the complete history of the project from conception to realisation and explaining the personnel changes over time.

Without doubt BWP is the most comprehensive reference work on the birds of the region to date, but it was, like all such works, out of date before it hit the bookshops due to the continual flow of new information.

In almost every part of the development of post-war ornithology in this country you do not have to dig very deep before Max Nicholson's name surfaces. Nicholson had many other interests, not least the governance of Britain – he displayed a long-felt despair with the way we are governed. He lived to be 98, and in all that time he received no national recognition for his contribution. Perhaps he refused, but it is more likely that he rocked too many boats. Yet in a career that spanned almost the whole of the twentieth century, he was continually working for birds.

THE POPULARISERS

The twentieth-century renaissance of ornithology in Britain was not un-connected with the successful way in which the subject was popularised. The films, radio and television programmes about birds inspired a post-war generation of birdwatchers, and this had two important long-term effects. First, and most obviously, it raised the profile of the birds and those who study them. Second, perhaps more subtly, it created a growing degree of interest among ordinary people that has been reflected in the expansion of organisations such as the RSPB and the BTO. Yet an equally, or possibly even more, important factor in the expansion of ornithology has been the radical change in the social structure of Britain that resulted from the upheaval of the two world wars, particularly the second. This social change enabled people from all backgrounds to pursue their interests, given the right motivation. In the 1950s the film shows of the Wildfowl Trust and the RSPB drew great crowds, but the attendance was still drawn mostly from the middle classes. It was television, with its greater emphasis on entertainment, which broke through the class barrier. Television sets rapidly appeared in homes, and by 1960 they were close upon ubiquitous. From the arrival of Independent Television the programming on ITV and BBC became a mixture of the serious and the entertaining, and bird programmes could be both! The vital ingredient for success was that there should be a presenter to whom the viewer could relate, a person with the ability to make the viewer feel that he or she was in the same room, a natural broadcaster. Birds were very lucky to have Peter Scott.

Peter Scott and James Fisher – the great communicators
Peter Scott (Fig. 202) could have been encumbered by the reputation of his father – sons of famous fathers invariably find their own achievements measured against those of the parent, usually unfavourably – but Peter ploughed his own furrow. If Scott's father's life was one of heroic failure, Peter's was one of considerable achievement, not just in one, but in four different fields of endeavour. As well as a conservationist and ornithologist he was an Olympic sailor, a glider pilot of international stature and an artist.

When it came to communication Scott had the magic. His weekly natural history programme, *Look*, began with Scott in the studio introducing the filmed topic or topics with an easy grace. He may have 'mugged up' on the subject matter prior to the broadcast but he always gave the impression that he was drawing casually from a wealth of knowledge, yet at no time did he appear condescending. The overwhelming impression was of a person excited by the subject who wanted to share his excitement with you. The films were usually of a high standard, and what might seem corny today was revolutionary then. Heinz Sielmann's *Year with the Woodpeckers*, where the German film-maker had cut away part of the tree in which the woodpeckers were nesting and placed a camera in a hide in its place, revealed the home life of these elegant birds, and

FIG 202. Peter Scott feeding
snow geese at Slimbridge.
From the Severn Wildfowl
Trust Annual Report, 1948.
(Sport and General)

Ron Eastman did the same for kingfishers. No doubt it helped to choose
attractive birds. When the films ended Scott, as if filmed by his own fireside,
would wrap up the programme with a summary, a few words of explanation or
a short statement to place the subject matter in the context of a conservation
message. There can be little doubt that many of those who watched as children
were enthused by what they saw: seeds were sown.

Peter Scott had been influenced by Kenneth Fisher, the headmaster at
Oundle School, where Peter was sent for his secondary schooling in 1923. Fisher
encouraged him in the study of natural history but also, and equally significantly,
in art. Scott went to Cambridge University to study biology but changed to art
and architecture, following his university education with periods at Munich
and the Royal Academy art schools. Perhaps the defining period came one
winter, when he rented an old lighthouse on the mouth of the River Nene in
Lincolnshire. There he worked with the decoymen at Borough Fen, catching
wildfowl, and painted. He developed an artistic style for the wide open skies,

with wildfowl crossing, and began his first motley collection of ducks and geese, largely injured birds. In 1933 he had two paintings in the Royal Academy exhibition, but it was his one-man exhibitions and the publication of two books, *Morning Flight* (1935) and *Wild Chorus* (1938), that provided financial success and wide recognition.

At the outbreak of war he joined the Royal Navy, and among his many contributions he put forward suggestions for the camouflage painting of warships, based on his observations of the way wildfowl were camouflaged on the water. When the war ended, as a result of the defences that had been built in the war, the lighthouse was now a mile away from the sea and Scott was forced to look for a place to keep his collection – and so to Slimbridge. It is a mark of how vital Scott was seen to be to the BBC that the organisation's Natural History Unit was moved to Bristol to be close to his base at Slimbridge. He went on to be a prime mover in the World Wildlife Fund: he designed the panda logo and came up with the idea for the Red Data books. He was knighted in 1973 and made a Companion of Honour and Fellow of the Royal Society in 1987. His death in 1989 marked the end of an era in which conservation was led by personalities.

Scott was not alone. He was one half of the story, and the other half was his friend and contemporary, the son of his former headmaster, James Fisher (Fig. 203). If Scott was the televised face of natural history, Fisher was the radio voice. He made over a thousand broadcasts on a very wide variety of subjects, but mainly about his first love, birds. Fisher's writings also played a significant part in the popularisation process, none more so than those published by Pelican, *Watching Birds* (1940) and *Bird Recognition* (1947–55). Fisher was educated at Eton and Oxford, where he began reading medicine but changed to zoology after travelling on a university expedition to Spitsbergen. In 1936 he became an assistant curator at the Zoological Society in London, encouraged to do so by Julian Huxley, a lifelong friend, and he remained at the zoo until the outbreak of World War II, whereupon he worked on the food of the rook for the Ministry of Agriculture, based in Oxford – first at the Bureau of Animal Population and then at the Edward Grey Institute, where he remained until 1946.

At this juncture it is quite possible that James Fisher might have gone on to be Director of the EGI. He had many good contacts and would have been an excellent 'front man', but the EGI remained within the framework of the university and there was some questioning of the scientific validity of the results of the rook survey work. In any case Fisher's scientific reputation could hardly compare with Lack's, so Fisher was passed over. Looking back, this was probably good for the future of British ornithology, as he was diverted into the publishing

FIG 203. James Fisher, photographed in 1970 by Eric Hosking. (Reproduced by kind permission of David Hosking)

and broadcasting that occupied him for the rest of his life. He became a founder member of the board of the New Naturalist series – and the tale, apocryphal or otherwise (Marren, 1995), has Fisher meeting Billy Collins by chance in an air-raid shelter in the war. Fisher apparently said that what the country needed was a good series of books on natural history to take people's minds from the carnage, whereupon Collins replied that if Fisher could find an editorial board he, Collins, would supply tea and buns! Whatever the truth, Fisher was undoubtedly one of the prime movers behind the New Naturalists. He produced the monograph on the fulmar (Fig. 204) in 1952, and with R. M. Lockley he wrote *Sea-Birds* (1954), the twenty-eighth book in the series and a forerunner of those books describing groups of birds that were to follow.

Fisher's interest in the history of both birds and ornithologists resulted in *The Shell Bird Book* (1966), of which a reviewer wrote that the title gave no hint of the content and that he thought it remarkable that Fisher could find new things to say about 'the most thoroughly documented avifauna in the world'. And all the time the radio broadcasts continued. Roger Peterson wrote that Fisher 'bridged the gap between the academic and the layman more effectively than any of his contemporaries', and he was said to hold audiences spellbound. Above all it was the combination of the relaxed style of broadcasting and the radiogenic voice that

FIG 204. Fulmar – one of James Fisher's favourite species. (Photograph by Rebecca Nason)

made Fisher such a success. Like Scott, he always seemed to be informing his audience about his enthusiasm, sharing his discoveries, never lecturing or talking down to the listener.

Fisher was greatly interested in new or neglected fields of study, fossil birds being one such, and he intended to write a book to be entitled *Early Birds*. He intended also to complete a monograph on his other favoured bird, the gannet, but it was not to be. He continued to serve the ornithological organisations, and his recognition of the importance and indeed significance of education echoes that of Scott. Almost uniquely he was awarded the main medal of all three ornithological organisations: the Union Medal of the BOU, the Tucker Medal of the BTO and the Gold Medal of the RSPB. Tragically he died in 1970 at the comparatively youthful age of 58. Bill Bourne, a fellow seabird enthusiast, wrote in the obituary of Fisher that appeared in *The Ibis* that 'together with Peter Scott he became identified in the public mind as the personal incarnation of natural history.'

The torch lit by Scott and Fisher was taken up by others. Pre-eminent among them is David Attenborough, who introduced the concept of the filmed series on a particular theme or topic. The Attenborough series *The Life of Birds*, broadcast in the late 1990s, was an excellent overview of the variety of the world's birds – but it also illustrated the overriding concern of general television broadcasting in never breaking from the simple or the entertaining into the more cerebrally challenging areas of, in this case, real ornithology. As such it was an opportunity missed, and that opportunity remains to be grasped, although the overriding concern with viewing figures makes a more detailed study unlikely at the present time.

The best person to make programmes of popular ornithology might have been Chris Mead (Fig. 205). A man of considerable physical proportions, Mead could always be relied upon for an authoritative opinion or explanation.

FIG 205. Chris Mead on the doorstep of Beech Grove, the headquarters of the BTO until the 1990s. The gannet features in the logo of the organisation. (BTO Collection)

Migration and bird ringing were his greatest loves, and his book on bird migration is beyond doubt the finest of its kind for the non-scientific reader. Like Yarrell, he had the art to extract the information that appealed to the public at large, to sift it and to regurgitate it in the most succinct and interesting way, whether by speech or writing. But sadly Chris Mead died in 2003, and ornithology remains outside the broadcasters' idea of serious science.

Last and by no means least, the arrival of the specialist monthly magazines saw the birth of *Bird Watching* in 1981. Glossy but not flash, filled with information about places and birds and most usefully containing excellent articles on the identification of birds that any birdwatcher might find in their local park or gravel pit, *Bird Watching* fulfilled the wishes of the enthusiastic birdwatcher for a magazine that reflects his or her interest. Initially some sceptics doubted its commercial viability. Not only have they been proved wrong, but a number of others have arrived on the scene, *Birdwatch* for one. All this publicity, on radio, on television, in magazines, has contributed to the public's interest in birds, and that great interest has enabled the subject to prosper and multiply in Britain.

CHAPTER 18

Post-War Ornithological Research

If I were to characterise British post-war ornithological research, I would point to its concentration on the living bird.

Niko Tinbergen, *The Ibis*, 1959

T HE PERIOD AFTER World War II saw a significant and far-reaching expansion in all science in Britain, and ornithology was no exception. The development of practical conservation exposed a need for scientifically reliable data that resulted in increasing employment for academically trained ornithologists. Oxbridge led the way. The Edward Grey Institute at Oxford was matched by the formation of a Sub-Department (of Zoology) of Animal Behaviour in Cambridge, and these two universities were the base of the three principal academic ornithologists of the immediate post-war period, David Lack, Bill Thorpe and Niko Tinbergen. These three inspired many, or even most, of the generation of British ornithologists at the end of the twentieth century.

THE WORK OF DAVID LACK

David Lack, born in London in 1910, began his bird studies while still at school. His father was descended from Norfolk farmers, and perhaps it was this that inspired the love of birds that saw him compile his first life list by the age of nine. There could scarcely be a better place to be sent away to school than Gresham's School at Holt in Norfolk. From Gresham's, Lack was able to visit Scolt Head, Cley, Blakeney and Hickling Broad, but it was at nearby Kelling and other local heaths that he conducted his studies, for which the school allowed him to take off games afternoons. At sixteen he won a competition at Gresham's for an essay on natural history with an account of three species found on Kelling Heath: nightjar, ringed plover (Fig. 206) and redshank. Studying nightjars for a season, he discovered they were not single-brooded, as the books stated, but double-brooded, and this work formed the basis of his first scientific paper in *British Birds* in 1930.

In 1930 he went to university at Cambridge, where he did not find his course stimulating – in fact quite the contrary. He found the Cambridge sewage farm more to his liking. Visiting it on his first day, he immediately added wood sandpiper to his life list, and he wrote a paper based on his observations at the site in *British Birds*. He also found people who could draw him out of his natural shyness, both in college (Magdalene) and in the town. There were the expeditions: in 1931 to St Kilda and in 1932 to Bear Island in the Arctic. To help organise the Bear Island expedition he invited T. G. Longstaff to lecture to the Cambridge Bird Club, and afterwards asked Longstaff his advice about the proposed expedition – which was 'the ideal number for an expedition is one and the party should consist of the minimum number above that to attain one's ends.'

FIG 206. Ringed plover, from John Gould's *Birds of Great Britain* (1862–73).

The following year he published two papers, 'Nesting conditions as a factor controlling breeding time in birds', based on observations from the Bear Island trip, and 'Habitat selection in birds with special reference to the effects of afforestation on the Breckland avifauna'. Both were treated dismissively in the reviews in *The Ibis* (see Chapter 12), but the latter has become something of a classic over the years and those poor reviews seem to have had no detrimental effect on the budding researcher. Next there was a paper in *British Birds*, 'Territory reviewed' (1933), written with his father. This paper alone went a long way to establishing David Lack's reputation. He was responsible for the publication of the first authentic *Birds of Cambridgeshire* in 1934. As a Cambridge graduate with a degree in natural sciences he had an opportunity to be a museum ornithologist, as a possible replacement in the British Museum Bird Room for Percy Lowe, but he decided to become a schoolmaster.

Julian Huxley suggested to Lack that there was a place for a master at Dartington College, a radical school in Devon where pupils were, among other things, allowed to choose whether or not to attend lessons. For Lack the job appealed since the teaching was combined with an opportunity to do research. When Lack visited the school he was surprised to find the pupils happy (contrary to his own experience), and he decided to take the job. His enjoyment was immediate and lasting, so that when the British Museum job finally came up Lack had no hesitation in turning it down. It is difficult to imagine what might have become of this solitary man if he had spent his productive life within the bird room, though at the time such employment was almost the only way to pursue a career in ornithology.

At Dartington Lack began to trap and colour-ring robins (Fig. 207), largely in an attempt to encourage interest from his pupils, whereupon he discovered that although each robin held a territory it freely trespassed into the territory of others. His study of robins was unofficially supervised by Julian Huxley, and Lack later stated that at the time Huxley was the only senior British zoologist who thought that ecology and behaviour were of any importance. Furthermore Huxley arranged for Lack to go to Tanzania to meet Reg Moreau during the summer holidays in 1934, and thus began a lifelong friendship based on mutual interests. The following summer Lack went to California, where he was 'amazed to find a university where ornithology was taught'. On his way home he met the American systematist, Ernst Mayr, in New York, and another lifelong friendship began with shared enthusiasm for Darwinian theory.

The robin work posed problems that Lack needed to address through research on other birds (all research leads to more research!), and reading Percy Lowe's paper on the Galapagos finches Lack thought they seemed an ideal

FIG 207. Robin, from George Graves's *British Ornithology* (1811–21).

subject. Huxley once more helped, with lots of encouragement and the essential financial backing, and eventually in autumn 1938 the expedition set off for the Galapagos Islands. Lack's summary of his time on Galapagos sounds distinctly uncomfortable; nevertheless it yielded results and set him off into another unexpected direction when he ended up again in California with some live specimens to study, as well as the skins in the museum there. This was followed by a stay with the Mayrs, where he received tuition on systematics and speciation.

Lack returned to Dartington in September 1939 but the atmosphere no longer worked its charm, perhaps because he had tasted the more heady wine of full-time research, and with the onset of World War II he signed up as a pacifist and left Devon to join a pacifist unit in London – where he was so put off by the pacifists' earnest attitudes, and so excited by the flashes and bangs, that he was immediately converted. During the war Lack was employed among the 'boffins', and despite his self-confessed weakness in the area of maths and physics he found himself working on developing the technical uses of radio. His first assignment (he volunteered, much to the relief of his fellow scientists) found him testing radio equipment in the ornithological paradise of Orkney, coincidentally in the breeding season. Back on the mainland, he joined the Operational Research Group, where he made two discoveries. The first was that he was more able than most to read the complex data files and to compress them into clearly written reports for his superiors, and the second was that birds could be detected by the radar used for aircraft.

The idleness of the long evenings in the war years provided the opportunity to spend time in discussion with scientists, particularly biologists, of a similar age and outlook, and his subsequent publications reflect the interests that Lack developed during the war. The free evenings also provided the time to complete his book *The Life of the Robin* (1943), the first of its kind, which brought to the public detailed knowledge of the country's most familiar bird. Writing it stimulated Lack to consider the usefulness of ringing data – first to look at mortality and, after the war, to consider survival in relation to brood size. When Lack announced at a meeting of the BOU that three-fifths of adult Robins die each year he reported that he was 'disbelieved by everyone present except Landsborough Thomson'.

When the war ended, Lack used his data on Galapagos finches to compile a book for sixth-form students about Darwinian principles – *Darwin's Finches* (1947). Writing the book caused him to review the literature particularly with regard to the principle of competitive exclusion – which suggested that competition between two similar species must in the end lead to the exclusion (or extinction) of one of the competitors (known as Gause's principle, after the man who proposed it). He also considered Julian Huxley's suggestion that size difference in related species had evolved for them to share the same habitat. At the time the accepted view was that most differences between species (and subspecies) were non-adaptive, i.e. not shaped by external factors, but Lack's *Darwin's Finches* expounded the now accepted view that they are very much adaptive, and it established his reputation in the scientific community, leading later to his election as a Fellow of the Royal Society. The distinguished zoologist Alistair Hardy thought it 'an outstanding study on the origin of species and the importance of adaptation in the differentiation of the various kinds. It was a small book but a great one.'

The subject that interested Lack now was population dynamics. He approached it from the simple but obvious equation that overall numbers were dictated by input versus outflow, in other words births and deaths: when birth rate equalled death rate the population remained stable, but any inequality must lead to population changes. A paper by Reg Moreau (1944) on the clutch sizes of African birds stimulated the idea that the clutch size of nidicolous birds (those that hatch naked and dependent, such as blackbird, as opposed to nidifugous birds, such as ducks, which hatch feathered) was manipulated by evolution to the capacity of each species to raise fledglings. In other words, birds lay the mean number of eggs that permit the maximum output of surviving young. This was the birth-rate side of the equation. Lack became equally interested in density-dependence as a regulator of death rate. Stated simply, do birds at higher densities suffer greater mortality, survival being harder due to increased competition for resources? In May 1944 Lack put together the rough draft of a book concerning these ideas, which subsequently became *The Natural Regulation of Animal Numbers* (1954).

The retirement of W. B. Alexander left the directorship of the Edward Grey Institute vacant. After some urging from Bernard Tucker and H. N. Southern, Lack accepted the post, so that, as he pointed out, at the age of 35, having written three books and exactly 50 papers, he became a professional ornithologist. To pursue the study of population dynamics he required a natural model, and he deserted his beloved robins for the great tit (Fig. 208) – a more practical species since it nested in boxes and thus made itself readily available for the collection of breeding data (Lack had seen Kluijver's nest-box studies in action in Holland).

Lack's work in the 1950s included swifts (Fig. 209), which had become an interest in the mid-1940s. With his wife Elizabeth he began a study of them in the tower of the University Museum (using adapted nestboxes), and this led to a number of papers and another excellent monograph, *Swifts in a Tower* (1956). This book, though perhaps less widely read than *The Life of the Robin*, was every bit as well written and every bit as readable.

In 1962 the hypothesis of density-dependence expounded in *The Natural Regulation of Animal Numbers* was countered by V. C. Wynne-Edwards in his book *Animal Dispersion in Relation to Social Behaviour*. Lack's view had been that numbers (of birds) were controlled by three main causes of mortality: disease, parasitic infestation and food shortage, all of which were dependent on the density of the population. Wynne-Edwards postulated that external or independent factors such as periods of hard weather could equally cause changes in population. The conflicting views included whether, as Lack thought, birds competed directly for food or, as Wynne-Edwards suggested, for status – which

FIG 208. Great tit by Archibald Thorburn, from Lilford's *Coloured Figures of the Birds of the British Islands* (1885–97).

FIG 209. Swift, from *Birds and Bird Keeping* (anon., late nineteenth century).

subsequently determined their success at feeding. Wynne-Edwards considered numbers to be limited by territorial behaviour so that given a minimum size of territory only a certain number could fit in a given area. Lack, on the other hand, thought that territories spaced out birds whose population level had already been determined. In 1966 Lack produced *Population Studies of Birds*, which was largely an attempt to reinforce the arguments put forward in *The Natural Regulation of Animal Numbers*. Bill Thorpe later commented that he thought Lack wasted time responding to Wynne-Edwards, whose points were valid, when he could have been doing more fieldwork. Perhaps the most useful feature of the later book was the appendix, which summarised the various arguments in population biology at that time. Lack's interest in population biology did not wane, and as late as 1970 he gave an introductory paper at the Symposium of the British Ecological Society entitled 'Animal populations in relation to their food sources'.

The discovery that migrating birds could be seen on radar opened up yet more lines of enquiry. Together with Kenneth Williamson, Lack became a proponent of the concept of 'drift migration' (see Chapter 14). His first migration paper 'The problem of partial migration' was published in 1944 and the last, 'Drift migration: a correction', in 1969.

Lack's last years saw the publication of two 'ecological' books, *Ecological Adaptations for Breeding in Birds* (1968) and *Ecological Isolation in Birds* (1971). The latter book was his last word on the way in which adaptation takes place, ecological isolation leading to divergence and thus structural and behavioural diversity. These were followed after his death by *Evolution Illustrated by Waterfowl* (1974) and *Island Biology* (1974).

Lack received many honours from various universities and scientific societies. His lack of interest in socialising notwithstanding, he was President of the British Ecological Society 1963–5 and Vice-President of the BOU from 1969 to 1972. A far more practical position was that of President of the XIVth International Ornithological Congress when it was held in Oxford in 1966. The two honours he prized most were the Godman–Salvin Medal of the BOU, awarded in 1958 (Fig. 210), and in the twilight of his life the Darwin Medal of the Royal Society. The citation for the latter stated that he had

greatly advanced our understanding of ecological speciation in birds, and of breeding habits and other factors that limit their numbers in natural populations and determine the separation of closely related species ... working with such distinction in a tradition of which Charles Darwin remains the prime exemplar. David Lack is pre-eminently fitted for the award of the Darwin Medal.

FIG 210. David Lack receiving his Godman–Salvin Medal from Bill Thorpe, 1958. From *The Ibis*.

He was sadly too ill to receive his medal in person. The greater shame since he would have received it from the physiologist and Nobel laureate Alan Hodgkin, at that time President of the Royal Society, who, as a fellow pupil at Gresham's, had helped Lack to find the nests of the nightjars all those years before.

Lack was described by Thorpe as 'an uncompromising individualist' who was 'always completely single-minded about his research', and he said that the only work that Lack enjoyed without reservation was fieldwork – 'and such people are seldom easy companions.' The consequences to British ornithology of Lack's early death from cancer in 1973 are impossible to assess. Had he been blessed with the length of life enjoyed by Newton, who knows what he might have achieved? Tinbergen stated that Lack liked to think of himself as 'the last of the amateurs' in bird ecology.

BILL THORPE, THE ETHOLOGIST

William Homan Thorpe (1902–86) spent the first part of his professional life as
an economic entomologist before he turned to birds as a means of pursuing
studies in ethology, in which he examined the relative importance of instinct
and learning, using bird song as his model. Thorpe was one of those unfortunate
children dogged by ill health, and this prevented him from becoming involved
in much social or sporting activity. He never really shone at school. After reading
of a need for economic entomologists, Thorpe went to Jesus College, Cambridge,
to read agriculture.

At Cambridge he was one of the founder members of the Cambridge Bird
Club. He also produced his first publications, including 'Some ecological aspects
of British ornithology' (1925), showing his interest in a 'new' topic. His course,
however, did not quite fulfil his hopes and he also attended lectures in zoology.
His degree in agriculture was far from the pinnacle of academic achievement
and hardly hinted at future success. After graduation Thorpe remained at
Cambridge, working in the Agriculture Department on economic entomology,
including 'biological races' of moths. After a spell at the Imperial Institute of
Entomology, he returned to Cambridge in 1932 as a Lecturer in Entomology in
the Zoology Department. From then until the close of World War II Thorpe
pursued his entomological research while maintaining an ornithological interest;
from 1943 he began to publish papers on such topics as learning in birds and
orientation.

By the late 1940s Thorpe was moving away from entomology to ethology,
mainly because of his interest in the relation between instinct and learning, and
eventually he became Professor of Animal Ethology at Cambridge. Thorpe's role
was described by Robert Hinde (1987):

> Bill played a unique role in establishing Ethology in the English-speaking world after
> the war. He was responsible for publicising Lorenz's views ... He was a founding
> member of the journal Behaviour [and] was largely responsible for a meeting in
> Cambridge in 1949 which was a forum for the presentation of Lorenz's and Tinbergen's
> post-war views, and Bill's own paper, 'The concepts of learning and their relation to
> those of instinct' was a foretaste of his later book.

Thorpe appreciated that if he was to be able to match Lorenz's studies of instinct
with studies of learning he needed a base away from the Zoology Department.
He found a place in Madingley, a village a few miles west of Cambridge, and in

1950 established an Ornithological Field Station there. It was at Madingley that Thorpe pursued his classic study of the mechanism by which songbirds develop their vocalisations, a process which Thorpe showed included elements of innate knowledge and subsequent learning. The study bird of choice was the chaffinch (Fig. 211), and as well as the ingenuity of the experiments Thorpe developed the use of the sound spectrograph to display and analyse each vocal output (Fig. 212).

This led him to look at other forms of vocalisation, including imitation in mynah birds – with amusing effects, as described by Hinde:

> *He asked members of the laboratory to take mynah birds home and train them to*
> *say particular phrases. Not surprisingly, the mynahs learnt things other than those*
> *they were taught. One of them, on returning to the laboratory, would very clearly*
> *repeat instructions to Bill to go away, though in very impolite language, and others*

FIG 211. Male and female chaffinch, from John Gould's *Birds of Great Britain* (1862–73).

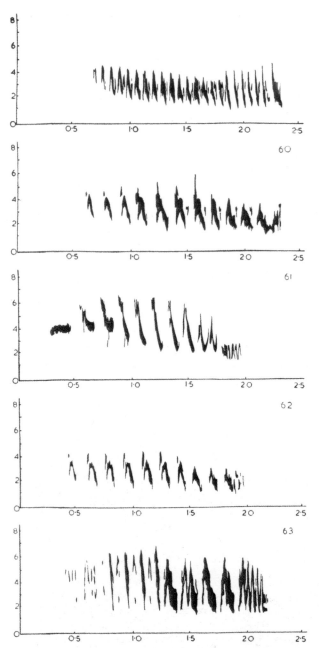

FIG 212. Spectrograph print-out of chaffinch song. From Thorpe, *The Ibis* (1958).

would reveal very interesting details of the domestic lives of those who had been looking after them.

Thorpe's research revolved around the sounds made by birds, including the lack of sound made by owls in flight. Among his books are *Learning and Instinct in Animals* (1956, with a second edition in 1963), and *Bird Song* (1961). In addition he contributed to many books across the whole behavioural theme.

It surprised Thorpe that Lack had not been an active conservationist, since the need to preserve the countryside was important to Thorpe. He played a part in many organisations (Fig. 213), particularly the International Council for Bird Preservation (ICBP) – now Birdlife International – of which he was Chairman of the British Section from 1965 to 1979. He was very active within East Anglia and was a stalwart on the local committee at Wicken Fen. He was entirely responsible for getting Chippenham Fen in Cambridgeshire preserved – it is now a National Nature Reserve – and he was involved in the management committees for Scolt Head and Blakeney Point in Norfolk and Woodwalton Fen in (old) Huntingdonshire. Thorpe worked for many societies, entomological, ethological and ornithological, serving as Vice-President and President of the BOU, President of the Zoology section of the British Association for the Advancement of Science and on the Council of the Royal Society. He was awarded the Godman–Salvin

FIG 213. Reg Moreau, Bill Thorpe and John Monk at the International Ornithological Congress, Ithaca 1962. From *The Ibis* (1970).

Medal of the BOU in 1968, the Frink Medal of the Zoological Society in 1980 and the Fyssen Prize for contributions to knowledge about the origin and nature of man's cognitive abilities in 1982.

Robert Hinde summarised Thorpe as slightly aloof: 'On most occasions, and for many people, his reputation for intellectual brilliance and his natural shyness formed an impenetrable barrier.' Yet he also commented on Thorpe's 'wonderful sense of humour, which sometimes appeared without warning, as when curtains are drawn back to reveal a brightly lit room.'

Thorpe's work was rooted in behaviour, and it was in the field of ethology that his followers worked. In addition, Cambridge did not at that time develop a base for ornithology, as Oxford did in the Edward Grey Institute, and it is perhaps for these reasons that the work of Bill Thorpe is not as well known as it should be amongst ornithologists.

THE BEHAVIOURAL STUDIES OF NIKO TINBERGEN

From an early age Nikolaas Tinbergen (1907–88) was a birdwatcher in the complete sense of the word, camping out in the dunes of Holland watching the behaviour of the wildlife, particularly the gulls. From the beginning almost to the end it was the gulls that enthralled him. Tinbergen was concerned with the fundamentals of the behaviours that he recorded, epitomised by his famous four whys:

> *Causation*: what causes the event – what internal or external factors provoke it?
> *Ontogeny*: why and how was this behavioural event developed – is it innate or learned?
> *Function*: what is the purpose, in other words, what is the survival value?
> *Evolution*: why and how did this behaviour evolve?

Tinbergen's creed was that if these four whys could be answered and explained then the investigator would have a biological understanding of the behaviour. Observation in the field was the key, and Tinbergen reasoned that only through observing creatures in their natural habitat, following their natural patterns of behaviour, could you hope to provide meaningful insights into what they did and why. His belief in this method of study gave him little confidence in the laboratory-based studies of the so-called animal psychologists.

Tinbergen (Fig. 214) was never academically inclined. Study at school seemed only to be an interruption in his birdwatching, and he was not beyond a little

FIG 214. Niko Tinbergen. From *The Ibis* (1969) on his award of the Godman–Salvin Medal.

truancy from time to time. Only ice skating and hockey, and above all photography, appealed beyond the natural world. When he left school he should have gone to university but it simply did not appeal. He was sent to the Vogelwarte Rossitten, the field station responsible for most of the early ringing data – and it must have been something that he saw there that made him realise that university life had something to offer after all. So Tinbergen returned to Leiden and to the university and a five-year course in biology.

The head of department, Jan Verwey, was only eight years older than Tinbergen. He was a marine biologist, but also a bird man, even if it was relegated to his spare time. Verwey was studying a nearby colony of herons and showed Tinbergen that it was possible to study social behaviour of birds in natural surroundings. With a group of like-minded enthusiasts Tinbergen became involved in studies in the dunes close to The Hague, and thus gulls became a focus of his interest.

In 1930 Tinbergen carried out the research studies for his degree, most notably on digger wasps. With no great enthusiasm he stayed in Leiden to do his PhD on the bee-hunting wasp, but in his spare time birds remained top of the agenda, and he conducted a study of the food of birds of prey, assisted by his younger brother Luuk. One vital development in his PhD studies occurred when, like Jenner, he began to conduct experiments in the field, such as changing markers that he believed the wasps used to find their burrows and to identify their prey. Setting up a circle of pine cones as markers for the wasps, Tinbergen would change their pattern or remove them to see how long the wasps took to find their burrow with the new arrangement. He showed that the wasps took honeybees only, and having removed the wasps' antennae he observed that they were unable to locate their prey without their sense of smell.

In July 1932 Niko Tinbergen went with his wife to Greenland as part of a Dutch expedition. His aim was to study glaucous gulls and compare their behaviour with the herring gull data; he also wanted to look at the territoriality of snow buntings, having recently read Eliot Howard's masterpiece. Howard had described territoriality in yellowhammers and reed buntings, but Max Nicholson on a previous visit to Greenland had suggested that snow buntings were non-territorial. In Greenland Tinbergen found a true wilderness, and living among the native people he became fully engaged in a lifestyle of hunting, far removed from the Dutch ethos of the sanctity of wildlife. Greenland also provided an opportunity for Tinbergen the photographer, and the year-long sojourn resulted in a book called *Eskimoland* (1934). The snow bunting study yielded a great deal of information, including the fact that they were as territorial as the other buntings (Nicholson had not been in Greenland at the right time of the year).

In 1935 Konrad Lorenz published his observations of instinctive behaviour of birds and the significance of imprinting, whereby newly hatched precocial birds are fixated on the first moving object they see – almost invariably their mother. Tinbergen was impressed. He wrote to Lorenz, and a correspondence began, so that after a coincidental meeting at a conference Tinbergen went to Austria to work with Lorenz in the summer of 1937. This period of the idyllic summer remained a high point in both their lives and cemented a lifelong friendship. Their main scientific project during Tinbergen's stay concerned the egg-rolling instinct of geese. When a goose sees an egg has escaped from the nest, and is not therefore being incubated, she stretches out her neck and tucks the egg under her chin, skilfully drawing it back into the nest. Tinbergen and Lorenz discovered that if the egg was removed from the goose halfway through the drawing-in process the goose continued the movement nevertheless. They followed this observation with Tinbergian experiments. First a model egg (wood) was presented, and the goose instinctively tried to pull it into the nest; then a model of a super-egg, and again despite the obvious disparity in size and the consequent difficulty of the task the goose persisted in trying to get the super-egg into the nest. It was a much-quoted elegant study of instinctive behaviour and the way that such behaviour persists beyond rationality.

Lorenz and Tinbergen always shared their interest in behaviour, but there were differences in their interpretation of cause: Lorenz tended towards black and white (behaviour was either innate or learned, nature or nurture), while Tinbergen was uncertain that it could be so simply dichotomised, and allowed for shades of grey, a combination of nature and nurture.

The following summer, 1938, Tinbergen went to America, where he spent time with many influential workers, not least among them Ernst Mayr. World War II interrupted Tinbergen's academic career in the Netherlands, and in 1942 he was interned by the Germans as part of a group of 'influential men', held as a kind of hostage. Incarcerated with politicians and scientists, there must have been ample time for reflection and planning. Once he was freed, he returned to his previous position at the University of Leiden, where he continued the study of territoriality, fighting and song in birds – and the 'why' questions began to emerge.

The herring gull work resumed, and he began to build a group of students around him. Further studies of digger wasps followed, once again with field experiments, and some of his students became involved in studies of stickle-backs, presenting the fish with models, increasingly crude, to determine which of the features – shape, movement or colour – was the stimulus for the male to attack. This work showed that behaviour could be broken down into units, each dependent on a sequence of events, and it led to the important concepts of sign stimuli and innate 'releasers'. Around this time, too, he began to record behaviours that seemed inappropriate, such as birds preening in the middle of a territorial dispute. Tinbergen suggested that these actions were designed to defuse the aggression, and they became known eventually as 'displacement activities'.

In 1946 Tinbergen travelled to England, visiting Lack in Oxford, Thorpe in Cambridge and finally Julian Huxley in London. Later the same year a series of lectures in Columbia University formed the basis of his most famous book, A Study of Instinct (1951). Tinbergen related behaviour to other biological specialties such as physiology, and to the more psychologically based animal studies. The kernel of the book dealt with the 'why' questions and considered the causal factors of behaviour before ending by covering the evolutionary and adaptive aspects of behaviour, learning and development. It also contained a distilled version of the idea of behaviour being separated into fragments within the hierarchical structure. Littered with the Tinbergen drawings (Figs 215, 216) and illustrations of practical research, A Study of Instinct reached a wide audience and undoubtedly achieved an important aim in that it made the work accessible beyond ethologists.

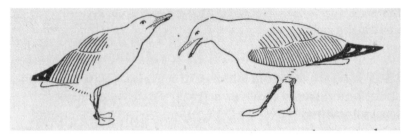

FIG 215. Drawing by Tinbergen to show the body postures of herring gulls: 'female (left) proposing to male'. From *Social Behaviour in Animals* (1953).

FIG 216. Drawing by Tinbergen to show the body postures of herring gulls: 'upright threat posture of male'. From *Social Behaviour in Animals* (1953).

Tinbergen's post-war travels indicated his restlessness. Although he remained highly productive in his research output, and despite being given a professorship in Leiden, he wanted to get away from Holland – and in the end, thanks particularly to Sir Alistair Hardy, then Professor of Zoology, he was offered a post at Oxford. Tinbergen's Oxford life appears to have been something of a curate's egg. His involvement with his group of research students and his continuing thread of research proved very positive, but the university politics made him ill at ease. One of his first pieces of writing in Oxford was *The Herring Gull's World* (1953). This book, probably more than *A Study of Instinct*, introduced Tinbergen to the naturalists of Britain.

Within a short space of time Tinbergen had begun to draw together a group of highly motivated, talented students, and he set them on the studies that continued the themes from his Leiden days: the sticklebacks, the wasps and above all the gulls. The students became known as 'the hard core' and their supervisor as 'the Maestro'. There were Friday-evening brainstorming sessions at the Tinbergen home and projects on gulls and terns in Norfolk and later the Farne Islands. Comparative gull studies included kittiwakes, which had adapted much of their behaviour to their cliff-nesting environment. At Ravenglass, a windswept duneland on the Irish Sea coast in Cumbria, he investigated how gulls deal with nest predators – a typical mixture of observation and experimentation. To confirm that the purpose of the colouration and pattern of gulls eggs was to camouflage them against predators, the team painted eggs, some black and some white, to contrast with the background and noted the relative rates of predation – much higher in painted eggs than in natural eggs. Next they placed objects close to the nest that also contrasted with the background, and as long as the nest contained eggs the adults would remove the objects, presumably seeing them as likely to attract the attention of predators. Finally in the late 1950s came the eggshell study. Having noted that adults removed the eggshells as soon as the chick had dried, the scientists presented a variety of objects that were variously white, like the inside of an opened eggshell, or frilly-edged, like an eggshell chipped open by an emergent chick. These both attracted predators and were subject to the same removal instinct.

By this time Tinbergen had expanded his photography beyond a still camera, becoming proficient with film. When new research started on lesser black-backed gulls on Walney Island, some 65 kilometres south of Ravenglass, Tinbergen teamed up with Hugh Falkus, a film director with BBC connections, and in the 1960s they produced films of the gulls, Falkus directing and Tinbergen filming and providing the science. This collaboration culminated in the Italia Prize-winning *Signals for Survival* film, one of the first films to show the science side of natural history studies turned into a story, and it spawned a companion book (1970) with photographs by Tinbergen and paintings by Eric Ennion (Fig. 217).

Oxford life was mainly a whirl of teaching and supervising, reading and writing. All the papers, articles, books and now films had made Tinbergen the nearest thing to a household name that a scientist can be. His work had been subject to criticism, some friendly, some dispassionate, some unfriendly. Towards the end of Niko's life his elder brother Jan (a Nobel laureate in economics) mildly reproved him for his lack of quantitative data, an Achilles heel that was the cause of much of the criticism.

He was in demand as a guest lecturer, and as a speaker at conferences and symposia (he was said to be the star performer at David Lack's student conferences). In 1962 he was elected to a Fellowship of the Royal Society, as well as receiving academic distinctions in Europe, America and South Africa during this period. He was the recipient of the BOU Godman–Salvin Medal in 1969. Then came the ultimate award when in 1973, to some surprise in the scientific community, Tinbergen, Lorenz and von Frisch (who had studied honeybees) were awarded the Nobel Prize in Physiology or Medicine. Looking back, it is still difficult to see how these pioneers of ethology fit in among the list of winners before and after. Nevertheless, it marked a point at which studies of birds had finally arrived in the scientific world.

Tinbergen was a naturalist, birdwatcher, ethologist, academic, communicator, photographer, film-maker, humanitarian, conservationist (not to mention skater), and very much beyond category. He drew a group of brilliant students such as Desmond Morris (*The Naked Ape*), Richard Dawkins (*The Selfish Gene*) and Aubrey Manning. Many others have become leaders in their fields of study. This slightly built man with his work ethic and simplicity of living, modest and egalitarian, was an inspiration to so many.

Tinbergen died in December 1988, having previously suffered a stroke. His former student Hans Kruuk described him as having 'a warm smile, enthusiasm, and a rich fund of stories and jokes', while others attested to his clear thinking and direct approach to his subject. Kruuk described 'a small, khaki-clad bespectacled and grey-haired man with his camera, following the track of a fox on some sandy slope, a curious naturalist whistling to himself'. Within three months, in March 1989, Konrad Lorenz too was dead.

Lack, Thorpe and Tinbergen were vital influences in the post-war shift to the study of birds as a part of fundamental biological investigation. Through the development of their respective units they left an expanding legacy of researchers. Few, if any, of today's ornithologists have not been influenced by them.

The free-roaming cattle cannot be expected to know the gulls' boundaries. The gulls accept them as local 'furniture', threatening them only when they graze too close to a nest. Although the cattle do not understand gull language, they soon learn how to avoid a sharp peck on the nose.

FIG 217. A watercolour by Eric Ennion from *Signals for Survival* by Tinbergen and Falkus (1970).

Oxford and Cambridge were not alone, and the contemporaries of these three included many ornithologists in other universities, such as Wynne-Edwards in Edinburgh. All these scientists played a part in the great academic ornithology boom that began in the 1960s and has continued ever since. A consequence has been the proliferation of published papers – not just in specific ornithological journals but also in more broadly based biology and science journals – the *Journal of Animal Ecology*, *Animal Behaviour* and more recently the *Proceedings of the Royal Society*. A bibliography of British ornithology, such as that of Irwin (1951), if written today would run into many volumes and would be practically a lifetime's work for anyone who attempted it. Academic ornithology, conservation ornithology and their peripherals have expanded to a degree and in a way that the likes of Witherby and Tucker could only have dreamed of during the 1940s.

CHAPTER 19

The British List and Problems with Fraud

Finally I come to the birds ... what should we do without them?

Harry Witherby, 1938

T HE BRITISH LIST as a concept originated from Yarrell's attempt to provide an assessment of the first occurrences of the uncommon British birds. This idea was taken up in the latter half of the nineteenth century, alongside the interest in county avifauna lists. In the twentieth century the British List served two functions. At the turn of the century it was intended to be a definitive list, not only of birds that had occurred in Britain, but also of their scientific nomenclature, and of course it included the various subspecies that had been identified. Latterly it has served, and been served by, those birdwatchers who devote their time to seeking and sighting rare birds.

It has never been easy to keep the List, and even now it is constantly under review as past records are re-examined in the light of new information. These re-examinations can lead to both positive and negative assessments. Old records may be reinstated, thus giving the first occurrence an earlier date, or deleted, thereby moving the first occurrence to a later date.

In the days of the collectors the principle of keeping a definitive list of British birds proved to be open to abuse simply because rare birds were worth more to the dealers than common ones. At the turn of the century there was a series of records that seemed too good to be true – the Hastings Rarities.

THE HASTINGS RARITIES

One of the functions that Witherby's journal *British Birds* assumed was the publication of records of rare birds. Often these were of local (county) importance but not infrequently they were national rarities, first or second occurrences. At the beginning of the twentieth century a number of records of rare birds were sent to *British Birds* for approval from an unusually confined area centred on the coastal town of Hastings in Sussex. Many of these were of birds recorded in Britain for the first time, and several for only the second time. Some, without precedent, were of several specimens of the same species – the so-called multiple sightings. All the records from the area became known as 'the Hastings Rarities'. Table 3 gives examples from two specimen years.

TABLE 3. Examples of the Hastings Rarities, from 1905 and 1915.

MONTH 1905		1915
Jan	(Thick-billed) nutcracker	(Cape Verde) little shearwater
		(Western large-billed) reed bunting
		Dusky thrush
		Black lark × 2
Feb	Snow finch × 2	Black lark
		Dusky thrush × 4
Mar		Dusky thrush × 2
Apr	Black headed bunting	Rock bunting
	(Thick-billed) nutcracker	Moustached warbler
May	Great reed warbler	(Western) black-eared wheatear
	(Western) black-eared wheatear	Sabine's gull
	Tawny pipit	Brown-backed warbler*
	[European] bee-eater	Olivaceous warbler
		Marsh sandpiper × 2
		Terek sandpiper × 3
June	Squacco heron	(North African) black wheatear
	[Oriental] pratincole	Great black-headed gull [Pallas's gull]
	[European] bee-eater × 2	
	Icterine warbler	
July	Masked shrike	Mediterranean gull × 5

TABLE 3. – *Cont.*

Aug	Whiskered tern × 6	Caspian tern × 2
	Aquatic warbler	Pectoral sandpiper
	Isabelline wheatear	
Sept	(White-spotted) bluethroat	Asiatic [Pacific] golden plover × 4
	[European] bee-eater	
	(Eastern) black-eared wheatear	
	Orphean warbler	
	Rustic bunting	
Oct	[European] bee-eater	Greater yellowlegs
	Pine grosbeak × 7	[European] roller
	[Northern] goshawk × 2	(Western) black-eared wheatear
Nov	Ruddy shelduck × 2	White-winged lark × 2
	Madeiran [storm] petrel	King eider
	(Madeiran) little shearwater	Mediterranean gull
		Killdeer × 3
Dec	(Eastern) little bustard	Balearic [Mediterranean] shearwater
	Wallcreeper	White's thrush
		Wallcreeper

(Brackets) indicate subspecies; [square brackets] indicate modern names.

* 'Brown-backed warbler' was the name given to a subspecies of what is now called the rufous-tailed scrub robin (Fig. 218).

FIG 218. Rufous-tailed scrub robin. (Photograph by Rebecca Nason)

What was the historical context of these records? First the compulsive desire for specimen collecting, and second the lack of a verification system. At that time the main source of records was dead specimens. Birds were shot to supply Victorian gentlefolk with stuffed fauna (mainly birds) with which to decorate their drawing rooms, and in some instances to provide specimens for the fanatical collectors. The trader in this situation was the taxidermist, who was often, as a result, a very knowledgeable person concerning the status of much of the local wildlife. In Cambridge, for example William Farren was a pillar of the Cambridge Natural History Society and made a considerable contribution to Lack's *Birds of Cambridgeshire* with his knowledge of the local avifauna – drawn far more from the specimens he had received and the information that went with them than from his own observations.

In the case of the Hastings Rarities the taxidermist was a man by the name of George Bristow, whose business was run from a shop at St Leonards-on-Sea. The system generally worked as follows. The bird was shot, often by a person of limited ornithological knowledge. The shooter would take the dead bird to the taxidermist, who would pay him, possibly on a sliding scale according to the perceived status of the specimen. The bird was then stuffed and in most cases mounted before being sold, either directly to a known collector or through display in the shop. Either the taxidermist or the ultimate owner, or on rare occasions the shooter, might inform the authorities of any rarity; and a bird that was the first of its species to be recorded in Britain was considered as great a prize then as it is today. For any (or all) of the three people involved (shooter, taxidermist and collector) there was greater commercial value in any bird that was 'listed', and naturally that value reached maximum for the first specimen of a new species for Britain.

Beginning around the 1890s, it took a little time for the Hastings records to arouse suspicion. Without the communications or indeed knowledge of rare birds of today, this is not that surprising. That the editors of *British Birds* (Witherby in particular) became concerned is evidenced by a remark in an article in *The Naturalist* in 1911:

> It has usually been a new British Bird seen in the flesh somewhere in Kent or Sussex, or thereabouts. We are relieved to learn now that the editors at last share the opinion of so many of their readers and throw doubt upon the records.

Officially, the editors said nothing, but when a single issue of *British Birds* for January 1916 listed six species new to Great Britain, all recorded from the Hastings area, a crisis point was reached. Almost all of these birds were 'examined', and submitted for addition to the list by amateur birdwatchers of varying degrees of competence after being shot and sometimes stuffed prior to examination. The examination seems to have been concerned only with establishing a correct identity for the specimen, nothing more.

Witherby was quite clearly disturbed, and in a letter to Parkin, one of the sponsors of the Hastings records, he commented, 'I suppose this will be another new Brit. Bird. Did you see it in the flesh? I cannot understand all these rarities being got at Westfield – it seems to me most fishy.' The reference to the village of Westfield is significant: an extraordinary aspect of these records is that many of them occurred not just in the same general area but in the same village.

Doubtless cognisant of the growing scepticism, Bristow, the taxidermist, wrote Witherby an unsolicited letter in June 1916. It is reproduced here in full because, together with the records themselves, it represents the only real evidence in the case.

Dear Sir,

For some considerable time I have had hints that you & other ornithologists entertain doubts as to the authenticity of some of the rare birds I get, & I must admit not without reason; I will endeavour to show you as briefly as possible how I get many; I am also the only gun and ammunition dealer in St. Leonards, consequently I get a great many persons in who use a gun, such as farmers, keepers, market gardeners &c, and as I have a good show of stuffed birds &c it causes conversation, and I invariably ask if any bird is seen out of the ordinary, to procure it for me, & many do so, naturally the great majority are no use, but I always give something for whatever is brought & now & then a good bird is brought. I will instance a few, about 10 or 12 years ago Mr. L. Curtis Edwards was in my shop, when a Mr. Morris a market gardener at Ninfield brought me a Red-throated Pipit, I believe Mr. Edwards recorded it in the Zoologist, I gave Morris 2/- for it, during the same year he brought from 30–40 Meadow Pipits that I purchased, so that took the profit of the other, but one morning on his journey down he picked up an Orphean Warbler under the telegraph wires, & has also shot a Rufous Warbler & 2 Meadow Buntings &c so in the end it pays to buy all they bring.

Another market gardener at Westfield generally brings some every week, two years ago he brought the two Ruppell's Warblers; but I do not remember any others but common, until last week he brought a Cetti's Warbler, Mr Parkin exd it in the flesh soon after.

Another at Rye Harbour, Saunders, I have had many birds from, amongst them generally a few Greenshanks every year, last year he sent a fine Greater Yellowshank, now you cannot expect me after buying a lot of birds unsaleable, to tell that man, or any other in a similar case, that particular bird is very rare; he thought it was a Greenshank & was satisfied with what I gave him, it is my living & I am entitled to do it in an honest way the best I can.

When I get any uncommon birds I generally show them at once in the flesh to some responsible person & I fail to see what else I can do to satisfy these doubts.

If I give the name of a person who shoots a rare bird & they are seen or written to, many would not like it, as probably they have no gun licence (or it is the close season) & have simply a .410 or No 3 saloon gun to kill birds on their allotments &c.

And there is also another side, I have given names at times & not always to my advantage, some years ago a man at Pett brought me an immature Squacco Heron & asked 5/- for it, a Mr Chapman of Rye who formerly had a collection of local birds saw it at my shop, and purchased it, but he required the name of the shooter simply as reference, the following Sunday he went & found the man, & asked him to send any other rare bird to him he would give more than Bristow, this bird was worth quite 20/- he told him.

A friend of yours also told a man from whom I bought an Avocet for 20/-, he would have given £5. I was considerably annoyed by these two men, coming saying I had swindled them.

Another case was a carrier from Robertsbridge named Glyde, he brought me a fine Kite with a message the owner would call in a few days for what I could give for it, if I did not want it, to mount it for him; soon after a young lady who was engaged to a Mr Studwick who has a collection of birds, called with a job and saw the Kite, I happened to say that a carrier from Robertsbridge had brought it, the next day he Studwick cycled over & ferreted out the man & bought the Kite for 5/- & I understand was considerably elated over dishing Bristow as he called it.

I have been told that the idea is I have birds sent over frozen, but that is preposterous, could I possibly get captains of ships and other officers to bother themselves over these little things? even if I could it would have been found out years ago, I have never had any birds this way with the exception of a captain of one of the Natal Line of Steamers whose home is here, and he sent me to mount 4 Albatrosses, a Gannet, a Cape Pigeon & a Hoopoe, these were caught on his ship at different times and placed in the refrigerator.

If you look over the birds that Mr M.J. Nichol collected & also those he only saw, & also the number Mr Alexander has seen lately in this neighbourhood, one need not be surprised at what is got here.

If you can suggest anything for me to do to allay these suspicions I should be glad to assist, but I cannot promise to give the names & addresses of every one if they object.

> *Apologising for troubling you*
> *I am yours faithfully*

GEO BRISTOW

P.S. I might add, all the rare birds I get are not recorded, some if I consider are escapes & some I mount for customers who do not wish them recorded, I do not say anything about them.

This year I have had a Saker Falcon & a very uncommon looking duck with white face chestnut breast I considered both might have escaped & I have also had as you are aware 2 Calandra Larks, but as they were a party of 5 I have no doubt they were genuine wild birds I saw 4 myself. I believe a single one or two has been here before.

The letter contains some vital points which will be discussed later. Witherby, no doubt delighted by the clear opportunity to bring a sense of order to the situation, replied with the following conditions:

- That all birds shall be shown in the flesh to Dr N. F. Ticehurst.
- That whenever required the bird shall be skinned before Dr Ticehurst and the body handed to him.
- That the name and address of the shooter shall always be sent by you to me.
- That I shall be allowed to make inquiries in such a way that no harm shall come to the shooter, and I will undertake that no offer or idea of the value of the bird shall be given to him.

Witherby went on to explain that the records were merely of interest and that the skins were of no scientific value before saying that 'there are a certain number of Ornithologists who do not credit these records and every bit of proof you can give is helpful.' And he ended by suggesting that if a mutually convenient time could be found he could pay a visit to the area and the shop, to be shown round by Bristow. This elicited a friendly response in which the taxidermist stated that he had no objection to the conditions and that in cases where the shooter might be sensitive it was better not to record the bird involved.

At this point one might reasonably expect that the records would become regularised using the criteria proposed by Witherby. In fact all contact and correspondence from Bristow ceased, and records continued trickling out from the area without any corroboration.

FIG 219. Red-throated pipit: a specimen supplied to George Bristow was one of the Hastings Rarities. (Photograph by Rebecca Nason)

FIG 220. Squacco heron, another Hasting species. (Photograph by Rebecca Nason)

In 1920 a second and decisive crisis point was reached when Witherby received a letter from another ornithologist–collector, J. B. Nichols (to whom Bristow had referred in his letter), requesting that records of four birds – two olivaceous warblers (Fig. 221) from St Leonards, and a pair of sharp-tailed sandpipers, the specimens of which he had recently added to his collection – be added to the *British Birds* list. Witherby replied that some time previously he had written to Bristow pointing out the conditions under which rare birds derived from him would be acceptable, and that Bristow had agreed to these conditions, which had also been explained to Nichols. As the conditions had not been complied with, the records would not be accepted for publication in *British Birds*. Nichols requested a copy of the conditions, and subsequently replied that he had understood that Butterfield (W. Ruskin Butterfield, curator of the local museum), who had examined the birds in question, was a person authorised by Witherby (presumably he was told this by Bristow), and that he (Nichols) had assumed that as Butterfield had seen the birds the records would meet the requirements. Nichols then declared his intention to take his enquiry to Bristow.

From that time the number of records declined and as a result the controversy gradually faded (publicly at any rate). In retrospect it seems odd that

FIG 221. Eastern olivaceous warbler by Archibald Thorburn, from his *British Birds* (1915–18).

no one attempted any real enquiry at that time. If any enquiry was made we do not know about it. Maybe, given the social standing of many of the collectors who bought birds from Bristow, it was considered politically or socially unwise. More likely, perhaps, any would-be enquirer could reasonably anticipate that the collectors would not cooperate in an investigation that might subsequently devalue their collections.

The methods of collecting bird records changed as the century progressed. The rise in field identification skills led to the British List receiving an ever-increasing number of additions, more and more of them sight records, but it remained permanently devalued by the presumed falsifications of the Hastings Rarities. Eventually the desire to produce a new version of the *Handbook* was the catalyst for a retrospective investigation, and in 1962 the August issue of *British Birds* was devoted entirely to the Hastings Rarities. There was a statistical analysis by J. A. Nelder, and a paper on the scientific acceptability of the contentious records by Max Nicholson and James Ferguson-Lees.

The paper by Nicholson and Ferguson-Lees included a comprehensive list of the records they considered to be suspect. In addition, they pointed out that a number of Hastings specimens labelled as British had found their way into the collections of various people or institutions unconcerned with 'registration', so that the total number of suspicious specimens was in fact likely to be greater. They began their examination by pointing out that in the period 1903–19 a total of 49 species and vagrant races was added to the British List, of which 32 (65 per cent) came from the Hastings area. The authors were at pains to point out that their interest lay solely in the scientific value of the records and they warned 'against the use of our investigation to seek to fasten any sort of guilt on any person or persons, living or dead'. Clearly they anticipated that there were those who would not only disagree but also seek to prove the innocence of friends or acquaintances (which, as we shall see, was in fact the case). Nicholson and Ferguson-Lees then worked systematically through the records, their possible causes and the evidence, essentially drawing out the following issues:

1. The extraordinary nature of the 'hinterland' group of records, where many rarities had occurred in a small area a few miles inland. The village of Westfield alone accounted for an eastern little bustard, two black larks, an eastern black-eared wheatear, a Cetti's warbler, a brown-backed warbler, a collared flycatcher (and another seen), a two-barred crossbill (and a flock of five seen), and a remarkable run of buntings including a black-headed (Fig. 222), a rock, and no less than three rustic in different years.

FIG 222. Black-headed bunting. (Photograph by Rebecca Nason)

2. The equally extraordinary nature of the records on so short a stretch of coastline, including the very high percentage of the total British occurrences around St Leonards/Pevensey.

3. The absence of really large birds in the list, which would have been more conspicuous and thus easier to discover and to shoot.

4. The presence of irruptive species such as pine grosbeak in non-irruptive years.

5. The presence of highly sedentary species such as masked wagtail, snow finch and thick-billed reed bunting, as well as Rüppell's warbler (Fig. 223) and masked shrike, which had not (even by 1962) been recorded beyond the Mediterranean region. Also the presence of the most unlikely collection of subspecies, such as brown-backed warbler (a subspecies of the rufous-tailed scrub robin from the Balkans and Asia Minor), North African black wheatear, Corsican woodchat shrike, Indian golden oriole – all of which were also sedentary.

6. The strange 'block' occurrences of certain species, with a number of records of the same species found within days of each other. For example in 1910 there were five sociable plovers and four slender-billed curlews; in 1911 there were five white-winged black terns; in 1912 there were four Terek sandpipers. For a block record to happen once would be strange (with all the modern enthusiasts out in the field it almost never happens, since vagrant birds are

FIG 223. Rüppell's warbler. (Photograph by Rebecca Nason)

by their very nature aberrant) – so for it to happen repeatedly is beyond any experience, even to the present day.

7. Comparison with the same area in the 1950s showed that although there had been a massive increase in interest and competence of birdwatchers the Hastings area had revealed nothing unusual in the pattern of rarities.

8. The anonymity of the people who collected the birds: 'Who then were the brilliant collectors who succeeded so spectacularly year after year where some of the best ornithologists were failing? The market gardener at Westfield who was sufficiently keen and skilful to obtain two Rüppell's warblers and a Cetti's within a couple of years remains a nameless and forgotten man.' Where people's names were appended to records they were usually too common to be checked, and Nicholson and Ferguson-Lees failed to find any trace of any person responsible for collecting any of the rarities in the field.

9. The value of the skins was likely to be high, and higher by rarity (thereby increasing the value of any fraud, although the authors forbore from stating it so baldly), £5–10 being paid for some birds – a substantial sum then.

10. It was technically possible to transport specimens by ship in a refrigerator – Bristow admitted that he had received some specimens in this way. Technical advice to the authors suggested that any independent examiner of a carcass who was not specifically looking for signs of recent thawing would be unlikely to notice much difference between a recently thawed specimen and one 'recently dead', which could sometimes mean up to two or three days old.

11. Most of the species in the list emanated from just one or two geographical

areas (there was a strong contingent of Mediterranean birds, for example), and thus could have been 'supplied' by the same source.

12. Finally there was the coincidence that following the correspondence between Witherby and Bristow in 1916–17 the flow of rarities slowed to about half, and after Witherby's letter rejecting Nichol's submissions in 1920 it virtually ceased.

Nelder's paper used statistical methods to examine, as scientifically as possible, the probability that the records as presented were genuine. To do this he segregated the data in several different ways:

1. He provided a second geographical area for comparison, the rest of Sussex and Kent, defining the 'Hastings area' as that within a twenty-mile (32 km) radius of Hastings Pier plus the whole of the Romney Marsh apart from Hythe.

2. He used two different eras: 1895–1924, designed to encompass all the Hastings records, and 1925–54, an equivalent period outside the Hastings records years.

3. He separated the records into three different classes:
   Class 1 – birds with fewer than 20 accepted British records
   Class 2 – birds with 20–99 accepted British occurrences
   Class 3 – birds which, although rare, were not sufficiently rare to have their occurrences listed in the *Handbook*

The analysis showed an extraordinarily high number of Class 1 rarities (of high value to the trade) in the Hastings area (243 in 1895–1924) compared with the remainder of the two counties (125 in the same period). Unsurprisingly, the difference in these figures was statistically significant. The Class 3 rarities (of low value) were by contrast much fewer in the Hastings area (165) than in the remainder of the two counties (255). Finally, comparison of the Hastings Class 1 rarities in the study years (243) with the control period of 1925–54 (54) was further clear evidence of something strange.

Nelder found 61 multiple occurrences in the Hastings area in the period 1895–1924 but only eight in 1925–54, and no more than four in the remaining parts of the two counties in either period. An examination of seasonal differences showed a disproportionately high number of winter records from the Hastings area in the study period (76, compared with 22 for the rest of the two counties) but not in the control period (15 and 19).

Nelder attempted to find a plausible explanation for the anomalies. He discounted the theory that the Hastings records were due to a dedicated band of observers working the area systematically since all the evidence – the curious distribution by class of rarity, the multiple occurrences, the strange seasonal distributions – was unique not only to the Hastings area but also to the period 1895–1924. Furthermore he pointed out that in Kent during the control period the number of observers increased without any of these effects. In his final paragraph he stated that the records 'appear so inherently unlikely as to call very seriously into question the basic assumption that all the [Hastings] records are genuine.'

The two papers were an excellent exposure of what was clearly a well-worked fraud, although no one said as much, even in the 1960s. Inevitably there was some protest, and one man, James Harrison, went so far as to make the case for the defence in a book entitled *Bristow and the Hastings Rarities Affair* (1968).

THE HARRISON DEFENCE

James Harrison, author of *The Birds of Kent*, must have been a young man at the time of Bristow's activities, and maybe he was influenced by a time spent with the many collectors who dealt with Bristow. Whatever his reasons, he was distressed by what he saw as an unwarranted accusation of dishonesty on the part of Bristow. This was despite the fact that Nicholson, Ferguson-Lees and Nelder had made deliberate efforts to examine the records rather than the personalities (although it was rather unrealistic of them to presume that one could be separated from the other). Harrison sought both to exonerate the taxidermist from allegations of impropriety and also to achieve reinstatement of the deleted records. The basis of his rebuttal was that in all their careful analysis Nicholson and Ferguson-Lees had simply been mistaken, and he employed a statistician to counter the claims of Nelder.

Unfortunately Harrison's statistician was not an ornithologist and his conclusions, together with Harrison's defence of Bristow, were more than adequately dealt with by the original writers in a follow-up paper published in 1969. They dismissed his evidence concerning Bristow as simply character testimony. They pointed out errors in the assumptions made by the statistician, largely due to his ignorance of ornithology. And they explained the lengths to which they had gone originally to establish the true origin of the birds that made up the Hastings records: facts which they had previously not published. These included an interview with one of the records' sponsors, H. W. Ford-Lindsay, a man described by James Harrison as 'exceptionally qualified', who had been responsible for the addition of three species to the British List: grey-rumped

FIG 224. Green woodpecker, from George Graves's *British Ornithology* (1811–21) – referred to by Harrison's 'exceptionally qualified' witness as a 'great green woodpecker'.

sandpiper, Rüppell's warbler and moustached warbler. Nicholson *et al.* reported that Ford-Lindsay

> *skilfully evaded giving any direct information and we formed the impression that he had made up his mind to regard the whole episode as one over which to draw a thick veil. Questioned concerning his first-hand ornithological experiences, he said that the rarest bird he had ever seen in the wild state in England was a Golden Oriole, and he spoke of 'the Great Green Woodpecker'. Yet this was one of the small band once more paraded by Dr Harrison as an 'acknowledged authority'.*

In the face of the overwhelming evidence gathered and reiterated by Nicholson *et al.*, very few, if any, dispassionate people doubted that the records were unacceptable and that sharp practice had taken place.

The raised standards of the last thirty years and the arrival of the super-birder only serve to confirm what anomalies these records were. Despite the present-day mania for rarities, nowhere in Britain has remotely recreated the cornucopia of records that came from the Hastings area in the first twenty years of the twentieth century, nor is ever likely to. The sad fact is that among them, almost certainly, were genuine occurrences. Nicholson *et al.*, together with a sadder but wiser Norman Ticehurst, appealed to everyone concerned to bring forward evidence that would validate any of the records. Little if anything emerged.

One point concerns the letter from Bristow to Witherby. Bristow referred in that letter to a carrier named Glyde who brought a 'fine kite'. The name Glyde is so similar to *glede* or *gled*, used in medieval times for the kite, that it was surely a rather obvious invention by Bristow. Can it be that no one noticed?

In 1970 it emerged in the national press, rather sensationalised, that a ship's steward had many years before admitted to being a witness to the transport of the bodies of birds on board ship, bodies that were destined to be stuffed and sold. Doubtless there were personal reasons why this information was suppressed for so long, but the emergence of this testimony just a few months before the death of James Harrison must surely have given the old man cause to doubt his vigorous defence of Bristow. The 1962 revision saw the removal of sixteen species and thirteen subspecies from the British List.

THE MEINERTZHAGEN AFFAIR

Richard Meinertzhagen (1878–1967) outwardly typified the character and attitudes of the higher echelons of society in Edwardian England. A lean, tall figure of a man, he served in World War I, much of the time as an intelligence officer, and in peacetime he was active, unofficially, on behalf of the Zionists seeking a state of Israel. His significance in the history of British ornithology rests on his collecting activities. The Meinertzhagen story, documented by Mark Cocker (1989), was pockmarked with incidents that were quite out of the ordinary.

Meinertzhagen (Fig. 225) was born into a wealthy family – his father was a merchant banker. He suffered greatly as a result of his difficult relationship with his mother and his treatment at school, and this was exacerbated by the early death of his brother Dan, with whom he had formed an unusually close bond.

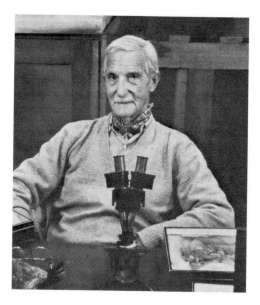

FIG 225. Richard Meinertzhagen in old age, from *The Ibis* (1967).

Whether this played any part in subsequent events it is no longer possible to say. Meinertzhagen joined the army and served in East Africa and in Palestine, where he earned great plaudits for his ruse of planting false plans in a satchel which he dropped in the desert as if by mistake when pursued by the enemy. This deceit played no small part in the subsequent success of General Allenby's attack on the Turkish forces at Beersheba and Gaza – the element of surprise being maintained. In Palestine Meinertzhagen came into contact with T. E. Lawrence (Lawrence of Arabia), and he is described in *The Seven Pillars of Wisdom* as:

> *a student of migrating birds drifted into soldiering … [He] knew no half measures. He was logical, an idealist of the deepest, and so possessed by his convictions that he was willing to harness evil to the chariot of good. He was a strategist, a geographer, and a silent laughing masterful man who took as blithe a pleasure in deceiving his enemy (or his friend) by some unscrupulous jest, as in spattering the brains of a cornered mob of Germans one by one with his African knob-kerri. His instincts were abetted by an immensely powerful body and a savage brain, which chose the best way to its purpose, unhampered by doubt or habit.*

With his private income, Meinertzhagen's life largely revolved around his natural history travelling, and collecting birds in particular. Yet there were incidents and rumours, colourful events, especially by today's standards, that may well have been, at the very least, embroidered by Meinertzhagen himself. One, almost certainly untrue, concerned a German officer who invited Meinertzhagen to dine with him in camp in East Africa. The German was unaware that war had been declared, and the story goes that at the conclusion of the meal Meinertzhagen informed his guest of the outbreak of hostilities, drew his revolver and shot the German in cold blood. Cocker suggests that this was derived from an incident in which Meinertzhagen consumed a Christmas dinner which he found in the tent of a German whom he had shot. With the passage of time, verification of this and many other stories remains almost impossible.

The circumstances of the death of Meinertzhagen's second wife, the ornithologist Annie Jackson, were also out of the ordinary. The Meinertzhagens had apparently been practising with their revolvers when, on their way back to the house, Anne accidentally shot herself. The only witness was her husband. Nothing has emerged beyond these bare facts, but for some people suspicions were aroused.

It is against this background that the ornithological side of the story begins. Meinertzhagen's first brush with authority came in 1919 when the guardians of the Bird Room at the British Museum accused him of removing some specimens without authorisation and failing to return them – theft, in normal language. Meinertzhagen made no attempt to deny that he had removed specimens, explaining that in his early days using the Bird Room, Sharpe had allowed him to remove specimens to his (Meinertzhagen's) home, and that he always returned them. The authorities took a very dim view of it and as a result of the breach of the rules Meinertzhagen was barred from using the facilities for a year. This incident has considerable significance later, but is particularly noteworthy in that it marked the commencement of a period of barely disguised mutual hostility between Meinertzhagen and the British Museum. This antipathy subsequently manifested itself whenever Meinertzhagen requested official support from the Museum for some expedition or other, or even when he wished to donate skins he had collected on one of his jaunts.

In 1931 a further incident occurred at the British Museum, this time involving two volumes of the Journal *Parasitology*. One volume went missing and another had some pages removed – and both volumes contained papers on *Mallophaga* (bird lice), a particular interest of Meinertzhagen's. A copy of the missing volume was found by the police at Meinertzhagen's house, but he claimed to have bought it from a dealer. Further evidence, from the bookseller and from a binder's invoice, was inconclusive, and the case against Meinertzhagen was considered not proven – though doubtless suspicions were not allayed. How many ornithologists knew of these incidents we cannot say, but they formed the basis of ill-disguised distrust on the part of the officials of the Bird Room.

In 1939 Meinertzhagen visited the island of Hoy, in Orkney, and the visit resulted in a publication in *The Ibis* on the birds of Hoy. This paper was attacked by Ralph Chislett, a well-known popular writer on natural history, who complained that the date given by Meinertzhagen for first breeding of the great skua (Fig. 226) was wrong. He further stated that there was no proof that the whimbrel bred on the island and that the red-necked phalarope had been included in Meinertzhagen's list without there being any records of its occurrence. Chislett next contested Meinertzhagen's assumptions regarding the predation rate of skuas on other birds, pointing out that birds formed only a part of the skua's diet. He ended by condemning Meinertzhagen's remarks concerning the Wild Birds Protection Act, which Meinertzhagen had suggested was too restrictive, presumably because it prevented the collection of specimens. Chislett implied that Meinertzhagen might have broken the law in order to collect specimens. This scarcely veiled accusation brought forth a most angry retort from the accused:

> *I have seen Mr Chislett's letter replete with misconceptions and carping criticism. To reply in detail would be a waste of space. Mr Chislett's hallmark is framed in his last sentence and this alone deserves reply, for it is libellous impertinence. The insinuation has not one grain of truth.*

FIG 226. Great skua. (Photograph by Rebecca Nason)

The fact that Meinertzhagen made no attempt to counter the criticisms put forward by Chislett beyond his bombastic response seems to suggest that they were justified. The paper on the birds of Hoy shows an example of a common thread in Meinertzhagen's output, publishing work consisting of surmise which he supposed to be fact simply because he believed it to be true.

That some ornithologists questioned Meinertzhagen's work is evident from this passage by Mark Cocker:

> *Those who have little faith in him as an ornithologist have also pointed to a number of errors, the most famous of which concerned the Razo Lark. This species is a single-island endemic from one of the Cape Verdes. In 1951 Meinertzhagen wrote of it in his 'Review of the Alaudidae' saying 'the short time during which I observed razae [Razo larks], they were constantly excavating for grubs and not surface-feeding for seeds.' Meinertzhagen's comments on its feeding behaviour, while largely accurate, were entirely anomalous, for having never been to the Cape Verdes, let alone Razo Island itself, he could never have seen the species.*

Cocker, in defence of his subject, went on to point out that 'such inexplicable mistakes' should not necessarily negate the huge volume of work that Meinertzhagen had contributed to ornithology. But in his treatment of the Razo lark Meinertzhagen displayed the same disregard for evidence as he had with the birds of Hoy. Much of the evidence of Meinertzhagen's life is contained in his 'diaries', which were typed on loose-leaf paper – a system which allowed pages to be easily replaced and, as we shall see, Meinertzhagen was quite capable of replacing supposedly archival information.

So we come to the re-examination of the Meinertzhagen redpoll skins in the Natural History Museum collection by Alan Knox (1993), who explained that his interest was directed to this particular species by remarks of Philip Clancey. Clancey, who had travelled on bird-collecting trips with Meinertzhagen, claimed that the Meinertzhagen collection contained the skin of a lesser redpoll *Carduelis flammea cabaret* (Fig. 227) said, by the label it carried, to have been shot by Meinertzhagen at Blois, France, in 1954. Yet this skin matched another in the museum collection prepared by Sharpe, 'made up by the same expert pair of hands at the one time with a date in the 1880s and a southeast England locality', and Clancey stated that Meinertzhagen had not visited Blois to collect birds in 1954.

Knox examined all the redpoll specimens in the Meinertzhagen collection and found seven or eight birds that had been 'relabelled with incorrect data' by Meinertzhagen. After his initial statement Knox declared what others had shrunk from saying:

Given the readiness with which Meinertzhagen falsified data on stolen specimens, one must question the authenticity of data on specimens he collected himself. None of the redpolls carries his original field labels. Redpolls dating from at least the 1890s through to the 1950s now have the same type of label and must have been completely relabelled at least once during Meinertzhagen's lifetime. This has made detection of further fraud much more difficult.

What might be the purpose behind Meinertzhagen's behaviour? Knox postulated that Meinertzhagen may have used such filched specimens to create an (artificial) series so as to be able to name a new race: in the case of the redpolls he suggested a new 'British' race *Carduelis flammea britannica*. It is also possible that he took specimens to enhance the quality of his collection and thus to raise his own status within ornithology. Whatever the reason it renders his entire collection open to question and thus, for scientific purposes, of little use. J. D. MacDonald, who was Head of the Bird Room at the Natural History Museum at a time when Meinertzhagen was offering his collection to them, recommended that rather than be incorporated within the Museum's collection the Meinertzhagen skins should be burnt. This echoed the comments of Charles Vaurie, who in a letter to

FIG 227. Redpolls (mealy to the left, lesser to the right) by Thorburn, from Coward's *Birds of the British Isles* (1920). The species that caused a re-examination of the Meinertzhagen collection.

F. E. Warr (quoted by Cocker) stated: 'I can say upon my oath that Meinertz-hagen's collection contains skins stolen from the Leningrad Museum, the Paris Museum, and the American Museum of Natural History ... He also removed labels, and replaced them by others to suit his ideas and theories.' This rather damning body of evidence bears out the assessment made of Meinertzhagen by Lawrence that he used his 'savage brain' to choose the best way to achieve his purpose, 'unhampered by doubt or habit'.

In the light of the history of suspicion surrounding Meinertzhagen one wonders why the BOU awarded him the prestigious Godman–Salvin Medal. Or was Meinertzhagen a major contributor to ornithology despite what Cocker called his 'inexplicable mistakes'? Only time will tell, but the pendulum has swung very much against him. If there was a nucleus of sound science it has been obscured by the blanket of deceit woven by a man whose motives must remain a matter for conjecture. It is true that his falsifications have not had the same dramatic effect as the Hastings Rarities, and the British List is not threatened by them at species level. But, as with the Hastings Rarities, it is possible, if not probable, that information that was valid has been discarded simply because of information that was fraudulent. The enigma that was Meinertzhagen continues to exercise us long after his death.

THE POST-HASTINGS ERA TO THE PRESENT – REGULARISATION OF SIGHT RECORDS

After Hastings there was a gradual change in the whole ethos of recording birds, brought about in no small part by the fact that shooting rare birds became less and less socially acceptable. Thus sight descriptions increased in importance, and the Protection of Birds Act of 1954 meant a final end to the slaughter of rarities. But the post-war increase in the number of reported sightings of rare and unusual birds gave rise to a question: how were the records to be dealt with without shot specimens? The answer was by committee.

Historically, the BOU List Committee dealt with taxonomy and nomenclature, while the journal *British Birds* published reports of new records. In the post-war era both organisations became involved in the regularisation of recording the British List, and this led to a conflicting arrangement, with two committees whose work overlapped. In December 1952 a new British List was produced, and in 1954 the (new) BOU Records Committee was formed (BOURC), evolving out of the old List Committee, 'to advise on the authenticity of records pro-posed for inclusion in the British List'. This committee became the accepted ultimate authority on what does and does not get added to the definitive British List.

Although there is considerable overlap between the BOURC and the *British Birds* Rarities Committee (BBRC), each has a separate role. The BOURC is responsible for the formal scientific control of the List, and for taxonomy and nomenclature, as before. The BBRC, on the other hand, receives and evaluates reported sightings and decides whether, on the balance of probability, the sighting as described was (a) correctly identified and (b) valid, i.e. not an escape. The BBRC had its origins in the increased submission of rarity sightings to *British Birds* in the mid-1950s, which led to the decision to collect the records together and publish them in the form of an annual report. The rare birds report required a process of scrutiny, and someone to take responsibility for collecting and collating the records. Thus in its August 1959 issue *British Birds* announced the formation of its Rarities Committee (BBRC), and the rare-bird records are still published in *British Birds* on an annual basis. That the membership of the committee is self-appointed, or at least is devoid of any democratic overseer, has been both a strength and a weakness. A great strength is that its membership is drawn from among the most knowledgeable identification and distribution experts in the country. Its weakness is that this has led to complaints of cronyism and a lack of transparency in its decisions, especially from people who have considered themselves to be 'outside the circle'.

STRUCTURAL CHANGES TO THE LIST

By the very nature of things, the British List is in a constant state of flux. Continual evaluation and re-evaluation of records is needed to ensure that the list consists only of those species for which there is categorical evidence of occurrence. It has, it is true, been complicated by the increasing number of escapes or feral species (Fig. 228), but nevertheless it remains a work of scientific respectability, and it is probably easier to get a bird removed than to get one added.

One of the most constructive changes occurred in 1971, when the list was divided into four categories:

Category A: species which have been recorded in an apparently wild state in Britain and Ireland at least once within the last fifty years.

Category B: species which have been recorded in an apparently wild state but not within the last fifty years.

Category C: species which, although originally introduced by man, have now
established a regular feral breeding stock which apparently maintains itself
without necessary recourse to further introductions.

Category D: species which have been recorded within the last fifty years and would
otherwise appear in Category A except that (1) there is a reasonable doubt that
they have ever occurred in a wild state, or (2) they have certainly arrived with
ship assistance, or (3) they have only ever been found dead on the tideline; also
species which would otherwise appear in Category C except that their feral
populations may or may not be self-supporting.

This change allowed the addition to the List of species such as Egyptian goose,
mandarin duck, ruddy shelduck, golden pheasant and Lady Amherst's pheasant,
in Category C. Birds in Category D have never been part of the British List: D
represents records of species that might be added at a later date if/when their
status changes.

However, as with everything else to do with the List, the original categories
have been the subject of constant revision and amendment. In 1986 Category D
was amended to include 'those species which certainly arrived with a

FIG 228. Egyptian goose: a species in Category C of the British List.

combination of ship and human assistance including provision of food or shelter', and in 1987 a new Category E was added to encompass 'those species which would otherwise appear in Category A or B but have only been recorded in British or Irish waters between 3 and 200 miles (4.8 and 320 km) from land'.

In 1992 further changes were made to the categories. Interchange between A and B happened often when a species had not been recorded for fifty years, only to pass back again with a new record. This was unsatisfactory, and to have greater stability a cutoff date of 31 December 1957 was introduced. Category E was abandoned (with only one species, Pacific swift, transferred to Category A) and Category D was slightly adjusted and subdivided. In 2005 a further review concluded that Category C, concerning wild populations derived from feral stock, needed some redefining, that Category D should be simplified, and that a new Category E was required. In addition, the British and Irish lists were separated, and the defining date in Categories A and B was changed, so that the present categories of the British List (Dudley et al., 2006) are:

Category A: species which have been recorded in an apparently wild state in Britain at least once since 1 January 1950.

Category B: species which have been recorded in an apparently wild state at least once up to 31 December 1949 but not subsequently.

Category C: species that, although introduced, now derive from the resulting self-sustaining populations.

C1 *Naturalised introduced species* – species that have occurred only as a result of introduction, e.g. Egyptian goose.

C2 *Naturalised established species* – species with established populations resulting from introduction by man, but which also occur in an apparently natural state, e.g. greylag goose.

C3 *Naturalised re-established species* – species with populations successfully re-established by man in areas of former occurrence, e.g. red kite.

C4 *Naturalised feral species* – domesticated species with populations established in the wild, e.g. rock pigeon (dove)/feral pigeon.

C5 *Vagrant naturalised species* – species from established naturalised populations abroad, e.g. sacred ibis from the naturalised French populations. There are currently no species in category C5.

C6 *Former naturalised species* – species formerly placed in C1 whose naturalised populations are no longer self-sustaining or are considered extinct, e.g. Lady Amherst's pheasant.

Category D: species which would otherwise appear in Category A except that there is a reasonable doubt that they have ever occurred in a natural state. Species placed in Category D only form no part of the British List, and are not included in the species totals.

Category E: species that have been recorded as introductions, human-assisted transportees or escapes from captivity, and whose breeding populations (if any) are thought not to be self-sustaining. Species in Category E that have bred in the wild in Britain are designated as E*. Category E species form no part of the British List (unless already included within Categories A, B or C).

The Appendix presents my own version of a British list, or rather two lists, a prehistoric one and one which starts with historical records and is complete up to the end of 2004. Perhaps the most remarkable aspect of all this is that we continue to find and record species new to Britain, although there is a suggestion that the number is slowing down, with only 14 in the 1990s compared with 40 in the 1980s, 27 in the 1970s, and 27 in the 1960s.

CHAPTER 20

New Slants on Old Problems

Nor should the impression be given that the behaviour of birds is fully explicable and their minds understood. We can only fathom them by patient and, above all, intelligent observation.

Max Nicholson, *How Birds Live* (1927)

T HIS BOOK IS A historical review of the many interlinking strands of ornithology in Britain, and as such it tells the story of the study of birds from earliest times up to close upon the present day. While deliberately refraining from examining the work of living ornithologists automatically closes the action in the 1980s, there are current trends that demonstrate only too well that history does indeed repeat itself. The need for sound scientific data on which to base conservation effort has its roots in the beliefs of Alfred Newton. If we thought we were done with names and orders, we were wrong: the controversial area of nomenclature and taxonomy, after a quiet period, has burst back into life via the tools of molecular research, and we continue our studies of migration using new technology. There never was as much ornithology in Britain as there is in the twenty-first century.

THE FRAMEWORK OF MODERN RESEARCH

The legacy of the Lack/Thorpe/Tinbergen era, combined with the huge demands of bird conservation, has seen a proliferation in Britain (and elsewhere) of ecological, evolutionary and behavioural studies of birds. In recent years Ian Newton at Monk's Wood, Chris Perrins at Oxford and Nick Davies at Cambridge have produced a body of work sufficiently respected by scientists for each of them to have been elected to Fellowship of the Royal Society, bringing British ornithology to the forefront of science. Applied studies into the lives of birds have helped to discover and define the precise conditions for survival required by threatened or endangered species. Studies of this sort have been combined with wider investigations into the conditions and management practices required for threatened habitats such as reedbeds and heathland. Some of this work is done by research officers employed by the various conservation organisations, but often it is carried out by contract workers or by academic staff. At the same time, basic studies concerning not just the biology of birds but biological principles more generally have revealed so many undreamed-of complications in what, a hundred years ago, seemed simple. How could the Victorians have foreseen such concepts as sperm competition, and what would they have made of the reproductive free-for-all revealed by modern ornithological methods?

THE CONSERVATION PROGRAMME

Bird conservation in Britain has never had a higher profile, and although not every conservation programme has been totally successful it is hard to think of a conservation programme that has actually failed. In addition to intensive habitat management, species such as bittern (Fig. 229), corncrake and great bustard are the current focus of attention, the last two both being the subject of reintroduction programmes. Is there really sufficient suitable habitat for corncrakes and great bustards to thrive?

Many species have been so successfully protected, or their populations artificially raised by human activities (cormorant, gull species, geese), that there is an increasing lobby for numbers to be controlled. Is conservation about control? Change in subsidy funding for farmers is embracing the effects of modern farming methods on wildlife for the first time, and as a result populations of some farmland birds appear to be stabilising, maybe even recovering. Yet which particular period in our history are we aiming to recreate – the 1930s? Should we consider greater planting of woodland, as a much more 'natural' habitat for this island? Should we go back to wildwood – when the skylark must have been an unusual bird? Which birds should we conserve and encourage? How many of them is the right number? All these questions are the inevitable consequence of the success of conservation organisations in mastering the art of population recovery and habitat restoration. Things that were

FIG 229. Bittern. This species more than any other typifies the combined use of background research linked to management of its habitat in an attempt to bring about a recovery in the decline of a vulnerable population. (Photograph by Rebecca Nason)

previously thought to be impossible have been done, and conservation is a hugely successful industry today.

The new conservation challenge is to embrace the 'big idea': the re-creation, not of isolated pockets of wildlife habitat, but of swathes of land like natural parks forty or fifty kilometres in each direction where land use favours wildlife, with wetland or woodland alongside traditional farming. Examples from the Netherlands suggest that this is possible, and several schemes are already gathering land together with this aim. The 'big ideas' are up and running.

MONITORING THE STATE OF THE NATION'S BIRDS

The BTO has continued to monitor the health of the nation's avifauna. New developments include an Integrated Population Monitoring Scheme in which the results of the many different surveys are pooled to give a more scientifically robust view of the status of our birds. In 1993 the second (New) Breeding Atlas was published, with enhanced information on density, and maps showing the putative changes in status from the original. The New Atlas is an important data source, and is soon to be updated once again in the forthcoming 2007–11 Atlas.

Last, and by no means least, in 2003 the mammoth *Migration Atlas* was published, summarising almost one hundred years of ringing data. Each species is given comprehensive coverage, and the results of all recoveries to and from Britain are presented on maps which indicate not just the locations but also the migratory routes taken. This achievement is another example of the BTO culture of using amateur, dedicated fieldworkers, in this case the ringers, to gather the data, giving it to scientists to analyse – precisely the sort of work that Nicholson, Tucker and Witherby dreamed of, and in many ways a tribute to their vision. The state of the nation's birds is now analysed annually and a small glossy document summarising changes is published by the conservation organisations.

THE NEW COLLECTORS – NOMENCLATURE AND TAXONOMY

A significant development of the post-war era has been the arrival of a new generation of collectors, the collectors of live bird sightings, the twitchers. This interest in collecting birds by way of observation and ticking them off on lists (life list, year list, country list, county list, …) has led to a remarkable advance in the techniques of bird identification. The spin-off has been that with a much more competent and informed body of birdwatchers there has been a significant increase in the number of vagrants discovered – suggesting that many were missed in the past. In many ways the twitchers of the twentieth century have replaced the collectors of the nineteenth. Since the national press is interested only in the more sensational side of life, rare birds are about the only items of ornithology that they report, giving a rather sadly lopsided view of bird study and its exponents.

Just as the collectors of dead birds in the early part of this century were obsessed with their systematics and nomenclature, so the present-day record collectors have returned to these contentious issues. A new set of English names has been introduced, so that names that have passed down through the ages, shaped by evolving language, have been rationalised to provide a defined nomenclature for the international birdwatcher. Partly this perceived need for change is due to the success of the Anglo-Saxon community in persuading the world to adopt English as an unofficial international language. The new names were not given universal approbation, and correspondence filled pages of the journals, but the committee voices prevailed and the names were introduced – recalling the words written by James Harting in 1918: 'I find birds that I have known all my life referred to by new and strange names.' The dunnock, for instance, is now the hedge accentor, a name that is factually correct but lacks the historical legacy. It must be said that most of these names show a lack of imagination, consisting largely of adding a prefix 'northern', 'common' or 'Eurasian' to the familiar name. Botanists and entomologists use scientific nomenclature preferentially – why should ornithologists be different?

An equally vexatious issue is the taxonomic position of many species and subspecies. Here we find the point of contention is the division between 'lumping' and 'splitting', exemplified by the case of the yellow wagtail (Fig. 230). With their many clear plumage differentiations, are yellow wagtails to be 'lumped' as one species with a myriad of subspecies, or are they to be 'split' so that each distinct plumage variation becomes a full species? This centres on the oldest taxonomic debate of all: how do you define a species? Of course to the 'lister' the possibility of splitting adds more species to your list, whereas lumping reduces its length! Possible help may be at hand in the shape of molecular analysis.

DNA FINGERPRINTING, PATERNITY AND GENOMIC CLASSIFICATION

Rather in the way that the police have been able to re-investigate unsolved cases from the past, advances in the technology of molecular biology have provided ornithology with a number of opportunities to open, or re-open, lines of research, mostly concerned with breeding biology. The most significant of these to date is the use of DNA 'fingerprinting' to identify the genetic make-up of an individual within a population. It is possible to use a sample of biological material, usually blood, to map out the DNA fingerprint of an individual. With DNA maps of the adults it is relatively straightforward to determine paternity by comparison with the maps of the young. This technique has revealed that the male parent of a nestling is not always the apparent male of a pair. The ability to discover biological paternity has led to a considerably revised view of the mating systems of what were hitherto considered to be mainly monogamous species. In fact research now shows that few common birds in Britain are exclusively monogamous, and that mating systems and mating strategies appear to be governed largely by Dawkins' suggestion of a 'selfish gene' principle – every bird for itself.

The use of molecular techniques is also being employed to give an empirical basis to taxonomy. In the immediate post-war period the order for presentation of birds was taken from the publications of the American ornithologist,

FIG 230. Yellow wagtail: heads of various subspecies by Henrik Gronvold, from *A Practical Handbook of British Birds* (1920–4).

Alexander Wetmore, and known as the Wetmore order. Following a complete review by the European systematist Charles Vaurie, some adjustment was made to Wetmore, and finally the work of Karl Voous gained acceptance in the 1970s as the prime source for the order of presentation of bird records. Molecular analysis has opened the door to a new approach, making it possible to unravel the evolutionary relationships of birds. A new classification was published in 1990 by the American ornithologists Sibley and Monroe, based on DNA–DNA hybridisation. This is a technique which compares DNA between species so that the degree of genetic divergence (or similarity) enables scientists to gauge the degree of relatedness. As genetic divergence takes time, the degree of difference in the DNA also indicates the time span of divergence. More recently a technique using mitochondrial DNA has been added to the armoury, and once again comparisons between birds have been used to determine genetic divergence. Molecular-level research has revealed a slightly altered (genetic) classification order, and after a period of relative stability in classification this area of study is delivering one or two surprises, such that birds with very similar appearance can be found not to be closely related! This now re-opens discussions on controversies such as the definition of species and subspecies, and we may yet return to Bullough's idea of physiological subspecies, although a more accurate description might be molecular subspecies. Like Clancey's never-ending divisions of fifty or more years ago, based on minute morphological character-istics which were totally unrecognisable in the field, we may yet find that some bird species can only be defined by using molecular techniques. This is hardly a satisfactory situation for today's birders, and it has already been suggested that we cannot place total reliance on molecular analysis.

SATELLITE TECHNOLOGY AND MIGRATION STUDIES

The use of electronics and the personal computer has been as revolutionary a tool in bird study as in any other walk of life. And the laptop takes it further. Ringing birds is now greatly enhanced by the facility to look up any retrapped bird on the computer and instantly to see its ringing and retrap history. The most exciting development in migration studies is the satellite tracking of individual birds. If we are finally to discover the detailed secrets of migration on a large scale then we need to be able to follow individual birds every step of the way. So far only large birds such as geese, swans, eagles and albatrosses have been tracked, but already this line of enquiry is yielding information about the routes, wintering grounds, ranges and movements of a number of species (Fig. 231). If, or

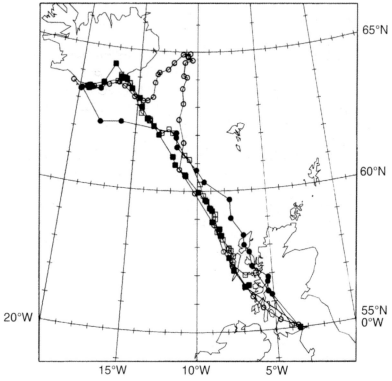

FIG 231. Flight lines of whooper swans in spring, monitored by satellite tracking. From Pennycuick *et al.* (1999).

more likely when, the technology is miniaturised we should be able to use it to unravel the final mysteries of migration in passerines, as well as to define both wintering and breeding grounds more precisely.

Developments in power sources such as solar batteries have also made fieldwork possible in ways undreamed of even twenty years ago. Particular uses include weighing birds, and/or their eggs, miles from any mains electricity with a greater degree of accuracy then ever before. Only a pessimist would imagine that this line of developments has reached an end.

CONCLUSION

Recently the reasoning ability of some of the most intelligent birds has been demonstrated, placing their abilities close to those of a two- or three-year-old child. Their sex lives, considered by the Victorians to be largely based on conventional monogamy, have been shown to be highly complicated, at times showing an uncomfortable parallel with those of humans. We have come a long way from the nineteenth-century view that all an ornithologist needed was a gun, a good stuffing technique, a large cabinet and a system for presenting the bodies. The ornithologists of the late nineteenth century, who seemed to lose sight of birds as biological entities, thought that they were at the cutting edge of science, whereas history shows they were about as far from it as they could be. Maybe in a hundred years the ornithology of today will appear to have been equally wide of the mark – but somehow it seems more likely that the present time will be seen truly as the golden age of ornithology in Britain.

The British List

The lists of British birds presented here are in 'recorded' order. In Part 1 (prehistoric records) that means the earliest available evidence from fossil or archaeological sources. In Part 2 (historical records) each species appears under the earliest date at which it occurred or (in the case of many of the commoner species) the first date it was named.

The list in Part 1 is drawn mainly from the work of the late Colin Harrison (Reid-Henry & Harrison, 1988) who described his work thus:

> The material providing information on Pleistocene birds is scrappy, and sporadic in occurrence. Much of it has only become available in recent years. It is based on bird bones that are usually single, and often broken or damaged; and in the past such objects proved difficult to identify. The bodies of birds are found in the sands, gravels or clays left as residual deposits. Single species or small groups of birds identified from bones preserved in this way have been found, usually by excavation for other reasons, or during natural erosion, mostly in lowland and coastal areas of eastern Britain, and more particularly in south-east England.

Using such material Harrison not only provided data on birds that we know, but he also discovered several new species, including north Atlantic albatross (*Diomedea anglica*), Storer's guillemot (*Cepphus storeri*), thick-legged eider (*Somateria gravipes*), European jungle fowl (*Gallus europaeus*), European crane (*Grus primigenia*) and western partridge (*Alectoris sutcliffei*). In addition he showed the presence of other species in unexpected places, almost certainly reflecting the climatic conditions of the time.

The list in Part 2 has a mixed provenance, the main sources being Fisher

(1966), Spencer (1983b) and Dudley *et al.* (2006). The earlier records are taken largely from Fisher's *Shell Bird Book*, although some subsequent research by myself and others has revealed new information. Fisher's list was the result of what must have been a monumental piece of historical research, and the source as described by Fisher appears alongside the species, wherever it is known. On occasions a source has been discovered that is earlier than that quoted by Fisher, and these are presented in square brackets. The list stops at 2004 because the process of scrutiny takes time and thus the official list is always a year or two behind the records.

It is important to bear in mind that neither of these lists is likely to be perfect. For the list in Part 1, there are doubtless many undiscovered sources of information that could change our knowledge of the past 10,000 years. The list in Part 2 begins with much supposition of the actual dates, since the Anglo-Saxon writings cannot always be dated with precision. And readers should bear in mind that the work of the BBRC and BOURC continues to examine, not just new records, but those from both the recent and the distant past, and not infrequently the status of a record is officially altered in the light of new information. For example the record of moustached warbler from Cambridgeshire in 1948 has just been excised (Melling, 2006). So a list is out of date within months – as this one will be. There is a clear danger that some records from the past can be seen to be unreliable by the standards of today, and they are vulnerable to being dismissed from the list because of it. While there is some justification for a considered approach one wonders whether, if the observers of the immediate post-war period had been aware of today's more exacting requirements, they might have recorded their discoveries in more detail. Once more an indication that being on the list at any one time does not guarantee posterity.

A further qualification is that during previous centuries a number of records were either undocumented, or else documented in such a way as to leave some doubt as to the true identification of the species. The dates quoted are always those from which we have *positive* evidence of occurrence, and it is possible, or even likely, that many of the species occurred, and were recognised, before the dates given in the list.

The English and scientific names are taken from the seventh edition of the BOU checklist (Dudley *et al.*, 2006). Each species has its scientific name appended when it is first mentioned, so that it is possible easily to determine those species in Part 2 that have no prehistoric records.

1. PREHISTORIC RECORDS

Pliocene

North Atlantic albatross (*Diomedea anglica*)

Lower (Early) Pleistocene (Ludhamian interglacial, Thurnian glaciation, Antian interglacial, Baventian glaciation)

Red-throated Diver (*Gavia stellata*), Long-tailed Duck (*Clangula hyemalis*), Willow Ptarmigan (Red Grouse) (*Lagopus lagopus*), Rock Ptarmigan (*Lagopus muta*), Sandwich Tern (*Sterna sandvicensis*), Eurasian Hobby (*Falco subbuteo*), Storer's Guillemot (*Cepphus storei*), Common Guillemot (*Uria aalge*), Razorbill (*Alca torda*), European Eagle Owl (*Bubo bubo*), Little Owl (*Athene noctua*), Barn Swallow (*Hirundo rustica*), Song Thrush (*Turdus philomelos*), Fieldfare (*Turdus pilaris*)

Middle Pleistocene (Pastonian interglacial, Beestonian glaciation, Cromerian interglacial, Anglian glaciation)

Great Cormorant (*Phalacrocorax carbo*), Whooper Swan (*Cygnus cygnus*), Tundra Swan (*Cygnus columbianus*), Greylag Goose (*Anser anser*), Mandarin Duck (*Aix galericulata*), Garganey (*Anas querquedula*), Mallard (*Anas platyrhynchos*), Eurasian Wigeon (*Anas penelope*), Eurasian Teal (*Anas crecca*), Northern Pintail (*Anas acuta*), Tufted Duck (*Aythya fuligula*), Common Pochard (*Aythya ferina*), Common Goldeneye (*Bucephala clangula*), Thick-legged Eider (*Somateria gravipes*), Black Scoter (*Melanitta nigra*), Smew (*Mergellus albellus*), Red-breasted Merganser (*Mergus serrator*), Common Buzzard (*Buteo buteo*) or possibly Rough-legged Buzzard (*Buteo lagopus*), European Jungle Fowl (*Gallus europaeus*), Hazel Grouse (*Bonasia bonasia*), Common Moorhen (*Gallinula chloropus*), Water Rail (*Rallus aquaticus*), Ringed Plover (*Charadrius hiaticula*), Green Sandpiper (*Tringa ochropus*), Blackbird (*Turdus merula*) or Ring Ouzel (*Turdus torquata*), Blue Tit (*Cyanistes caeruleus*) or Coal Tit (*Periparus ater*), Great Tit (*Parus major*), Wood Nuthatch (*Sitta europea*), Eurasian Jay (*Garrulus glandarius*), Common Starling (*Sturnus vulgaris*)

Penultimate (Hoxnian) interglacial of Pleistocene

Northern Shoveler (*Anas clypeata*), Garden Warbler (*Sylvia borin*), European Serin (*Serinus serinus*)

Penultimate (Wolstonian) glaciation of Pleistocene

Greater White-fronted Goose (*Anser albifrons*), Common Shelduck (*Tadorna tadorna*), Goosander (*Mergus merganser*), White-tailed Eagle (*Haliaeetus albicilla*), Common Kestrel (*Falco tinnunculus*), Western Capercaillie (*Tetrao urogallus*), Western Partridge (*Alectoris sutcliffei*), White Stork (*Ciconia ciconia*), Rook (*Corvus frugilegus*), Carrion Crow (*Corvus corone*), Common Raven (*Corvus corax*), Common Crossbill/Scottish Crossbill (*Loxia curvirostra/Loxia scotica*) [could be either]

Last (Ipswichian) interglacial of Pleistocene

Cory's Shearwater (*Calonectris diomedea*), Bean Goose (*Anser fabalis*), Red-breasted Goose (*Branta ruficollis*), Ruddy Shelduck (*Tadorna ferruginea*), Gadwall (*Anas strepera*), Common Eider (*Somateria mollissima*), Red Kite (*Milvus milvus*), Spotted Crake (*Porzana porzana*), Common Coot (*Fulica atra*), European Crane (*Grus primigenia*), Golden Plover (*Pluvialis apricaria*), Dunlin (*Calidris alpina*), Ruddy Turnstone (*Arenaria interpres*), Sky Lark (*Alauda arvensis*), Tree Pipit (*Anthus trivialis*), Pied Wagtail (*Motacilla alba*), Northern Wheatear (*Oenanthe oenanthe*), Red-billed Chough (*Pyrrhocorax pyrrhocorax*)

Last (Devensian) glaciation of Pleistocene

Grey Heron (*Ardea cinerea*), Barnacle Goose (*Branta leucopsis*), Brent Goose (*Branta bernicla*), Pink-footed Goose (*Anser brachyrhynchus*), Osprey (*Pandion haliaetus*), Northern Goshawk (*Accipiter gentilis*), Merlin (*Falco columbarius*), Peregrine Falcon (*Falco peregrinus*), Black Grouse (*Tetrao tetrix*), Grey Partridge (*Perdix perdix*), Northern Lapwing (*Vanellus vanellus*), Grey Plover (*Pluvialis squatarola*), Common Snipe (*Gallinago gallinago*), Eurasian Curlew (*Numenius arquata*), Whimbrel (*Numenius phaeopus*), Black-tailed Godwit (*Limosa limosa*), Common Redshank (*Tringa totanus*), Greenshank (*Tringa nebularis*), Red Knot (*Calidris canutus*), Long-tailed Skua (*Stercorarius longicaudus*), Mew Gull (*Larus canus*), Black-legged Kittiwake (*Rissa tridactyla*), Atlantic Puffin (*Fratercula arctica*), Little Auk (*Alle alle*), Black Guillemot (*Cepphus grylle*), Stock Pigeon (*Columba oenas*), Rock Pigeon (*Columba livia*), Common Wood Pigeon (*Columba palumbus*), Barn Owl (*Tyto alba*), Tawny Owl (*Strix aluco*), Long-eared Owl (*Asio otus*), Short-eared Owl (*Asio flammeus*), Snowy Owl (*Bubo scandiacus*), Common Kingfisher (*Alcedo atthis*), Lesser Spotted Woodpecker (*Dendrocopos minor*), House Martin (*Delichon urbicum*), Crested Lark (*Galerida cristata*), Horned Lark (*Eremophila alpestris*), Meadow Pipit (*Anthus pratensis*), Rock Pipit (*Anthus petrosus*), Yellow Wagtail (*Motacilla flava*), Grey Wagtail (*Motacilla cinerea*), Stonechat (*Saxicola torquatus*), Whinchat (*Saxicola rubetra*), Common Redstart (*Phoenicurus phoenicurus*), Black Redstart (*Phoenicurus ochruros*), European Robin (*Erithacus rubecula*), Bohemian Waxwing (*Bombycilla garrulus*), Winter Wren (*Troglodytes troglodytes*), Hedge Accentor (*Prunella modularis*), White-throated Dipper (*Cinclus cinclus*), Mistle Thrush (*Turdus viscivorus*), Redwing (*Turdus iliacus*), Willow Warbler (*Phylloscopus trochilus*), Common Chiffchaff (*Phylloscopus collybita*), Blackcap (*Sylvia atricapilla*), Common Nightingale (*Luscinia megarhynchos*), Spotted Flycatcher (*Muscicapa striata*), Long-tailed Tit (*Aegithalos caudatus*), Eurasian Jackdaw (*Corvus monedula*), Black-billed Magpie (*Pica pica*), House Sparrow (*Passer domesticus*), Chaffinch (*Fringilla coelebs*), European Goldfinch (*Carduelis carduelis*), European Greenfinch (*Carduelis chloris*), Common Linnet (*Carduelis cannabina*), Hawfinch (*Coccothraustes coccothraustes*), Common Bullfinch (*Pyrrhula pyrrhula*), Pine Grosbeak (*Pinicola enucleator*), Lapland Longspur (*Calcarius lapponicus*), Snow Bunting (*Plectrophenax nivalis*), Yellowhammer (*Emberiza citrinella*), Reed Bunting (*Emberiza schoeniclus*), Corn Bunting (*Emberiza calandra*)

Last glaciation of Pleistocene or Early Holocene
(Species with identifiable bone fragments which are impossible to place accurately in any one era)

Common Quail (*Coturnix coturnix*), Golden Eagle (*Aquila chrysaetos*), Eurasian Sparrowhawk (*Accipiter nisus*), Purple Sandpiper (*Calidris maritima*), Great Spotted Woodpecker (*Dendrocopos major*)

Early Holocene (Mesolithic, Neolithic)
Manx Shearwater (*Puffinus puffinus*), Dalmatian Pelican (*Pelecanus crispus*), Great Bittern (*Botaurus stellaris*), Corn Crake (*Crex crex*), Great Bustard (*Otis tarda*), Eurasian Woodcock (*Scolopax rusticola*), Ruff (*Philomachus pugnax*), Great Black-backed Gull (*Larus marinus*)

Bronze Age
Great Crested Grebe (*Podiceps cristatus*), Mute Swan (*Cygnus olor*)

Iron Age
Little Grebe (*Tachybaptus ruficollis*), Velvet Scoter (*Melanitta fusca*), Eurasian Marsh Harrier (*Circus aeruginosus*)

2. HISTORICAL RECORDS

Sixth Century
c.530 European Robin [source: St Serf]
c.570 Common Crane (*Grus grus*) [source: St Columba]

Seventh Century
mid-600s Eurasian Spoonbill, Common Eider
c.650 Northern Gannet (*Morus bassanus*), Whooper Swan, Whimbrel, Black-legged
Kittiwake, Common Tern (*Sterna hirundo*), Common Cuckoo (*Cuculus canorus*)
[source: *Seafarer*]
c.662 White-tailed Eagle, Carrion Crow [source: St Cuthbert]
c.685 Common Wood Pigeon, Barn Swallow, Common Nightingale, Chaffinch
[Aldhelm]
c.699 Common Raven, Hooded Crow (*Corvus cornix*)
c.700 Common Quail
[sources: mainly *Beowulf* and *Seafarer*, as well as other Anglo-Saxon reports such as
those of Aldhelm, Cuthbert and Guthlac]

Eighth Century
Mute Swan, Greylag Goose, Barnacle Goose, Mallard, Willow Ptarmigan, Great
Crested Grebe, European Shag (*Phalacrocorax aristotelis*), Great Bittern, Grey
Heron, Red Kite, Eurasian Sparrowhawk, Gyr Falcon (*Falco rusticolus*), Peregrine
Falcon, Common Kestrel, Northern Lapwing, Eurasian Woodcock, Common
Snipe, Herring Gull (*Larus argentatus*), Tawny Owl, Common Kingfisher, Green
Woodpecker (*Picus viridis*), Sky Lark, Sand Martin (*Riparia riparia*), House
Martin, White Wagtail, Winter Wren, Hedge Accentor, Common Redstart,
Common Blackbird, Song Thrush, Mistle Thrush, Long-tailed Tit, Blue Tit,
Great Tit, Red-backed Shrike (*Lanius collurio*), Rook, Common Starling, House
Sparrow, European Goldfinch, Common Linnet, Yellowhammer
[source: *Anglo-Saxon Chronicle*]

Tenth Century
c.975 European Turtle Dove (*Streptopelia turtur*) [Fisher gives no source]
c.992 White stork [Aelfric, see below]
c.998 Red-breasted Merganser, Little Grebe, Northern Goshawk, Golden Eagle,
Common Moorhen, Common Coot, European Golden Plover, Rock Pigeon,

European Nightjar (*Caprimulgus europaeus*), Great Spotted Woodpecker, Blackcap, Coal Tit, Black-billed Magpie, Red-billed Chough [all from Archbishop Aelfric's Vocabulary]
Undated Osprey [Fisher does not give the source – mentions tenth or eleventh century]

Eleventh Century

1059 Grey Partridge, Common Pheasant [source: Waltham – Fisher]
Undated Common Buzzard, Corn Crake, Eurasian Curlew, Stonechat, Northern Wheatear, Fieldfare, Eurasian Treecreeper (*Certhia familiaris*) [Fisher – no source given]

Twelfth Century

1150 Eurasian Jackdaw [Fisher gives no source]
1186 Greater White-fronted Goose, Western Capercaillie, Eurasian Hobby, Merlin [sources: Giraldus Cambrensis, although from his Irish journey, & Gurney]
1191 Eurasian Golden Oriole (*Oriolus oriolus*) [Giraldus Cambrensis]
Undated Great Cormorant [Fisher stated records from 1382], Common Guillemot [Reginald of Durham]

Thirteenth Century

1225 Barn Owl [Fisher – no souce given]
1251 Common Crossbill [Mathew Paris]
1275 Eurasian Teal [Edward I]

Fourteenth Century

1337 Atlantic Puffin [Fisher notes 'Inquisitions']
1369 Eurasian Siskin (*Carduelis spinus*), Common Bullfinch [Fisher quotes *Romaunt of the Rose*]
1382 Eurasian Jay [Chaucer]
1384 Black-tailed Godwit [*Liber albus*]

Fifteenth Century

1427 Black Grouse
1450 Common Shelduck, Water Rail, Eurasian Dotterel (*Charadrius morinellus*), Mew Gull, Stock Pigeon, Ring Ouzel, Wood Nuthatch, Corn Bunting
1452 Red Knot
1460 Northern Shoveler, Great Bustard [Fisher indicates 'J. Russell'], Reed Bunting

1465 Ruff [Neville banquet order]
1473 Wood Lark [based on the founding of St Catharine's College, Cambridge, by
  a Robert Woodlark]
1500 Common Redshank

Sixteenth Century

1508 Brent Goose [Phyllyp Sparrowe], Eurasian Wigeon [*Boke of Kurynge*]
1520 Bar-tailed Godwit (*Limosa lapponica*) [Hunstanton rolls]
1523 Grey Plover [Hunstanton rolls]
1525 Ringed Plover [Fisher states *Libri Emprium*]
1527 Eurasian Oystercatcher (*Haematopus ostralegus*) [Hunstanton rolls]
1531 Dunlin [Hunstanton rolls]
1532 European Greenfinch
1536 Black-headed Gull (*Larus ridibundus*) [Hunstanton rolls]
1537 Common Scoter [Hunstanton rolls]
1544 Common Pochard, Hen Harrier (*Circus cyaneus*), Eurasian Marsh Harrier,
  Common Sandpiper (*Actitis hypoleucos*), Black Tern (*Chlidonias niger*), Long-eared
  Owl, Common Swift (*Apus apus*), Eurasian Wryneck (*Jynx torquilla*), White-
  throated Dipper, Meadow Pipit, Common Whitethroat (*Sylvia communis*),
  Goldcrest (*Regulus regulus*), Great Grey Shrike (*Lanius excubitor*), Brambling
  (*Fringilla montifringilla*) [all from Turner]
1555 Common Goldeneye [Fisher's notes say simply 'Scottish']
1562 Twite (*Carduelis flavirostris*)
1599 Rock Ptarmigan
c.1600 Pied Avocet (*Recurvirostra avosetta*), Sanderling (*Calidris alba*), Jack Snipe
  (*Lymnocryptes minimus*), Hoopoe (*Upupa epops*), Yellow Wagtail, Redwing [Fisher
  quotes 'Breviate']

Seventeenth Century

1634 Great Northern Diver (*Gavia immer*)
1638 Pink-footed Goose [Fisher states 'Oddsson']
1644 European Roller (*Coracias garrulus*) [Browne]
1652 Great Auk (*Pinguinus impennis*) [Martin Martin]
1660 Manx Shearwater [Browne]
1661 Razorbill, Black Guillemot [both Willughby/Ray]
1662 Garganey, Tufted Duck, Goosander, Bohemian Waxwing, Bearded Tit
  (*Panurus biarmicus*) [all Browne]
1666 Gadwall, Smew, Black-necked Grebe (*Podiceps nigricollis*), Little Bittern
  (*Ixobrychus minutus*), Stone-curlew (*Burhinus oedicnemus*), Great Skua (*Stercorarius*

skua), Lesser Spotted Woodpecker, Spotted Flycatcher, Hawfinch [all in Merrett]

1668 Red-legged Partridge (*Alectoris rufa*), European Bee-eater (*Merops apiaster*), [both mentioned by Charleton]

1671 Sandwich Tern, Little Tern (*Sternula albifrons*)

1672 Northern Pintail, Greater Scaup (*Aythya marila*)

1675 European Honey Buzzard (*Pernis apivorus*)

1676 Greater Canada Goose (*Branta canadensis*), Velvet Scoter, European Storm-petrel (*Hydrobates pelagicus*), Ruddy Turnstone, Green Sandpiper, Red-necked Phalarope (*Phalaropus lobatus*), Little Auk, Eurasian Reed Warbler (*Acrocephalus scirpaceus*), Garden Warbler, Wood Warbler (*Phylloscopus sibilatrix*), Pied Flycatcher (*Ficedula hypoleuca*) [all Willughby/Ray]

1678 Bean Goose, Common Greenshank, Great Black-backed Gull, Short-eared Owl, Grey Wagtail, Whinchat, Common Grasshopper Warbler (*Locustella naevia*), Common Chiffchaff, Marsh Tit (*Poecile palustris*), Crested Tit (*Lophophanes cristatus*), Snow Bunting, Lesser Redpoll (*Carduelis cabaret*) [all Willughby/Ray]

1684 Black Kite (*Milvus migrans*), Black-winged Stilt (*Himantopus himantopus*), Eurasian Eagle Owl [not on the official BOU List] [all three mentioned in Sibbald's *Prodromus*]

1694 Long-tailed Duck [Ray]

1697 Northern Fulmar (*Fulmarus glacialis*) [Martin Martin]

Eighteenth Century

1713 Arctic Skua (*Stercorarius parasiticus*), Eurasian Tree Sparrow (*Passer montanus*) [Ray]

1718 Willow Warbler [Derham]

1738 Tree Pipit [Albin]

1743 Black-throated Diver (*Gavia arctica*), Black Redstart, Rosy Starling (*Sturnus roseus*) [all in Edwards]

1745 Mandarin Duck [officially added to the List in 1971]

1751 Little Bustard (*Tetrax tetrax*) [Edwards]

1753 Spotted Nutcracker (*Nucifraga caryocatactes*) [Pennant]

1757 Grey Phalarope (*Phalaropus fulicarius*) [Edwards]

1766 Spotted Crake, Rock Pipit, Sedge Warbler (*Acrocephalus schoenobaenus*) [Pennant]

1771 Red-throated Diver, Spotted Redshank (*Tringa erythropus*) [Tunstall]

1773 Dartford Warbler (*Sylvia undata*) [Latham]

1775 Squacco Heron (*Ardeola ralloides*) [Latham]

1776 Red-breasted Goose, Ruddy Shelduck [officially added to the list in 1971] [both Latham], Slavonian Grebe (*Podiceps auritus*) [Pennant], Little Stint (*Calidris minuta*), Great Snipe (*Gallinago media*) [both Pennant], Ortolan Bunting (*Emberiza hortulana*) [Brown]

1780 Lesser Whitethroat (*Sylvia curruca*) [White]

1782 Black-crowned Night Heron (*Nycticorax nycticorax*) [Latham]

1784 Wood Sandpiper (*Tringa glareola*) [Pennant]

1785 Cream-coloured Courser (*Cursorius cursor*) [Latham]

1786 Curlew Sandpiper (*Calidris ferruginea*) [Latham]

1787 Red-necked Grebe (*Podiceps grisegena*), Purple Heron (*Ardea purpurea*), Glossy Ibis (*Plegadis falcinellus*) [all Latham]

1791 Little Crake (*Porzana parva*)

1792 Rough-legged Buzzard, Wallcreeper (*Tichodroma muraria*) [both Montagu]

1798 Purple Sandpiper [Montagu]

1800 Cirl Bunting (*Emberiza cirlus*) [Montagu]

Undated Egyptian Goose (*Alopochen aegyptiaca*) [officially added to the List in 1971]

Nineteenth Century

1801 Long-billed Dowitcher (*Limnodromus scolopaceus*)

1802 Montagu's Harrier (*Circus pygargus*) [Montagu], Kentish Plover (*Charadrius alexandrinus*), Lesser Black-backed Gull (*Larus fuscus*), Two-barred Crossbill (*Loxia leucoptera*)

1804 American Bittern (*Botaurus lentiginosus*)

1805 Cattle Egret (*Bubulcus ibis*), Eurasian Scops Owl (*Otus scops*)

1806 Ferruginous Duck (*Aythya nyroca*)

1807 Collared Pratincole (*Glareola pratincola*)

1808 Snowy Owl, Little Owl

1812 Tengmalm's Owl (*Aegolius funereus*), Richard's Pipit (*Anthus richardi*)

1813 Little Gull (*Larus minutus*), Gull-billed Tern (*Gelochelidon nilotica*), Roseate Tern (*Sterna dougallii*)

1814 Black Stork (*Ciconia nigra*)

1817 Alpine Accentor (*Prunella collaris*)

1818 Red-crested Pochard (*Netta rufina*), Leach's Storm-petrel (*Oceanodroma leucorhoa*), Pomarine Skua (*Stercorarius pomarinus*), Arctic Tern (*Sterna paradisaea*), Parrot Crossbill (*Loxia pytyopsittacus*)

1819 Baillon's Crake (*Porzana pusilla*)

1822 Glaucous Gull (*Larus hyperboreus*), Sabine's Gull (*Larus sabini*), Ivory Gull (*Pagophila eburnea*), Aquatic Warbler (*Acrocephalus paludicola*)

1823 Iceland Gull (*Larus glaucoides*)

1824 Great Egret (*Ardea alba*), Tundra Swan

1825 Caspian Tern (*Hydroprogne caspia*)

1826 Little Egret (*Egretta garzetta*), Buff-breasted Sandpiper (*Tryngites subruficollis*), Bluethroat (*Luscinia svecica*), Lapland Longspur

1828 Sooty Shearwater (*Puffinus griseus*), White's Thrush (*Zoothera dauma*)

1829 Yellow-billed Diver (*Gavia adamsii*), Alpine Swift (*Apus melba*)

1830 Steller's Eider (*Polysticta stelleri*), Red-footed Falcon (*Falco vespertinus*), Pectoral Sandpiper (*Calidris melanotos*), Northern Hawk Owl (*Surnia ulula*), Horned Lark

1831 Pine Grosbeak

1832 King Eider (*Somateria spectabilis*), Temminck's Stint (*Calidris temminckii*), Long-tailed Skua, Yellow-billed Cuckoo (*Coccyzus americanus*), Firecrest (*Regulus ignicapilla*)

1835 Savi's Warbler (*Locustella luscinioides*)

1836 White-rumped Sandpiper (*Calidris fuscicollis*), Broad-billed Sandpiper (*Limicola falcinellus*), Whiskered Tern (*Chlidonias hybrida*)

1838 Wilson's Storm-petrel (*Oceanites oceanicus*), American Wigeon (*Anas americana*), Yellow-browed Warbler (*Phylloscopus inornatus*)

1839 Great Shearwater (*Puffinus gravis*)

c.1840 Green-winged Teal (*Anas carolinensis*)

1841 Greater Short-toed Lark (*Calandrella brachydactyla*)

1843 Rufous-tailed Rock Thrush (*Monticola saxatilis*)

1845 Crested Lark

1846 Surf Scoter (*Melanitta perspicillata*), White-throated Needletail (*Hirundapus caudatus*)

1847 Macqueen's Bustard (*Chlamydotis macqueenii*), Great Reed Warbler (*Acrocephalus arundinaceus*)

1848 Sharp-tailed Sandpiper (*Calidris acuminata*), Icterine Warbler (*Hippolais icterina*)

1850 Capped Petrel (*Pterodroma hasitata*), Bonaparte's Gull (*Larus philadelphia*), Little Plover (*Charadrius dubius*)

1851 Upland Sandpiper (*Bartramia longicauda*), Lesser Grey Shrike (*Lanius minor*)

1852 Eskimo Curlew (*Numenius borealis*), Sooty Tern (*Onychoprion fuscata*), European Serin

1853 Least Sandpiper (*Calidris minutilla*), White-winged Black Tern (*Chlidonias leucopterus*)

1854 Lesser Yellowlegs (*Tringa flavipes*), Red-throated Pipit (*Anthus cervinus*), Rufous-tailed Scrub Robin (*Cercotrichas galactotes*)

1855 Arctic Redpoll (*Carduelis hornemanni*)

1856 Red-necked Nightjar (*Caprimulgus ruficollis*)

1858 Blue-winged Teal (*Anas discors*), Macaronesian Shearwater (*Puffinus baroli*), Tawny Pipit (*Anthus campestris*)

1859 Balearic Shearwater (*Puffinus mauretanicus*), Killdeer (*Charadrius vociferus*), Pallas's Gull (*Larus icthyaetus*), Pallas's Sandgrouse (*Syrrhaptes paradoxus*)

1860 Greater Spotted Eagle (*Aquila clanga*), Sociable Lapwing (*Vanellus gregarius*)

1862 Harlequin Duck (*Histrionicus histrionicus*)

1863 Red-breasted Flycatcher (*Ficedula parva*)

1864 Sora (*Porzana carolina*), Little Bunting (*Emberiza pusilla*)

1866 Spotted Sandpiper (*Actitis macularia*), Mediterranean Gull (*Larus melanocephalus*)

1867 Lesser Kestrel (*Falco naumanni*), Rustic Bunting (*Emberiza rustica*)

1868 Egyptian Vulture (*Neophron percnopterus*), Dark-throated Thrush (*Turdus ruficollis*), Black-headed Bunting (*Emberiza melanocephala*)

1869 White-winged Lark (*Melanocorypha leucoptera*), Common Rosefinch (*Carpodacus erythrinus*)

1870 Pacific Golden Plover (*Pluvialis fulva*), Solitary Sandpiper (*Tringa solitaria*), Great Spotted Cuckoo (*Clamator glandarius*)

1871 Snow Goose (*Anser caerulescens*), Marsh Warbler (*Acrocephalus palustris*)

1875 Black-eared Wheatear (*Oenanthe hispanica*)

1879 Barred Warbler (*Sylvia nisoria*)

1880 Desert Wheatear (*Oenanthe deserti*)

1881 Greater Flamingo (*Phoenicopterus ruber*) [now in Category D]

1882 Blyth's Pipit (*Anthus godlewskii*)

1883 Egyptian Nightjar (*Caprimulgus aegyptius*)

1886 Lesser White-fronted Goose (*Anser erythropus*)

1887 Marsh Sandpiper (*Tringa stagnatilis*), Isabelline Wheatear (*Oenanthe isabellina*)

1889 Green Heron (*Butorides virescens*), Oriental Turtle Dove (*Streptopelia orientalis*)

1890 Caspian Plover (*Charadrius asiaticus*), Baltimore Oriole (*Icterus galbula*)

c.1890 Golden Pheasant (*Chrysolophus pictus*) [released and breeding in East Anglian Brecks but only added to the List in 1971]

1894 Subalpine Warbler (*Sylvia cantillans*)

1896 Pallas's Leaf Warbler (*Phylloscopus proregulus*), Greenish Warbler (*Phylloscopus trochiloides*)

1897 Black-browed Albatross (*Thalassarche melanophris*), White-faced Storm-petrel (*Pelagodroma marina*), Melodious Warbler (*Hippolais polyglotta*), Willow Tit (*Poecile montanus*)

1898 Radde's Warbler (*Phylloscopus schwarzi*)

Twentieth Century

1902 Allen's Gallinule (*Porphyrula alleni*), Arctic Warbler (*Phylloscopus borealis*), Rock Bunting (*Emberiza cia*)

1903 Red-flanked Bluetail (*Tarsiger cyanurus*)

1905 Sandhill Crane (*Grus canadensis*), Yellow-breasted Bunting (*Emberiza aureola*), Dusky Thrush (*Turdus naumanni*)

1906 Cory's Shearwater (*Calonectris diomedea*), Greater Yellowlegs (*Tringa melanoleuca*), Red-rumped Swallow (*Cecropis daurica*)

1908 Brünnich's Guillemot (*Uria lomvia*), Belted Kingfisher (*Ceryle alcyon*), Lanceolated Warbler (*Locustella lanceolata*)

1909 White-throated Sparrow (*Zonotrichia albicollis*), Black-winged Pratincole (*Glareola nordmanni*), Pied Wheatear (*Oenanthe pleschanka*)

1910 Buff-bellied Pipit (*Anthus rubescens*), Blyth's Reed Warbler (*Acrocephalus dumetorum*)

1911 Madeiran Storm-petrel (*Oceanodroma castro*), Baird's Sandpiper (*Calidris bairdii*), Thrush Nightingale (*Luscinia luscinia*), Pine Bunting (*Emberiza leucocephalos*)

1913 Dusky Warbler (*Phylloscopus fuscatus*)

1920 Bufflehead (*Bucephala albeola*)

1921 Blue-cheeked Bee-eater (*Merops persicus*)

1923 Laughing Gull (*Larus atricilla*)

1925 Pechora Pipit (*Anthus gustavi*), Paddyfield Warbler (*Acrocephalus agricola*)

1927 Common Nighthawk (*Chordeiles minor*)

c.1930 Lady Amherst's Pheasant (*Chrysolophus amherstiae*) [released in Bedfordshire, added to the List in 1971]

1931 Pallid Harrier (*Circus macrourus*), Bridled Tern (*Onychoprion anaethetus*)

1932 Black-billed Cuckoo (*Coccyzus erythrophthalmus*)

1936 Ross's Gull (*Rodostethia rosea*), Booted Warbler (*Hippolais caligata*), Black-and-white Warbler (*Mniotilta varia*)

1947 Collared Flycatcher (*Ficedula albicollis*)

1948 Olive-backed Pipit (*Anthus hodgsoni*), Western Bonelli's Warbler (*Phylloscopus bonelli*)

1949 Pallas's Grasshopper Warbler (*Locustella certhiola*)

1950 Isabelline Shrike (*Lanius isabellinus*)

1951 Terek Sandpiper (*Xenus cinereus*)

1952 Eurasian Collared Dove (*Streptopelia decaocto*), American Robin (*Turdus migratorius*)

1953 Ascension Frigate Bird (*Fregata aquila*), Semipalmated Sandpiper (*Calidris pusilla*), Gray-cheeked Thrush (*Catharus minimus*)

1954 Stilt Sandpiper (*Calidris himantopus*), Wilson's Phalarope (*Phalaropus tricolor*), Citrine Wagtail (*Motacilla citreola*), Siberian Thrush (*Zoothera sibirica*), Common Yellowthroat (*Geothlypis trichas*)

1955 Ring-necked Duck (*Aythya collaris*), Thick-billed Warbler (*Acrocephalus aedon*), Orphean Warbler (*Sylvia hortensis*), Sardinian Warbler (*Sylvia melanocephala*), Yellow-rumped Warbler (*Dendroica coronata*)

1956 American Golden Plover (*Pluvialis dominica*), Western Sandpiper (*Calidris mauri*), Southern Grey Shrike (*Lanus meridionalis*)

1957 Summer Tanager (*Piranga rubra*)

1958 (American) Purple Gallinule (*Porphyrula martinica*), Northern Waterthrush (*Seiurus noveboracensis*)

1959 Syke's Warbler (*Hippolais rama*), Song Sparrow (*Melospiza melodia*)

1960 Slender-billed Gull (*Larus genei*), Dark-eyed Junco (*Junco hyemalis*)

c.1960 Ruddy Duck (*Oxyura jamaicensis*) [first bred in the wild and added to the List in 1971]

1961 Calandra Lark (*Melanocorypha calandra*), Cetti's Warbler (*Cettia cettia*), River Warbler (*Locustella fluviatilis*), Fox Sparrow (*Passerella iliaca*), Blackburnian Warbler (*Dendroica fusca*)

1962 Bimaculated Lark (*Melanocorypha bimaculata*), Red-eyed Vireo (*Vireo olivaceus*), Bobolink (*Dolichonyx oryzivorus*)

1963 Pied-billed Grebe (*Podilymbus podiceps*)

1964 Eyebrowed Thrush (*Turdus obscurus*), Yellow Warbler (*Dendroica petechia*)

1965 Royal Tern (*Sterna maxima*)

1966 Brown Thrasher (*Toxostoma rufum*), Hume's Leaf Warbler (*Phylloscopus humei*), Eurasian Penduline Tit (*Remiz pendulinus*), Spanish Sparrow (*Passer hispaniolensis*), Northern Parula (*Parula americana*), Eastern Towhee (*Pipilo erythrophthalmus*), Rose-breasted Grosbeak (*Pheucticus ludovicianus*)

1967 American Black Duck (*Anas rubripes*), Swainson's Thrush (*Catharus ustulatus*), American Redstart (*Setophaga ruticilla*), Eastern Olivaceous Warbler (*Hippolais pallida*), Cretzschmar's Bunting (*Emberiza caesia*)

1968 Blackpoll Warbler (*Dendroica striata*)

1969 Evening Grosbeak (*Hesperiphona vespertina*), Short-toed Treecreeper (*Certhia brachydactyla*)

1970 Long-toed Stint (*Calidris subminuta*), Franklin's Gull (*Larus pipixcan*), Veery (*Catharus fuscescens*), Asian Desert Warbler (*Sylvia nana*), Hooded Warbler (*Wilsonia citrina*), Scarlet Tanager (*Piranger olivacea*)

1971 Trumpeter Finch (*Bucanetes githagineus*)

1972 Iberian Chiffchaff (*Phylloscopus ibericus*)

1973 Ring-billed Gull (*Larus delawarensis*), Ovenbird (*Seiurus aurocapilla*)

1975 White-tailed Lapwing (*Vanellus leucurus*), Yellow-bellied Sapsucker (*Sphyrapicus varius*), Siberian Rubythroat (*Luscinia calliope*), Hermit Thrush (*Catharus guttatus*), Tennessee Warbler (*Vermivora peregrina*), Yellow-browed Bunting (*Emberiza chrysophrys*)

1976 American Kestrel (*Falco sparvensis*), Zitting Cisticola (*Cisticola juncidis*), Pallas's Bunting (*Emberiza pallasi*)

1977 Eleanora's Falcon (*Falco eleonorae*), Rüppell's Warbler (*Sylvia ruppelli*), Cape May Warbler (*Dendroica tigrina*), White-crowned Sparrow (*Zonotrichia albicollis*)

1978 Semipalmated Plover (*Charadrius semipalmatus*), Greater Sand Plover (*Charadrius leschenaultii*), Pallid Swift (*Apus pallidus*)

1979 Aleutian Tern (*Onychoprion aleutica*), Barrow's Goldeneye (*Bucephala islandica*)

1980 Forster's Tern (*Sterna forsteri*)

1981 Oriental Pratincole (*Glareola maldivarum*), Hudsonian Godwit (*Limosa haemastica*), Grey-tailed Tattler (*Heteroscelus brevipes*), Little Swift (*Apus affinis*), Pacific Swift (*Apus pacificus*), Rock Sparrow (*Petronia petronia*), Magnolia Warbler (*Dendroica magnolia*), Lark Sparrow (*Chondestes grammacus*)

1982 Little Curlew (*Numenius minutus*), Lesser Crested Tern (*Sterna bengalensis*), Chimney Swift (*Chaetura pelagica*), Northern Mockingbird (*Mimus polyglotta*), Varied Thrush (*Zoothera naevia*), White-tailed Wheatear (*Oenanthe leucopyga*), Marmora's Warbler (*Sylvia sarda*), Savannah Sparrow (*Passerculus sandwichensis*)

1983 Rose-ringed Parakeet (*Psittacula krameri*) [added to the List as a result of escaped birds setting up a wild breeding population], Cliff Swallow (*Petrochelidon pyrrhonota*)

1984 Black Lark (*Melanocorypha yeltoniensis*)

1985 Cedar Waxwing (*Bombycilla cedrorum*), Blue Rock Thrush (*Monticola solitarius*), Brown Shrike (*Lanius cristatus*), Chestnut-sided Warbler (*Dendroica pensylvanica*), Wilson's Warbler (*Wilsonia pusilla*)

1986 Red-necked Stint (*Calidris ruficollis*), Woodchat Shrike (*Lanius serrator*)

1987 Lesser Scaup (*Aythya affinis*), Black Scoter (*Melanitta americana*), Water Pipit (*Anthus spinoletta*) [previously considered a subspecies of Rock Pipit but added to the list when the taxonomic split was agreed], Eastern Phoebe (*Sayornis phoebe*), Wood Thrush (*Hylocichla mustelina*), Eastern Bonelli's Warbler (*Phylloscopus orientalis*), Philadelphia Vireo (*Vireo philadelphicus*)

1988 Eurasian Crag Martin (*Ptyonoprogne rupestris*), Moussier's Redstart (*Phoenicurus moussieri*), Brown-headed Cowbird (*Molothrus ater*)

1989 Swinhoe's Storm-petrel (*Oceanodroma monorhis*), Double-crested Cormorant (*Phalacrocorax auritus*), Great Knot (*Calidris tenuirostris*), Red-breasted Nuthatch (*Sitta canadensis*), Golden-winged Warbler (*Vermivora chrysoptera*)

1990 Ancient Murrelet (*Synthliboramphus antiquus*), Tree Swallow (*Tachycineta* *bicolor*), White-throated Robin (*Irania gutturalis*), Yellow-throated Vireo (*Vireo flavifrons*)

1992 Lesser Short-toed Lark (*Calandrella rufficens*), Spectacled Warbler (*Sylvia conspicillata*)

1994 Black-faced Bunting (*Emberiza spodocephala*)

1995 Bay-breasted Warbler (*Dendroica castanea*)

1996 Redhead (*Aythya americana*), Canvasback (*Aythya valisineria*), American Coot (*Fulica americana*), Indigo Bunting (*Passerina cyanea*)

1997 Lesser Sand Plover (*Charadrius monglus*)

1998 Slender-billed Curlew (*Numenius tenuirostris*)

1999 Short-toed Eagle (*Circaetus gallicus*), Short-billed Dowitcher (*Limnodromus griseus*), Mourning Dove (*Zenaida macroura*)

2000 Siberian Blue Robin (*Luscinia cyane*), Long-tailed Shrike (*Lanius schach*), Common Redpoll (*Carduelis flammea*) [occurred long before this but was given separate species status in this year]

2001 Fea's Petrel (*Pterodroma feae*), Red-billed Tropicbird (*Phaethon aethereus*), Snowy Egret (*Egretta thula*), Grey Catbird (*Dumetella carolinensis*)

2003 Audouin's Gull (*Larus audouinii*), Taiga Flycatcher (*Ficedula albicilla*)

2004 Rufous-tailed Robin (*Luscinia sibilans*), Masked Shrike (*Lanius nubicus*)

2005 Yellow-legged Gull (*Larus michahellis*) [added to the list by the Taxonomic Subcommittee of the BOU]

References and Further Reading

Some of the items in this list are not referred to directly in the text but have been used as sources of information, and those with an asterisk are suggested further reading for the interested reader.

The Ibis had a rather confusing notation early in its existence. For a while the volumes were described in series (first series up to fourteenth series), with six volumes in each. Then in 1943 the notation became volume 85. So to trace the early works from the journal the most valuable information is the date of publication. In 1982 the title was shortened simply to *Ibis*. The references here remain faithful to these changes. *British Birds* began by notating their volume numbers in roman numerals, but they are presented here uniformly as arabic numerals.

Ackworth, B. (1930) *This Bondage: A Study of the Migration of Birds, Insects and Aircraft, with Some Reflections on Evolution and Relativity.* Murray, London.

Albin, E. (1731–8) *A Natural History of Birds.* London.

Aldrovandi, U. (1610–35) *Ornithologiae hoc est de avibus historia libri XII–XX.* Frankfurt.

Alexander C. J. & Alexander, H. G. (1909) On a plan of mapping migratory birds in their nesting areas. *Brit. Birds* **2**: 322–6.

Alexander, H. G. (1935) A chart of bird song. *Brit. Birds* **29**: 190–8.

Alexander, H. G. (1974) *Seventy Years of Birdwatching.* Poyser, Berkhamsted.

Alexander, W. B. (1945–7) The woodcock in the British Isles. *The Ibis* **87**: 512–50; **88**: 1–24, 159–79, 271–86, 427–44; **89**: 1–28.

Alford, C. E. (1920) Some notes on diving ducks. *Brit. Birds* **14**: 106–10.

Allen, D. E. (1976) *The Naturalist in Britain.* Penguin, Harmondsworth.*

Anon. (c.1400) *The Sherborne Missal.*

Anon. (1419) *Liber albus*

Anon. (late 19th century) *Birds and Bird Keeping.* The Country Library. Warne, London.

Aristotle *The History of Animals* (various editions).

Armstrong, E. A. (1942) *Bird Display: an Introduction to the Study of Bird Psychology.* Cambridge University Press, Cambridge.

Artedi, P. (1738) *Philosophia icthyologia.* Leiden.

Audubon, J. J. (1827–38) *The Birds of America.* Edinburgh & London.

Audubon, J. J. (1831–9) *Ornithological Biography, or an Account of the Habits of the Birds of the United States of America.* 5 vols. A. Black, Edinburgh.

Audubon, J. J. (1845–6) *The Viviparous Quadrupeds of America.* New York.

Bain, I. (ed.) (1979) *Bewick: a Memoir.* Oxford University Press, Oxford.*

Baker, R. A. (1996) The Great Gun of Durham. Canon Henry Baker Tristram, FRS: an outline of his life, collections and contribution to natural history. *Arch. Nat. Hist.* **23**: 327–41

Barber, L. (1980) *The Heyday of Natural History, 1820–1870.* Jonathan Cape, London.*

Barclay-Smith, P. (1959) The British contribution to bird protection. *The Ibis* **101**: 115–22.

Barrington, D. (1771) An essay on the periodical appearing and disappearing of certain birds at different times of the year. *Phil. Trans. Roy. Soc.* **62**: 265–326.

Bartholomeus Anglicus (1260) *De proprietatibus rerum.* Cologne.

Baxter, E. V. & Rintoul, L. J. (1953) *The Birds of Scotland.* Oliver & Boyd, Edinburgh.

Belon, P. (1555) *L'Histoire de la nature des oyseaux.* Paris.

Berkenhout, J. (1769–71) *Outlines of the Natural History of Great Britain and Ireland.* London.

Bernes, J. (1486) *Boke of St Albans containing treatises of hawking, hunting and cote armour.* St. Albans.

Berthold, P. (2001) *Bird Migration: a General Survey.* 2nd edn. Oxford University Press, Oxford.

Bewick, T. (1797–1804) *History of British Birds.* Newcastle upon Tyne.

Bewick, T. (1820) *The History of Quadrupeds.* Newcastle upon Tyne.

Bircham, P. M. M. (1992) John Legg: an advanced and neglected ornithologist. *Arch. Nat. Hist.* **20**: 147–55.*

Birchley, S. (1909) *British Birds: for Cages, Aviaries and Exhibition.* 2 vols. Sherratt & Hughes, London.

Blackburn, J. (1989) *Charles Waterton, 1787–1865: Traveller and Conservationist.* The Bodley Head, London.*

Blackwall, J. (1822) Tables of the various species of periodical birds observed in the neighbourhood of Manchester. *Proc. Lit. Phil. Soc. Manchester.*

Blackwall, J. (1822) Observations on the notes of birds. *Proc. Lit. Phil. Soc. Manchester.*

Blackwall, J. (1824) *Observations Conducive Towards a More Complete History of the Cuckoo.* Printed for the author by the Executors of S. Russell, Deansgate.

Blackwall, J. (1824) *Capability of the Periodical Birds to become Torpid.* Printed for the Author by the Executors of S. Russell. Deansgate.

Blackwall, J. (1833) On the instincts of birds. *Edin. New Phil. Journ.* **XIV**: 241–261

Blackwall, J. (1834) Remarks on the swallow tribe. In *Researches into Zoology.* London.

Blackwall, J. (1834) Remarks on the diving of aquatic birds. In *Researches into Zoology.* London.

Blackwall, J. (1861–4) *A History of the Spiders of Great Britain and Ireland.* London.

Blomfield L. (formerly Jenyns) (1885) *Reminiscences of Prideaux John Selby & Twizell House.* Privately printed.

Boisseau, S. & Yalden, D. W. (1998) The former status of the crane *Grus grus* in Britain. *Ibis* **140**: 482–500.

Bolton, J. (1794) *Harmonia ruralis, or an Essay Towards a Natural History of British Songbirds.* London.

Bourne, W. R .P. (1981) The birds and animals consumed when Henry VIII entertained the King of France and the Count of Flanders at Calais in 1532. *Arch. Nat. Hist.* **10**: 331–3.

Bourne, W. R .P. (2003) Fred Stubbs, egrets, brewes and climatic change. *Brit. Birds* **96**: 332–9.

Boyd, A. W. (1931) On some results of ringing greenfinches. *Brit. Birds* **24**: 329–37.

Brooke, M de L. & Davies, N. B. (1987) Recent changes in host usage by cuckoos *Cuculus canorus* in Britain. *J. Anim. Ecol.* **56**: 873–83.

Brown, L. (1976) *British Birds of Prey*. New Naturalist 60. Collins, London.

Brown, P. (1776) *New Illustrations of Zoology*. London.

Buffon, G. L. L. de (1770–83) *Histoire naturelle des oiseaux*. 9 vols. Paris.

Bullough, W. S. (1945) Physiological races and nomenclature. *The Ibis* **87**: 44–8.

Burkitt, J. P. (1924–6) A study of robins by means of marked birds. *Brit. Birds* **17**: 294–303; **18**: 97–103, 250–7; **19**: 120–4; **20**: 91–101.

Buxton, J. (1950) *The Redstart*. New Naturalist Monographs. Collins, London.

Caius, J. (1570) *Ioannis Caii Britanni de rariorum animalium atque stirpium historia liber unus*. London.

Carew, R. (1602) *The Survey of Cornwall*. London.

Catesby, M. (1731–43) *A Natural History of Carolina*. London.

'Caw Caw' (1872) *The Pipits*. James Maclehose, Glasgow.

Chance, E. (1922) *The Cuckoo's Secret*. Sidgwick & Jackson, London.

Chance, E. (1940) *The Truth about the Cuckoo*. Country Life, London.

Chancellor, J. (1978) *Audubon: a Biography*. Weidenfeld and Nicholson, London.*

Charleton, W. (1668) *Onomasticon zoicon*. London.

Childrey, J. (1661) *Britannia Baconica*. London.

Clancey, P. A. (1947–8) Notes on birds of the Western Palearctic region. *The Ibis* **89**: 509, 652; **90**: 331, 468.

Clarke, W. E. (1896–1903) *Bird Migration in Great Britain and Ireland*. Report of the British Association.

Clarke, W. E. (1902) A month on the Eddystone: a study in bird migration. *The Ibis* **44**: 245–69.

Clarke, W. E. (1912) *Studies in Bird Migration*. 2 vols. Gurney & Jackson, London.

Clarke, W. E. (1914) On some migratory birds observed at Fair Island during spring and autumn of 1913. *Scottish Naturalist*.

Cocker, M. (1989) *Richard Meinertzhagen: Soldier, Scientist and Spy*. Secker & Warburg, London.*

Collinge, W. E. (1913) *The Food of Some British Wild Birds: a Study in Economic Ornithology*. Dulau, London. 2nd edn, York, 1924–7.

Cooper, T. (1563) *Thesaurus linguae Romanae et Britannicae*. London.

Cornwallis, R. W. & Smith, A. E. (1960) *The Bird in the Hand*. BTO Field Guide 6.

Coward, T. A. (1920) *The Birds of the British Isles and Their Eggs*. Frederick Warne, London.

Cramp, S., Simmons, K. E. L. & Perrins, C. M. (eds) (1977–95) *Handbook of the Birds of Europe, the Middle East and North Africa. The Birds of the Western Palearctic*. Oxford University Press, Oxford.

Crossley-Holland, K. (1984) *The Anglo-Saxon World: an Anthology*. Oxford University Press, Oxford.

Daglish, E. F. (1948) *Birds of the British Isles*. Dent, London.

Dance, P. (2003) *Letters on Ornithology*

1804–1815, between George Montagu and Robert Anstice. Privately published.

Darwin, C. (1839) *Journal of Researches into the Geology and Natural History of the Various Countries Visited by H.M.S. 'Beagle'.* Henry Colborn, London.

Darwin, C. (1859) *On the Origin of Species by Natural Selection.* Murray, London.

Darwin, C. (1868) *The Variation of Animals and Birds under Domestication.* Murray, London.

Darwin, E. (1794–6) *Zoonomia, or the Laws of Organic Life.* London.

Dawkins, R. (1976) *The Selfish Gene.* Oxford University Press, Oxford.

Delamain, J. (1934) Obituary: Edmund Selous. *Alauda* 6: 388–93.

Denham, J. F. (1850) *Memoir of Francis Willughby.* Reprinted from Jardine's Naturalist's Library, vol. 16.

Derham, W. (1713) Life of John Ray. In *Memorial of John Ray* (1846). Ray Society, London.

Dewar, J. H. (1922) Ability of the oyster-catcher to open oysters and its bearing upon the history of the species. *Brit. Birds* 16: 215–16.

Donovan, E. (1794–1819) *The Natural History of British Birds.* London.

Dresser, H. E. (1871–96) *A History of the Birds of Europe.* 9 vols. London.

Dresser, H. E. (1910) *Eggs of the Birds of Europe.* London.

Dudley, S. P., Gee, M., Kehoe, C., Melling, T. M. and the British Ornithologists' Union Records Committee (BOURC) (2006) The British List: a checklist of the birds of Britain (7th edition). *Ibis* 148: 526–63.

Eastwood, E. (1963) Bird migration in southeastern England. *Proc. X111 Int. Orn. Congr.* 390–5. American Ornithologists' Union.

Eastwood, E. (1967) *Radar Ornithology.* Methuen, London.

Edwards, G. (1743–51) *A Natural History of Birds.* 4 vols. London.

Edwards, G. (1758–64) *Gleanings of Natural History.* 3 vols. London.

Elliot, D. G. (1870–2) *A Monograph of the Phasianidae or Family of the Pheasant.* New York.

Elwes, H. J. (1922) Modern nomenclature and subspecies. *The Ibis* 64: 314–22.

Ely, Thomas of (11th century) *Liber Eliensis.*

Evans, A. H. (1903) *Turner on Birds: a Short and Succinct History of the Principal Birds Noticed by Pliny and Aristotle.* Cambridge University Press, Cambridge.

Farber, P. L. (1997) *Discovering Birds: the Emergence of Ornithology as a Scientific Discipline, 1760–1850.* Johns Hopkins University Press, Baltimore, MD.

Fisher, J. (1940) *Watching Birds.* Pelican Books. Penguin, Harmonsdworth.

Fisher, J. (1947) *Bird Recognition 1.* Pelican Books. Penguin, Harmonsdworth.

Fisher, J. (1951) *Bird Recognition 2.* Pelican Books. Penguin, Harmonsdworth.

Fisher, J. (1952) *The Fulmar.* New Naturalist Monographs. Collins, London.

Fisher, J. (1966) *The Shell Bird Book.* Michael Joseph, London.

Fisher, J. (1967) *Thorburn's Birds.* Michael Joseph, London.

Fisher, J. & Lockley, R. M. (1954) *Sea-Birds.* New Naturalist 28. Collins, London.

Forster, T. (1808) *Observations on the Brumal Retreat of the Swallow.* London.

Fuller, R. J. (1982) *Bird Habitats in Britain.* Poyser, Calton.

Fürbringer, M. (1888) *Untersuchungen zur Morphologie und Systematik der Vögel.* 2 vols. Jena and Amsterdam.

Gadow, H. (1892) On the classification of birds. *Proc Zoo. Soc. Lond.* 229–56.

Gadow, H. (1898) *A Classification of Vertebrata Recent and Extinct.* Black, London.

Garmonsway, G. N. (ed.) (1939) *Aelfric's Colloquy*. Exeter.

Gesner, C. (1555) *Historia animalium. Book III. De avium natura*. Zurich.

Gesner, C. (1560) *Icones animalium*. Zurich.

Gibbons, D. W., Reid, J. B. & Chapman, R. A. (1993) *The New Atlas of Breeding Birds in Britain & Ireland: 1988–1991*. Poyser, London.

Giraldus Cambrensis (1185) *The Itinerary of Archbishop Baldwin Through Wales*.

Giraldus Cambrensis (1187) *The Topography of Ireland, its Miracles and Wonders*.

Gladstone, H. S. (1919) John Hunt 1777–1842. *Brit. Birds* **XI** 125–37, 148–55.

Gladstone, H. S. (1924) Seventeenth century names for some British birds. *Brit. Birds* **XVII**: 50–4.

Gladstone, H. S. (1928a) An early work on bird-migration. *Brit. Birds* **21**: 220–6.

Gladstone, H. S. (1928b) Notes on a Discourse on the Emigration of Birds: 1780. *Brit. Birds* **22** 34–35.

Glegg, W. E. (1942) A comparative consideration of the status of the hoopoe in Great Britain and Ireland over a period of a hundred years (1839–1938). *The Ibis* **84**: 390–433.

Godman, F. C. (1870) *A Natural History of the Azores*. Van Voorst, London.

Godman, F. C. (1907–10) *A Monograph of the Petrels*. Witherby, London.

Godwin, F. (1638) *The Man in the Moone: or a Discourse of a Voyage Thither by Domingo Gonzales*. London.

Gough, J. (1812) Remarks on the summer birds of passage and on migration in general. *Proc. Lit. Soc. Manchester*.

Gould, J. (1830–31) *A Century of Birds from the Himalaya Mountains*. London.

Gould, J. (1832–7) *The Birds of Europe*. 5 vols. London.

Gould, J. (1833–5) *A Monograph of the Ramphastidae or Family of Toucans*. London.

Gould, J. (1836–8) *A Monograph of the Trogonidae or Family of Trogons*. London.

Gould, J. (1840–48) *The Birds of Australia*. 7 vols. London.

Gould, J. (1849–61) *A Monograph of the Trochilidae or Humming-birds*. 5 vols. London.

Gould, J. (1850–83) *The Birds of Asia*. 7 vols. London.

Gould, J. (1862–73) *The Birds of Great Britain*. 5 vols. London.

Gould, J. (1875–88) *The Birds of New Guinea and Adjacent Papuan Islands*. 5 vols. London.

Graves, G. (1811–21) *British Ornithology*. London.

Greene, W. T. (1898) *Birds of the British Empire*. Imperial Press, London.

Gurney, J. H. (1921) *Early Annals of Ornithology*. Witherby, London.

Gwinner, E. (1967) Circannuale Periodik der Mauser und der Zugunruhe bei einern Vogel. *Naturwiss.* **54**: 447.

Hale, W. G. (1980) *British Waders*. New Naturalist 65. Collins, London.

Hammond, N. (1983) Royal Society for the Protection of Birds. In Hickling, R. A. O. (ed.) *Enjoying Ornithology*. Poyser, Calton.

Harrison, J. M. (1968) *Bristow and the Hastings Rarities Affair*. Privately published, St Leonards-on-Sea.

Hartert, E. (1903–22) *Die Vögel der Paläarktischen Fauna*. Berlin & London.

Hartert, E. (1907) On birds represented in the British Isles by peculiar forms. *Brit. Birds* **1**: 208–22.

Hartert, E., Ticehurst, N. F., Witherby, H. F. & Jourdain, F. C. R. (1912) *A Hand-List of British Birds*. Witherby, London.

Harvie-Brown, J. A. (1906) *A Vertebrate Fauna of the Tay Basin and Strathmore*. Douglas, Edinburgh.

Harvie-Brown, J. A. & Buckley, T. E. (1887)

A Vertebrate Fauna of Sutherland, Caithness and West Cromarty. Douglas, Edinburgh.

Harvie-Brown, J. A. & Buckley, T. E. (1892) *A Vertebrate Fauna of Argyll and the Inner Hebrides.* Douglas, Edinburgh.

Harvie-Brown, J. A. & Buckley, T. E. (1896) *A Vertebrate Fauna of the Moray Basin.* Douglas, Edinburgh.

Harvie-Brown, J. A. & Macpherson, H. A. (1904) *A Vertebrate Fauna of the North-West Highlands and Skye.* Douglas, Edinburgh.

Hayes, W. (1775) *A Natural History of British Birds.* London.

Hickling, R. A. O. (1983) *Enjoying Ornithology.* Poyser, Calton.

Hill, D. (1988) *Turner's Birds: Bird Studies from Farnley Hall.* Phaidon, Oxford.

Hinde, R. A. (1987) William Homan Thorpe. *Biog. Mem. Fell. R. Soc.* **33**: 619–39.

Holloway, S. (1996) *The Historical Atlas of Breeding Birds in Britain and Ireland 1875–1900.* Poyser, London.

Howard, H. E. (1907–14) *The British Warblers.* 2 vols. Porter, London.

Howard, H. E. (1920) *Territory in Bird Life.* Murray, London.

Howard, H. E. (1929) *An Introduction to the Study of Bird Behaviour.* Cambridge University Press, Cambridge.

Howard, H. E. (1935) *The Nature of a Bird's World.* Cambridge University Press, Cambridge.

Howard, H. E. (1940) *A Waterhen's World.* Cambridge University Press, Cambridge.

Hudson, W. H. (1900) *Nature in Downland.* Longmans, London.

Hunt, J. (1815–22) *British Ornithology.* Norwich.

Huxley, J. (1914) The courtship habits of the Great Crested Grebe. *Proc. Soc. Zool. Lond.* **2**: 491–562.

Huxley, J. S. (1926) *Essays in Popular Science.* Pheonix Library.

Huxley, J. S. (1939) Clines: an auxiliary

method in taxonomy. *Bild. Dierk.* **27**: 491–520.

Huxley, J. S. (1940) *The New Systematics.* Clarendon Press, Oxford.

Huxley, J. S. (1942) *Evolution: the Modern Synthesis.* Allen & Unwin, London.

Huxley, J. S. (1964) *Essays of a Humanist.* Chatto & Windus, London.

Huxley, T. H. (1867) On the classification of birds; and on the taxonomic value of the modifications of certain of the cranial bones observable in the class. *Proc. Zool. Soc. Lond.* 415–72.

Irwin, R. A. (1951) *An Index to British Ornithology AD 1481 – AD 1948.* Grafton, London.

Irwin, R. A. (ed.) (1955) *Letters of Charles Waterton.* Rockliff, London.

Jackson, C. E. (1975) *Bird Illustrators: Some Artists in Early Lithography.* Witherby, London.

Jackson, C. E. (1978) H. C. Richter, John Gould's unknown bird artist. *Journal for the Society for the Bibliography of Natural History.* **9**: 10–14

Jackson, C. E. (1987) W. Hart: John Gould's second unknown bird artist. *Arch. Nat. Hist.* **14**: 237–41.

Jackson, C. E. (1992) *Prideaux John Selby: a Gentleman Naturalist.* Spredden Press, Stocksfield.

Jackson, C. E. & Davis, P. (2001) *Sir William Jardine: a Life in Natural History.* Leicester University Press, Leicester.*

Jardine, W. (1838–43) *Birds of Great Britain and Ireland.* In *The Naturalist's Library,* vols V, VII & X. Edinburgh.

Jardine, W. (1839) *Illustrations of the Duck Tribe.* Dumfries.

Jardine, W. (1848–52) *Contributions to Ornithology.* 5 vols. Edinburgh.

Jardine, W. & Selby, P. J. (1825–43) *Illustrations of Ornithology.* Edinburgh.

Jenner, E. (1788) Observations on the

natural history of the cuckoo. *Phil. Trans. Roy. Soc.* 221–237.

Jenner, E. (1824) Some observations on the migration of birds. *Phil. Trans. Roy. Soc.* **64**: 11–44.

Johnson, W. (1928) *Gilbert White.* John Murray, London.*

Jones, W. R. D. (1988) *William Turner: Tudor Naturalist, Physician and Divine.* Routledge, London & New York.*

Jonstonus, J. (1650) *Historia naturalis de avibus.* Frankfurt.

Kaup, J. J. (1854) Einige Worte über die systematische Stellung der Familie der Raben, Corvidae. *Journal für Ornithologie* **2**: 47–57.

Knox, A. (1993) Richard Meinertzhagen: a case of fraud examined. *Ibis* **135**: 320–35.

Kruuk, H. (2003) *Niko's Nature.* Oxford University Press, Oxford.

Lack, D. L. (1930) Double-brooding of the nightjar. *Brit. Birds* **23**: 242–4.

Lack, D. L. (1930) The spring migration 1930 at the Cambridge Sewage Farm. *Brit. Birds.* **24**: 145–54.

Lack, D. L. (1933a) Habitat selection in birds with special reference to the effects of afforestation on the Breckland avifauna. *J. Anim. Ecol.* **2**: 239–62.

Lack, D. L. (1933b) Nesting conditions as a factor controlling breeding time in birds. *Proc. Zool. Soc. Lond.* 23–7.

Lack, D. L. (1934) *The Birds of Cambridgeshire.* Cambridge Bird Club, Cambridge.

Lack, D. L. (1937) Review of bird census work and bird population problems. *The Ibis* **89**: 369–95.

Lack, D. (1940) The behaviour of the robin: population changes over four years. *The Ibis* **90**: 299–324.

Lack, D. L. (1943) *The Life of the Robin.* Witherby, London.

Lack, D. L. (1944) The problem of partial migration. *Brit. Birds* **37**: 122–30, 143–50.

Lack, D. L. (1947) *Darwin's Finches.* Cambridge University Press, Cambridge.

Lack, D. L. (1954) *The Natural Regulation of Animal Numbers.* Clarendon Press, Oxford.

Lack, D. L. (1956) *Swifts in a Tower.* Methuen, London.

Lack, D. L. (1959) Some British pioneers in ornithological research 1859–1939. *The Ibis* **101**: 71–81

Lack, D. L. (1966) *Population Studies of Birds.* Clarendon Press, Oxford.

Lack, D. L. (1968) *Ecological Adaptations for Breeding in Birds.* Methuen, London.

Lack, D. L. (1969) Drift migration: a correction. *The Ibis* **111**: 253–5.

Lack, D. L. (1971) *Ecological Isolation in Birds.* Blackwell, Oxford.

Lack, D. L. (1974) *Evolution Illustrated by Waterfowl.* Blackwell, Oxford.

Lack, D. L. (1974) *Island Biology: Illustrated by the Land Birds of Jamaica.* Blackwell, Oxford.

Lack, D. L. & Lack, L. (1933) Territory reviewed. *Brit. Birds* **27**: 179–99.

Lambourne, M. (1987) *John Gould, Bird Man.* Osberton, Milton Keynes.*

Latham, J. (1781–1801) *A General Synopsis of Birds.* 3 vols. London.

Latham, J. (1790) *Index ornithologicus.* London.

Latham, J. (1821–8) *A General History of Birds.* London.

Latham, S. (1615–18) *Falconry, or the Faulcons Lure and Cure.* London.

Lawrence, T. E. (1935) *The Seven Pillars of Wisdom.* Jonathan Cape, London.

Lear, E. (1832) *Illustrations of the Family of Psittacidae.* London.

Legg, J. (1780) *Discourse on the Emigration of British Birds.* Salisbury.

Legg, J. (1780) *A New Treatise on the Art of Grafting and Innoculation.* Salisbury.

Legg, J. (1789) *Meditations and Reflections on the most important subjects, or serious* soliliquies on Life, Death, Judgement, and Immortality. Salisbury.

Leigh, C. (1700) The Natural History of Lancashire, Cheshire and the Peak District of Derbyshire. Oxford.

Leslie, A. S. & Shipley, A. E. (1912) The Grouse in Health and Disease: the Report of the Committee of Enquiry on Grouse Disease. 2 vols. Smith, Elder & Co., London.

Lewin, W. (1789–94) The Birds of Great Britain with their Eggs Accurately Figured. London.

Lilford, Lord (1885–97) Coloured Figures of the Birds of the British Islands. 7 vols. Porter, London.

Linnaeus, C. (1735 etc) Systema naturae. 1st edn 1735, 10th edn 1758, 12th edn 1766. Stockholm.

Lister, M. D. (1939) An account of the lapwing population on a Surrey farm. Brit. Birds 32: 260–71.

Lockley, R. M. & Russell, R. (1953) Bird-ringing. Crosby Lockwood & Son, London.

Lord, T. (1791) Entire New System of Ornithology, or Oecumenical History of British Birds. London.

Lorenz, K. (1935) Der Kumpan in der Umwelt des Vogels. Journal für Ornithologie 83: 137–213, 289–413.

Lyons, H. (1944) The Royal Society 1660–1940. Cambridge University Press, Cambridge.

Mabey, R. (1986) Gilbert White: a Biography of the Author of The Natural History of Selbourne. Century Hutchinson, London.*

MacGillivray, W. (1836) Descriptions of the Rapacious Birds of Great Britain. MacLachlan & Stewart, Edinburgh.

MacGillivray, W. (1837–52) A History of British Birds, Indigenous and Migratory. 5 vols. London.

MacGillivray, W. (1838–43) History of British Quadrupeds. Jardine's Naturalist's Library.

MacGillivray, W. (1843) A History of the Molluscous Animals of the Counties of Aberdeen, Kincardine and Banff. Cunningham & Mortimer, London.

MacGillivray, W. (1855) The Natural History of Deeside and Braemar. London.

MacLeay, W. S. (1819) Horae entomologicae; or Essays on the Annulose Animals. London, Bagster.

Manson-Bahr, P. (1959) Recollections of some famous British ornithologists. The Ibis 101: 53–64.

Marchant, J. H., Hudson, R., Carter, S. P., & Whittington, P. (1990) Population Trends in British Breeding Birds. BTO, Tring.

Martin, M. (1698) A Late Voyage to St. Kilda. London.

Martin, M. (1703) A Description of the Western Islands of Scotland. London.

Masson, P. W. (1930) Night soaring of swifts. Brit. Birds 24: 48–50.

Matthews, G. V. T. (1955) Bird Navigation. Cambridge University Press, Cambridge.

Matthews, G. V. T. (1968) Bird Navigation. 2nd edn. Cambridge University Press, Cambridge.

Mattingley, A. H. E. (1946) Orientation in birds. The Ibis 88: 512–17.

Mead, C. (1983) Bird Migration. Country Life, Feltham.

Meinertzhagen, R. (1921) Some thoughts on sub-species and evolution. The Ibis 63: 528–37.

Meinertzhagen, R. (1939) A note on the birds of Hoy, Orkney. The Ibis 81: 258–64.

Meinertzhagen, R. (1951) Review of the Alaudidae. Proc. Zoo. Soc. Lond. 121: 81–132.

Meinertzhagen, R. (1959) Nineteenth century recollections. The Ibis 101: 46–52.

Melling, T. (2006) Time to get rid of the moustache: a review of records of the moustached warbler. Brit. Birds 99: 465–78.

Merrett, C. (1666) Pinax rerum naturalium Britannicarum. London.

Miall, L. C. (1912) *The Early Naturalists, Their Lives and Work 1530–1789*. Macmillan, London.

Montagu, G. (1798) Descriptions of three rare species of British birds. *Trans. Linn. Soc.* **IV**: 35–43.

Montagu, G. (1802–13) *Ornithological Dictionary, or Alphabetical Synopsis of British Birds*. 2 vols & supplement. London.

Montagu, G. (1807) Some interesting additions to the natural history of *Falco cyaneus* and *pygargus*, together with remarks on some other British birds. *Trans. Linn. Soc.* **IX**.

Montagu, G. (1811) Observations on some peculiarities observable in the structure of the gannet, *Pelecanus bassanus*, and an account of a new and curious insect, discovered to inhabit the cellular membrane of that bird. *Mem. Wernerian Nat. Hist. Soc. (Edinburgh)* **1**: 176–193.

Montagu, G. (1817) Some remarks on the natural history of the black stork, for the first time captured in Britain. *Trans. Linn. Soc.* **XII**: 19–23.

Moore, N. W. (1957) The past and present status of the buzzard in the British Isles. *Brit. Birds* **50**: 173–97.

Moore, N. W. (1987) *The Bird of Time*. Cambridge University Press, Cambridge.

Moreau, R. E. (1944) Clutch size: a comparative study with special reference to African birds. *The Ibis* **86**: 286–347.

Moreau, R. E. (1972) *The Palaearctic–African Migration Systems*. Academic Press, London.

Morgan, C. L. (1896) *Habit and Instinct*. Arnold, London.

Morgan, C. L. (1912) *Instinct and Experience*. Methuen, London.

Morgan, C. L. (1923) *Emergent Evolution*. Williams & Norgate, London.

Morgan, C. L. (1926) *Life, Mind, and Spirit*. Williams & Norgate, London.

Morgan, C. L. (1929) *Mind at the Crossways*. Williams & Norgate, London.

Morgan, C. L. (1930) *The Animal Mind*. Arnold, London.

Morgan, C. L. (1933) *The Emergence of Novelty*. Williams & Norgate, London.

Morris, D. (1967) *The Naked Ape*. Jonathan Cape, London.

Morris, F. O. (1851–7) *A History of British Birds*. 6 vols. Groombridge. London.

Morton, C. (1701) *An essay towards the probable solution of this question: whence come the Stork and the turtle, the crane and the swallow, when they know and observe the time of their coming*. London. (originally said to be by Francis Roberts).

Moss, S. (2004) *A Bird in the Bush: a Social History of Birdwatching*. Aurum Press, London.

Mountfort, G. (1957) *The Hawfinch*. New Naturalist Monographs. Collins, London.

Mountfort, G. (1959) One hundred years of the British Ornithologists' Union. *The Ibis* **101**: 8–18.

Muffet, T. (1655) *Health's Improvement*. London.

Muirhead, G. (1889–95) *The Birds of Berwickshire*. Edinburgh.

Mullens, W. H. (1908a) Some early British ornithologists and their works. II. Richard Carew. *Brit. Birds* **2**: 42–50.

Mullens, W. H. (1908b) Some early British ornithologists and their works. III. Christopher Merrett (1614–1695). *Brit. Birds* **2**: 109–163.

Mullens, W. H. (1908c) Some early British ornithologists and their works. IV. Martin Martin (ob. 1719). *Brit. Birds* **2**: 173–82.

Mullens, W. H. (1909a) Some early British ornithologists and their works. V. Robert Plot (1641–1696). *Brit. Birds* **2**: 218–25.

Mullens, W. H. (1909b) Some early British ornithologists and their works. VI.

Thomas Pennant (1726–1798). *Brit. Birds* 2: 259–66.

Mullens, W. H. (1909c) Some early British ornithologists and their works. VII. John Ray (1627–1705) and Francis Willughby (1635–1672). *Brit. Birds* 2: 290–300.

Mullens, W. H. (1909d) Some early British ornithologists and their works. VIII. Thomas Bewick (1753–1828) and George Montagu (1751–1815) *Brit. Birds* 2: 351–61.

Mullens, W. H. (1909e) Some early British ornithologists and their works. IX. William MacGillivray (1796–1852) and William Yarrell (1784–1853). *Brit Birds* 2: 389–99.

Mullens, W. H. (1911) Walter Charleton and his Onomasticon Zoicon. *Brit. Birds* 5: 64–71.

Mullens, W. H. (1912a) Thomas Muffat 1553–1604. *Brit. Birds* 5: 262–78.

Mullens, W. H. (1912b) Robert Sibbald and his Prodromus. *Brit. Birds* 6: 34–57.

Mullens, W. H. (1922) Review of J. H. Gurney's *Early Annals of Ornithology. Brit. Birds* XV: 161–8.

Mullens, W. H. & Swann, H. K. (1916–17) A *Bibliography of British Ornithology*. 2 vols. Macmillan, London.

Murton, R. K. (1965) *The Wood Pigeon*. New Naturalist Monographs. Collins, London.

Neckam, A. (1863) *De naturis rerum*. Rolls series 4. Longman, London. (Facsimile of original.)

Nelder, J. A. (1962) A statistical examination of the Hastings Rarities. *Brit. Birds* 55: 283–97.

Newton, A. (1844) Notes on the arrival of summer birds at Elveden and its vicinity. *Zoologist* ii: 722–3.

Newton, A. (1861a) On the possibility of taking an ornithological census. *The Ibis* 3: 190–6.

Newton, A. (1861b) Abstract of Mr J. Wolley's researches in Iceland respecting the

Gare-fowl or Great Auk. *Zoologist* 374–99.

Newton, A. (1864–1907) *Ootheca Wolleyana*. London.

Newton, A. (1868) The zoological aspect of game laws. *Proc. Brit. Assoc. Adv. Sci.* August 1868.

Newton, A. (1878) The rooks and London rookeries. *Zoologist*.

Newton, A. (1892) Errors concerning the sanderling (*Calidris arenaria*). *The Ibis* 34.

Newton, A., Gadow, H. *et al.* (1896) *A Dictionary of Birds*. Black, London.

Newton, I. (1972) *Finches*. New Naturalist 55. Collins, London.

Nicholson, E. M. (1926) *Birds in England*. Chapman and Hall, London.

Nicholson, E. M. (1927) *How Birds Live*. Williams & Norgate.

Nicholson, E. M. (1929) Report on the 'British Birds' census of heronries 1928. *Brit. Birds* 22: 270–323, 334–73.

Nicholson, E. M. (1931) *The Art of Bird-Watching: a Practical Guide to Field Observation*. Witherby, London.

Nicholson, E. M. (1951) Obituary: Bernard William Tucker (1901–1950). *Brit. Birds* 44: 40–6.

Nicholson, E. M. (1959) The British approach to ornithology. *The Ibis* 101: 394–5.

Nicholson, E. M. (1983) The Trust: origins and early days. In Hickling, R.A.O. (ed.) *Enjoying Ornithology*. Poyser, Calton.

Nicholson, E. M. & Ferguson-Lees, I. J. (1962) The Hastings Rarities. *Brit. Birds* 55: 299–384.*

Nicholson, E. M., Ferguson-Lees, I. J. & Nelder, J. A. (1969) The Hastings Rarities again. *Brit. Birds* 62: 364–81.*

Nicholson, E. M. & Koch, L. (1936) *Songs of Wild Birds*. Witherby, London.

Nicholson, E. M. & Koch, L. (1937) *More Songs of Wild Birds*. Witherby, London.

Noblett, W. (1982) Pennant and his

publisher: Benjamin White, Thomas Pennant and 'of London'. *Arch. Nat. Hist.* **11**: 61–68.

North, M. & Simms, E. (1954) *Witherby's Sound Guide to British Birds.* Witherby, London.

O'Connor, R. J. & Shrubb, M. (1986) *Farming and Birds.* Cambridge University Press, Cambridge.

Owen, J. H. (1926–36) [The sparrowhawk.] *Brit Birds* **20**: 114; **25**: 151, 238; **26**: 34; **30**: 22.

Owen, J. H. (1948) The larder of the red-backed shrike. *Brit. Birds.* **41**: 200–3.

Papi, F. & Pardi, L. (1982) Olfaction and homing in pigeons: ten years of experiments. In Papi, F. & Wallraff, H. G. (eds) *Avian Navigation.* Springer, Berlin.

Pashby, B. S. (1985) *John Cordeaux Ornithologist.* Spurn Bird Observatory.

Pierce-Duncombe, A. (1983) The Scottish Ornithologists' Club. In Hickling, R.A.O. (ed.) *Enjoying Ornithology.* Poyser, Calton.

Pennant, T. (1766) *The British Zoology.* London.

Pennant, T. (1771) *Synopsis of British Quadrupeds.* Chester.

Pennant, T. (1773) *Genera of Birds.* Edinburgh.

Pennant, T. (1781) *A History of British Quadrupeds.* Chester.

Pennant, T. (1784–7) *Arctic Zoology.* London.

Pennant, T. (1793) *The Literary Life of the Late Thomas Pennant Esq by Himself.* London.

Pennycuick, C. J., Bradbury, T. A. M., Einarsson, O. & Owen, M. (1999) Response to weather and light conditions of migrating whooper swans *Cygnus cygnus* and flying height profiles observed with the Argos satellite system. *Ibis* **141**: 434–43.

Perrins, C. (1979) *British Tits.* New Naturalist 62. Collins, London.

Peterson, R. T., Mountfort, G. & Hollom, P. (1954) *A Field Guide to the Birds of Britain and Europe.* Collins, London.

Pike, O. (1900) *In Bird-Land with Field Glasses and Camera.* Unwin, London.

Pliny (c. AD 77) *Historia naturalis.* Various editions.

Plot, R. (1677) *The Natural History of Oxfordshire.* Oxford

Plot, R. (1686) *The Natural History of Staffordshire.* Oxford.

Prater, A . J. (1981) *Estuary Birds in Britain and Ireland.* Poyser, Berkhamsted.

Pycraft, W. P. (1910) *A History of Birds.* Methuen, London.

Rackham, O. (1986) *The History of the Countryside.* Dent, London.

Ralph, R. (1993) *William MacGillivray.* HMSO, London.

Ratcliffe, D. A. (1963) The status of the peregrine in Great Britain. *Bird Study* **10**: 56–90.

Ratcliffe, D. A. (1965) The peregrine situation in Great Britain 1963–64. *Bird Study* **12**: 66–82.

Raven, C. E. (1942) *John Ray, Naturalist: His Life and Works.* Cambridge University Press, Cambridge.

Raven, C. E. (1947) *English Naturalists from Neckam to Ray.* Cambridge University Press, Cambridge.

Ray, J. (1660) *Catalogus plantarum circa Cantabrigiam nascentium.* London.

Ray, J. (1670) *Catalogus angliae.* London.

Ray, J. (1686) *Historia piscium.* London.

Ray, J. (1713) *Synopsis methodica avium et piscium: opus posthumum.* London.

Reid-Henry, D. & Harrison, C. (1988) *The History of the Birds of Britain.* Collins/Witherby, London.

Rintoul, L. J. & Baxter, E. V. (1918) The birds of the Isle of May, a migration study. *The Ibis* **247**.

Ryves, B. H. & Ryves, B. H. (1934) Supplementary notes on the breeding-habits of the corn bunting as observed in North Cornwall in 1934. *Brit. Birds* **28**: 154–64.

Salvin, O. & Godman, F. C. (1879–1904) *Biologia Centrali-Americana*. London.

Samstag, T. (1988) *For Love of Birds*. RSPB, Sandy.

Saunders, H. (1866) The birds of Walney, the Lakes & Farne Islands. *Zoologist* ser 2. 178–88.

Saunders, H. (1879) On the geographical distibution of gulls and terns. *J. Linn. Soc. Lon.* **14**: 390–406.

Saunders, H. (1887) *A List of British Birds*. London. 2nd edition 1907.

Saunders, H. (1889) *An Illustrated Manual of British Birds*. Van Voorst, London.

Saunders, H. (1907) Additions to the List of British birds since 1899. *Brit. Birds* **1**: 4–16.

Saxby, H. L. (1874) *The Birds of Shetland*. Edinburgh.

Sclater, P. L. (1858) On the general geographical distribution of the members of the Class Aves. *J. Proc. Linn. Soc. Zoology* **2**: 130–45.

Scott, P. (1935) *Morning Flight*. Country Life, London.

Scott, P. (1938) *Wild Chorus*. Country Life, London.

Seebohm, H. (1880) *Siberia in Europe: a Visit to the Valley of the Petchora*. Murray, London.

Seebohm, H. (1882) *Siberia in Asia: a Visit to the Valley of Yenesay in East Siberia*. Murray, London.

Seebohm, H. (1883–5) *A History of British Birds, with Coloured Illustrations of Their Eggs*. 4 vols. Porter, London.

Seebohm, H. (1887) *The Geographical Distribution of the Family Charadriidae*. London & Manchester.

Seebohm, H. (1890) *The Classification of Birds: an Attempt to Diagnose the Subclasses, Orders, Suborders and Some Families of Existing Birds*. Porter, London. Supplement, 1895.

Seebohm, H. (1893) *Geographical Distribution of British Birds*. Porter, London.

Seebohm, H. (1896) *Coloured Figures of the Eggs of British Birds*. Edited by R. B. Sharpe. Pawson & Brailsford, Sheffield.

Seebohm, H. (1902) A *Monograph of the Turdidae or Family of Thrushes*. Edited and completed by R. B. Sharpe. Sotheran, London.

Selby, P. J. (1825 & 1833) *Illustrations of British Ornithology*. 2 vols. Edinburgh.

Selous, E. (1899) Observational diary of the habits of nightjars mostly of a sitting pair. *Zoologist* **3**: 388, 486.

Selous, E. (1901) *Bird Watching*. Dent, London.

Selous, E. (1905) *Bird Life Glimpses*. Allen, London.

Selous, E. (1905) *The Bird Watcher in the Shetlands*. Dent, London.

Selous, E. (1927) *Realities in Bird Life*. Constable, London.

Selous, E. (1931) *Thought Transference (or What?) in Birds*. Constable, London.

Selous, E. (1933) *Evolution of Habit in Birds*. Constable, London.

Sharpe, R. B. (1868–71) *A Monograph of the Alcedinidae, or Family of Kingfishers*. James Murie, London.

Sharpe, R. B. (ed.) (1874–98) *Catalogue of the Birds in the British Museum*. 27 vols. British Museum, London.

Sharpe, R. B. (1891) *A Review of Recent Attempts to Classify Birds*. International Ornithological Congress, Budapest & London.

Sharpe, R. B. (1894–7) A *Hand-Book to the Birds of Great Britain*. 4 vols. Allen, London.

Sharpe, R. B. (1898) *Sketch-Book of British Birds*. SPCK, London.

Sharpe, R. B. (1898) *Wonders of the Bird World*. Wells Gardner, London.

Sharpe, R. B. & Walpole, B. (eds) (1900)

Gilbert White's Natural History of Selborne. London.

Sharpe, R. B. & Wyatt, C. W. (1885–94) *A Monograph of the Hirundinidae or Family of Swallows.* 2 vols. Sotheran, London.

Sharrock, J. T. R. (ed.) (1976) *The Atlas of Breeding Birds in Britain and Ireland.* Poyser, Berkhamsted.

Sibbald, R. (1684) *Scotia illustrata sive Prodromus historiae naturalis.* 3 vols.Edinburgh.

Sibley, C. G. & Monroe, B. L. (1990) *Distribution and Taxonomy of Birds of the World.* Yale University Press, New Haven.

Simms, E. (1978) *British Thrushes.* New Naturalist 63. Collins, London.

Simms, E. (1985) *British Warblers.* New Naturalist 71. Collins, London.

Smith, A. C. (1894) Memoir of Mr John Legg of Market Lavington Wilts. *Wiltshire Archeological and Natural History Magazine* **28:** 1–9.

Smith, S. (1950) *The Yellow Wagtail.* New Naturalist Monographs. Collins, London.

Snow, D. W. (1958) *A Study of Blackbirds.* George Allen & Unwin, London.

Southwell, T. (1902) *Notes and Letters on the Natural History of Norfolk, More Especially on the Birds and Fishes: from the MSS of Sir Thomas Browne ...* Jarrold, London.

Spencer, R. (1983a) The Trust from 1951 to 1982. In Hickling, R. A. O. (ed.) *Enjoying Ornithology.* Poyser, Calton.

Spencer, R. (1983b) Our changing avifauna. In Hickling, R. A. O. (ed.) *Enjoying Ornithology.* Poyser, Calton.

Stearn, W. T. (1981) *The Natural History Museum at South Kensington.* Heinemann, London.

Stockman, S. & Garnett, M. (1923) Bird migration and the introduction of foot and mouth disease. *Journal of the Ministry of Agriculture* **30:** 681.

Stresemann, E. (1950) The development of theories which affected the taxonomy of birds. *The Ibis* **92:** 123–31.

Stresemann, E. (1975) *Ornithology: from Aristotle to the Present.* Harvard University Press, Cambridge, MA.

Swainson, W. S. (1820–3) *Zoological Illustrations. First series: Ornithology.* London.

Swainson, W. S. (1822) *The Naturalist's Guide for Collecting and Preserving All Subjects of Natural History and Botany.* Baldwin Craddock, London.

Swainson, W. S. (1834) *A Preliminary Discourse on the Study of Natural History. Lardner's Cabinet Cyclopaedia.* Longman, London.

Swainson, W. S. (1836–7) *The Natural History and Classification of Birds.* London

Swainson, W. S. (1840) *Taxidermy with the Biographies of Zoologists.* London.

Swaysland, W. (1883–8) *Familiar Wild Birds.* 4 vols. Cassell, London.

Teversham, T. F. (1942–7) *A History of the Village of Sawston.* Crampton, Sawston.

Thomson, A. L. (1926) *The Problems of Bird Migration.* Witherby, London.

Thomson, A. L. (1936) Recent progress in the study of bird migration, a review of the literature 1926–35. *The Ibis* **78:** 472–530.

Thomson, A. L. (1936) *Bird Migration.* Witherby, London.

Thomson, A. L. (1959) The British contribution to the study of bird migration. *The Ibis* **101:** 82–9.

Thomson, A. L. (1964) *A New Dictionary of Birds.* Nelson, London.

Thorburn, A. (1915–18) *British Birds.* 4 vols. Longman, London.

Thorpe, W. H. (1925) Some ecological aspects of British ornithology. *Brit. Birds* **19:** 106–19.

Thorpe, W. H. (1956) *Learning and Instinct in Animals.* Methuen, London.

Thorpe, W. H. (1958) The learning of song patterns by birds, with especial reference to the song of the chaffinch *Fringilla coelebs*. *The Ibis* **100**: 535–70.

Thorpe, W. H. (1961) *Bird Song: the Biology of Vocal Communication and Expression in Birds*. Cambridge University Press, Cambridge.

Thorpe, W. H. (1974) David Lambert Lack. *Biog. Mem. Fell. R. Soc.* **20**: 271–93.

Ticehurst, C. B. (1932) *A History of the Birds of Suffolk*. Gurney & Jackson, London.

Ticehurst, C. B. (1938) *A Systematic Review of the Genus Phylloscopus*. London.

Ticehurst, N. F. (1923) Some British birds in the fourteenth century. *Brit. Birds* **17**: 29–35.

Tinbergen, N. (1934) *Eskimoland*. Van Sijn & Zonen, Rotterdam.

Tinbergen, N. (1939) Field observations of East Greenland birds II. The behaviour of the snow bunting (*Plectrophenax nivalis subnivalis*) in spring. *Trans. Linn. Soc N.Y.*, **5**: 1–94.

Tinbergen, N. (1951) *A Study of Instinct*. Clarendon Press, Oxford.

Tinbergen, N. (1953) *The Herring Gull's World*. New Naturalist Monographs. Collins, London.

Tinbergen, N. & Falkus, H. (1970) *Signals for Survival*. Clarendon Press, Oxford.

Tomkins, S. (1998) The Kingfisher's Bridge Wetland Creation Project: a report from the project's inception to autumn 1996. *Nature in Cambridgeshire* **40**: 37–53.

Topsell, E. (1607) *The Historie of Four-footed Beastes*. London.

Topsell, E. (1608) *The Historie of Serpents*. London.

Topsell, E. (1972) *The Fowles of Heauen or History of Birds*, ed. T. P. Harrison & F. D. Hoeniger. University of Texas, Austin.

Tree, I. (1991) *The Ruling Passion of John Gould*. Barrie & Jenkins, London.*

Tristram, H. B. (1859) On the ornithology of North Africa. *The Ibis* **1**: 153–62, 277–301, 415–35.

Tristram, H. B. (1860) *The Great Sahara: Wanderings South of the Atlas Mountains*. London.

Tristram, H. B. (1867) *The Natural History of the Bible*. London.

Tristram, H. B. (1884) *Flora and Fauna of Palestine*. Palestine Exploration Fund, London.

Tucker, B. M. (1949) Species and subspecies. *Brit. Birds* **42**: 129–34, 161–74, 193–205.

Tunstall, M. (1771) *Ornithologia Britannica*. London.

Turner, W. (1538) *Libellus de re herbaria*. London.

Turner, W. (1544) *Avium praecipuarum quarum apud Plinium aet Aristotelem mentio est brevis & succincta historia*. Cologne.

Turner, W. (1551 & 1562) *Libellus de re herbaria novus Pts 1&2*.

Vigors, N. (1825) Observations on the natural affinities that connect the orders and families of birds. *Trans. Linn. Soc.* **XIV**: 395–517.

Walcott, J. (1789) *Synopsis of British Birds*. London.

Wallace, A. R. (1876) *The Geographical Distribution of Animals*. Macmillan, London.

Wallace, I. (2004) *Beguiled by Birds*. Christopher Helm, London.

Walters, M. (2003) *A Concise History of Ornithology*. Christopher Helm, London.*

Waterton, C. (1837) *Wanderings in South America*. London.

Waterton, C. (1837) *An Ornithological Letter to William Swainson*. Wakefield.

Waterton, C. (1838) *Essays on Natural History, Chiefly Ornithology*. London.

Wernham, C., Toms, M., Marchant, J., Clark, J., Siriwardena, G. & Baillie, S. (2003) *The Migration Atlas: Movements of the Birds of Britain and Ireland*. Poyser, London.

White, G. (1789) *The Natural History and Antiquties of Selborne in the County of Southampton*. London.

Wilkins, J. (1640) *The Discovery of a World in the Moone*. London.

Williamson, K. (1960) *Identification for Ringers 1. The Genera Cettia, Locustella, Acrocephalus and Hippolais*. British Trust for Ornithology.

Williamson, K. (1962) *Identification for Ringers 2. The Genus Phylloscopus*. British Trust for Ornithology.

Williamson, K. (1964) *Identification for Ringers 3. The Genus Sylvia*. British Trust for Ornithology.

Willughby, F. (1676) *Ornithologiae libri tres*. London.

Wilson, A. (1808–14) *American Ornithology*. 9 vols. Philadelphia, PA.

Winstanley, D. R., Spencer, R. & Williamson, K. (1974) Where have all the whitethroats gone? *Bird Study* **21**: 1–14.

Witherby, H. F., Hartert, E., Jackson, A. C., Jourdain, F. C. R., Oldham, C. & Ticehurst, N. F. (1920–4) *A Practical Handbook of British Birds*. 3 vols. Witherby, London.

Witherby, H. F. & Leach, E. S. (1931) Movements of ringed birds from abroad to the British Isles and from the British Isles abroad. *Brit. Birds* **25**: 174–92.

Witherby, H. F., Jourdain, F. C. R., Ticehurst, N. F. & Tucker, B. W. (1938–42) *The Handbook of British Birds*. 5 vols. Witherby, London.

Wolf, J. (1861) *Zoological Sketches*. Henry Graves, London.

Wollaston, A. F. R. (1921) *Life of Alfred Newton, Professor of Comparative Anatomy, Cambridge University, 1866–1907*. John Murray, London.

Wormald, H. (1910) The courtship of the mallard and other ducks. *Brit. Birds* **4**: 2–7.

Wynne-Edwards, V. C. (1962) *Animal Dispersion in Relation to Social Behaviour*. Oliver & Boyd, Edinburgh.

Yapp, W. B. (1982) Birds in captivity in the Middle Ages. *Arch. Nat. Hist.* **10**: 479–500.

Yarrell, W. (1836) *A History of British Fishes*. London.

Yarrell, W. (1837–43) *A History of British Birds*. 3 vols. Van Voorst, London.

Yeates, G. (1934) *The Life of the Rook*. Philip Allen, London.

Yeates, G. (1946) *Bird Photography*. Faber and Faber, London.

Yeates, G. (1947) *Bird Haunts in Southern England*. Faber, London.

Yeates, G. (1951) *Bird Haunts in Northern England*. Faber, London.

Index

Plot, Robert 80, 189
plovers 18, 20, 405
  American golden 443
  Asiatic golden 397
  Caspian 441
  European golden 435
  golden 38, 57, 433
  greater sand 444
  grey 38, 57, 226, 433, 437
  Kentish 439
  lesser sand 445
  little 440
  Pacific golden 441
  ringed 38, 57, 77, 374, 432,
    437
  semipalmated 444
plumage
  species identification 142
  studies 267, 284, 285
  trade 318, 333
Plumage League 318
Pluvialis apricaria 433
  dominica 443
  fulva 441
  squatarola 433
pochards 89
  common 432, 437
  red-crested 164, 439
Podiceps auritus 439
  cristatus 434
  grisegena 439
  nigricollis 437
Podilymbus podiceps 443
Poecile montanus 441
  palustris 438
pole traps 322
Polysticta stelleri 440
population
  biology of 378, 380
  censuses 268–73, 275
  counting 283–4
  regulation 12
Porphyrula alleni 442
  martinica 443
Porter, Captain 119
Portland, Duchess of 318
Porzana carolina 441
  parva 439

porzana 433
  pusilla 439
poulterers 13, 20
Powys, Thomas *see* Lilford,
  Lord
Poyser, Anna 358
Poyser, Trevor 358
Prater, Tony 357
pratincoles
  black-winged 442
  collared 145, 439
  oriental 396, 444
Prestt, Ian 331–2
The Private Life of Gannets
  (film) 347
*Proceedings of the Royal
  Society* (journal) 394
protection of birds 274,
  314–33, 358, 416
  species reintroduction
  332
  see also RSPB
Protection of Birds Act
  (1954) 330, 416
Prunella collaris 439
  modularis 434
Psittacula krameri 444
ptarmigans 45
  rock 432, 437
  willow 435
Pterodroma feae 445
  hasitata 440
Ptyonoprogne rupestris 444
puffins 22, 34, 35, 55, 64–5
  as food 37
  Atlantic 433, 436
Puffinus baroli 441
  gravis 440
  griseus 440
  mauretanicus 441
  puffinus 434
Pycraft, William 222
Pye-Smith, G. R. H. 259–60
Pyrrhocorax pyrrhocorax 433
Pyrrhula pyrrhula 434

quail 12, 16, 22, 27, 28, 39, 45,
  50, 434, 435

as food 20
  migration 132
Quinary system 210–13, 211

Rackham, O. 4
radar, tracking birds 306,
  308–10, 377, 380
radio programmes 274, 368,
  369–70
Radipole Lake, Dorset 321
rail, water 432, 436
Rallus aquaticus 432
Ralph, Robert 147
Ramsey, Wales 321
rare species 396–408, 416,
  417
Ratcliffe, Derek 327, 354,
  358
Raven, C. E. 9, 12, 63, 69–70
ravens 5, 12, 40, 43, 50, 433,
  435
  white 32
Ravensglass, Cumbria 391
Ray, John 40, 44, 46, 58,
  59–81, 60, 73, 98, 162
  classification systems 63–7,
  70, 84, 92
  Ornithology 63–71, 81, 82,
  83–4
Ray Society 69
razorbill 55, 432, 437
Reading Museum,
  Berkshire 324
records 396–404
  during medieval period 18
  early 2–23
  recording birds 416–17
  Wetmore order 427
  see also avifaunas; lists
Recurvirostra avosetta 437
red-footed falcon 264, 440
redhead 445
redpolls 44, 57, 414–15
  arctic 440
  common 445
  greater 294
  lesser 274, 414, 415, 438
  mealy 415

The New Naturalist Library